M

EXPLORING

ADVANCES IN CONSCIOUSNESS RESEARC

ADVANCES IN CONSCIOUSNESS RESEARCH provides a forum for sch from different scientific disciplines and fields of knowledge who study consc ness in its multifaceted aspects. Thus the Series will include (but not be limit the various areas of cognitive science, including cognitive psychology, lingui brain science and philosophy. The orientation of the Series is toward develc new interdisciplinary and integrative approaches for the investigation, descri and theory of consciousness, as well as the practical consequences of this res for the individual and society.

Series B: Research in Progress: Experimental, descriptive and clinical resear consciousness.

Volume 23

Dan Zahavi (ed.)

Exploring the Self

Philosophical and psychopathological perspectives on self-experience

EXPLORING THE SELF

PHILOSOPHICAL AND PSYCHOPATHOLOGICAL PERSPECTIVES ON SELF-EXPERIENCE

Edited by

DAN ZAHAVI
University of Copenhagen

JOHN BENJAMINS PUBLISHING COMPANY
AMSTERDAM/PHILADELPHIA

The paper used in this publication meets the minimum requirements of American National Standard for Information Sciences — Permanence of Paper for Printed Library Materials, ANSI Z39.48–1984.

Library of Congress Cataloging-in-Publication Data

Exploring the self: philosophical and psychopathological perspectives on self-experience / ed
by Dan Zahavi.
p. cm. -- (Advances in consciousness research, ISSN 1381-589X ; v. 23)
Papers presented at a conference held in May 1999 at the University of Copenhagen.
Includes bibliographical references and index.
1. Self--Congresses. 2. Psychology, Pathological--Congresses. 3. Self (Philosophy)--Congre
4. Schizophrenia--Congresses. I. Zahavi, Dan. II. Series.
RC455.4.S42 E97 2000
616.89--dc21 00-039
ISBN 90 272 5143 6 (Eur.) / 1 55619 666 0 (US) (Pb; alk. paper)

John Benjamins Publishing Co. • P.O.Box 75577 • 1070 AN Amsterdam • The Netherlands
John Benjamins North America • P.O.Box 27519 • Philadelphia PA 19118-0519 • USA

Table of Contents

PART IV

Preface

In May 1999, an interdisciplinary conference took place at the University of Copenhagen. The aim of the conference was to discuss recent research into self-experience and its disorders, and to contribute to a better integration of the different empirical and conceptual perspectives.

Among the topics discussed were questions like 'What is a self?,' 'What is the relation between the self-givenness of consciousness and the givenness of the conscious self?', 'How should we understand the self-disorders encountered in schizophrenia?' and 'What general insights into the nature of the self can pathological phenomena provide us with?'

This volume is comprised of papers presented on that occasion. In addition to an introductory chapter by the two organizers, the volume has been divided into four parts. The papers by Butterworth, Strawson, Zahavi, and Marbach are general in nature and address different psychological and philosophical aspects of what it means to be a self. Next Eilan, Parnas, and Sass turn to schizophrenia and ask both how we should approach and understand this disorder, and, more specifically, what we can learn about the nature of selfhood and existence from psychopathology. The papers by Blakemore and Gallagher present us with a defense and a criticism of the so-called model of self-monitoring, respectively. The final three papers by Cutting, Stanghellini, Schwartz and Wiggins represent anthropologically oriented attempts to situate pathologies of self-experience.

I am much indebted to Josef Parnas, the co-organizer of the conference. Without his help this volume would never have seen the light of the day. Project coordinator Lotte Wehding Møller was of invaluable assistance in the organization and practical conduct of the conference. The conference was financially supported by the Danish Medical Research Council and the Danish Research Council for Humanities. Additional and necessary financial help was generously provided by Pfizer A/S, Denmark. Finally, thanks are due to Maxim Stamenov, the editor of *Advances in Consciousness Research*, and Bertie Kaal from John Benjamins Publishing Company for their help with the preparation of the volume.

The link: Philosophy – Psychopathology – Phenomenology

Josef Parnas and Dan Zahavi
University of Copenhagen

How can philosophical reflections on consciousness, mind, and self possibly be of any value to the psychiatrist, how can these highly abstract concerns increase her comprehension of concrete pathological cases, and how can psychopathological disorders be anything but insignificant empirical oddities to the philosopher? This apparent independence and indifference between the two fields is not only increasingly being questioned by recent interdisciplinary projects. Already in the beginning of the century, Karl Jaspers — an influential scholar and master of both disciplines — claimed that philosophy could contribute to a better psychiatry, and that familiarity with the methods and viewpoints of philosophy were useful for the psychiatrist.

Let us first give an outline of how philosophy might be of value for psychopathology, and then reverse the question. At the end we will then take a brief look at phenomenology and make some suggestions to why this tradition might be particularly suited in facilitating a dialogue between philosophy and psychopathology.

1. The importance of philosophy for psychopathology

Psychopathology as a discipline in its own right followed the development and maturation of clinical psychiatry since the second half of the 19th century. Through its medical nature and roots, psychopathology borders on an array of natural sciences such as genetics, epidemiology, neurobiology, neuroscience, neuropsychology, experimental- and developmental psychology. Its history is also marked by affinities to the humanities, such as sociology and philosophy. In one sense then, psychopathology is an umbrella-term, covering a multitude of empirical and theoretical approaches. The strength and potential productiveness of this interdisciplinary nature is mixed with a sense of insecurity concerning the status of psychopathology as an autonomous, self-subsistent practical science and theoretical discipline. This sense of insecurity stems from a pervasive lack of a suitable meta-framework, which could allow for a unified discourse; a discourse both liberated from dogmatic metaphysical commitments and faithful to the investigated phenomena, and on which professionals could agree, thus providing a common basis for multiple scientific approaches (Janzarik 1976; Pichot 1999). Precisely this search for a unified discourse was the principal motive behind the most comprehensive effort ever undertaken by the German psychiatrist (and later, a professional philosopher) Karl Jaspers, who in 1922 published a third revised edition of his 900 pages long *General Psychopathology* (the first edition appeared in 1913). In his memoirs he described his initial psychiatric experience (of early 1900-) in the following way:

> …the same things were discussed in different terms…in the most obscure manner. Several schools had each its own terminology….There seemed to be no such thing as a common scientific psychiatry uniting all those engaged in psychiatric research. (Jaspers 1957/1981)

This need for a unified framework makes the relation philosophy-psychopathology particularly important. Moreover, it is our contention that this importance is even more clearly perceptible today than ever before. We will elaborate this contention through a brief historical sketch of the unifying attempts and an assessment of their contemporary context and significance.

Psychopathology, in a general sense, refers to the empirical and theoretical study of anomalous *experience, expression and action*; indeed this was the very definition proposed by Jaspers. The goal is a description, typology and a comprehension of anomalous mental states. To attain it, Jaspers considered philosophy as an indispensable tool or ingredient of psychopathology:

> the psychiatrist's competence is really commensurate with how far his education and knowledge would qualify him to belong to the philosophic faculty. (Jaspers 1957/1981)

Jaspers believed that the methods and viewpoints of philosophy (and other fields in the human sciences) had a special value for psychiatry. He hoped that such erudition would foster a curious and sophisticated attitude of mind, one allergic to "platitudinous speculation, dogmatic theorizing, and absolutism in every form".

General Psychopathology provided a first systematic description of anomalous mental phenomena, usually presented upon the corresponding descriptive background of normal experience (e.g. the discussion of delusion followed the exposition of the sense of reality).[1] Phenomenological exposition of anomalous subjective experience, followed by the chapters on disorders of expression (*Ausdruckspsychologie*) and performance (*Leistungspsychologie*) comprised the first, core section of the book. *General Psychopathology* also contained a thorough presentation of basic philosophical concepts relevant for psychiatry as well as a critical review of the pertinent biological, psychological and sociological theories and factual evidence.

The impact of *General Psychopathology* was however quite limited outside Germany. In France it was almost ignored: the first translation appeared already in 1928 but was rather infrequently quoted. The major reason for this negative reception was the rather anti-theoretical, case-oriented clinical-descriptive French tradition, inherently skeptical towards "German theorizing and a tendency to abstract classifications" (Pichot 1999). Eugéne Minkowski, a naturalized Frenchman, was, however, untouched by this bias. Trained in Poland, Germany, and Switzerland, he was thoroughly familiar with Jaspers' contribution. Influenced partly by phenomenology and partly by Bergsonian philosophy, Minkowski (1927) performed what is probably the best-to-date analysis of the clinical features of schizophrenia. He redescribed the schizophrenic autism (Bleuler 1911) as a loss of "contact vital"- a disturbance in the pre-reflective intentional flow — rather than, as originally defined by Bleuler, a withdrawal to boundless fantasy of pure immanence.

A much later French counterpart to *General Psychopathology, Traité des hallucinations* by an eminent psychopathologist and a prolific author, Henri Ey, was published in 1973. The title is misleading, because this extremely informative book (1500 pages) provides a systematic description not only of hallucinations but, more generally, of anomalous subjective experience. Clinical material is presented in the framework of phenomenology and philosophy of mind, and one third of the book is devoted to contemporary neuroscientific models and theories.

The first publication of *General Psychopathology* in the English translation took place fifty years after its original German publication. It remained virtually unnoticed in the US, almost never quoted in the standard textbooks nor required by any training curriculum. In the British psychiatry, *General Psychopathology* was much more appreciated, reflecting a widespread familiarity with the continental psychiatric literature (e.g., Hamilton 1962).

General Psychopathology is, of course, not free of shortcomings, even when judged upon its own historical context. Some of its concepts were uncritically carried over from the 19th century psychiatry. Despite these shortcomings, however, *General Psychopathology*'s potential for creating a basis for a unified discourse in psychopathology was never, even approximatively, exploited on a wider, international scale by the psychiatric community. Not only are the sophisticated descriptions of single pathological experiences frequently unheard of; the main methodological declaration of Jaspers (that of a faithful, "from within", description of anomalous experience) is universally neglected in the scientific psychiatry of today.[2]

Psychopathology of today, taken in its mainstream, international appearance, is in a state of crisis or fragmentation; in fact one may even question to what extent we can still speak of psychopathology as a unified field at all. This critical assessment can be expanded into the following aspects:

1. In our view, the minimum of what psychopathology has to be equipped with is a *conceptual* framework for conceiving and grasping the phenomena of experience and behavior, and it is on that point that philosophy may be especially helpful. The meager conceptual resources are particularly manifest in the absence of a vocabulary suitable to address the phenomenology of the first-person perspective. In fact, no major English-language textbook of psychiatry provides even a descriptive sketch of what it means to entertain conscious states. Psychopathology is committed to a self-proclaimed so-called "a-theoretical" discourse, *de facto* amounting to common-sense, naive-realistic assumptions about the nature of experience and the world (Mishara 1994). It is now dominated by the requirements of logical positivism, which were presented by Carl Hempel in his influential address to the American Psychiatric Association in 1962 (Hempel 1965). Psychiatric terms should be "operationally defined", on analogy with physics. An "operational definition" provides rules whose application links the concept with its referent (e.g., ice can be defined as a certain amount of water which changes into solid state if brought to appropriate temperature under given barometric pressure). However, since "operations" are not feasible in psychopathology, the increasing

domination of positivistic epistemology has led to a dramatic simplification of the psychopathologic concepts and elimination of vast areas of human experience as simply "non-existent" because they resisted formulation in a "reliable" way (e.g., the notion of self and identity) (Parnas and Bovet 1995).

2. There are at least three essential psychopathological domains of questioning, which permeate and perhaps even found the entire psychopathological enterprise. These questions stand today largely unresolved and in need of philosophical assistance. First, *how* and *to what extent* is a psychiatrist able to access the patient's mind and reconstruct his experience? Jaspers has little to say on the issue of intersubjectivity (except emphasizing first/third person epistemic asymmetry) and this question is systematically evaded in the standard psychiatric texts (even in the texts specifically devoted to psychiatric interviewing). Second, central to many psychopathological disorders, are the notions of self, self-identity, agency, ownership etc. and apparent disorders and dissociations in these domains: In other words, notions that all refer to the issue of subjectivity and the first-person perspective. Since philosophy has traditionally been thematically concerned with these issues, it should come as no surprise that its investigations can help conceptualize the disorders, and refine and supplement the terminology and overall framework of psychiatry. Third, how do we comprehend the issue of *mental causation*. This needs a careful reappraisal in all its different ramifications. Psychopathology only implicitly confronts the mind-brain issue. The (modular) type-type identity thesis is tacitly taken for granted, resulting in a phrenological discourse, mixed up with cognitivist ideas on information processing and quite ignorant of the potential difficulties and rival paradigms (Hasker 1999). This tacit and pervasive domination of physicalism results in a scientific atmosphere in which empirical findings appear as "unquestionably objective", only open to methodological critique, but remaining immune to a more fundamental and substantive theoretical questioning because the theory is invisible.

3. As a result of these basic deficiencies, current psychopathological discourse reflects a confused *mixture of approaches*: purely descriptive statements are frequently contaminated by functionalist, neuroscientific or other extraclinical concepts. Especially numerous are references to hypothetical subpersonal "computational" (unconscious) processes, claimed to exist between the neural and the phenomenal level. A paradigmatic example of such a hybrid concept is the notion of delusion. Delusion is defined as a false

personal belief based upon *incorrect inference* about external reality (APA 1994). This is clearly not a descriptive definition. In the majority of cases, faulty inference does not belong to the phenomenology of delusion formation but is a notion more linked to a pathogenetic hypothesis. This type of mixture of discourses, mainly inspired by cognitivistic assumptions, is so pervasive that it makes the field referentially opaque, preventing critical dialogue and impeding resolution of debates.

It is, however, important not to overlook some promising recent developments, aimed at a better integration of philosophical concepts in psychiatry. Spitzer and colleagues (1988, 1990, 1992) published three successive anthologies addressing these issues. In 1994, two more volumes were published by Graham and Stephens, and Sadler, Wiggins and Schwartz. In 1996, Bolton and Hill made a thorough exposition of analytic philosophy in relation to psychopathology, and in 1997 a significant and detailed *Principles of Psychopathology* appeared which contains some of the long missing conceptual analyses (Cutting 1997).

To summarize: Psychiatry is not simply facing a number of factual and empirical problems, but a central part of its undertaking involves conceptual and epistemological issues as well. In order to classify something as a delusion, a hallucination, an obsession, or a self-disorder, the psychiatrist cannot avoid relying upon his tacit understanding of the nature of 'reality', 'rationality', 'personal identity' etc. That is, he must constantly make reference to philosophical issues, and since this is inevitably the case, why not benefit from the analyses that philosophy can provide. Philosophy can help in creating a sophisticated framework for description of *experience and existence*, a framework stripped from distorting hidden theoretical commitments and enabling the psychiatrist to address concrete psychopathological questions with a deeper understanding of the overarching issues such as time, space, mind, self etc. Terminological clarity can only be achieved on the basis of a conceptual clarity, which in turn requires a critical attitude towards the foundation of the scientific discourse. Thus, apart from this positive contribution, philosophy might also have a more negative or critical impact. Just like every other science, psychiatry makes a number of assumptions about the nature of reality, the status of consciousness and the process of scientific investigation. Here the skeptical eye of philosophy might prevent psychiatry from falling prey to unwarranted reifications, scientism and a too facile reductionism.

2. The importance of psychopathology for philosophy

If we now reverse the direction and ask how philosophy might profit from psychiatry, it might again be useful to distinguish between a negative or critical contribution and a positive one. Let us start with the critical aspect.

One of the customary ways to test the validity of philosophical analyses has been to look for invalidating counter-examples. If none could be found, so much the better for the proposed thesis. This search has often been carried out by means of imagination. We don't necessarily have to come across (f)actual counter-examples. It is sufficient if we can imagine them. Thus *imaginability* has often been taken as a mark of *possibility*: If something is imaginable, then it is, if not practically, or physically possible, at least possible in principle, that is conceptually or metaphysically possible. And if that is the case, then the exceptions are relevant, and should be taken into account when assessing the universalistic pretensions of the philosophical analysis.

If we look at much contemporary philosophy, particularly analytical philosophy of mind, it abounds with thought experiments meant to test and challenge our habitual assumptions about the nature of consciousness, the mind-body relation, personal identity etc. Thus one often comes across references to zombies, brain-transplantations, twin-earths and teletransporters etc. To illustrate how these thought experiments are being put to use, let us consider a concrete example.[3] Let us imagine that I (DZ) have a double, who is a molecule-by-molecule duplicate of me, and that each of us is sitting in two adjacent rooms. Let us further imagine that the two halves of my brain are slowly separated from each other and from the brainless body and that the nerves connecting the two halves with each other and with the body are replaced by radio communicators, so that the communication between all three parts continues as before. Let us further imagine that a similar 'zippering' operation is performed on my identical double. By now we have four separated brain halves and two brainless bodies. Let us then finally imagine that the wavelengths of the radio communicators are manipulated in such a fashion that the left brain half of my double starts communicating with my right brain half, whereas my left brain half starts communicating with my double's right brain half. It has been claimed that we, at this point, are faced with a situation where two different persons are having not only qualitatively but numerically identical experiences, that is it has been claimed that we are presented with a situation where two people are actually sharing each others experience. Since this scenario is imaginable, it must be (metaphysically) possible, and the claim has therefore been that it can serve as a valid counter-example to the thesis that experiences cannot be shared, but are always and necessarily private in the sense of belonging to a specific and singular subject.

This way of doing philosophy has, to put it mildly, not been met with universal approval.[4] One understandable reaction has been to ask whether it is really legitimate to draw such substantial philosophical conclusions from the fact that certain scenarios are imaginable. Is our imagination always trustworthy, does it always attest to metaphysical possibility, or might it occasionally reflect nothing but our own ignorance?

As Wilkes has pointed out, if thought experiments are to be of any value they have to be conducted with as much care to detail and with as many stringent constraints as real experiments in the laboratory. One of the important requirements is that we are in the clear about the background conditions against which the experiment is set. In other words, we need to know exactly what is being altered and what remains the same in the imagined scenario when compared to the actual world. If there are too many variables, if too many parameters are changed, we would not know which of them were responsible for the outcome, and it would consequently be impossible to draw any clear conclusion from the experiment (Wilkes 1988: 2, 6). Another prerequisite is that we actually know something about the topic under discussion. Otherwise we might easily end in a situation where we think that we have succeeded in imagining a possible state of affairs, whereas we in reality have done nothing of the sort, as we will realize when we acquire more information and are able to think the scenario through more carefully.

To illustrate: If we ask somebody whether he can imagine a candle burning in a vacuum, or a gold bar floating on water, and if the answer is yes, should we then conclude that there must be some possible world where gold bars have a different molecular weight, while remaining gold bars, and where candles can burn despite a lack of oxygen, or should we rather conclude that the person has only succeeded in imagining something that superficially resembles gold bars and burning candles? It definitely seems necessary to distinguish between imagining something in the sense of having a loose set of fantasies and imagining it in the sense of thinking it through carefully, and surely only the latter is of any value if we wish to establish whether a certain scenario is possible or not. In other words, it does seem necessary to distinguish between apparent imaginability/possibility and real imaginability/possibility (Tye 1995: 190) and the lesson to learn is undoubtedly, that the more ignorant we are, the easier it will seem to imagine something, since "the obstructive facts are not there to obtrude" (Wilkes 1988: 31). What seemed to be an imaginable possibility might by closer examination turn out to be an impossibility in disguise. But if we wish to derive any interesting conclusions from our thought experiments we need to assure ourselves that we are not faced with such impossibilities. And obviously we are not entitled to conclude that we are faced with a possible scenario, just because we do not know for a fact that it is impossible. Ignorance is a poor justification for any conclusion (Wilkes 1988: 20). Thus, as Dennett has put it: "When philosophical fantasies become too outlandish — involving time machines, say, or duplicate universes or infinitely powerful deceiving demons — we may wisely decline to conclude *anything* from them. Our conviction that we understand the issues involved may be unreliable, an illusion produced by the vividness of the fantasy." (Dennett 1981: 230)

Wilkes' suggestion, a suggestion we heartily endorse, is that since so many details have to be taken care of if a thought experiment is really to be conclusive, it might occasionally be better to abandon fiction altogether and instead pay more attention to the startling facts that can be found in the actual world. Real life deviations can serve the same function as thought experiments. They can also probe and test our concepts and intuitions, and they can do so in a far more reliable way, since the background conditions are known to us. Being real phenomena, they do not harbor any concealed impossibilities.

Our criticism should not be misunderstood. Thinking about exceptional cases "is indispensable if we wish to avoid mistaking accidental regularities for regularities which reflect a deeper truth about the world" (Gendler 1999: 463). However, given that thought experiments can be deceptive it might at times be more informative to search for actual rather than imaginary exceptions, and it is of course at this point that psychiatry can make its entry. If we are looking for phenomena that can shake our ingrained assumptions, and force us to refine, revise or even abandon our habitual way of thinking, there is no need to get lost in farfetched and unreliable fantasies. All we have to do is to turn to psychopathology (along with neurology, developmental psychology, ethnology etc.), since all of these disciplines present us with rich sources of challenging material. And of course, anomalous phenomena are very real. They constitute actual and not merely possible or hypothetical paradoxes and puzzles. To put it differently, if we wish to test our assumptions about the unity of mind, the privacy of mental states, the nature of agency, or the role of emotions, far more can be learned from a close examination of pathological phenomena such as depersonalization, thought-insertion, multiple personality disorder, cases of apraxia, or states of anhedonia than from thought experiments involving zipped brains.

Having said this, a word of caution might be appropriate. Pathological phenomena and other empirical findings are of course open to interpretation. Their interpretation will usually depend upon the theoretical framework one is operating within. Thus, the theoretical impact of an empirical case is not necessarily something that can be easily determined.[5]

Another question that also needs to be considered is how much significance one should actually attribute to these anomalous phenomena? Should we consider them to be mere marginal cases? Are they so to speak the exceptions that prove the rule? Or should they rather force us to abandon our habitual typification of behavior and experience with the realization that the normality that has been our point of departure has no centrality, but is just one variation among many?

These are certainly issues in need of further clarification, and we will not attempt to answer them here. One stance, though, that must be rejected as unacceptable is the following: It will not do simply to dismiss the anomalous phenomena or even the empirical findings with the argument that they are irrelevant from a philosophical point of view given their pathological and/or empirical status. Even if it might be too much to demand that a philosophical account should actually be able to explain deviating phenomena, it cannot simply ignore them; i.e., it will not do to advocate a theory that implicitly denies the possibility of these disorders. The chosen theory must remain compatible with their existence, it must be able to accommodate them.

So far we have mainly been calling attention to the negative or critical contribution of psychiatry. Its description of pathological disorders can challenge a number of philosophical platitudes. However, as we also mentioned, in some cases the confrontation with these case-stories might not force us to reject, but rather to revise or refine our analysis. It is of course at this point that the positive contribution of psychiatry comes to the fore. The very notion of deviant and anomalous states, the very grasp of these states as being deviant and anomalous, obviously implies a contrast to the normal modes of experience and existence from which they differ. It is exactly due to this contrastive feature that an examination of psychopathological disorders might help shed light on the elemental configurations of the normal modes. The normal is often so familiar to us that it remains practically unnoticed; it is so pervasive that it becomes elusive. But as both Wittgenstein and Heidegger have remarked, one of the tasks of philosophy is exactly to call attention to and elucidate those fundamental aspects of existence and reality that are so taken for granted, that we often fail to realize their true significance and might even deny their existence. However, exactly because psychopathological disorders involve such profound deviations from normal human experience, they can bring forth usually taken-for-granted, unnoticed conditions of normal daily experience. That is, the elemental conditions and configurations of normal existence, be it on the level of intentionality, intersubjectivity or self-experience, can be sharply illuminated through a study of their pathological distortions. Thus, it is no coincidence that all of the main figures of phenomenological philosophy have at some point written about psychopathological phenomena.

3. The contribution of phenomenology

Let us conclude with a few words about why we think that phenomenology might be particularly well suited to act as the philosophical 'Gesprächs-partner' of psychiatry. It seems to us (as it has seemed to generations of continental psychopathologists) that a crucial first step in dealing with a psychiatric disorder is to recreate its experiential dimension: If we wish to understand what depersonalization, perplexity or compulsion is, we have first to investigate what it feels like, that is, we have to take the first-person perspective seriously. Without a proper description of the central features of the disorder any subsequent attempt at explaining it, i.e., giving a causal account, will be doomed to failure. Given a misdescription, the explanation will be either worthless or misleading.

This problem arises already at the level of nosographic classification. Operationalistic psychopathology defines disorders in a polythetic manner (i.e. by a specified number of operational criteria). Such mode of classifying, ignoring prototypicality of a given disorder, which is linked to the essential aspects of a given disorder, is at variance with the *de facto* clinical processes, and has been detrimental to the etiologic research (Parnas 1999).

When it comes to acute and refined experiential descriptions, this is exactly one of the central tasks of phenomenology. The focus and the principal aim of phenomenological investigation is the description of the lived experience, a description of phenomena just as they present themselves or are given in experience. In further steps phenomenology asks about conditions of such experience and its mode of constitution. Phenomenology has therefore developed a series of methodological approaches to protect this investigative process from inadvertent contamination by theoretical or commonsensical prejudices, which may deform the description. In view of our assessment of the current status of psychopathology (see above), and more specifically of the prevalence of mixed, confusing discourse, it seems that a search for purity in the process of description should be a goal with high priority, and a sufficient reason to appreciate phenomenology.

Moreover, if we look closer at some of the central experiential categories that are afflicted in a manifold manner in different psychopathological conditions, such as the structure of time and space, the demarcation between self and non-self, the experience of one's own body, the question of unity and identity of self, the nature of intersubjectivity, then the relevance of phenomenological resources becomes obvious. Phenomenology has devoted extensive analyses to an understanding of such issues. These analyses might contain valuable material for a psychiatrist attempting to understand and conceptualize the patient's experiences.

This is not to say, however, that all is well with phenomenology. If this philosophical tradition is to remain of contemporary relevance, it will not do for it simply to continue down the narrow path of text-exegetical analysis — regardless of how much there still is to learn from authors such as Husserl or Merleau-Ponty. Phenomenology will have to overcome its phobic tendencies and enter into a critical dialogue with analytical philosophy, cognitive science, and the behavioral sciences. Moreover, such a dialogue will only be possible if those trained in phenomenology make more of an attempt to formulate their reflections in a relatively untechnical manner, thus making phenomenology accessible to people not already thoroughly familiar with its complex terminology.[6]

At the same time, one should not overlook some recent promising steps of rapprochement taken by analytical philosophy of mind. The issues of subjectivity, phenomenal consciousness, and selfhood are now once again respectable philosophical topics. It is almost commonplace to argue that the subjective dimension of experience must be taken seriously, since an important and non-negligible feature of consciousness is exactly the way in which it is experienced by the subject.[7] Lately, it is even being acknowledged that the investigation of the first-person perspective calls for a disciplined approach, and that there are existing resources to draw upon, with many refined analytical and systematical descriptions of lived consciousness. As David Chalmers has recently written: "the development of more sophisticated methodologies for investigating first-person data and of formalisms for expressing them is the greatest challenge now facing a science of consciousness."(Chalmers 1999: 10).[8]

Another encouraging development is the fact that a number of analytically trained philosophers with a background that includes Kant, Wittgenstein, P.F. Strawson, Gibson, and Evans, have begun to draw upon resources from cognitive science, psychopathology, neurology, and developmental psychology (e.g., Campbell 1995; Cassam 1997; Bermúdez 1998). They have reached conclusions, particularly on issues such as the role of the body, the connection between perception (exteroception) and proprioception, and the existence of pre-linguistic understanding, that bears a striking resemblance to some of the views found within phenomenology.[9]

It is our hope that this communication between phenomenology, analytical philosophy, and the empirical sciences will continue to improve. If that were to happen, psychopathology and empirical psychiatric research would be provided with the much needed conceptual resources.

Notes

1. For an insightful discussion of the difference between the descriptive term 'anomal' which merely signifies the discordant and the term 'abnormal' which has normative connotations cf. Steinbock 1995, 132.

2. In the German speaking psychiatry, the philosophy-psychiatry link continued to be cultivated and seen as crucial for academic psychiatry, with many important contributions, but unfortunately it hardly ever penetrated out of Germany (e.g. Hans Kunz, Zutt, Wyrsch, Müller-Suur, Klaus Conrad and others). In general, it was phenomenology and phenomenological anthropology, which dominated the philosophy-psychiatry link. Along these lines, the work of Ludwig Binswanger and Wolfgang Blankenburg deserves special attention; both made a permanent imprint on the continental psychiatric thinking (Parnas and Bovet 1991). Especially Binswanger explicitely searched for a meta-theory, capable of providing a foundational role for psychopathology (see Valdinoci 1986).

3. This thought experiment can be found in Unger 1990, and is discussed in Tye 1995: 78–79.

4. For a sustained criticism that we are indebted to, cf. Wilkes 1988.

5. To mention a few examples. On the one hand, it has often been claimed that pathological phenomena such as depersonalization and thought-insertion confront us with clear cut exceptions to the thesis that experiential phenomena are as such characterized by a quality of *myness*. There are, however, other interpretations possible (cf. Gallagher in this volume, and Zahavi 1999: 153–156). On the other hand, the puzzling case of blindsight is also open to interpretation. To mention but two of the most predominant ones: Blindsight has been taken both as a case of visual *consciousness* that simply lacks self-awareness, but it has also been understood as a case of *unconscious* information-processing that enables the subject to perform certain visual discriminatory tasks (cf. Van Gulick 1994).

6. For some attempts to make phenomenology more accessible without however losing what is essential to it, i.e., without simply transforming phenomenology into a subdiscipline of analytical philosophy, cf. Drummond 1990; Marbach 1993; Zahavi 1999; Sokolowski 2000.

7. See Nagel 1986; Searle 1992; Strawson 1994, and Flanagan 1992 for important contributions to this revival.

8. The *Journal of Consciousness Studies* has played a non-negligible role in this development. See for instance Varela and Shear 1999; Gallagher and Shear 1999. For another important contribution, cf. Petitot et al., 2000.

9. The "Joint Philosophy and Psychology Project on Consciousness and Self Consciousness" located at the department of Philosophy, University of Warwick, is at the forefront of this development. For some publications related to this project see Bermúdez et al. 1995; Eilan et al. 1999.

References

American Psychiatric Association (1994). *Diagnostic and Statistical Manual for Mental Disorders-IV edition*. Washington.

Bermúdez, J.L., Marcel, A.J., Eilan, N. (eds.) (1995). *The Body and the Self*. Cambridge, MA: MIT Press.

Bermudez, J.L. (1998). *The Paradox of Self-Consciousness*. Cambridge, MA: MIT Press.

Bleuler, E. (1911). Dementia praecox oder Gruppe der Schizophrenien. In G. Aschaffenburg (ed.). *Handbuch der Psychiatrie*. Spezieller Teil, 4. Abteilung, 1. Hälfte. Leipzig: Deuticke.

Bolton, D., Hill, J. (1996). *Mind, Meaning and Mental Disorder*. Oxford: Oxford University Press.

Campbell, J. (1995). *Past, Space and Self*. Cambridge, MA: MIT Press.

Cassam, Q. (1997). *Self and World*. Oxford: Oxford University Press.

Chalmers, D. (1999). First-person methods in the science of consciousness. *Consciousness Bulletin*, Fall 1999: 8–11.

Cutting, J. (1997). *Principles of Psychopathology. Two Worlds — Two minds — Two hemispheres*. Oxford : Oxford University Press.

Drummond, J.J. (1990). *Husserlian Intentionality and Non-foundational Realism*. Dordrecht: Kluwer Academic Publishers.

Eilan, N., McCarthy, R., Brewer, B. (eds.) (1999). *Spatial Representation*. Oxford: Clarendon Press.
Ey, H. (1973). *Traité des hallucinations*. Paris: Masson.
Flanagan, O. (1992). *Consciousness Reconsidered*. Cambridge MA: MIT Press.
Gallagher, S., Shear, J. (eds.) (1999). *Models of the Self*. Thorverton: Imprint Academic.
Gendler, T.S. (1999). Exceptional Persons: On the Limits of Imaginary Cases. In Gallagher, S. and Shear, J. (eds.): *Models of the Self*. Imprint Academic, Thorverton, 447–465.
Graham, G., Stephens, G.L. (eds.) (1994). *Philosophical Psychopathology*. Cambridge, MA: MIT Press.
Hamilton, M. (ed.) (1962). *Fish's Schizophrenia*. Bristol: John Wright & Sons.
Hasker, W. (1999). *The Emergent Self*. Ithaca: Cornell University Press.
Hempel, C. G. (1965). *Aspects of scientific explanations and other essays in the philosophy of science*. New York: Free Press.
Hofstadter, D.R., Dennett, D.C. (eds.) (1981). *The Mind's I*. London: Penguin Books.
Janzarik, W. (1976). Die Krise der Psychopathologie. *Nervenarzt*, 47:73–80.
Jaspers, K. (1922). *Allgemeine Psychopathologie*. 2. Auflage. Berlin: Springer.
Jaspers, K. (1957/1981). *Philosophical Autobiography*. In Schilpp, P.A. (ed): *The Philosophy of Karl Jaspers* (The Library of Living Philosophers). La Salle, Illinois: Open Court, 3–94.
Marbach, E. (1993), *Mental Representation and Consciousness. Towards a Phenomenological Theory of Representation and Reference*. Kluwer Academic Publishers, Dordrecht.
Minkowski, E. (1927). *La schizophrénie*. Psychopathologie des schizoïdes et des schizophrènes. Paris: Payot.
Mishara, A. (1994). A phenomenological critique of commonsensical assumptions in DSM-III-R: The avoidance of the patient's subjectivity. In Sadler, J.Z., Wiggins, O.P., Schwarz, M.A. (Eds.): *Philosophical Perspectives on psychiatric diagnostic classification*. Baltimore: Johns Hopkins University Press, 129–147.
Mishara, A., Parnas, J., Naudin, J. (1998). Forging the links between phenomenology, cognitive neuroscience and psychopathology. *Current Opinion in Psychiatry* 11:567–573.
Nagel, T. (1986). *The View from Nowhere*. Oxford: Oxford University Press.
Parnas, J., Bovet, P. (1991). Autism in schizophrenia revisited. *Comprehensive psychiatry* 32:7–21.
Parnas, J., Bovet, P. (1995). Research in psychopathology: Epistemological issues. *Comprehensive Psychiatry* 36:167–181.
Parnas, J. (1999). The boundaries of the schizotypal disorders and schizophrenia. (Plenary Lecture). In J. Lopez-Ibor et al (eds.): *One World, One Language — Paving the Way to Better Perspectives for Mental Health*. (Proceedings of X-th World Congress of Psychiatry). Hogrefe & Huber Publishers, 164–169.
Petitot, J., Varela, J., Pachoud, B., Roy, J.-M. (2000). *Naturalizing Phenomenology: Issues in Contemporary Phenomenology and Cognitive Science*. Stanford: Stanford University Press.
Pichot, P. (1999). Introduction. L'approche clinique en psychiatrie. In P. Pichot, W. Rein (eds.): *L'approche clinique en psychiatrie*. Paris: Institut Synthélabo, 7–25.

Sadler, J.Z., Wiggins, O.P., Schwartz, M.A. (Eds.): *Philosophical Perspectives on psychiatric diagnostic classification*. Baltimore: Johns Hopkins University Press.
Searle, J. (1992). *The Rediscovery of the Mind.* Cambridge, MA: MIT Press.
Sokolowski, R. (2000), *Introduction to Phenomenology*. Cambridge: Cambridge University Press.
Spitzer, M., Ühlein, F.A., Oepen, G. (eds.) (1988). *Psychopathology and Philosophy* Berlin: Springer.
Spitzer, M., Maher, B.A. (eds.) (1990). *Philosophy and Psychopathology*. Berlin: Springer
Spitzer, M., Ühlein, F., Schwartz, M.A. (eds.) (1992). *Phenomenology, Language & Schizophrenia*. Berlin: Springer.
Strawson, G. (1994). *Mental Reality*. Cambridge, MA: MIT Press.
Tye, M. (1995). *Ten Problems of Consciousness*. Cambridge, MA: MIT Press.
Unger, P. (1990). *Identity, Consciousness, and Value*. Oxford: Oxford University Press.
Valdinoci, S. (1986). Binswanger: une Metaphysique de la Psychiatrie. In P. Fédida (ed.): *Phénoménologie, Psychiatrie, Psychanalyse*. Paris: Echos-Centurion.
Van Gullick, R. (1994). Deficit Studies and the Function of Phenomenal Consciousness. In Graham, G., Stephens, G.L. (eds.): *Philosophical Psychopathology*, Cambridge, MA: MIT Press, 25–49.
Varela, F., Shear, J. (eds.) (1999). *The View from Within. Journal of Consciousness Studies* 6.
Wilkes, K.V. (1988). *Real People. Personal Identity without Thought Experiments*. Oxford: Clarendon Press.
Zahavi, D. (1999), *Self-awareness and Alterity. A phenomenological Investigation*. Evanston, Northwestern University Press.

PART I

An Ecological Perspective on the Self and its Development

George Butterworth
University of Sussex

1. Introduction: The ecological approach to self

James Gibson (1966, 1979) is best known for promoting the ecological approach to perception. His fundamental insight was that perception consists in detecting information concerning the relation between an active perceiver and a structured physical and social environment. Unlike most traditional theories the ecological approach proposes that the self exists objectively from the outset and is revealed in the dynamic structure of information available to perceptual systems. This perspective leads one to search for evidence of the origins of self in processes of self-perception. Self-perception is distinguished here from the self-concept which may be defined as a cognitive representation based on reflective self-awareness. The question with which the ecological approach is concerned is whether antecedents of the self-concept may be observed in self-perception and how development between the perceptual and conceptual levels of self-awareness occurs. Putting the question in William James (1890) terms we ask whether there is evidence for an existential subject, the I or agent of activity in early infancy and for a categorical self, or the me as the object of my own awareness. If we consider the problem in terms of self-conscious awareness, then we are looking for evidence of "primary consciousness" as Edelman defined it. Primary consciousness is the state of being aware of things including the self as an object situated in the physical and social world. Primary consciousness is based in perception, it depends on being embodied and situated in a physical and social environment. Ulric Neisser (1988) described these aspects of self-awareness as the ecological and interpersonal aspects of self.

Some characteristics of the ecological self that have been listed by Neisser (1988) are: (a) It is specified by objective information (b) Much of the information is kinetic and is available to several perceptual systems at once (c) The ecological self is veridically perceived from infancy. This most elementary form of self-awareness can be distinguished developmentally from higher order, secondary consciousness or reflective self-awareness. Let us begin therefore with a distinction between the ecological self defined as an object of one's own perception and the reflective self as an object of one's own cognition.

How can the self be an object of one's own perception? In most developmental theories until recently, the newborn baby was considered to be undifferentiated from the world in her own awareness. Piaget (1954) spoke of the infant existing in an adualistic confusion unable to distinguish between sensory experiences which change as a result of the infant's own activity and those which are independent of action. In Piaget's theory (Piaget 1954, 1962) and other major theories such as the Freudian account, development proceeds from total lack of differentiation (adualistic confusion) to proximal sensitivity (awareness of the kinaesthetic qualities of the infant's own body) and finally to distal spatial sensitivity. By about 18 months, largely as a result of the onset of independent locomotion, the infant becomes aware of herself as a totality contained within an encompassing space. Adualistic confusion is a necessary consequence of the assumption that visual space perception develops as a result of co-ordination of touch with vision and motor activity.

An alternative view, "natural dualism", was first put forward by the philosopher, Thomas Reid (1764). Natural dualism has been defined as "an immediate knowledge by mind of an object different from any modification of its own….the ego and the non-ego are thus given in an original synthesis, as conjoined in the unity of knowledge and in an original antithesis, as opposed in the contrareity of existence" (Baldwin 1901. Contrareity is defined as the relationship between two contraries, an opposition between one thing and another). James Gibson (1987) may have been influenced by Reid in formulating his theory of direct perception. Gibson's (1966) theory stands in contrast to adualistic theories. Direct perception means that information both about objects (including the self) and events in the environment, as they relate to behavior, is preserved in the energy patterns that impinge on perceptual systems. The ecological level of perception of reality is defined as follows by Gibson (1987a):

> Awareness of the persisting and changing environment (perception) is concurrent with the persisting and changing self (proprioception in my extended use of the term). This includes the body and its parts and all its activities from locomotion to thought, without any distinction between the activities called "mental" and those called "physical". Oneself and one's body exist along with the environment, they are co-perceived (418).

Gibson departs from Sherrington (1906) in explaining awareness of the bodily self. According to Gibson (1987b), proprioception is considered a general function of perceptual systems, regardless of modality, rather than a specifically kinaesthetic sense. In the traditional, Sherringtonian account, proprioception is given internally by muscle and joint receptors. Gibson (1987b) extended proprioception to include external feedback arising as a normal correlate of the exploratory activity of perceptual systems. Instead of kinaesthesis being considered a special sense, proprioception becomes a general, self-specifying, aspect of the information seeking functions of perceptual systems. Thus proprioception is a mechanism of self-sensitivity, common to all perceptual systems. Awareness of one's own movements can be obtained through vision or audition, as well as through the muscles and joints. Just as a bat may fly using echo-location to guide it, feedback from the visual environment may help the infant gain control of posture and hence be informative about the self. Proprioceptive information is available even to babies since perceptual systems are simultaneously proprioceptive and exteroceptive in the co-perception of self and environment.

Contemporary research strongly puts into question the assumption of an initial adualism in early infant experience, in favor of Reid's natural dualism. Infants demonstrate more than a rudimentary differentiation between self and the physical environment. Recent sources of information for self-specification in early infancy come from studies using video-feedback whereby the baby sees her own arm or leg movements, not directly, but over a TV monitor, either in correct perspective or reversed (Bahrick and Watson 1985; Van der Meer, Van der Weel and Lee 1995). These studies show that very young babies prefer the view which corresponds to their own perspective and is congruent with self-generated kinaesthetic information. Van der Meer et al. (1995) showed that a newborn baby would keep a weighted arm aloft when the limb was visible on a TV monitor but would allow the arm to drop when the camera showed the other, non-weighted arm. This achievement requires more than simple detection of a contingent relation between kinaesthetically specified limb motion and visual feedback. It requires perception of the correspondence between the kinaesthetic output of one's own limbs and the patterned visual feedback consistent with that motion. The embodied aspect of self is constituted in perceiving the identity of patterning between kinaesthetic and visual proprioceptive processes. Other examples show babies differentiate aspects of self in tactile self-exploration (Kravitz et al. 1978), and in the coordination between hand and mouth (Butterworth and Hopkins 1988). They also differentiate between self and the social environment, as evidenced by neonatal imitation (Meltzoff and Moore 1977). They show previously unsuspected inter-sensory co-ordinations e.g., between seeing and hearing (Castillo and Butterworth 1981) and between vision and touch (Meltzoff and Borton 1979) to cite just a few examples. These show that even newborns can relate information obtained through different perceptual systems to the same external objects. Such observations put into question the assumption that early perceptual experience is uncoordinated with respect to the self or with respect to external referents.

2. Visual proprioception and posture

The assumption that development begins from profound adualism ultimately rests on the assertion that the infant cannot tell the difference between sensory stimulation that is independent of her own activity and sensory feedback that is contingent on activity. According to Piaget (1954), there is no information in the structure of sensory stimulation to allow response contingent feedback to be differentiated from independent sensory data. The essential problem for the baby is to differentiate a change of place from a change of state of an object and this amounts to perceiving the difference between position changes that are reversible by a movement of the observer (change of place of a stable object) and those that are not (change of state of an object). To make this discrimination requires a distinction between observer and observed and a monitoring of object (or self) movement with respect to an external stable spatial framework.

Gibson (1966) coined the term visual proprioception to describe the kinaesthetic functions of vision. At any station point a continuous flow of optical information accompanies movement of the observer. Whether an observer actively moves or is passively moved through a stable visual environment, there arises a systematic flow of patterned optical information at the retina. In the case of forward locomotion the optical texture flows outwards, from a stationary central point which gives the direction in which the observer is moving. Under normal conditions, where the ground and surroundings may be considered stable, such a flow pattern can only arise when the observer is moving. Hence, within the co-perception of self and environment, it is sufficient to specify the distinction between self and the world and to form one of the foundations for the ecological self.

Visual proprioception offers a critical test for traditional accounts since the theory states that the optic flow field simultaneously provides differentiated information both for the movements of the observer and for the stability of the perceived environment, with no suggestion of adualistic confusion. The first demonstration that infants use visual proprioception to monitor their posture was made by Lee and Aronson (1974). Infants who had recently learned to stand were tested inside a "moving room" comprising three walls and a ceiling suspended just above the ground. The infants stood facing the interior end wall of the room and the whole room, except the floor, was moved so the end wall slowly approached or receded (and the side walls moved in the periphery). Babies compensated for a non-existent loss of balance and they swayed, staggered or fell in a direction appropriate to compensating for visually specified instability. For example, when the end wall receded, thus providing information consistent with backward instability, infants compensated and fell forward.

This rather spectacular demonstration certainly showed that babies are susceptible to visual proprioception but it remained ambiguous with respect to the origins of the proprioceptive functions of vision. It is possible that locomotion by crawling or walking might have given visual feedback its informative function. This possibility was examined in a series of studies with younger babies by Butterworth and Hicks (1977), Butterworth and Cicchetti (1978) and by Pope (reviewed in Butterworth and Pope 1983) which showed that babies too young to walk or crawl nevertheless monitor the stability of the standing posture, the sitting posture and even the stability of head control at 2 months, using visual proprioceptive feedback. Babies lose balance in the moving room when standing or sitting and at 2 months, before they can sit unsupported, their heads will sway in compensation for visually specified instability. Jouen (1990) has shown that newborns distinguish between visual and vestibular sources of information for passive acceleration. This suggests that internal and external information for self-motion are differentiated.

For good measure we recently tested 24 hour old chicks in a moving room and showed that they also monitor their posture with respect to the stability of the visual surround (Butterworth and Henty 1992). Thus altricial species, like human infants and a precocial species, like the early locomoting chicks, both make use of the visual flow field in similar ways in the early control of posture. It seems very likely that visual proprioception comprises an innate feedback loop which informs the organism of its relation with the natural environment.

What are the implications for the traditional concept of adualism? The infant's involuntary compensation to the misleading optic flow field can be thought of as an attempt to reverse a perceived change of place of her own body in order to maintain postural stability. By inverting the normal conditions of the ecology and inducing a change of state of the surround, moving room studies reveal that the baby normally does make the distinction between a change of place and a change of state. There is no question of adualistic confusion, the young infants invariably perceive the visual information as signifying a change of place of their own body.

In what sense does visual proprioception imply a form of self-awareness? Neisser (1988) argues that the ecological self does imply a form of unreflective consciousness but it is not what is ordinarily termed "self-consciousness" since the ecological self is not an object of reflective thought. Nevertheless, it does amount to an irreducible, basic form of self-awareness. Later in development, at about 14 months, the ability partially to overrule discrepant optic flow patterns can be observed as the baby turns to see what made the room move (Butterworth and Cichetti 1978). This later behavior does seem to reflect the kind of explicit self-consciousness normally implied by the term, where the baby shows that the event is understood to have occurred outside her own agency.

Even so, the difference between self-awareness and self-consciousness is only a matter of degree. Adults in an unfamiliar posture can easily be unbalanced in the face of discrepant visual feedback and they presumably have elaborated self-concepts (Lee and Lishman 1975). This implies that in addition to specification of self through visual proprioception there arises a form of self-knowledge which can, at least in part, overrule what is specified visually under non-ecological conditions. Normally these different aspects of self-awareness would be congruent and there is no reason to suppose that we ever grow out of relying on ecological specification of self. The developmental transition may be om optical specification of agency in the normal ecology to an autonomous lf-consciousness which comprehends its own agency over the optic flow eld. Self-specification remains embedded in the latter type of self-knowledge.

Visual proprioception may have a particularly important part to play in e acquisition of skills in infancy. Since the ground is normally an extremely able external referent, visual proprioception might serve to calibrate other inaesthetic systems. In developing organisms, where there is inherent vari-bility introduced by growth, a stable external referent may serve a particu-rly important ongoing calibrating function. Posture, perception and action re closely linked phenomena, with control of posture often acting as the rate miting factor in development. Acquiring control over head and trunk enables ew skills to be acquired, such as reaching and grasping. Such skills them-lves depend on the establishing of a "platform" of postural stability and this ill have implications for the infant's developing bodily self-awareness Rochat and Bullinger 1994). The onset of independent locomotion also epends on good prior control of static postures. Each of these motor skills has prolonged period of development and it is not surprising that infants with isual impairments are also delayed in postural control and the onset of ocomotion (Fraiberg 1977). Postural factors also enter into the social relation-hips between the infant and the adult, for example, as the baby moulds herself the body of the mother in feeding (Rochat and Bullinger 1994) or as the ightly older baby offers herself to the mother communicating her desire to be icked up (Fogel 1993). Perhaps the main implication for the origins of self is hat in acquiring skilled, goal directed activity the infant can discover more bout the agency of self. As Neisser (1988) puts it "We perceive as we act and hat we act; often, our own actions constitute the very characteristics of the cological self that we are simultaneously perceiving"(40).

Recall that we found negatively accelerated slopes with increasing xperience of the posture, with a particularly sharp decline in the effects of the iscrepant flow field after the onset of independent locomotion through crawl-ng. It seems possible that the optic flow pattern serves to calibrate each osture, so that the infant gains fine control over the body segments in a uccession of stages culminating in active locomotion. The transition from tatic to active postures places a particular premium on the visual system and he use of information for fine motor control. This precise form of self-control evelops only gradually, with experience of autonomous locomotion, as Held nd Hein showed (1960).

3. Perception, communication, and the interpersonal self

Some aspects of direct perception, such as detecting the information th specifies the elasticity or rigidity of objects, may have primary application i social perception (Walker et al. 1982). Fogel (1993) lists 14 different ways i which the dynamics of social interaction may be based on a rather sma number of variant and invariant properties of perceptual information. Thes coupled with the capacity for perception of emotional expressions may consti tute a large part of the necessary repertoire of perceptual abilities for soci interaction in babies.

Perhaps the best evidence of the infant's pre-adaptation for social experi ence comes from studies of imitation in early infancy. Precocious imitatio was long ago called "participation" by Baldwin (1913). His terminolog emphasizes imitation as a mechanism for realizing the socially constitute aspects of self. The importance of imitation for the origins of self is th consciousness of mutual, human relations provides the most direct feedbac about one's own personhood. MacMurray (1933) put it as follows: "Complet objectivity depends on our being objectively related, in action as well as i reflection, to that in the world which is capable of calling into play all th capacities of consciousness at once. It is only the personal aspect of the worl that can do this" (134). Baldwin (1913) agreed that imitation plays a centr role in the development of self knowledge "My sense of myself grows by m imitation of you and my sense of yourself grows in terms of myself (185)".

Notwithstanding its controversial status in contemporary psycholog there is now extensive evidence for neonatal imitation. Imitation in huma newborns has been shown for tongue protrusion, mouth opening, lip pursing sequential finger movements, blinking, vocalisation of vowel sounds an emotional expressions (Maratos 1982; Meltzoff and Moore 1983; Field et 1985; Kugiumutzakis 1985; Reissland 1988). Vynter (1986) showed th newborn infants imitate the dynamics (not the statics) of the acts they observ they need to see the act in progress in order to imitate. By the end of the fir year of life however it is sufficient for the infant to see the end state (e.g tongue protruded) in order to imitate. By one year of age imitation can als take on symbolic properties, it is no longer merely participation in the liter act, as in the neonate. Neonatal imitation is just the first level of a developin system of inter-personal relatedness which may contribute in important way to acquiring self-knowledge. Although imitation of remembered events als levelops, as shown by the capacity for deferred imitation which increases with age (Meltzoff 1988; Vynter 1986) newborn imitation can be taken as evidence for direct, primary consciousness of an inter-personal self.

How is neonatal imitation possible when it involves parts of the body the infant cannot see? The appropriate type of explanation would appear to require a theory of perception-action coupling to explain how the patterns of behavior observed can be elicited by the models presented to the newborn. A number of theories of basically similar type exist. Meltzoff and Borton (1981) argue that the mechanism of imitation, with its essential defining property of "transfer" of information from vision to action is logically equivalent to matching information across modalities of input. This is the active inter-modal matching AIM hypothesis (Meltzoff and Moore 1997, 1999). Meltzoff and Moore (1997) have recently elaborated this argument to suggest that some behaviours, such as tongue protrusion, entail organ identification which allow the baby to reproduce an observed target behaviour in a goal directed fashion.

The essential features are that prenatal activity, which Meltzoff and Moore (1997) term "body babbling" (by analogy with mechanisms know to be implicated in the development of speech), yields a repertoire of co-ordinated acts, which are simultaneously perceived proprioceptively in the self and exteroceptively in the model. A test-operate-test-exit comparator process, similar to Miller Galanter and Pribram's TOTE unit, allows progressive matching of action to the model. Other authors have made similar theoretical claims e.g. Trevarthen (1999) argues for "transfer of an amodal perceptual effect"; Donald (1991) also postulated a supra-modular "mimetic controller"; Kugiumutzakis (1985) argued that face recognition must occur, perhaps through a facial memory engram, between the visual exploration of the facial model and before the first effort to imitate. His point is perhaps similar to Meltzoff and Moore's hypothesis that imitation responses can be divided into phases, one of which is organ selection.

It may be sufficient, as James Gibson (1987) suggested, that the dynamics of perceptual systems always carry both exteroceptive and proprioceptive information. On this theory, the amodal system identified as necessary for imitation by all major theories is actually the general proprioceptive component of perception, regardless of which sensory channel carries it. Much of this information is kinetic in structure and equivalent across several perceptual systems. Despite a broad measure of agreement as to the necessity for an intermodal process to explain neonatal imitation, there are nevertheless many points of detail which still remain to be resolved. For instance, are we to think of the pre-natal patterns of activity as a form of learning, or are these movement patterns genetically determined? What is the range of pre-natal activity and how does it map onto post-natal imitation? To what extent is memory for an observed action pattern implicated in the newborn? Is it necessary to invoke representation from the outset? Does imitation begin with dynamic input and only later move onto imitation of end state models?

4. Prenatal development

Resolving these question will entail a theory of the embodied foundations of self-perception, which can then be extended to the special case of interpersonal perception. One possibility is to take into account evidence from pre-natal development. Ultra-sonic scanning studies of fetuses have shown that at least fifteen different, well co-ordinated movement patterns can be discerned as early as fifteen weeks gestational age (De Vries, Visser and Prechtl 1984). These include independent finger movements, rapid and slow mouth opening, movements of the hand, repetitive contacting of the mouth with the fingers, opening and closing the jaws, and co-ordinated independent leg movements. Movements of the fused eyelids are observed at twenty weeks, and conjugate lateral eye movements with open eyelids by 24–25 weeks. Finely modulated facial expressions can also be observed in fetuses of twenty four weeks (Hofer 1981). That is, complex sequences of co-ordinated activity can be observed in fetuses as young as 12 weeks of age and species typical facial expressions. Some of these are the very behaviors that have been reported in neonatal imitation studies.

Contemporary theories of brain development suggest that the detailed circuitry of the nervous system may depend on feedback from intra-uterine activity and sensory feedback (Purves 1994). Such activity and experience-dependent growth processes may begin very early in development. There is a high level of activity (estimated to be as many as 20,000 movements per day in the fetus to 15 weeks). Given the very early appearance of co-ordinated movements it is apparent that much fetal behavior must be regulated by systems within the spinal cord, brain stem and mid-brain. The neural basis for the complex action patterns reported in neonatal imitation studies may therefore be well established long before birth.

In summary, our analysis suggests that the infant is capable of imitating visual auditory and proprioceptive information because prenatal patterns of activity have been involved in selectively laying down the mid-brain structures at the heart of the embodied action system which give rise to patterned movement. These contribute to the control of manual, vocal and facial systems of expression in the newborn. Since the individual functions as an organized totality, the information controlling action, from whatever modality it is obtained, can be self-specifying and self-referent, or indeed, other specifying and other referent. As Andrew (1998) has argued once an ability has evolved sufficiently to be controlled by feedback, whether auditory or visual, the byproduct of that form of motor control is the ability to copy the sounds or movements of a con-specific.

5. Hand-mouth co-ordination

Hand-mouth co-ordination is an example of pre-natal organization of behavior which may be important for understanding newborn imitation and innate aspects of proprioceptive function. Newborn babies will make repetitive movements of the hand to the mouth which give every impression of being goal directed. With video-technology it is now possible closely to study behavior in the newborn and this shows that about 15% of the spontaneous arm movements of the awake, alert newborn infant result in the hand contacting the mouth. Butterworth and Hopkins (1988) observed that the newborn, lying with the head to the right side, opens the mouth and then moves the ipsilateral hand, so that the hand touches the mouth. The mouth "anticipates" the arrival of the hand which, incidentally, can find its way to the mouth by a variety of trajectories and without visual guidance. If the hand misses the mouth, but lands in the perioral region, it is very likely to move directly to the mouth. The action system has basic intentionality, it is not merely a mechanical reflex. Hand and mouth function in the newborn as a well organized system which may have benefitted from practice in utero (Butterworth 1989b). Others have described a consistent order of emergence of movements of the hand to the face in the hours after birth, starting with movements to the mouth (167 minutes after birth) then the face (192 minutes) the head (380 minutes) the ears (469 minutes), the nose (598 minutes) and the eyes (1491 minutes, median values, Kravitz, Goldenberg and Neyhus 1978). Observations such as these suggest a particularly early onset of tactile self exploration. That is, the mouth seems to know its own hand and there is no necessity for visual guidance. As we mentioned earlier, similar behaviors occur about 50 times per hour in the fetus from the 15th week of gestational age before the cortex is differentiated in the fetus so it is probably a function of mid-brain organization.

Recently, Ramachandran, Rogers-Ramachandran & Steward (1992) made the observation that adults who have had an arm amputated experience phantom limbs when the mouth is touched. Gallagher, Butterworth, Lew and Cole (1998), reviewed the literature in search of congenital aplisics to establish whether they also experience phantom limbs. We found 5 reports of such phenomena, totaling 18 cases in all, of children born without one or both arms who experienced phantom arms later in childhood. We interpreted this finding to mean that even in the absence of the arms, phantom limbs may arise because there is a pre-existing but unfulfilled co-ordination laid down between hand and mouth. That is hand mouth co-ordination may be a basic, genetically determined aspect of the body scheme.

Subsequently, we became aware of a case of congenital tetramelia reported by Brugger and colleagues (1998) of a 44 year old woman born with neither arms, nor legs, who has experienced vivid phantoms throughout her life, of the arms, legs, fingers and toes. She reported phantom hands which even gesticulate during speech. In an ingenious study using fMRI scanning these authors showed that imaginary tasks performed by the phantom limbs resulted in bilateral activation of the premotor and parietal areas of the cortex whereas the cortical areas for somatotopic representation of the hand in the primary motor cortex was not activated in any of 15 tasks. Brugger et al. also conclude that the basic perceptual experience of having a body must be at least in part, genetically determined. We are now debating whether phantom legs may arise because there is also a motor synergy linking the feet with the genital area in the typical legs crossed fetal posture of later pregnancy, since patients report phantom legs when the genitals are touched.

To return to the question of amodal perception in self-specification, a recent study by Botvinick and Cohen (1998) showed that normal adults will mislocate their own invisible arm in the direction of a visible rubber arm placed on the table in front of them, when both the real and rubber arm are stroked synchronously. They suggest that this illusion involves a constraint satisfaction procedure such that the normal correlations operating between vision, touch and proprioception are reconciled spuriously through a distortion of position sense. Ramachandran and Blakeslee (1998) also review a number of studies in which providing mirror image visual feedback of the arm enabled patients to gain movement control over their paralyzed phantom limbs. These studies dramatically attest to the role of proprioception in specification of the embodied self.

In summary, the arguments presented here have been for the unity of perceptual experience from the outset, that the motor organization laid down in utero has long term implications for motor control even when some components of the body are missing, that proprioception is provided by all perceptual systems and that infants are well to make use of visual aspects of proprioception as soon as it becomes available.

6. The interpersonal self and communication

Kugiumutzakis (1992) draws on evidence from neonatal preference for the sound and affective tone of the voice to suggest that imitation reflects an innate motive for communication. He agrees with Trevarthen (1993), that newborns show an “innate intersubjectivity” and they distinguish between self and others from the outset. This may be a necessary but insufficient condition for perception of an interpersonal self since the relationship lacks any emotional significance when stated so baldly. The infant’s capacity for emotional expression may also play an important part in early communication.

Evidence for such finely attuned behavior, and for the sharing of affect, between two month infants and their mothers has been obtained by Murray and Trevarthen (1985).They have studied the mutual co-regulation of activity in mother-infant pairs, the fine synchrony of movements, vocalisations and expressions of pleasure as the behaviors of the partners which form an indissociable whole. Stern (1985, 1993) has described a similar process he calls “affect attunement” whereby the mother matches the infant’s feelings with her own. If the baby is expressing joy, the mother does so too, perhaps by a different form of non-verbal expression but in a manner precisely synchronised with the infant’s emotional expression. The emotions form an invariant constellation of feeling qualities which are experienced as belonging to the self, while interaction with others is the eliciting condition for such self specifying experience.

Trevarthen distinguishes innate primary intersubjectivity (infant’s conscious awareness of mother, especially in relation to emotion) from secondary (infant's conscious joint awareness with mother of the world of objects). Primary intersubjectivity consists in the exchange of feelings, a common code of cooing noises, facial and hand movements, concentration, pleasure, and surprise which manifest even in very early social interactions between the two month old infant and the mother (Trevarthen 1991: 3). Primary intersubjectivity, Trevarthen argues, can be thought of as a directly perceived, conversational consciousness where communication occurs through the dynamic, transient shifts of emotion, as revealed in emotional expression of infant and adult alike. Toward the end of the first year of life the infant achieves secondary intersubjectivity, based on jointly constructed meaning, the negotiation of conventional knowledge and common purposes and communication through symbols (Sperry and Trevarthen 1991; Trevarthen 1991, 1992).

Secondary intersubjectivity in behavioral terms concerns how an infant knows where someone else is looking, how a baby knows where someone else is pointing and how babies produce pointing for other people. In studying the foundations of referential communication (how babies share objects with other people) the definition of self-consciousness which might apply is of joint awareness of public objects. That is, the object in the world offers an opportunity for minds to meet in joint attention to its properties. There is no doubt that babies as young as 6 months are able to change their own line of sight to follow a change in the attention of another person. Contrary to the traditional assumption that infants are totally egocentric (i.e., lost in an undifferentiated self) and therefore unaware of other minds, babies will take a change in the focus of attention of their social partner as indicating a potentially interesting sight. In our carefully controlled studies, an adult turns slowly and deliberately, to look at one of several targets positioned around the room. Babies can find the target the adult is looking at and we have described the ecological, geometric and representational mechanisms of joint attention, which arise during the first 18 months of life (Butterworth and Jarrett 1992).

One of the most striking phenomena we have discovered is that the ability to look where someone else is looking in the first year of life is circumscribed by the boundaries of the infant's own visual field. With the laboratory in front of the baby stripped bare and the potential targets only being located behind the infant babies do not search behind them when the mother changes her line of gaze (Butterworth and Cochran 1980). Instead, on the adult's signal, the baby turns through about 40 degrees within their own visual field and failing to encounter a target, the baby gives up. Only at 18 months does the baby succeed in searching in the invisible space behind him or herself, when the adult looks there.

These data suggest that the infant takes her own visual field to be held in common with others. Of course, if objects are noisy, then the baby can turn behind to locate them but this merely illustrates the different properties of the auditory and visual systems with respect to the ecological processes of spatial orienting. Visual perception necessarily originates at a particular viewpoint but the infant behaves as if others have a perspective on a common visual space. The boundaries of joint attention are defined by the periphery of the visual field. Even after 12 months when the baby begins to comprehend manual pointing this still does not extend the boundaries of joint attention. Grover (1988, and Butterworth and Grover 1988, 1989) showed that babies fail to search beyond the boundaries of the visual field even when the mother looks and points behind the baby.

Infants produce pointing at about 14 months and we know that this is an important, species-specific gesture which bridges non-verbal and verbal communication. Pointing, with the typical extended index finger posture of the hand is species specific to humans and may reflect the adaptation to communication of the specialised morphology of the hand (Butterworth 1991). In our most recent studies we have examined the production of pointing in babies. We use remotely controlled doll figures which move their arms and legs. Babies find these objects very interesting, they will point at them and they will often check that the adult has taken notice. Checking reveals a concern for the effectiveness of communication. We were particularly interested to find recently that 14 month old babies, when placed in pairs also point for each other and check that their message has been received (Franco, Perruchina and Butterworth 1992).

William James (1946) argued that joint visual attention depends on expressive movements which lead unrelated minds to terminate in the same perception. Objects, he said, are coterminous, mutual aspects of experience. Indeed, he argued that other minds are known only by virtue of the body's expressive movements and their effects on one's own perception. A change in another person's visual orientation, or manual pointing, signals to an observer an object of potential interest in shared visual space. Just as the moving room experiments show that the primary sense of the embodied self is directly, perceptually tied to the stability of the visual environment, joint attention studies suggest that interpersonal communication, or secondary intersubjectivity, also depends on a shared, stable visual space, which serves as the frame of reference for the change of posture of the partner to be perceived as a signal referring to an event within a shared space.

Neisser (1988) defines the interpersonal self as the self engaged in immediate, unreflective social interaction with another person. He argues that the essential information for the interpersonal self comes into existence only when inter-personal behaviors become synchronized. There arises a mutuality of experience (or intersubjectivity) which is confirmed by the reciprocal effects of gestures, emotions and expressions on the partner. The interpersonal aspect of self is brought into existence through the information created by these forms of early communication.

Stern (1985) has described how a co-ordination of emotional experience between mother and baby occurs in terms of the dynamics of emotional expression. Stern argues that through experiences such as these, the baby comes to be aware of the variants and invariants of the emotional relationship with the partner and of the organization and manifestation of each species typical form of emotional expression. The emotions form an invariant constellation of feeling qualities which are experienced as belonging to the self, while interaction with others is the eliciting condition for such self-specifying experience.

7. Direct perception and the core sense of self

These various pieces of evidence based on the ecological perspective may now be drawn together to give an account of the origins of self in infancy. One possibility is to follow Stern (1985) who has argued that a core sense of self comprises four components:

i. self-agency, the sense of the authorship of ones actions;
ii. self-coherence, the sense of being a physical whole with boundaries;
iii. self-affectivity, experiencing affect correlated with other experiences of self;
iv. and self-history, having the sense of enduring by noting the regularities in the flow of events.

In Stern's view, the core sense of self is an integration of these four self-invariant aspects of experience into a social, subjective perspective, with volition as the most fundamental invariant in a core sense of self. To the extent that acquisition of skilled action is accompanied by the sense of volition, by proprioceptive feedback and by predictable consequences the infant gains information about the authorship of her own activity. Perceptual systems provide the means to identify the consistent aspects of experience (invariants) which give rise, eventually, to the remembered self. The core sense of self is not a cognitive construct, nor is it a concept of self, nor is it linguistic, nor even self-knowledge. It is the foundation, in perception, action and emotion, for the more elaborated aspects of self which are yet to be developed.

Fogel (1993) agrees that a coherent core of self-related experience might be identified at the intersection of various sources of information for self. However, he suggests that the self is "the dialogic relationship between the point of observation, the rest of the body and the perceptual flow field in which the body is immersed"(143). The roots of the dialogic self, which give the distinction between the I and the me, lie in the co-perception of self and world and the co-regulation of social encounters. In self-directed exploratory action, for example, the existential self (I) specifies through touch an aspect of the categorical self (me). In social interaction, the dialogic aspect of self is particularly obvious. Fogel argues that this process of self-awareness is dialogic in the sense that there will always be self-specific feedback, of different kinds. Imitation too is dialogic because it requires self-action to be carried out in relation to another's action. The self in imitation is initially perceived in relation to the other as an aspect of embodied cognition, only at the end of infancy does the dialogic self become an aspect of the work of the imagination. The dialogical self exists from the outset in the inherently relational information available to perception.

In conclusion, the ecological approach to perception has revealed many unsuspected aspects of the original abilities of babies. There is now emerging a view of the origins of self both as a process and product of embodied perception. It is this essential advance that offers a new foundation for theories of the emergence of higher order forms of self-consciousness.

References*

Andrew, R (1962). Evolution of intelligence and vocal mimicking. *Science* 137:585–589.
Bahrick, L. and Watson, J. S. (1985). Detection of intermodal proprioceptive-visual contin-

* Due to the sudden and untimely death of George Butterworth this list of references remains incomplete. (DZ)

gency as a potential basis of self perception in infancy. *Developmental Psychology* 21/6:963–973.
Baldwin, J.M. (1901). *Dictionary of philosophy and psychology Vol 1*. New York and London: Macmillan and Co.
Baldwin J.M. (1913). *Social and ethical interpretations in mental development: a study in social psychology.* 5th edn. New York: MacMillan.
Botvinick, M. and Cohen, D. (1998). Rubber hands "feel" touch that the eyes see. *Nature* 391:759.
Brugger, P. and Regard, M. (1998). Phantom limbs in congenital tetramelia: a case report. (abstract) *Journal of the International Neuropsychological Society* 206.
Butterworth, G.E. (1989a). Events and encounters in infant perception. In A. Slater and G. Bremner (Eds.), *Infant development*. Hove: Lawrence Erlbaum, 73–84.
Butterworth, G.E. (1989b). On U shaped and other transitions in sensori-motor development. In A. de Ribaupierre (ed.), *Transition mechanisms in child development*. Cambridge: Cambridge University Press, 283–296.
Butterworth, G.E. (1992 a). Origins of self perception in infancy. *Psychological Inquiry* 3/2:103–111. (See also 10 peer commentaries pages 112–133).
Butterworth, G.E. (1992b). Self perception as a foundation for self knowledge. *Psychological Inquiry* 3/2:134–136.
Butterworth, G.E. and Cicchetti, D. (1978). Visual calibration of posture in normal and motor retarded Down's syndrome infants. *Perception* 7:513–525.
Butterworth, G.E., Cochran, E. (1980). Towards a mechanism of joint visual attention in human infancy. *International Journal of Behavioural Development* 3:253–272.
Butterworth, G.E. and Henty, C. (1991). Origins of the proprioceptive function of vision: Visual control of posture in one day old domestic chicks. *Perception* 20:381–386.
Butterworth, G.E. and Hicks, L. (1977). Visual proprioception and postural stability in infancy: A developmental study. *Perception* 6:255–262.
Butterworth, G.E. and Pope, M. (1983). Les origines de la proprioception visuelle chez le nourisson. In S. de Schonen (ed.), *Le developpement dans la premiere annee*. Paris: Presses Universitaires de France, 107–127.
Castillo, M. and Butterworth, G.E. (1981). Neonatal localisation of a sound in visual space. *Perception* 10:331–338.
DeVries, J.I.P., Visser, G.H.A. & Prechtl, H.F.R.(1984). Fetal motility in the first half of pregnancy. In H.F.R. Prechtl (Ed.), *Continuity of neural function from prenatal to postnatal life*. London: Spastics International Medical Publications, 46–64.
Edelman, G. M. (1989). *The remembered present*. New York: Basic Books.
Field, T., M. Woodson, R., Greenberg, R and Cohen, D. (1982). Discrimination and imitation of facial expressions in neonates. *Science* 218:179–181.
Fogel, A. (1993). *Developing through relationships. Origins of communication, self and culture.* Hemel Hempstead: Harvester Press.
Fraiberg, S. (1977). *Insights from the blind.* New York: Basic Books.
Gallagher, S., Butterworth, G.E., Lew, A. and Cole, J. (1998). Hand-mouth co-ordination, congenital absence of limb and evidence for innate body schemas. *Brain and Cognition* 38:53–65.
Gibson, J.J. (1966). *The senses considered as perceptual systems.* Boston: Houghton-Mifflin.

Gibson, J.J. (1987a). A note on what exists at the ecological level of reality. In E. Reed, and R. Jones (Eds.): *Reasons for Realism: Selected essays of James J. Gibson*. Hillsdale NJ: Erlbaum, 416–418.

Gibson, J.J. (1987b). The uses of proprioception and the detection of propriospecific information. In E. Reed, and R. Jones (Eds.): *Reasons for Realism: Selected essays of James J. Gibson*. Hillsdale NJ: Erlbaum, 164–170.

Held, R. and Hein, A. (1963). Movement produced stimulation in the development of visually guided behaviour. *Journal of Comparative and Physiological Psychology* 56:872–876,

Hofer, M.A. (1981). *The Roots of Human Behavior*. San Francisco: Freeman.

Jouen, F. (1990). Early visual-vestibular interactions and postural development. In H. Bloch and B.I Bertenthal (eds.), *Sensory-motor organisation and development in infancy and early childhood*. Dordrecht: Kluwer, 199–216.

Kravitz, H., Goldenberg, D. and Neyhus, A. (1978). Tactual exploration by normal infants. *Developmental Medicine and Child Neurology* 20:720–726.

Kugiumutzakis, G. (1985). *The origin, development and function of early infant imitation*. PhD thesis. Department of Psychology, University of Uppsala, Sweden.

Kuhl, P. & Meltzoff, A. N. (1982). The bimodal perception of speech in infancy. *Science* 218:1138–41.

Kuhl, P. & Meltzoff, A. N. (1986). The intermodal representation of speech in infants. *Infant Behaviour and Development* 7:361–381.

Lee, D. and Aronson, E. (1974). Visual proprioceptive control of standing in human infants. *Perception and Psychophysics* 15:529–532.

Lee, D. and Lishman, J.R. (1975) Visual proprioceptive control of stance. *Journal of Human Movement Studies* 1:87–95.

MacMurray, S. (1933). *Interpreting the universe*. London: Faber.

Maratos, O. (1973). *The origin and development of imitation during the first 6 months of life*. PhD thesis, University of Geneva.

Meltzoff, A.N. (1988). Infant imitation and memory: Nine month olds in immediate and deferred tests. *Child Development* 59:217–225.

Meltzoff, A. and Borton, R.W. (1979). Intermodal matching by human neonates. *Nature* 282: 403–404.

Meltzoff, A.N. & Moore, M.K (1977). Imitation of facial and manual gestures by human neonates. *Science* 198:75–8.

Meltzoff, A.N. & Moore, M.K (1997). Explaining facial imitation: a theoretical model. *Early Development and Parenting* 6:179–192.

Michaels, C. and Carello. C. (1981). *Direct perception*. New York: Appleton.

Murray, L. and Trevarthen, C. (1985). Emotional regulation of interactions between two month olds and their mothers. In T.M.Field and N.A. Fox (eds.), *Social perception in infants*. Norwood New Jersey: Ablex, 101–125.

Neisser, U. (1988). Five kinds of self knowledge. *Philosophical psychology* 1/1:35–59.

Piaget, J. (1954). *The construction of reality in the child*. New York: Basic Books.

Piaget, J. (1962). *Play Dreams and Imitation in the child*. New York: Norton.

Ramachandran, V.S., Rogers-Ramachandran, D. & Steward, M. (1992). Perceptual correlates of massive cortical reorganisation. *Science* 258:1159–1160.

Ramachandran, V.S. and Blakeslee, S. (1998). *Phantoms of the mind*. London: Fourth Estate.

Reissland, N. (1988). Neonatal imitation in the first hour of life. Observations in rural Nepal. *Developmental Psychology* 24: 464–469.

Rochat, P. and Bullinger, A. (1994). Posture and functional action in infancy. In A.Vyt, H. Bloch and M. Bornstein (eds.), *Francophone perspectives on structure and process in mental development*. New Jersey: Lawrence Erlbaum, 15–34.

Sherrington, C.S (1906). On the proprioceptive system, especially in its reflex aspect. *Brain* 29: 467–482.

Stern, D. (1985). *The interpersonal world of the infant*. New York: Basic Books.

Van der Meer, A., Van der Weel, F.R. and Lee, D.N. (1995). Lifting weights in neonates: Body building in progress. *Science* 267:693–695.

Von Hofsten, C. (1988). Transition mechanisms in sensorimotor development. In A. de Ribaupierre (ed.), *Transition mechanisms in child development*. Cambridge: Cambridge University Press, 233–258.

Vynter, A. (1986). The role of movement in eliciting early imitation. *Child Development* 57: 66–71.

Walker, A., Owlsley, C J., Megaw-Nyce, J., Gibson, E.J. and Bahrick, E. (1980). Detection of elasticity as an invariant property of objects by young infants. *Perception* 9:713–718.

The Phenomenology and Ontology of the Self

Galen Strawson
Oxford University

1. Introduction

I am interested in two questions. One is ontological: 'Do selves exist, and if so, what are they?' The other is phenomenological: 'What is the nature of self-experience? What is the nature of experience that has the character of being experience of a self, whether or not there are such things.' Self-experience certainly exists, whether or not selves do. It exists although people have very different views about what it is, and about what is important in it.

It is difficult to know where to begin, because there are many different notions of the self. Among those I have recently come across are the cognitive self, the conceptual self, the contextualized self, the core self, the dialogic self, the ecological self, the embodied self, the emergent self, the empirical self, the existential self, the extended self, the fictional self, the full-grown self, the interpersonal self, the material self, the narrative self, the philosophical self, the physical self, the private self, the representational self, the rock bottom essential self, the semiotic self, the social self, the transparent self, and the verbal self. I am not going to go through them all here. In a way I love them all, but when I talk about selves, and ask whether or not they exist, I mean selves as classically conceived: internal mental things, internal mental presences. I start from the assumption that whatever a self is, it is certainly (a) a *subject of experience*, although it is certainly (b) *not* a human being considered as a whole. My question is: Do such things exist? I'm inclined to answer Yes. Many, however, may feel that my Yes amounts in effect to a No. And I am aware that the way I approach the question of the self may seem unhelpful —

pointless — to many psychologists. This is because they and I have very different concerns.

I think ontology and phenomenology are tightly connected when it comes to the self, in a way that I will try to explain. First, though, let me make it clear that I take the term 'phenomenology' to be a completely general name for the study of the character of experience. I use it in the standard non-aligned sense which has nothing to do with the special use that derives from Husserl and his school.

As for basic ontology, I am a materialist. I take it that every thing and event in the universe, including consciousness, is physical. So I certainly don't think that selves are Cartesian egos, or immaterial souls.

2. The relation between ontology and phenomenology

The argument that ontology and phenomenology are tightly connected when it comes to the problem of the self goes as follows.

i. The idea or sense of the mental self is vivid for us, and it is this that creates the problem of the self. It is this that leads us to ask whether selves exist.
iii. But clearly we need to know what sort of things we are asking about before we can begin trying to find out whether they exist.
iii. The question is then this: Where should we look to establish what sort of things we are asking about?
iv. The best answer seems to be that we should look to self-experience, because it is self-experience that gives rise to the problem, by giving us a vivid sense that there is such a thing as a self. In fact, I propose, self-experience is the source of the problem of the self in such a way that when we ask whether selves exist, what we are asking is (necessarily): Does anything like the sort of thing that is figured in self-experience exist?[1]

And if this is right, then

v. Before we ask the *ontological* question 'Do selves exist?' we have to answer the *phenomenological* question 'What sort of thing is figured in self-experience?'

I think this is at first best taken as a question about human beings, as the *local* phenomenological question 'What sort of thing is figured in ordinary human self-experience?' Once we have an answer to the *local* question we can go on to the *general* phenomenological question: 'Are there other possibilities, so far as self-experience is concerned? What is the *minimal* form of genuine self-experience?' And once we have an answer to the general phenomenological question we can go back to the ontological question 'Do selves exist?', which now has two versions: 'Do selves exist as figured in ordinary human self-experience?' and 'Do selves exist as figured in the minimal form of self-experience?' I believe that the best answer to the first question is No, and that the best answer to the second question is Yes.

As remarked, different people mean very different things by 'self-experience', but they can all use the general procedure outlined above. They can begin with phenomenology and take the ontological problem of the self to be set by the outcome of the phenomenology. Note, though, that some hold that the transition from phenomenology to ontology is immediate. They hold that the phenomenology of the self constitutes the existence of the self. Zahavi and Parnas make this move, stating that 'there is no difference between the . . . phenomenon of self and its metaphysical (or ontological) nature. Reality here is the same as appearance' (1998: 263).[2] Others hold, as I do, that the ontology of the self is not identical to the phenomenology of the self. And yet I agree with Zahavi and Parnas (where many might not) that what is phenomenally given in self-experience is at least *part* of what a self's existence consists in — if indeed selves exist. I differ from them only because I also think that there must be more to a self: A self cannot be just what is phenomenally given, any more than a subject of experience can itself be a merely experiential phenomenon.[3]

Many psychologists who study self-experience, and in particular disorders of self-experience, simply do not have any further ontological concerns, when it comes to 'the self'. And they may wish to express this by saying, in Zahavi and Parnas's words, that 'reality here is the same as appearance'. That's fine by me. It means that their concerns are different from mine.

Clearly a great deal depends on what one means by 'self-experience'. So let me say again that I mean the vivid sense that people have of themselves as being a self in the sense of an inner mental presence or being, a single mental something that is a conscious subject of experience: 'my self, that which I most intimately am' in the words of Colin McGinn; a 'living, central, ... inmost I', in the words of Arthur Hugh Clough, a nineteenth-century poet; 'a secret self … enclosed within', in the words of Thomas Traherne, a seventeenth-century poet; 'my self, my inward self I mean …', in the words of Edmund Spenser, a sixteenth-century poet; 'my inmost self', in the words of St Paul. I don't for a moment believe that this is a peculiarly modern, Western experience, a product of the Romantic movement (or whatever), or of an unusually leisured or intellectual life. It is part of what Cicero had in mind when he said '*Mens cuiusque is est quisque*' — 'the mind of a person *is* that person', and it is something that has been explicitly discussed in the Eastern tradition of thought for thousands of years.[4]

3. Human experience

My main concern is with the ontological question 'Do selves exist?', but in order to generate a clear version of this question I have first to answer the phenomenological question about self-experience. For this purpose I will draw on some already published conclusions about the basic structure — the basic conceptual framework — of self-experience (cf. Strawson 1997, 1999).

In the case of the local question about ordinary human experience, a self tends to be figured as

(1) a *subject of experience*, a conscious feeler and thinker
(2) a *thing*, in some interestingly robust sense
(3) a *mental* thing, in some sense
(4) a thing that is *single* at any given time, and during any gapless or hiatus-free period of experience
(5) a *persisting* thing, a thing that continues to exist across gaps or hiatuses in experience
(6) an *agent*
(7) something that has a certain character or *personality*.

This list raises many questions, but I will make only four brief comments.[5]

The first is that, as I understand them, these seven clauses record features of the ordinary human mental condition that are universal. They are situated below any level of plausible cultural variation, although their force may vary considerably from person to person on account of individual (intracultural) differences.

The second is that to focus on the basic *conception* of the self implicit in self-experience as I am doing is in no way to downplay the importance of *affective* factors in self-experience, as some have thought. I think it plausible that emotional phenomena are the fundamental source — the fundamental engines — of self-experience, at least so far as humans are concerned, and may be in some way constitutive of self-experience, in some cases.[6] But they are not my present subject.

Now for two comments about specific items on the list. First, as far as (4) is concerned, I take the idea of a hiatus-free period of thought or experience as primitive. The conscious entertaining of a thought like 'the cat is on the mat', in which the elements *cat*, *on*, and *mat* are bound together into a single thought, is perhaps, a paradigm example of such a period of experience. So is looking up and seeing a face and seeing it as such. Like Dennett, I take it that such periods are almost always short in the human case, and I believe that there is considerable experimental support for this view.

Condition (2), the proposal that a self is experienced as a thing in some sense, has been widely challenged and is wide open to misunderstanding, but the general idea is simply this: Normal self-experience does not figure a self as (merely) a state or property of something else, or as an event, or some sort of process, as 'process' is ordinarily understood. To that extent, there is nothing else for a self to seem to be, other than a thing of some sort. Obviously it is not thought of as being a thing in the way that a stone or a chair is, but it is none the less figured as a thing of some kind — something that can *undergo* things and *do* things and, most simply, *be in some state or other*. None of these things can be true of processes as ordinarily conceived of. Kant's discussion of this in the presentation of the First Paralogism in the *Critique of Pure Reason* is hard to beat, and I will say no more about it today (cf. Kant 1781–7: A349, B407, B419–20).

So (1)–(7) offer a description of the basic conception of the self implicit in ordinary human self-experience. I think such self-experience comes to every normal human being, in some form, in early childhood. The realization of the fact that one's thoughts are unobservable by others, the experience of the sense in which one is alone in one's head or mind, the mere awareness of oneself as thinking: These are among the very deepest facts about the character of human life. Many psychologists and philosophers are rightly concerned to stress the embedded, embodied, 'ecological' or 'Triple-E' aspects of our experiential predicament as social and organic beings situated in a physical environment; but they risk losing sight of the respect in which self-experience as I understand it — the experience of oneself as a specifically mental something — is, for all this, one of the most central and fundamental ways (and arguably the most central way) in which human beings experience themselves. We may have some constant background awareness of our bodies, but this is fully compatible with our thinking of ourselves centrally as mental things, and those who stress somatic awareness may forget that it is just as true to say that there is constant background (as well as foreground) awareness of our minds. Kinaesthetic experience and other forms of proprioceptive experience of body are just that — experience — and in so far as they contribute constantly to our overall sense of ourselves, they not only contribute awareness of body, they also contribute awareness of themselves, i.e. awareness of experience. The notion of background awareness is imprecise, but I think that there is certainly never *less* background awareness of awareness (i.e., of mind) than there is background awareness of body, and unprejudiced reflection reveals that in general awareness of mind, background or foreground, vastly predominates over awareness of body. (Even if background awareness of body is indispensable for self-experience in creatures like human beings, it does not follow, and is not true, that such self-experience figures the self *as* embodied in any way.)[7]

In stressing the sense of mental self, I am not saying that our experience of ourselves as embodied human beings isn't also central to our lives. Obviously it is. And I am certainly not saying that self-experience involves any belief in anything like a non-physical soul.

4. Self-experience — the minimal case?

The first phenomenological claim, then, is that the ordinary human case of self-experience is captured by (1)–(7). What about the minimal case of self-experience? Using a mixture of thought experiment and reference to actual but unusual human cases, some of which tend to be classified as pathological, I propose that (5), (6), and (7), are not essential, and that in the minimal case of self-experience a self is figured just as

(1) a *subject of experience*, a conscious feeler and thinker
(2) a *thing*, in some interestingly robust sense
(3) a *mental* thing, in some sense
(4) a thing that is *single* at any given time, and during any gap-free period of experience.

In other words, I claim that it is in the limiting case possible for a being to lack any significant sense of itself as an agent, and as something that has a personality, and as something that has long-term persistence, and still experience itself as a self or mental subject at a given time.

Many disagree — the claim requires considerable defence (cf. Strawson 1997: 417–21). I won't say more about it now, except to note that there are recognized pathologies that can involve the weakening or loss of all three of these aspects of ordinary human self-experience — aboulia, apraxia, depersonalization, passivity phenomena in schizophrenia, autism, and loss of time sense (consequent on damage to the dorsolateral prefrontal cortex, for example, or bilateral lesions of the medial temporal lobe and damage to the hippocampus).[8]

Lack of a significant sense of the self as persisting, or as an agent, or as having personality, is likely to be called a disorder of self-experience — a 'self-disorder'(Zahavi and Parnas 1998: 265). It is not, however, clear that it will always be harmful, or always involve unhappiness. For it is likely to involve abnormality of what one might, drawing on the Hindu-Buddhist tradition, call the 'I-Me-Mine' emotional structure, and although the I-Me-Mine structure is certainly part of the normal human mental endowment, it is a familiar thought that it is also the principal source of human unhappiness. And this suggests that abnormalities of the I-Me-Mine structure, inherited or acquired, may in certain cases be a good thing.[9]

Obviously there may be I-Me-Mine-driven abnormalities of the I-Me-Mine structure — exacerbations or hypertrophies of one or other of its elements that make it an even more potent source of unhappiness than before; and no doubt one can suffer as a result of an abnormality of the I-Me-Mine structure, and feel socially isolated on account of it, even when the abnormality involves a potentially liberating weakening of the I-Me-Mine structure, and has many features in common with a state of detachment that others, seeking to improve their lives, strive to attain. But neither of these points undermines the possibility that the weakening of the sense of the self as having personality (or as having long-term diachronic continuity, or as being an agent) can be a good thing. Pathology aside, human beings can differ dramatically, so far as the strengths of the seven different elements of self-experience are concerned. In these respects, as in all other psychological and physiological respects, we lie along a long spectrum of difference. A certain psychological set can be abnormal, or even highly abnormal — like red hair, or very red hair — without being in any way pathologically abnormal — again like red hair, or very red hair. There are many deeply different forms of a good human life, and the ethical tradition deriving from Plato and Aristotle has done no good in so far as it has tended to imply that there is some single human optimum. Everybody, perhaps, has some psychological peculiarity or other, and one does not have to glorify mental abnormality in the manner of some Laingians in order to find good in it. It can be a gift or a curse according to context, inner or outer, psychological, social or economic. Some, for example, have a gift for detachment — even, perhaps, for enlightenment. Others, perhaps, find their propensity to detachment a curse.

5. SESMETs

Be that as it may, I want now to consider the ontological question that is delivered by the answer to the general phenomenological question in the last section. According to this answer, (1)–(4) give the minimal case of self-experience. And if this is right, then the basic ontological question is: Does anything actually exist that has the four properties listed in (1)–(4)? That is: Do there in fact exist (1) subjects of experience that are (4) single (3) mental (2) things during any gap-free period of experience, whether or not they can persist across gaps in experience?

I think there are, and since I don't want to argue about whether they should be called 'selves' or not, I will call them SESMETS (**S**ubjects of **E**xperience that are **S**ingle **ME**ntal **T**hings). This will allow me to put the case for their existence while leaving open the question of whether it would be right or best to call them 'selves'.

As already remarked (p. 43), I think that gap-free periods of experience are always short in the human case — a matter of a few seconds at most. So I think that many SESMETS exist in the case of a human being. In all essentials, in fact, I agree with William James — in spite of his advocacy of the deeply dubious phrase 'the stream of consciousness'. He holds that 'the same brain may subserve many conscious selves' that are entirely distinct — numerically distinct — substances. Using the word 'thought' in the wide Cartesian sense to cover all types of conscious episodes, he claims that each '"perishing" pulse of thought' is a self. In a famous but puzzling phrase, he says that 'the thoughts themselves are the thinkers' (1890: 401, 371; 1892: 191). I think that it is better and clearer to say that the existence of each 'thought' or conscious episode involves a self, or consists in the existence of a self or SESMET or subject of experience entertaining a certain mental content, but the basic idea is the same. On this view, the apparent continuity of our conscious experience, such as it is, and the general consistency of perspective shown by successive selves in a single body, derives from the fact that SESMETs 'appropriate' — in James's word — the experiential content of their predecessors' experiences. They do so in a way that is entirely unsurprising in so far as they arise, like jets or gouts of water from a rapidly sporadic fountain, from brain conditions that have considerable similarity from moment to moment even as they change. (Here there are two very different points. First, given short-term or 'working' memory, the immediately preceding experiential contents form part of the context in which new experiential contents arise in every sense in which features of the external environment do. Second, the features of the brain that constitute a human being's basic epistemic and cognitive outlook and basic conative and emotional outlook are likely to remain highly stable from moment to moment, and indeed over long periods of time.)

According to James

> the *I* is a *thought*, at each moment different from that of the last moment, but *appropriative* of the latter, together with all that the latter called its own. All the experiential facts find their place in this description, unencumbered with any hypothesis save that of the existence of passing thoughts or states of mind.[10]

In my terms: a SESMET is a subject of experience present and alive in the occurrence of an experience. It is a real, concretely existing mental unity of a certain sort.[11] It is, equally, a physical unity of a certain sort (for the mental is physical). It is as Triple-E — as environmentally embedded, embodied and ecological — as anyone could wish.

It seems to me that SESMETs are the best candidates there are for the name 'selves', if we take the ontological question 'Do selves exist?' at face value and in a classical fashion and consider the human case. And since I have no doubt that SESMETs exist, I am happy to answer Yes to the question 'Do selves exist?'

Some think that selves must at the very least be SESMEPETS — subjects of experience that are single, mental, *persisting* things. They think that nothing can deserve the name 'self' unless it has considerable diachronic continuity (while still being something that is not a human being considered as a whole). And this is clearly a view that needs to be discussed in any general treatment of the theory of the self. Here it suffices to note that an argument for SESMETS can leave open the possibility that SESMETS — or at least some of them — are also SESMEPETS. It seems to James and me, though, that there is no evidence for the existence of SESMEPETS as opposed to SESMETS and persisting brains, in the human case, and it is this that leads us to embrace what one may call the 'Transience' view of human selves: we feel that 'all the experiential facts find their place in this description, unencumbered with any hypothesis save that of the existence of passing thoughts or states of mind'.

Most of those who want to defend the idea of 'the' self find this view disappointing. It does not give them what they want — it makes 'the' self (whatever that is) fleeting and insubstantial. Nor does it connect with popular and deeply rooted psychotherapeutic uses of the notion of self. What's more, it looks like one of those philosophical views that can perhaps be defended and made consistent and even shown to have certain theoretical advantages, but that remains ultimately boring because it is too far removed from what we feel and what we want. I disagree, however. I think the Transience view can be made compelling and shown to be natural and true to life. But I realize that deep differences of temperament make this hard for some people to see, and I will now say a little more about it.

6. The Transience view

Let me introduce Louis, a representative human being. I will call the portion of reality that consists of Louis the 'Louis-reality', or the 'L-reality' for short. The notion of the L-reality is rough, because as a physical being Louis is enmeshed in wide-reaching physical interactions and is not neatly separable out as a single portion of reality, but it will do for present purposes.

Consider, then, the L-reality. According to the Transience view, many SESMETS exist in the L-reality, for a SESMET exists in the L-reality whenever there is an episode of conscious experience in the L-reality.

How long does a given SESMET last? As long as the experientially unitary period of experience of which it is the subject. How many are there? There are exactly as many SESMETS in the L-reality as there are experientially unitary periods of experience. For each experientially unitary period of experience must have a subject *for whom* it is a unitary, bound experience, a subject that holds it together in such a way that it constitutes an experientially unitary experience — the grasping of a thought-content, the seeing of a bird and the seeing of it as a bird, and so on. If distinguishing and counting such experientially unitary periods of experience is an irreducibly uncertain business, epistemologically speaking, so be it. The same goes for the counting of SESMETS. It certainly does not follow that there is any *ontological* indeterminacy when it comes to the question of how many there are (though it may well be rather unimportant how many there are).

I take it, then, that there are many SESMET-involving bindings, in the case of the life of a human being, and that for the most part they exist successively and in a non-overlapping fashion, although I agree with William James that there is no theoretical difficulty in the idea that they may also exist concurrently. The conscious experience — the conscious mental life — of a human being is just the living — the inhabitings — of these bindings. When we consider a human being as a persisting whole, we naturally speak in terms of there being just one subject of experience. It is only when we decide to take on the Problem of the Self, and press the metaphysical question of the existence of the self, that we do better to say that there are many subjects of experience — or SESMETS — or selves.

The Transience view is so called because of its application to the human case. It does not claim that SESMETS are necessarily of relatively short duration. It is only relative to everyday human standards of temporal duration that they appear short-lived, in any case, and it is not a necessary feature of their nature.[12] There may perhaps be beings whose periods of hiatus-free experience extend for hours, or for the whole of their existence. This is how I'd expect the divine SESMET to be, if I believed in God. We, however, are not like this. It may be that meditation or music can engender longer periods of hiatus-free thought in human beings, but the basic form of our consciousness is that of a gappy series of eruptions of consciousness out of non-consciousness, although the gaps are usually not apparent to casual inspection.[13]

It is crucial to the present position that there is no SESMET in the Louis-reality — the L-reality — when there is no conscious experience in the L-reality. A SESMET is present only when there is actual experience or consciousness. So it cannot be identified with a human being considered as a whole, or with a brain, or with a relatively enduring brain structure: It has quite different identity conditions. Many people use the term 'subject of experience', which is one of the components of the term 'SESMET', in such a way that a subject of experience can be said to exist in the absence of any experience, and many have grown so accustomed to this use, and to identifying subjects of experience with human beings (or other creatures) considered as a whole, that they can no longer hear the extreme naturalness of my present use, according to which there is no *subject of experience* if there is no *experience*; according to which a subject of experience cannot exist at time *t* unless experience exists at *t* for it to be a subject *of*. I hope that those who find this natural use of 'subject of experience' odd will accustom themselves to it. It is only a matter of terminology, after all, and it is only this indubitably real phenomenon — the subject of experience considered as something that is alive and present in consciousness at any given moment of consciousness — that concerns me at the moment. Obviously a subject of experience in this sense cannot be said to exist at all when there is no experience or consciousness.

7. 'What then am I?'

But what then am I?, you ask; as Descartes once asked. What am I if the mental subject of experience is not the same thing as the human being? What is the relation between Louis and a SESMET that exists in the L-reality? Am I a SESMET, or short-lived self?

In one sense No. I am a human being. In another sense Yes, that is precisely what I am, as I speak and think now.

But what then am *I*? Am I two different things, $I_{\mathrm{H(uman\ being)}}$ and $I_{\mathrm{S(ESMET)}}$, at a given time? Surely that is an intolerable conclusion, logically and metaphysically?

Not at all. It is simply a reflection of how the word 'I' works. 'I' is not univocal in ordinary thought and talk, and can refer to two different things. More precisely, its referential reach can expand outwards in a certain way, so that it can refer to more or less. The same is true of 'here' and 'now', with which 'I' is often contrasted, but 'I' does not expand outwards in a continuous fashion like 'now' and 'here'.[14] Rather, it moves between two fixed positions. 'I' refers to an object, unlike 'now' and 'here', and the phrase 'the castle' provides a better analogy, given that we are concerned with objects. Thus sometimes 'the castle' is used to refer to the castle proper, and sometimes it used to refer to the ensemble of the castle and the ground and buildings located within its outer walls. Similarly, when I think and talk about myself, my reference sometimes extends only to the SESMET that I then am, and sometimes it extends further out, to the human being that I am. The castle proper is not the same thing as the castle in the broad sense, but it is a (proper) part of the castle in the broad sense. The same is true in the case of a SESMET and a human being.

'But what *is* a SESMET, exactly? You, Galen Strawson, say you're a materialist, and you accordingly say that a SESMET is a physical unity of some sort, but you haven't actually given any account of what it's made of, or how it relates to the brain.'

This question leads into the 'mind-body' or 'consciousness-matter' problem. To begin with, it requires an account of what it is to be a genuine or realistic materialist, that is, someone who, like me, is (a) an outright realist about consciousness, thinks (b) that everything is physical, and therefore also thinks (c) that consciousness is physical. I could express the realistic materialist position dramatically by saying that I'm inclined to think that consciousness is a form of matter. And if anyone were to say that this is implausible I would reply that they must think they know more about the nature of matter than they do. For present purposes, though, I will try to give an idea of what is involved in realistic materialism by making one brief comment about the standard use of the word 'brain'.

When philosophers and psychologists discuss the brain they almost always slide into supposing that the word 'brain' somehow refers only to the brain non-mentally and non-experientially considered — the brain-as-revealed-by-current-physics-and-neurophysiology, for example. But the word 'brain', used to refer to a living brain, does just that. It refers to the living brain considered as a whole, the brain in its total physical existence. And if you're a realistic materialist you hold that this total physical existence is *constituted,* at least in part, by consciousness phenomena, in every sense in which it's constituted, in part, by non-consciousness phenomena characterizable by physics.

With this very brief introduction to realistic materialism, I can give a further answer to the question what a SESMET is.[15] Taking the term 'an ultimate' to denote the fundamental constituents of reality, whatever they are (I could talk of fundamental particles or strings, but 'ultimates' is a better term because it is theoretically uncommitted), I hold that Louis is identical with (or is constituted at any time by) a set of ultimates in a certain active relation, and, similarly, that a SESMET existing in the L-reality for a period of time *t* (a two-second interval, say) is identical with (or is constituted at any time by) a set of ultimates in the L-reality in a certain active relation.

This is not any sort of 'reductionist' claim, because the same remarks apply to the phrase 'a set of ultimates in a certain relation' as apply to the word 'brain'. If one is a realistic materialist, the phrase 'a set of ultimates in a certain relation' does not refer only or even especially to non-mental, non-consciousness phenomena that can be described by current physics or something like it. It refers just as it says: to a set of ultimates in a certain dynamic relation, ultimates whose existence in relation is, in the case of a SESMET, and as all realistic materialists must agree, as much revealed and constituted by consciousness phenomena as by any non-consciousness phenomena characterizable by physics.

A SESMET, then, is a peculiarly shaped thing that has both experiential being and non-experiential being — consciousness being and non-consciousness being. (I say it is peculiarly shaped because it is peculiarly shaped when considered spatially or non-experientially, involving — say — ultimates in the intralaminar nuclei of the thalamus, the reticular activating system, and so on. It is not peculiarly shaped when it is considered experientially, for then it has the familiar shape — or unity — of a conscious experience.) As for the relation between a SESMET in the L-reality (an object with, say, a 2-second existence) and Louis the human being (an object with, say, a seventy-year existence) is a straightforward part-whole relation, like the relation between Louis and one of his toes — or the relation between a morning glory plant and one of its flowers, or between Louis and one of his fortunately transient pimples.

That, I take it, is how things are, physically and metaphysically in the case of SESMETs. And I am strongly inclined to call SESMETs 'selves', because I think that SESMETs are located at the centre of what we must mean to be talking about when we talk about 'the self' — in a way that trumps or overrides all other claims to the word 'self'. Obviously talk of SESMETs leaves out a great deal of what some have in mind when they talk of selves; but the central component of the idea of the self is the idea of an inner subject of experience, and in the human case, or so I believe, the existence of inner subjects of experience is, as a matter of empirical fact, just the existence of SESMETs. I think it is a deep and difficult truth, fundamental to the Buddhist tradition and prepared for, in the Western tradition, by Hume and William James, that these short-term selves are what we are really talking about when we talk about *the* self.

There is a lot to be said about the similarity relations between the SESMETs or selves that exist in the L-reality across time — and that give rise to the experience, or the illusion (as I am now inclined to say), of the persisting self. But that is a question for another time.

Notes

1. I use 'figured' in a highly general sense that carries no implication of picturing.
2. Brook also holds that the self considered as a metaphysical entity is a kind of phenomenologically constituted entity: 'the self is simply what one is aware of when one is aware of oneself (and specifically of one's mental features) from the inside' (1998: 41).
3. It is arguable (but doubtful) that William James takes the opposite view in his well known, and very difficult paper 'Does Consciousness Exist?'
4. McGinn 1999: 172; Clough (1862) and Traherne (1637–74, first published 1903) are quoted by Kenny (1989: 86); Spenser c. 1594: xlv.3; St Paul *Romans* 7: 22; Cicero 54–51 BC: vi. 26.
5. For more, see Strawson 1997: 8–19, 1999: 496–8.
6. Cf. Damasio 1999; note his broad construal of the word 'emotion'.
7. For clear early expressions of the point about embodiment see e.g. Wundt 1874, James 1890: 1.303.
8. For cases that may involve loss of a sense of self as persisting in time, see e.g. Knight and Grabowecky 1995; Scoville and Milner 1975; Squire and Kandel 1999.
9. On the 'I-Me-Mine' complex see e.g. Austin 1998: 43–47.
10. The word 'all' is surely too strong.
11. It is not a merely transcendental unity, in the Kantian sense.
12. Although 10^{-34}th of a second is a short time by human standards, it 'seems by the standards of early-universe physics as interminable as an indifferent production of *Lohengrin*' (Ferris 1997: 237).
13. See Strawson 1997: 17–19 for a sketch of this view.
14. According to context, 'here' can refer to this room, this town, this country, this solar system, and so on.
15. I discuss realistic materialism at length in Strawson (forthcoming).

References

Austin, J. (1998). *Zen and the Brain*. Cambridge, MA: MIT.

Brook, A. (1998). Unified Consciousness and the Self. In S. Gallagher & J. Shear (Eds.) *Models of the Self*. Imprint Academic.

Cicero (54–51 BC/1929). *De Republica* . Translated by G. Sabine & S. Smith. Columbus OH: Ohio State University Press.

Clough, A. H. (1862/1974). The Mystery of the Fall. In *Poems*. Oxford: Oxford University Press.

Damasio, A. (1999). *The Feeling of What Happens: Body and Emotion in the Making o Consciousness*. New York: Harcourt Brace.

Ferris, T. (1997). *The Whole Shebang*. London: Weidenfeld & Nicolson.

Gallagher, S. & J. Shear (Eds.) *Models of the Self*. Thorverton: Imprint Academic.

James, W. (1890/1950). *The Principles of Psychology*, Volume 1. New York: Dover.

James, W. (1892/1984). *Psychology: Briefer Course*. Cambridge, MA: Harvard University Press.

James, W. (1904/1996). Does Consciousness Exist? in *Essays in Radical Empiricism* Lincoln, Nebraska: University of Nebraska Press.

Kant, I. (1781–7/1996). *Critique of Pure Reason*. Translated by W. S. Pluhar. Indianopolis Hackett.

Kenny, A. (1989). *The Metaphysics of Mind*. Oxford: Clarendon Press.

Knight, R. T. & M. Grabowecky (1995). Escape from Linear Time: Prefrontal Cortex an Conscious Experience. In M. Gazzaniga (Ed.), *The Cognitive Neurosciences*. Cambridge, MA: MIT.

McGinn, C. (1999). *The Mysterious Flame*. New York: Basic Books.

Scoville, W. B. & B. Milner (1957). Loss of recent memory after bilateral hippocampa lesions. *Journal of Neurology, Neurosurgery, and Psychiatry* 20: 11–21.

Spenser, E. (c. 1594/1989). Amoretti. In *Shorter Poems*. New Haven: Yale University Press.

Squire, L. & E. Kandel (1999). *Memory: From Mind to Molecules*. New York: Scientifi American Library.

Strawson, G. (1997). "The Self". In S. Gallagher & J. Shear (Eds.), *Models of the Sel* Imprint Academic.

Strawson, G. (1999). The Self and the SESMET. In S. Gallagher & J. Shear (Eds.), *Models o the Self*. Imprint Academic.

Strawson, G. (forthcoming). Realistic materialism. In L. Antony & N. Hornstein (Eds.) *Chomsky and his Critics*. Oxford: Blackwell.

Traherne, T. (1903). *Poetical Works*. London.

Wundt, W. (1874/1911). *Principles of Physiological Psychology,* translated by E. B Titchener. New York: Macmillan.

Zahavi, D. & J. Parnas (1998). Phenomenal Consciousness and Self Awareness: A Phenomenological Critique of Representational Theory. In S. Gallagher & J. Shear (Eds.) *Models of the Self*. Imprint Academic.

Self and Consciousness

Dan Zahavi
University of Copenhagen

> Suppose the mind to be reduc'd even below the life of an oyster. Suppose it to have only one perception, as of thirst or hunger. Consider it in that situation. Do you conceive of any thing but merely that perception? Have you any notion of *self* or *substance*? If not, the addition of other perceptions can never give you that notion. – David Hume

In his recent book 'Kant and the Mind' Andrew Brook makes a distinction between two types of self-awareness. The first type, which he calls *empirical* self-awareness, is an awareness of particular psychological states such as perceptions, memories, desires, bodily sensations etc. One attains this type of self-awareness simply by having particular experiences and being aware of them. To be in possession of empirical self-awareness is, in short, simply to be conscious of one's occurrent experience. The second type of self-awareness he calls *apperceptive* self-awareness. This type of self-awareness entails an awareness of oneself as the subject of experience. For this type of self-awareness to obtain, it would not be enough merely to be conscious of, say, an occurrent perception of a chair, one would also have to be aware that it was oneself who was perceiving the chair. And as Brook adds, when I am self-aware in this way, I am not only aware of being the subject of a single experience, but also aware of myself as the common subject of other psychological states (Brook 1994: 55–57).

I find Brook's distinction illuminating, but it raises a question which I would like to pursue in this paper. When we speak of self-awareness, do we then necessarily also speak of a self, is there so to speak always a self involved in self-awareness, or is it rather the case, as Brook's notion of empirical self-awareness might suggest, that there are types of self-awareness which are 'selfless', or to use two other related terms 'subjectless' or 'non-egological'? Is *self*-awareness always to be understood as an awareness of *a self*, or can it be understood simply as the awareness which a specific experience has of *itself*? Ultimately, I believe an answer to these questions are important, both when it comes to an understanding of what exactly self-awareness amounts to, and also when it comes to a proper understanding of what a self is. To be more precise, I believe that an examination of self-awareness contains a key towards what it means to be a self.

1. The non-egological challenge

Let me illustrate the two alternatives by using Gurwitsch's well-known distinction between an egological and a non-egological theory of consciousness (Gurwitsch 1941). An *egological* theory would typically claim that when I watch a movie by Hitchcock, then I am not only intentionally directed at the *movie*, nor merely aware of the movie being *watched*, I am also aware that it is being watched by *me*, i.e., that *I* am *watching* the *movie*. In short, there is an object (the movie), there is an experience (the watching), and there is also a subject, myself, the one having the experience. Thus, an egological theory would typically claim that it is a conceptual and experiential truth that any episode of experiencing necessarily includes a *subject of experience* (Shoemaker 1968: 563–564). In contrast, a *non-egological* theory (also known as the *no-ownership* view (Strawson 1959: 95)) would deny that every experience is for a subject. It would, in other words, omit any reference to a subject of experience, and simply say that there is an awareness of the watching of the movie. Experiences are basically egoless. They are not states or properties of anyone, but mental events which simply occur, so that self-awareness properly speaking must be understood as the anonymous acquaintance which consciousness has of *itself*, and *not* as an awareness of an experiencing *self*.

If one examines some recent influential accounts of self-awareness, it is not difficult to find arguments against the egological theory and in favor of a non-egological position. Let me start by giving a brief account of arguments to be found in Dieter Henrich and Ulrich Pothast, and then turn to Sartre's classical position.

According to Henrich and Pothast, any egological theory claiming that self-awareness is properly speaking an awareness of my*self*, as a self, subject or ego takes self-awareness as a kind of object-awareness, and is therefore prone to all the devastating problems confronting the so-called reflection theory of elf-awareness.[1] Furthermore, to speak of a self or ego is normally to speak of n *agent*, that is, some principle of activity and volition. Basic pre-reflective elf-awareness, however, is not something that is initiated or controlled by a ubject, it is something that precedes all performances, and it should consequently not be attributed to an ego, but rather be understood as an anonymous nd egoless occurrence. Finally, if one conceives of the ego qua subject of xperience as something which *has* the experience, one obviously makes a istinction between the ego and the experience. They are not identical. In this ase, however, it is difficult to understand why the ego's awareness of the xperience should count as a case of *self*-awareness. Against that background, Ienrich and Pothast conclude that it is better to avoid introducing any ego into ıe structure of basic self-awareness, and they consequently state that selfwareness is originally egoless and anonymous (Henrich 1970: 276, 279; 'othast 1971: 76, 81; cf. Frank 1991: 252; Cramer 1974: 573).

This view is fairly close to the position advocated by Sartre. In his work *a transcendance de l'ego* Sartre basically employs three different arguments, ttempting to show that the ego is neither *necessary*, *possible*, nor *actual*. To tart with, Sartre takes issue with the tradition, and argues that the ego is *uperfluous*. It has often been assumed that the mental life would dissipate into chaos of unstructured and separate sensations if it were not supported by the nifying, synthesizing and individuating function of a central and atemporal go. But as Sartre points out, this reasoning misjudges the nature of the stream f consciousness. It does not need an exterior principle of individuation, since is *per se* individuated. Nor is consciousness in need of any transcendent rinciple of unification, since it is as such an ecstatic flowing unity. It is xactly qua temporalizing that consciousness unifies itself. Thus, a correct ccount of time-consciousness will show that the contribution of an ego is nnecessary, and it has consequently lost its *raison d'être*.[2]

Secondly, Sartre claims that the ego for essential reasons cannot possibly e a part of consciousness. As is well known, Sartre takes consciousness to be haracterized by a fundamental transparency. Its being consists in selfivenness or self-manifestation, and there is consequently no part of consciousess which at any time remains hidden. The ego, however, is opaque. It is omething whose nature has to be unearthed gradually and which always ossesses aspects yet to be disclosed. Since it is never given in its entirety and onsequently never given adequately, it lacks the transparency of consciousess, and cannot be part of it.

Sartre's third and final argument is to demonstrate that a correct phenom enological description of lived consciousness will simply not find any ego understood as an inhabitant in or possessor of consciousness. One occasion ally says of a person who is absorbed in something that he has forgotte himself. This way of speaking contains a truth. When I am absorbed in readin a story, I have a consciousness of the narrative, and a pre-reflective self awareness of the reading, but according to Sartre, I do not have any awarenes of an ego, nor of the reading being done by me. Thus, Sartre seems to accep Lichtenberg's critique of Descartes. The traditional rendering of the cogit affirms too much. What is certain is not that 'I am aware of this chair', but tha 'there is awareness of this chair' (Sartre 1936: 31–32, 37).

According to Sartre, pre-reflective consciousness has no egological struc ture. As long as we are absorbed in the experience, *living* it, no ego will appea This only happens when we adopt a distancing and objectifying attitude to th experience in question, that is, when we reflect upon it. But even then we are no dealing with an I-consciousness, since the reflecting pole remains non egological, but merely with a consciousness *of* I. As Sartre puts it: the appearin ego is the object and not the subject of reflection. When I engage in a reflectiv exploration of this object, I will be examining it as if it were the ego of an othe That is, I will assume the perspective of an other on myself, and naturally thi perspective will never reveal the original self-givenness of my own subjectivit (Sartre 1936: 65, 69). Thus, Sartre can write: "L'attitude réflexive est exprimé correctement par cette fameuse phrase de Rimbaud (dans la lettre du voyant) 'J est *un autre*'."(Sartre 1936: 78).

Sartre's argumentation apparently supports the position of Henrich an Pothast. But is it really convincing? Is it really legitimate to attribute *self* awareness to an impersonal and non-egological stream of consciousness, o does one not rather reduce the experience to a third-person entity if one insist on speaking of it in strict non-egological terms? It is obviously possible t speak of the self or ego the way Henrich, Pothast and Sartre do. That is, as a active principle, as an owner of experiences, or as a person with habits character traits, persisting convictions etc. But is that the only appropriat way?

In the following I will argue that it is not only possible but also necessar to operate with a more basic notion of self than the one criticized by Sartre Henrich and Pothast. To be more precise, I wish to argue that it is appropriat to ascribe a fundamental type of *egocentricity* or *ipseity* to experiential phe nomena as such, and that any theory of self-awareness which fails to do so is inadequate. My argumentation will make use of some of Husserl's reflections on the matter, since they contain important insights both when it comes to an understanding of what it means to be a self, but also when it comes to a comprehension of the relation between self and self-awareness.

Before I proceed, just one terminological remark. In the following I will use the terms 'self' and 'ego' interchangeably. I realize that there might be objections to this, since the terms are occasionally used with different connotations, but to simplify things, I have chosen to ignore these differences.

2. An egological reply

2.1. *The ipseity of first-personal givenness*

Initially, that is, in *Logische Untersuchungen*, Husserl started out with a non-egological conception of consciousness (a conception which resembles the one adopted by Sartre in *La transcendance de l'ego*), but he later abandoned this position. As Marbach has shown, one of Husserl's principal reasons for this change was the difficulties his theory encountered when it came to a phenomenological analysis of *intersubjectivity* (Marbach 1974: 77, 90)! A condition of possibility for investigating intersubjectivity is that one operates with a conception of subjectivity that allows one to demarcate one consciousness from another, thereby allowing for plurality. But as long as Husserl held on to a non-egological theory, which operated with anonymous experiences belonging to nobody (Husserl 1973e: 40), and which took the unity of consciousness to be nothing but the sum total of all contiguous experiences, he was faced with difficulties of the following kind: if we imagine a situation in which I am puzzled by the unexpected anger of a taxidriver, we would say that I am puzzled not by my own anger but by the anger of another. But it is exactly this distinction which will evade me as long as I opt for a non-egological theory. As Marbach puts it:

> Die Analyse phänomenologischer Erfahrung bringt einen kardinalen Unterschied zur Geltung: ich habe Bewußtseinserlebnisse, die ich als 'eigene' bezeichne, und ich habe Bewußtseinserlebnisse *von* Bewußtseinserlebnissen, welche *nicht* 'eigene', vielmehr 'fremde' sind. Soll Klarheit herrschen, kann nicht mehr von 'niemandes' Erlebnissen gesprochen werden. (Marbach 1974: 100)

In my encounter with the taxidriver's anger, I am both self-aware and aware of somebody else. I am conscious of two different subjects. What is it that permits me to distinguish between my own experience (of puzzlement) and the other's experience (of anger)? In contrast to physical objects which can exist regardless of whether or not they *de facto* appear for a subject, experiences are essentially characterized by having a subjective 'feel' to them, i.e., a certain (phenomenal) quality of 'what it is like' or what it 'feels' like to have them (Nagel 1986: 15–16; Jackson 1982; James 1890: I/478). Whereas the object of my perceptual experience is intersubjectively accessible in the sense that it can in principle be given to others in the same way that it is given to me, my perceptual experience itself is only given directly to me. It is this first-personal givenness of the experience which makes it *subjective*. And it is clear why I do not mix up my own experience with the other's experience (Husserl 1962: 416). When I am aware of a pain, perception or thought from the first-person perspective, the experience in question is felt immediately, non-inferentially and non-criterially as *mine*, i.e., I do not first scrutinize a specific perception or feeling of pain, and subsequently identify it as being mine. If I am puzzled, I can neither be in doubt nor mistaken about who the subject of that experience is, and it is nonsensical to ask whether I am sure that I am the one who is puzzled, or to demand a specification of the criteria being used by me in determining whether or not the felt puzzlement is really mine. But whereas my own experience is given to me originarily in a first-personal mode of presentation, this is obviously not the case with the driver's anger. In fact the first-personal givenness of the other's experience is in principle inaccessible to me. It is exactly for that reason that the other is characterized by a fundamental alterity and transcendence. It is exactly therefore that the other is given to me as an other. As Husserl writes: If I had direct access to the other's experiences, they would become part of my own subjectivity, and the difference between the two of us would disappear (Husserl 1973a: 139; Husserl 1973d: 12).

When Husserl realized this, he abandoned his non-egological theory. Every conscious experience belongs to a subject, i.e., either to me or to somebody else. It cannot belong to nobody. Whether a certain experience is experienced as mine or not, does not, however, depend upon something apart from the experience, but exactly upon the givenness of the experience. If the experience is given originarily, in a first-personal mode of presentation, it is experienced as *my* experience, otherwise not (Klawonn 1991: 5, 141–142;

James 1890: I/226–227; Smith 1989: 93). Obviously, this form of egocentricity must be distinguished from any explicit I-consciousness. I am not (yet) confronted with a thematic or explicit awareness of the experience as being owned by or belonging to myself. Nevertheless, the particular primary presence of the experience makes it mine, and distinguishes it from whatever experiences others might have (Husserl 1959: 175 1973b: 28, 56, 307, 443).

> Das ursprünglichst Meine ist mein Leben, mein 'Bewusstsein', mein 'ich tue und leide', dessen Sein darin besteht, mir als fungierendem Ich ursprünglich vorgegeben, d.i. im Modus der Originalität, des Es-selbst zugänglich erfahrbar, erschaubar zu sein. All mein Leben ist original für mich erschaubar, es ist fungierendes und dann anonymes Leben oder aktuell erschautes und dann thematisches. (Husserl 1973c: 429)

Thus, Husserl ultimately ends up equating the first-personal mode of givenness, self-awareness, and a certain basic sense of egocentricity or ipseity.[3] One way to capture this point is by replacing the phrase 'subject of experience' with the phrase 'subjectivity of experience'. Whereas the first phrasing might suggest that the self is something that exists apart from or above the experience, and for that reason something that might be encountered in separation from the experience and even something the experience might occasionally lack, the second phrasing excludes these types of misunderstanding. It hardly makes sense to say that the subjectivity of the experience is something that can be detached from or isolated from the experience, nor for that matter that it is something the experience can simply lack. But to stress the subjectivity of experience is not an empty gesture, but is on the contrary to insist upon the basic egocentricity of experiential phenomena.

A possible objection might be that this reading makes the thesis concerning the self in self-awareness acceptable, but also quite trivial. However, as long as the thesis is routinely denied by advocates of the different impersonality theses, i.e., by adherents to the no-ownership view, the radical anonymity thesis, the non-egological account, etc., it does not seem superfluous to make the point. Moreover, as both Wittgenstein and Heidegger have remarked, one of the tasks of philosophy is exactly to call attention to and elucidate those fundamental aspects that are so familiar to us, so taken for granted, that we often fail to realize their true significance and might even deny their existence.

If we look back, the non-egological theory would claim that it is possible to have strictly *impersonal* experiences, which do not include any reference, not even an implicit reference, to oneself as the subject of the experience.

Thus, even if one had to concede that two persons, who had two simultaneous and qualitatively identical experiences, would still have two numerical distinct experiences, this would not be the case because each of the experiences had a different *subject*, but simply because, to quote Parfit, "one of these experiences is *this* experience, occurring in *this* particular mental life, and the other is *that* experience, occurring in *that* other particular mental life."(Parfit 1987: 517. Cf. 1987: 252).

An objection to this position comes to mind the moment one adopts a first-person perspective. Is it really true that the primary difference between my perception and my friend's perception is that my perception is *this* one and his *that* one? Is this not, as Klawonn has argued, a parasitic and derived characterization? Is it not rather the case that an experience is *this* one exactly because it is *mine*, i.e., given in an irreducible *first-personal mode of presentation*, whereas the other's experience is not given in a first-personal mode for *me*, and exactly therefore no part of *my* mental life? (Klawonn 1991: 28–29).

I have earlier mentioned Pothast's argument against an egological theory of self-awareness: If the ego is conceived as something standing opposed to or above the experience, it is difficult to understand why the ego's awareness of the experience should count as a case of *self*-awareness. As Husserl's discussion of the originary givenness of my own experiences has shown, however, one does not need to conceive of the ego as something standing apart from or above the experience, nor to conceive of the relation between self and experience as an external relation of ownership. It is also possible to describe the very first-personal givenness of an experience, that is its very self-givenness or self-manifestation, as the most basic form of egocentricity. In this case the ego would not be something standing opposed to the stream of consciousness but be an essential part of its structure.[4]

For this reason, Sartre's position must be criticized as well. One has to question Sartre's revised paraphrase of the cogito. It does not seem adequate to render the cogito as "there is a perception of a chair," nor for that matter as "somebody perceives a chair" (Merleau-Ponty 1945: 249, 277) since the two formulations overlook one significant detail. If I and the reader are looking at the same chair, these two perceptions of the chair might very well be anonymous in the sense of lacking any explicit self-thematization. In fact, on the pre-reflective level there is probably no explicit awareness of the experience being mine. But the two perceptions are definitely *not* anonymous in the sense of being undifferentiated and indistinguishable, regardless of whether this is taken to imply strict numerical identity (in which case the two streams of consciousness would have merged) or merely qualitative identity. On the contrary, the moment we take the first-person perspective seriously, it is obvious that there is a vital difference between the two perceptions. Only one of them is given in a first-personal mode of presentation for me. To acknowledge this is to acknowledge that experiential phenomena are as such characterized by a basic level of ipseity. To deny this, i.e., to argue for radical anonymity in the sense of *undifferentiatedness*, seems utterly absurd. Thus, a thorough consideration of the alternative, increases the plausibility of the egocentric position.

A further argument given in defense of the radical anonymity thesis relates to the problem of *intersubjectivity*. It has been claimed that the only way to avoid the threat of solipsism is by conceiving of the difference between self and other as a founded and derived difference, as a difference arising out of a common and shared undifferentiated anonymous life. I think this solution is much too radical. Properly speaking it does not solve the problem of intersubjectivity, but dissolves it. To speak of a fundamental anonymity prior to any distinction between self and other obscures that which has to be clarified, namely intersubjectivity understood as the relation between subjectivities. On the level of radical anonymity there is neither individuation or selfhood, but nor is there any differentiation, alterity, or transcendence, and there is consequently room for neither subjectivity nor intersubjectivity. To put it differently, the radical anonymity thesis threatens not only our concept of a self-given subject, it also threatens our concept of the transcendent and irreducible other. I consequently think that it is more than doubtful whether this radical anonymity with its latent solipsism can help us understand the possibility of intersubjectivity. On the contrary, it seems to present us with one of those cases where the medicine turns out to be part of the sickness it was supposed to cure, and in the end just as deadly.

To avoid possible misunderstandings, let me emphasize once again that I am by no means denying the existence of what has often been described in the phenomenological literature as *anonymous experiences*. I am just criticizing a certain concept of anonymity. For an experience to be anonymous is for the experience in question to lack any explicit self-awareness; it is not for it to lack self-givenness, individuation or first-personal givenness altogether. To suggest something like that is to conceive of the first-personal givenness of the experiential phenomena as something quite incidental to their being, as a mere varnish that the experiences could also lack without ceasing to be experiences. And I believe that to be a radical mistake (cf. Searle 1992: 172; Smith 1989: 95; Chalmers 1996: 4; Strawson 1994: 71). If, however, the thesis were maintained, it would be necessary to explain how something like first-personal self-givenness could eventually arise out of this undifferentiated dimension of anonymity. Here I believe the radical anonymity thesis is basically faced with all the difficulties confronting the reflection theory of self-awareness — difficulties which I also very much doubt can be solved.

The problem with Sartre's argumentation is consequently that he (just like Henrich and Pothast) operates with too narrow a concept of the ego. However, it might be argued that Sartre eventually came to realize this deficit himself. For whereas he in *La transcendance de l'ego* characterizes the pre-reflective, non-egological field of consciousness as *impersonal*, he describes this view as mistaken in both *L'Être et le néant* and in the important article 'Conscience de soi et connaissance de soi'. It is, as he says, not the ego which personalizes consciousness, it is consciousness which by means of its fundamental self-givenness or selfhood (*ipséité*) allows the ego to appear: "…si la conscience n'a pas une ego au niveau de l'immédiat et de la non-réflexivité, elle n'en est pas moins personnelle. Elle est personnelle parce qu'elle renvoi, malgré tout, à soi."(Sartre 1948: 63; cf. Sartre 1943: 114, 142–143, 284, 1936: 19, 78–79). At this point the difference between Husserl's and Sartre's positions no longer seems substantial, and one might merely object to Sartre's terminology. I think it would have been more reasonable to ascribe a fundamental egocentricity or ipseity to consciousness as such, and reserve the term 'personal' for the socially constituted self.

To recapitulate: To have egocentric self-awareness is not to apprehend a pure self apart from the experience, but to be acquainted with an experience in its first-personal mode of presentation, that is, from 'within'. It is exactly the primary presence or first-personal givenness of a group of experiences which constitutes their *myness*, i.e., make them belong to a particular subject. The subject or self referred to in *self*-awareness is consequently not something apart from or beyond the experience, but simply a feature or function of its givenness. One advantage of this view is that it incidentally makes it clear that self-awareness is not to be conceived of as an awareness of an isolated worldless self. To be self-aware is not to withdraw to some self-enclosed interiority. It is not to interrupt the experiential interaction with the world in order to turn the gaze inside. On the contrary, subjectivity is open towards and engaged in the world, and it is in this openness that it reveals itself.[5]

2.2. *Identity in difference*

So far I have argued that the self-givenness or first-personal givenness of an experience entails some basic type of selfhood, and that this fact constitutes an argument against a non-egological theory of consciousness.

The notion of self discussed so far is, admittedly, a very minimalistic notion. Nevertheless, it still strikes me as fundamental in the sense that nothing which lacks it deserves to be called a self. When this is said, it would, however, be an obvious mistake to think that this is all there is to the relation between self and self-awareness. There are obviously also other notions of self, and more complex forms of self-awareness, to be considered. If one had any doubts, one would only have to read Strawson's article 'The Self and the SESMET' where he sums up some of the recent discussions in *Journal of Consciousness Studies* by enumerating no less than 21 different concepts of self. In what follows I will not attempt to elucidate this manifold, but simply draw attention to a further quite crucial aspect of the relation between self and self-awareness which I have not mentioned so far. Once again I will use Husserl's reflections as a clue.

Husserl not only speaks of self in terms of the self-givenness or first-personal givenness of an experience. He also operates with the notion of an act-transcendent ego in the sense of an identity-pole which is shared by all experiences belonging to the same stream of consciousness.[6] As Husserl points out, the ego cannot be identified with the experiences, since it preserves its identity, whereas the experiences arise and perish in the stream of consciousness, replacing each other in a permanent flux (Husserl 1952: 98, 1974: 363). But as he then emphasizes, although the ego must be distinguished from the experiences in which it lives and functions, it cannot in any way exist independently of them. It is a transcendence, but in Husserl's famous phrase: *a transcendence in the immanence* (Husserl 1976: 123–124, 179, 1952: 99–100, 1973c: 43, 1973b: 246).

What is crucial about this characterization? Obviously the attempt to *differentiate* between the ego and the experiences. Despite my earlier reservations this differentiation seems to be warranted the moment we pass beyond a narrow investigation of the self-givenness and egocentricity of a single experience, and instead consider the kind of self-awareness at stake when a plurality of experiences is involved. After all, it is not only possible to be aware of one's own burning pain, it is also possible to be aware of oneself as the common subjectivity of a manifold of simultaneous experiences, just as one might be self-aware across temporal distance, and recall a past experience as one's own. In these latter cases it is necessary to distinguish the self from the occurrent experience since the self can retain its identity although the experience change. And any account of the relationship between self and self-awareness which ignores this feature must be characterized as defective. In other words, if there are forms of self-awareness which bridge the gap between numerical different experiences, these forms must also be accounted for, (and this incidentally appears particular difficult for a non-egological account, since such an account cannot recur to any act-transcendent principle).

Since I am pursuing the relation between self and self-awareness, the question I would like to raise is: How are we aware of this ego? How is it given to consciousness? Or to phrase the question in a way that makes it clear that we are in fact dealing with a new type of self-awareness, and not simply returning to the one treated in the discussion of the first-personal mode of presentation: When does my self-awareness contain a reference to an *act-transcendent* identity? I think a plausible answer would be that the self-givenness of a single experience is a necessary but not a sufficient condition for this type of self-awareness to occur. The latter entails more than a simple and immediate self-awareness, it also entails a difference or distance which is bridged, that is, it involves a *synthesis*. Why is that? Because the self cannot be given as an act-transcendent identity in a *single* act (Kern 1989: 60–62, 1975: 66; Marbach 1974: 110, 112). It is only when we are acquainted with a manifold of different acts which are then compared that we can encounter something that is given as the same despite the change in experiences. It is only then that we can encounter something transcendent that retains its identity through changing experiences.[7] In short, we only need to operate with a difference between experience and self, the moment we realize that the self retains its identity through different experiences. But this realization cannot occur as long as we stick to a single experience, but only in the moment we relate and compare several different experiences, that is, the moment a synthetization takes place.[8]

I hardly need to point out that we are presently approaching something that is very close to Brook's notion of apperceptive self-awareness. Brook wrote that when one was in possession of apperceptive self-awareness one was not merely aware of being the subject of a single experience, but also aware of oneself as the common subject of other psychological states. The point now being made is of course that this reference to a plurality of experiences is not merely incidental, but quite essential for something like apperceptive self-awareness to occur.[9]

One question that has to be asked concerns the relation between the earlier description of the self involved in first-personal givenness, and the present description of the act-transcendent identity of the self. What is the connection? It could be claimed that there is in fact no connection, since the present description insists upon the difference between self and experience, whereas the earlier description attempted to abolish this difference. However, this claim would be mistaken. As a closer examination reveals there are in fact good reasons for insisting upon the *difference* between our singular and transitory acts and the abiding dimension of first-personal experiencing, between *die Erlebnisse* and *das Erleben* (Husserl 1980: 326; Husserl 1973c: 46). After all, it makes perfect sense to say that I had an experience of joy which has now passed. I might even completely forget about it and only recall it much later. But whereas the act can become past and absent, the dimension of experiencing that allows for presence and absence cannot itself become past and absent (for me). Whereas we live through a number of different experiences, the first-personal experiencing itself remains as an unchanging dimension. To use a striking image by James, it stands permanent, like the rainbow on the waterfall, with its own quality unchanged by the events that stream through it (James 1890: I/630). Of course, this should not be misunderstood. Distinguishability is not the same as separability. We are not dealing with a pure or empty field of experiencing upon which the concrete experiences subsequently make their entry. After all, the field of experiencing is nothing apart from the concrete experiences. Nevertheless, the moment we expand the focus to include more than a single experience it becomes not only legitimate but highly appropriate to distinguish the strict singularity of the field of first-personal givenness from the plurality of changing experiences (Klawonn 1994: 143; Brough 1972: 316). To use a nice formulation by Klawonn, the latter are exposed in it (Klawonn 1991: 77, 128). It is their exposure in this field of first-personal givenness which makes them mine. And of course this exposure is not something incidental to their being. It is not a mere superficial varnish, but that which makes them conscious experiential phenomena.

Granted that it is their exposure in the same field of first-personal givenness which makes different experiences belong to one and the same self, it is possible to explain, both how self-awareness can be established across numerical different acts, and more specifically how self-awareness can bridge temporal distance and allow me to remember a former experience as *mine*. The relationship between my present and past experience cannot be compared to the one entertained by two different beads on one and the same string of pearls. Whereas it is possible to examine the beads without being aware of their relation to each other or to the string, and whereas we would need to assure ourselves that they were in fact joined by an uninterrupted string in order to be certain that they are connected, this is not the case for the two experiences. In order to determine whether a past experience is really mine, I do not first need to assure myself of the uninterrupted, temporal continuity between my present recollection and the past experience, but can do so immediately. Or to be more exact, I do not have to do anything, since no criterial self-identification is involved (cf. Strawson 1966: 164). If an experience is reflectively accessible to me in recollection, it is automatically given as *my past* experience. (Obviously this is not to say that episodic memory is infallible — I might have false beliefs about myself — but only that it is not subject to the error of misidentification (cf. Campbell 1994: 98–99)). To argue against the unity of mind by pointing to alleged interruptions in the stream of consciousness (such as dreamless sleep, coma, etc.) is consequently pointless, since one thereby makes the erroneous assumption that it is the *contiguity* between two experiences that makes them part of the same subjectivity, rather than their shared manner of givenness.

But let me return to the question concerning the relation between the two notions of self. Although the act-transcendent identity of the self only reveals itself in acts of synthesis, the identity in question does not arise out of the blue, but is clearly grounded in the pervasive dimension of first-personal experiencing.

3. Conclusion

Let me conclude. In the beginning I posed the following question: is there an intimate link between self and self-awareness. Is there always a self involved when we are self-aware, or is it also possible to speak of self-awareness without assuming the existence of anyone being self-aware? In short is *self*-awareness to be understood as an awareness of *a self*, or rather as the awareness which a specific experience has of *itself*? On closer examination, however, this way of putting the question turned out to be misleading. First of all, it presents us with a false alternative. Self-awareness is not *either* an awareness of a self, *or* the awareness which an experience has of itself. On the contrary, it must be realized that there are different kinds of self-awareness. I can be pre-reflectively self-aware of my current perception, and I can reflect and thematize this perception. But I can also reflect upon myself as the subjectivity of experience, that is, I can reflect upon myself as the one who thinks, deliberates, resolves, acts and suffers. If I compare that which is given in two different acts of reflection, say a perception of birds, and a recollection of a walk, I can focus upon that which has changed, namely the intentional acts, but I can also focus upon that which remains identical, namely the subjectivity of experience. Secondly, the formulation suggests that if self-awareness were merely a matter of the awareness which an experience had of itself, we would be dealing with a non-egological or subjectless type of self-awareness. But, as I hope to have made clear, this suggestion is mistaken, since it overlooks the egocentricity involved in first-personal givenness. (For which reason the initial Gurwitschian definition of the difference between an egological and a non-egological theory also turned out to be too crude). Thus, my conclusion is that there is selfhood or ipseity involved whenever there is self-awareness. And there is self-awareness not only when I realize that *I* am perceiving a candle, but whenever I am acquainted with an experience in its first-personal mode of givenness, that is whenever there is a 'what it is like' involved with its inherent 'quality' of *myness*. As Flanagan puts it: "...all subjective experience is self-conscious in the weak sense that there is something it is like for the subject to have that experience. This involves a sense that the experience is the subject's experience, that it happens to her, occurs in her stream." (Flanagan 1992: 194). Needless to say if this is true it has some obvious consequences for the attribution of both self and self-awareness to infants and animals (cf. Husserl 1973d: 173). But it is just as obvious that there are also higher forms of self-awareness which the newborn infant (and most, if not all, animals) lacks, for instance the apperceptive self-awareness mentioned above.[10]

Notes

1. For a criticism of the reflection theory cf. Zahavi 1999.

2. Sartre 1936: 21–23. Referring to Husserl's investigations in *Zur Phänomenologie des inneren Zeitbewußtseins*, Sartre mentions in passing that the *Längsintentionalität* unites the chain of retentions, but he does not elaborate on this (Sartre 1936: 22).

3. Husserl 1985: 193, 1973b: 184, 1952: 252, 350, 1973c: 151. For a profound investigation of Husserl's notion of *life* cf. Montavont 1999.

4. Henry 1963: 580–581, 1965: 53, 1989: 55. For the very same reason, it is bizarre to argue against an egological theory of self-awareness by pointing out that pre-reflective self-awareness is a passive, given state which precedes all egological initiative (Henrich 1970: 276). The very same thing can be said about our selfhood. To be a self in the most basic sense is a gift, the result of a happening (*Ereignis*), and not something that we decide to become (Henry 1966: 31).

5. Space does not allow me to show this in detail, but I think this account is easily compatible with the Gibsonian notion of an ecological self and with his idea about the way in which the different sensory modalities provide us with self-specifying information. Cf. Gibson 1986: 115, 126.

6. Husserl 1973b: 248, 1962: 207, 1952: 277. In his repeated characterization of the ego as a *pole or center of action and affection*, Husserl also calls attention to the ego's function as a *structuring principle or principle of focus* (Husserl 1952: 310, 1962: 315). If we look at experiences such as concentrating on a task, making a decision, suffering a slight, feeling ashamed, scolding somebody, these experiences do not only entail a reference to an object, but also a reference to the subject as the *agent* or *patient* of the act. And ultimately, an adequate investigation of egological consciousness would have to undertake a detailed taxonomy, since the precise character of the ego-involvement differs from act-type to act-type. The ego is present in voluntary acts in a different way than in involuntary acts just as one must distinguish the egological character of, for instance, experiences where I am formally present such as perceptions or recollections, experiences where I am emotionally engaged and responding with feelings of joy, indignation or hatred, and acts that I am responsible for and the author of (cf. Hart 1992: 68–69).

7. Husserl 1973b: 318, 1962: 208, 1966: 309–310. Cf. Fink 1992: 114, 117. In fact, Husserl more specifically speaks of the importance of presentifying acts, i.e. acts involving a sort of self-displacement. I have chosen to downplay that part of his theory, since Marbach gives an excellent account in his article in this volume.

8. Cf. Marbach 1974: 117–119; Bernet 1985: xliv. As Bernet has pointed out, Husserl's notion of a pure ego cannot simply be taken as a manifestation and confirmation of his adherence to a metaphysics of presence, since Husserl only introduced the pure ego the moment he started taking intentional acts characterized by self-division, self-absence and self-alienation seriously (Bernet 1994: 303–304).

9. Let me stress that this should not be taken as an argument in favor of Sartre's thesis concerning the ego being a product of reflection. It is true that reflection confronts us with an emphatic type of I-consciousness, but this is due to the identity across difference which it reveals, and not to the self-objectivation peculiar to it. Moreover, whereas Sartre claimed that reflection presents us with a consciousness of I, and not with an I-consciousness, since the appearing ego was the object and not the subject of reflection, it is in fact the entire process of reflection which is egological (Kern 1975: 65–66). When I reflect, I am not simply confronted with some indefinite individual who perceives something. If I did, I would not say 'I perceive a black billiard ball', but 'Somebody perceives a black billiard ball'. By saying 'I', I am affirming the identity between the reflecting and the reflected subject.

10. Speaking of infants, results from contemporary developmental psychology seem to corroborate the thesis I have defended above. Until recently it was customary to claim that the infant initially lived in a kind of *adualism* where there were no distinction between self, world, and other. Thus 'adualism,' 'primary narcissism' or 'symbiosis' were terms used to describe the first period of the infant's life, a life where there were not yet supposed to be any boundary between experience and reality, not yet any differentiation between self and non-self (Piaget & Inhelder 1969: 22). Thus, it was assumed that the infant were originally incapable of distinguishing itself from the caregiver, not only in the obvious sense that it were unable to *conceptualize* the difference between self and other, but in the sense that the infant existed in a "state of undifferentiation, of fusion with mother, in which the 'I' is not yet differentiated from the 'not-I' and in which inside and outside are only gradually coming to be sensed as different."(Mahler, Pine & Bergman 1975: 44. Cf. Spitz 1983: 217, 249). This state of symbiosis was then assumed to be the milieu from which the infant gradually separated itself in order to reach a sense of the difference between self and other, only thereby acquiring self-awareness. This traditional hypothesis, which mirrors the views I have been criticizing above, since it takes the infant's experience to be initially impersonal and anonymous has been rejected by dominant positions in contemporary developmental psychology. On the basis of numerous experimental data it is now assumed that the infant already from birth begins to experience itself, and that it never passes through a period of total self/other indifferentiation. As both Stern and Neisser have argued, there is no symbiotic-like phase, and there exists no systematic and pervasive confusion between the child's experience of self and other, nor between the child's experience of the other and the world (Neisser 1988: 40; Stern 1983: 51; Stern 1985: 10; Butterworth 1995: 90). However, although this conclusion seems to corroborate my criticism of the non-egological position, it also raises questions of its own, particular when it concerns the way in which the infant is supposed to be able to distinguish between self and other. Stern has suggested that the infant is not initially overwhelmed by a surge of unstructured sensations, but that it on the contrary has inborn capabilities which permit it to discriminate different gestalt constellations of stimuli in such a fashion that it can distinguish the patterns of stimuli that only arise on the occasion of its own actions or mental processes from the patterns that belong to the movement and actions of particular others (Stern 1983: 56–62, 1985: 7, 65, 67). It is obvious, however, that this account is insufficient. Even if the infant is able to distinguish between different constellations in such a way that no confusion takes place, this does not answer the key question: How does the infant 'identify' one of these experiential configurations as *itself*? But, of course, if one is forced to ask this question, thereby implying that self-awareness is the result of a successful criterial self-identification, something is wrong. The infant does not first scrutinize a specific experience and subsequently identify it as its own. To suggest something like that is to commit the error of conceiving of self-awareness in terms of criterial object-identification. To put it differently, the problem of self-awareness is not primarily a question of a specific 'what', but of a unique 'how'. It does not concern the specific content of an experience, but its unique mode of givenness. As a consequence, even prior to any conceptual discrimination between self and world or self and other, the child is self-aware due to the unique first-personal mode of givenness of its experiences, that is, due to the intrinsic self-manifesting character of its consciousness. This is a fact that Stern perhaps realizes himself, since he acknowledges that the infant's (direct and immediate) experience of proprioception and volition is of crucial importance (Stern 1983: 65).

References

Bernet, R. (1994). *La vie du sujet.* Paris: PUF.

Bernet, R. (1985). Einleitung. In E. Husserl, *Texte zur Phänomenologie des inneren Zeitbewußtseins (1893–1917).* Hamburg: Felix Meiner, xi-lxvii.

Brook, A. (1994). *Kant and the Mind.* Cambridge: Cambridge University Press.

Brough, J.B. (1972). The Emergence of an Absolute Consciousness in Husserl's Early Writings on Time-Consciousness. *Man and World* 5:298–326.

Butterworth, G. (1995). An Ecological Perspective on the Origins of Self. In J.L. Bermúdez, A. Marcel and N. Eilan (Eds.), *The Body and the Self.* Cambridge, MA: MIT Press, 87–105.

Campbell, J. (1994). *Past, Space, and Self.* Cambridge, MA: MIT Press.

Chalmers, D.J. (1996). *The Conscious Mind. In Search of a Fundamental Theory.* New York: Oxford University Press.

Cramer, K. (1974). 'Erlebnis'. Thesen zu Hegels Theorie des Selbstbewußtseins mit Rücksicht auf die Aporien eines Grundbegriffs nachhegelscher Philosophie. In H.-G. Gadamer (Ed.), *Stuttgarter Hegel-Tage 1970.* Bonn: Hegel-Studien. Beiheft 11, 537–603.

Fink, E. (1992). *Natur, Freiheit, Welt.* Würzburg: Königshausen & Neumann.

Flanagan, O. (1992). *Consciousness Reconsidered.* Cambridge, MA: MIT Press.

Frank, M. (1991). *Selbstbewußtsein und Selbsterkenntnis.* Stuttgart: Reclam.

Gibson, J.J. (1986). *The Ecological Approach to Visual Perception.* Hillsdale, N.J.: Lawrence Erlbaum Associates.

Gurwitsch, A. (1941). A Non-egological Conception of Consciousness. *Philosophy and Phenomenological Research* 1:325–338.

Hart, J.G. (1992). *The Person and the Common Life.* Dordrecht: Kluwer Academic Publishers.

Henrich, D. (1970). Selbstbewußtsein, kritische Einleitung in eine Theorie. In R. Bubner, K. Cramer, R. Wiehl (Eds.), *Hermeneutik und Dialektik.* Tübingen: Mohr, 257–284.

Henry, M. (1963). *L'essence de la manifestation.* Paris: PUF.

Henry, M. (1965). *Philosophie et phénoménologie du corps.* Paris: PUF.

Henry, M. (1966). Le concept d'âme a-t-il un sens? *Revue philosophique de Louvain* 64:5–33.

Henry, M. (1989). Philosophie et subjectivité. In A. Jacob (Ed.), *Encyclopédie Philosophique Universelle, Bd.1.: L'univers philosophique.* Paris: PUF, 46–56.

Hume, D. (1888). *A Treatise of Human Nature.* Oxford: Clarendon Press.

Husserl, E. (1952). *Ideen zu einer reinen Phänomenologie und phänomenologischen Philosophie II* [Husserliana IV]. Den Haag: Martinus Nijhoff.

Husserl, E. (1959). *Erste Philosophie II (1923–24)* [Husserliana VIII]. Den Haag: Martinus Nijhoff.

Husserl, E. (1962). *Phänomenologische Psychologie* [Husserliana IX]. Den Haag: Martinus Nijhoff.

Husserl, E. (1966). *Analysen zur passiven Synthesis* [Husserliana XI]. Den Haag: Martinus Nijhoff.

Husserl, E. (1973a). *Cartesianische Meditationen und Pariser Vorträge* [Husserliana I]. Den Haag: Martinus Nijhoff.

Husserl, E. (1973b). *Zur Phänomenologie der Intersubjektivität I* [Husserliana XIII]. Den Haag: Martinus Nijhoff.

Husserl, E. (1973c). *Zur Phänomenologie der Intersubjektivität II* [Husserliana XIV]. Den Haag: Martinus Nijhoff.

Husserl, E. (1973d). *Zur Phänomenologie der Intersubjektivität III* [Husserliana XV]. Den Haag: Martinus Nijhoff.

Husserl, E. (1973e). *Ding und Raum* [Husserliana XVI]. Den Haag: Martinus Nijhoff.

Husserl, E. (1974). *Formale und Transzendentale Logik* [Husserliana XVII]. Den Haag: Martinus Nijhoff.

Husserl, E. (1976). *Ideen zu einer reinen Phänomenologie und phänomenologischen Philosophie I* [Husserliana III/1–2]. Den Haag: Martinus Nijhoff.

Husserl. E. (1980). *Phantasie, Bildbewußtsein, Erinnerung* [Husserliana XXIII]. Dordrecht: Kluwer Academic Publishers.

Husserl, E. (1985). *Erfahrung und Urteil.* Hamburg: Felix Meiner.

Jackson, F. (1982). Epiphenomenal Qualia. *Philosophical Quarterly* 32:127–136.

James, W. (1890). *The Principles of Psychology I-II.* London: Macmillan and Co.

Kern, I. (1975). *Idee und Methode der Philosophie.* Berlin: de Gruyter.

Kern, I. (1989). Selbstbewußtsein und Ich bei Husserl. In G. Funke (Ed.), *Husserl-Symposion Mainz 1988.* Stuttgart: Akademie der Wissenschaften und der Literatur, 51–63.

Klawonn, E. (1991). *Jeg'ets Ontologi.* Odense: Odense Universitetsforlag.

Mahler, M.S., Pine, F., Bergmann, A. (1975). *The psychological birth of the human infant.* New York: Basic Books.

Marbach, E. (1974). *Das Problem des Ich in der Phänomenologie Husserls.* Den Haag: Martinus Nijhoff.

Merleau-Ponty, M. (1945). *Phénoménologie de la perception.* Paris: Éditions Gallimard.

Montavont, A. (1999). *De la passivité dans la phénoménologie de Husserl.* Paris: PUF.

Nagel, T. (1986). *The View from Nowhere.* Oxford: Oxford University Press.

Neisser, U. (1988). Five Kinds of Self-knowledge. *Philosophical Psychology* 1(1):35–59.

Parfit, D. (1987). *Reasons and Persons.* Oxford: Clarendon Press.

Piaget, J., Inhelder, B. (1969). *The Psychology of the Child.* New York: Basic Books.

Pothast, U. (1971). *Über einige Fragen der Selbstbeziehung*. Frankfurt am Main: Vittorio Klostermann.

Sartre, J.-P. (1936/1988). *La transcendance de l'ego.* Paris: Vrin.

Sartre, J.-P. (1943). *L'Être et le néant.* Paris: Tel Gallimard.

Sartre, J.-P. (1948). Conscience de soi et connaissance de soi. *Bulletin de la Société Française de Philosophie* XLII:49–91.

Searle, J.R. (1992). *The Rediscovery of the Mind.* Cambridge, MA: MIT Press.

Shoemaker, S. (1968). Self-reference and Self-awareness. *The Journal of Philosophy* LXV:556–579.

Smith, D.W. (1989). *The Circle of Acquaintance.* Dordrecht: Kluwer Academic Publishers.

Spitz, R.A. (1983). *Dialogues from infancy. Selected papers*, ed. R.N. Emde. New York: International Universities Press.

Stern, D.N. (1983). The early development of schemas of self, other and 'self with other'. In J.D. Lichtenberg & S. Kaplan (Eds.), *Reflections on self-psychology*. Hillsdale: Analytical Press, 49–84.
Stern, D.N. (1985). *The interpersonal world of the infant.* New York: Basic Books.
Strawson, G. (1994). *Mental Reality.* Cambridge, MA: MIT Press.
Strawson, G. (1999). The Self and the SESMET. In S. Gallagher, J. Shear (Eds.), *Models of the Self,* Thorverton: Imprint Academic, 483–518.
Strawson, P.F. (1959). *Individuals.* London: Methuen.
Strawson, P.F. (1966). *The Bounds of Sense.* London: Methuen.
Zahavi, D. (1998a). Self-awareness and Affection. In N. Depraz & D. Zahavi (Eds.) *Alterity and Facticity. New Perspectives on Husserl*, Dordrecht: Kluwer, 205–228.
Zahavi, D. (1998b). The Fracture in Self-awareness. In D. Zahavi (Ed.), *Self-awareness Temporality, and Alterity*, Dordrecht: Kluwer, 21–40.
Zahavi, D. (1999a). *Self-awareness and Alterity. A Phenomenological Investigation.* Evanston, Northwestern University Press.
Zahavi, D. (1999b). Michel Henry and the Phenomenology of the Invisible. *Continental Philosophy Review* 32/3: 223–240.
Zahavi, D. & Parnas, J. (1998). Phenomenal Consciousness and Self-Awareness: A Phenomenological Critique of Representational Theory. *Journal of Consciousness Studies* 5: 687–705.

The Place for an Ego in Current Research

Eduard Marbach
University of Bern

> To be sure, this is an important question that I have evaded too much, the evidence of the I as an identical, which therefore can surely not consist in the bundle. (Husserl 1907)

In this paper, I would like to put forward some reflections on the phenomenon of the self in a theoretical orientation, the substance of which I owe to familiarity with Husserl's phenomenology. A good way of getting a sense of Husserl's enterprise, especially for those of you who are not familiar with his somewhat counterintuitive way of raising questions, is to take account of, and to keep in mind, a fundamental distinction between two attitudes towards reality or, if you like, towards what there is.

I will, therefore, first briefly sketch these two attitudes, one of which is adopted in Husserl's philosophy. In order to give you then right away an idea of how I intend to discuss the question of the place for an Ego, I will refer to a well-known point of David Hume's theory of mind in *A Treatise of Human Nature* (1739); for Husserl's conception of our conscious experiences that guides my reflections stands arguably just in opposition to the influential Humean conception. In the main part of my talk, I will proceed by doing some phenomenology for you. I will develop a phenomenological analysis of conscious experiences of real people, particularly of the experience of remembering something, and more briefly of imagining something. Here, as I understand the phenomena, the claim for an Ego or I makes very good sense. In discussing these matters, I have much profited from recent and current work by Iso Kern (1975, 1989, and 2000). Finally, even though I will come to the conclusion that there is some good evidence at least for a *phenomenological* place for an Ego or I, I feel pretty much at a loss when it comes to saying something more about the metaphysical status of the purely subjective unity 'I' that I will be concerned with. I certainly have more questions than illuminating answers regarding the metaphysics of the 'I', as I will indicate at the end.

1. The naturalistic attitude versus the phenomenological attitude towards reality

I turn now to my first point, regarding two fundamental attitudes towards reality.[1] We can take [1] the *naturalistic* attitude, or we can take [2] the *phenomenological* attitude towards reality. Putting it simply, given [1], we presuppose the natural world, the objective physical space-time, as so to speak the encompassing framework within which everything else occurs and can occur. *Within* this frame and among very many other things and events, there are also creatures with various finely developed types of conscious experiences, considered as late products of evolution by natural selection. Moreover, there are physical things or processes that are able to stimulate consciousness via the body and the brain of those creatures. On such a view, characteristic of the natural sciences and of naturalistically minded philosophy, the natural world and physical time obviously come first — having originated some 13 to 14 billion years ago -, and conscious experiential phenomena, if they are at all to be preserved within the causal scheme of things and not given up to "epiphenomenalism or outright eliminativism", will have to be preserved "as part of the physical world" (e.g., Kim 1998: 120) by being held to be "wholly physical phenomena", even when "considered specifically in respect of their qualitative-experiential character" (e.g., Strawson 1999: 504). On such an objective or third-person approach, consciousness is taken as consciousness of this or that organism alike, at times it is studied more specifically as consciousness of a non-human or of a human animal, or of some artificial mind, etc. In short, consciousness is itself considered a portion of reality and as such it is, "in some sense", set "out there" *in* the natural world, *in* the objective space-time and *in* the objective causality among physical objects or processes.

Given [2], by contrast, the reverse is the case. The phenomenological question in its Husserlian conception now is, How is the natural world out there appearing or given *in consciousness*? More specifically, how is space, ime, causality, how are organisms, among them other human beings and I nyself with my body, etc. given *in consciousness*? What are the conditions of he possibility that something like the natural world and human beings therein an be given, or can become conscious for me or, intersubjectively, for us? In articular, what makes it possible that the natural world and human beings herein can appear or become conscious for us in the ways the modern nathematized natural sciences (physics, biology, neurosciences, etc.) conider them, and consider them in contrast to our everyday pre-scientific ways f experiencing the world out there? In a nutshell, Husserl's chief philosophial interest was to make *consciousness purely in itself and as such* the theme or systematic investigation or, as he liked to say, to consider it *absolutely*, i.e., ot putting it in an alien frame, but rather trying with the help of reflection to xplain what consciousness is and does out of itself, and to consider all ossible objects of consciousness just *in so far as* they are *given to consciousess* in one way or another. If consciousness is thus no longer straightforvardly considered as inserted *into* the natural world, as a more or less nysterious annexe of the physical, if instead it is first taken as *consciousness n the pure sense* (or as *pure consciousness),* we must be prepared to be in eed of novel categories and concepts in order to do justice to its own essential ature *(Eigenwesentlichkeit),* instead of simply transferring the conceptual cheme from the natural world to the study of consciousness.

A very far-reaching aspect of the phenomenological attitude [2], only radually clarified by Husserl himself, concerns the *proper treatment of the bjects* that are considered in so far as they are given to consciousness. In this egard it is crucial not to misinterpret the phenomenologically reflective turn owards the pure conscious experiences in such a way that we, so to speak, lose ight of the things "out there". When we are doing phenomenology in Husserl's ense, we do *not* retreat to some sphere of isolated pure consciousness, *nor* do ve, by taking into account the intentionality of consciousness as consciousness of something, introduce so-called *intentional objects* "in" the conscious mind s *substitutes* for, or *representations* of, the things outside of consciousness. nstead, as Husserl made it very clear, when we are adopting the phenomenoogical attitude [2], we have to turn away from dealing *straightforwardly* with he things "out there" in order to study *these very things* in the modified sense of "correlates" of conscious experiences. Using Husserl's technical language, he point can be succinctly put like this: when we are doing phenomenology we ave to do "not with objects *simpliciter* in an unmodified sense, but with noemas as correlates of noeses" (Husserl 1982: § 133). Quite generally, then, th phenomenological question of how something or other is given to conscious ness can always be put like this: How is consciousness presenting itself, or hov is it structured that something or other — for example, an Ego or I — come about in such and such a way in my experience?

2. Hume's theory of 'successive perceptions only' in contrast to Husserl's theory of 'intentional implication and modification'

Let me now turn to Hume's theory of mind and consciousness. Hume's worl *A Treatise of Human Nature*, by the way, was considered by Husserl to be th first systematic attempt to develop something like a phenomenology of th mind, and this, precisely, within a wholly naturalistic attitude [1]. My poin now is that in Hume's view it is "*successive perceptions only*, that constitut the mind" (Hume 1967: 253, emphasis mine), that "all our particular percep tions ... are different, and distinguishable, and separable from each other, an may be separately consider'd, and may exist separately" (252; cf. 634) furthermore, that "if perceptions are distinct existences, they form a whol only by being connected together. But no connexions among distinct exist ences are ever discoverable by human understanding. We only *feel* connexion or determination of the thought, to pass from one object to an other"(635). As Hume (1967: 634) illustrates:

> when I view this table and that chimney, nothing is present to me but particular perceptions, which are of a like nature with all the other perceptions. This is the doctrine of philosophers. But this table, which is present to me, and that chimney, may and do exist separately. This is the doctrine of the vulgar, and implies no contradiction. There is no contradiction, therefore, in extending the same doctrine to all the perceptions.

Against such a conception of our perceptions or experiences that appears to b modeled after spatial *partes-extra-partes* relations in the physical world ou there, and to regard perceptions as obviously an analogue of physical natura events, Husserl (e.g., 1977: 26) forcefully defended the view that

> instead of spatial mutual externality, spatial intermingling and interpenetration, and spatial totality, it pertains to the essence of conscious life to contain an intentional intertwining, motivation, mutual implication by meaning, and this in a way which in its form and principle has no analogue at all in the physical.

Using a first-person reflective methodology,[2] Husserl was able to describe the fact that certain mental acts of consciousness *intentionally imply*, i.e., *contain in themselves*, other mental acts of consciousness. I am thinking here of very common everyday mental acts of re-presenting (*vergegenwärtigen*) something, which Husserl had analyzed, such as remembering a past event, imagining something, picturing something, thinking of (or trying to understand) someone else's experiences of perceiving, remembering or imagining something, etc. In such cases, the intentional structure of the experiences is such that a conscious experience that is intentionally implied in an encompassing mental act of consciousness *could not exist without* this act. This is a crucial reflective phenomenological finding, and I will return to it shortly in more detail. The reason for its being crucial for my present purposes is, of course, that the reflecting mind may here just have the opportunity to "perceive some *real connexion*" among our perceptions or experiences, sibyllicly hinted at by Hume himself (Hume 1967; Appendix: 636).[3]

It is, indeed, my conviction that what Husserl described as intentional implication and modification belonging to the conscious experiences of mentally re-presenting something that is not actually given here and now speaks exactly to this problem of an intimate connection among conscious experiences. And it is, after all, precisely in the context of reflectively analyzing the multiple intentional components that are implied in these phenomena of re-presentation that Husserl claimed a place for the Ego or I as something like an identical subjectively unifying reference-point, discoverable — *pace* Hume — "when I turn my reflexion on *myself*" (Hume 1967: 634), as I will presently try to develop.

3. A detailed phenomenological analysis of structures of re-presentational consciousness and the place for an Ego or I

In the main part of the paper, to which I now turn, I want to present a somewhat detailed phenomenological analysis of the consciousness of re-presentation, with the help of which I aim at showing that a place for an Ego or I makes good phenomenological sense. Soon after having cleared the way for doing phenomenology of pure consciousness in a first-person methodology, Husserl noted in a manuscript from 1907 with regard to "*the I* which, in the flux of the subjective time, has its life in these acts" of consciousness: "To be sure, this is an important question that I have evaded too much, the evidence c the I as an identical, which therefore can surely not consist in the bundle" (M B II 1: 22b). Husserl then asked himself whether he had not to acknowledg that *the I* was something experiencable, "perceivable", something "phenom enologically evident", that it was "an apperception, but one that was precisel in contrast to what is empathized, in contrast to other I's" ("*andere Ich*").

The decisive progress regarding the issue of the I as an identical cam about when Husserl deepened his analysis of the structures of mental acts c re-presenting something, and more specifically when he elaborated what i common to re-presentations of one's own experiences as against re-presenta tions of others' experiences. I would like to proceed by analyzing concret examples of experiences of re-presenting something, thereby moving our wa up to the question of how to distinguish between experiences of my own a against experiences of someone else. To begin with, I develop the case i some detail on the basis of an example of remembering something. I the present, much more briefly, elements of the analysis of imagining something before I finally turn to the contrast with re-presenting someone else's experi ences.

For what I intend to discuss now, any common act of thinking by onesel rememberingly of a thing, a person, or an event will do. Let's take somethin nice! Thus suppose that I am thinking, say, of my sitting at the Caffè Florian i Venice during a visit there a few years ago. Note that, appropriately modified the example could also be construed as thinking of a possible visit at the Caffè leaving it open when it would take place. Similarly, it could be construed a thinking of another visit there at some time in the future. Again, with appropri ate modifications, an example of this type could even be conceived of a thinking purely imaginatively of an event located at some imaginary time an space, etc. And, of course, the object or event of the remembering etc. coul just as well be something else. What, with Husserl, I take these modes o thinking to have in common is that in all of them the thinking can b performed in such a way that the thinking person intentionally refers to a object (i.e., a person, thing, event, situation) by way of representing a percep tion of the object thought about, regardless of whether the object is to be foun somewhere in the real, intersubjectively shared world, or whether the object i merely imagined.

Let us examine the example of my remembering an episode in Venic more closely. This helps to make vivid what the problem of the I as a lentical is. As I am now remembering the visit at the Caffè Florian from the rst-person perspective, I am, as it were, sitting there at a small table with my ife to the right, close to the door where the waiters go in and out, enjoying, as were, a glass of wine; I am, as it were, looking out at the musicians who are laying under the nearby awning slightly to the left of our table, and at the rowd sitting at the tables on the large square outside of the arcades. I am also ware again more or less clearly of the spatial layout of part of the town and ome of its buildings and waterways in particular, even though they are not, as were, visible in the way the immediate surroundings of the Caffè are. esides my recalling how things are spatially oriented from my point of view the situation that I recall, I am also temporally aware of having come here ite at night after attending a concert at the Goldoni, and I can readily conjure p the subsequent walk in the light of the full moon over the large square owards the Church of San Marco and along the Palazzo Ducale, over the onte dei Sospiri and into the narrow street to the Hotel…

So far, my account is pretty close to real life talk about past events, I ink. Now, in Husserl's phenomenological perspective, the main task consists in capturing the structure or form of the conscious experience that is alive the act of remembering the episode. By speaking of the structure or form of ie conscious experience, I intend to highlight that to be conscious is not just ome ineffable quality, feeling or what-it-is-likeness accompanying my cogniive act of remembering. Rather, when I am remembering, I am conscious of inking of something in a certain way, as distinct from, e.g., imagining a ossible event or anticipating a future one, which each would exhibit a istinctly different form of consciousness. However, the form of my concious experience can only be made explicit with the help of my reflecting pon the act when it is no longer performed but only re-presented.

How do I (and each of you for herself or himself) do this? Crucially, it is ie *object* of my conscious experience that provides what Husserl called the uiding thread ("Leitfaden") for the analysis. Ask yourself, how the object is *iven* to you (appears to you) in order to unpack the hidden multiple constitunt parts of the mental act of consciousness in question. Proceed step by step order to elaborate the corresponding unified structure of conscious experince.

Applied to the case at hand, such reflection permits to point out a number f constituent parts of the form of my remembering the episode in Venice. irst of all, my rememberingly referring to the episode can be characterized as *quasi-direct referring* to the event in the following way. Qualifying the way of referring as '*quasi*-direct' serves to make us understand that in thinking rememberingly of the episode it is consciously as if I were directly bodily in contact with the things there etc., *not actually though*, rather only *as it were*, i.e. *quasi*. That my being there is only a *quasi*-being there can readily be seen by observing that in remembering the episode I am able, for instance, to see, as it were, *now* the table at the Caffè in front of me, *now, instantly thereafter*, the entrance of the Hotel which, in reality, is located at quite some distance from the Florian so that I could not *actually* have seen one instantly after the other as I can when remembering the episode. And yet, as reflection helps to make explicit, I do intentionally refer quasi-*directly*, quasi-*immediately* to the table etc. Speaking this way is meant to emphasize that in thinking rememberingly of the episode it is consciously as if *the table etc. itself appeared* to me. Put in another way, it is as if I *as perceiver* were bodily present there. Clearly, however, the represented table in its surroundings (the arcades, the square etc.) does not appear in correlation with my *actual* perceptual position, here and now; for actually I am sitting at my desk at home, not seeing that table and those arcades etc.... Instead, when I now think rememberingly of the episode the table itself in its surroundings at the Caffè appears as if it were seen and touched from the position I occupied there and then. Thus the table appears as it were to the *re-presented* perceptual point of view in correlation with which the table in its surroundings would actually be found to appear. The sense of directness or immediacy of my intentional referring to the object is due to the fact that the very correlation between an object's ways of appearing and this or that perceptual point of view that is characteristic for acts of *perceiving* obtains here, too, although consciously modified as *quasi*-directness, given that the act of perceiving is here only re-presented by me and not actually performed. To the extent, then, that in such a mode of thinking I am involved in one or several *bodily quasi-occupied point(s) of view* in correlation with the (visually, tactually, etc.) appearing object, I would like to say, with Husserl, that I am *intuitively*, i.e. non-conceptually, referring to the represented object and I am doing so more or less clearly and vividly.

An important feature of my thinking rememberingly, whether vividly or not, of the episode at the Florian is at any rate that I preserve the *belief* that was inherent in the past perceptual situation when I now quasi-perceive again, say, the musicians playing under the awning or think of our subsequent walking over San Marco square etc. This character of belief pertaining to my remem ering the episode at the Caffè etc. can easily be highlighted by contrasting the ct with a modification of the act to the effect of thinking merely imaginatively f, say, my walking over to the piano player and talking to him before leaving ne scene… When I do this, as I readily can, my conscious experience is adically different from what it is when I remember our visit at the Caffè; for I an no longer preserve a belief regarding the represented acts of walking over nd talking to the pianist as having actually occurred in the past, given that — s I remember — they never took place! To be sure, in thinking ememberingly of the evening in Venice, my belief can — without being ntirely suspended — be inhibited or restrained as soon as I start hesitating doubting, questioning, etc.) whether I was really active in the ways I now nink I was. Such restrain would, however, not be consciously equivalent to ninking merely imaginatively of something. If the validity of my act is uestioned, if doubts of my own arise or if someone else — my wife, in our xample — gives me reason to believe that what I remember to have been the ase may actually have been different, then I will search for better confirmed epresentations of belief-bestowed experiences with regard to the remembered vent — as far as I can. Thus, restrain in my otherwise straightforward belief-reserving performance of the act of thinking rememberingly of the episode in Venice will continue to take place, so to speak, in the milieu of belief.

I now want to turn to another crucial point regarding the structure or form f the conscious experience of remembering that has already been discussed in etail by the early Husserl (1980) and that is also to be found in the conscious xperience of imagining to be discussed below. The point is this: When I am hinking rememberingly of the past episode I continue at the very same time to e aware of actually perceiving my present surroundings. Perhaps I remain onscious of the present only dimly; namely when I am much absorbed by my ividly thinking of the past event. However, to be intentionally referring to omething past can only make sense if, *at the same time*, I am also intentionally referring to something else that is presently given. It is a necessary part of ny act of rememberingly thinking of the episode in Venice that in my onscious experience some position of mine is established in the presently iven world here and now. On the view that I am defending, such a position is, ndeed, established in virtue of the perceptual awareness of my lived body *Leib*) which is tactually, visually and otherwise directly in contact with my resently, bodily given surroundings. Note that if in my conscious experience he contact to my actual presently given surroundings were not preserved, my experience would be one of dreaming (daydreaming), or even of hallucinating to be in Venice. But then, as again Husserl already discussed the matter, what I would intentionally be referring to in such experiences of dreaming etc. would have the property of being taken to be actually itself present and supplied with the character of belief. The episode at the Caffè would no longer only be given with the quality of my being there *as it were again*, unlike what obtains with my rememberingly thinking of it while *simultaneously* maintaining contact with the presently given surroundings.

Fundamentally, then, in my act of rememberingly thinking of the episode in Venice, there is at once, *uno actu*, a two-fold time-awareness. For one thing there is awareness of my present situation, the here and now where I am doing my rememberingly thinking of the event. And for another, *simultaneously operative* in my conscious experience but contrasting with the awareness of the present time, there is my awareness of some more or less determined past time in Venice. To be sure, this aspect of time-consciousness would deserve much closer analysis; this would, however, lead us way beyond the scope of this paper.

Now, as Husserl already had observed, there occurs a phenomenon of *overlapping* (*Verdeckung*) or *interference* among my intuitive acts that is most relevant for my discussion. To the extent that I am really actually thinking of the past episode in the way described above, that is, by rememberingly conjuring up an experience of seeing *as it were again* the table etc. at the Caffè in Venice from the re-presented perceptual point of view, I can no longer *at the very same time* actually see my present surroundings from my actually occupied present perceptual point of view with any degree of clarity and distinctness. My *quasi*-seeing interferes with, or it overlaps, my simultaneous actual seeing, say, the Lake and the mountains out there, and vice versa. The more I get attentively involved in seeing and hearing as it were again, say, the musicians under the awning, and the less am I able simultaneously to keep alive some actual seeing and hearing of something in my present surroundings; and the more I get attentive visually and otherwise to what there is around me at present, the less can I continue my experience of being *as it were again* there at the Florian.

As I understand this phenomenon, it shows that to be actually intuitively or non-conceptually *thinking of* something — be it rememberingly, as in our example, or be it imaginatively or anticipatorily — always involves *my being as it were co-present there and then*. Thinking of something *intuitively*, then oes not allow me truly *to detach myself* from the situation thought of; rather, ne re-presented situation itself is given in relation to a co-represented point of iew *of mine*, as if *I* were present there and then in person. And this can only ccur at the cost of a full presence of mine in the here and now. Instead of eferring to the re-presented event only from a certain *distance*–as it would ften seem to be the case when we are linguistically reporting something — I m, as it were, returning there again or re-presenting myself as being, as it vere, co-present there, more or less intensely absorbed, and accordingly oosening my contact with the present surroundings. Importantly, in view of ne central topic of this paper, the Caffè etc. does not appear as it were again to *ust any indeterminate* spatial position there and then, or to *just anyone's* erceptual position. Instead, it appears quite precisely relative to *my position* nere and then, i.e., it appears relative to that position which I now, errone-usly or not, believe to have occupied in the past (at some point in the past, or t just that day of a particular year, etc.), with or without awareness of ertainty, or probability etc. Degrees of certainty or uncertainty are of course art of the experience, and errors of various sorts are always possible, too.

But now, consider once again that I am of course *not really, actually* there nd then when I now rememberingly think of the event. *But am* I *really, ctually, here, only and exclusively?* My *body* is here, and as I am now emembering the episode in its being given to me *then*, I know that my body *as there*. Bodily positions are really always only actual positions. The Caffè vould not as it were *appear* (again) to me without a consciousness (e. g., a onscious experience of remembering, more generally of re-presenting) to the ffect of *my being as it were displaced there and then*–that is, without a *iodified* consciousness of bodily perceiving: instead of a consciousness of ctually seeing the table etc. itself, one of seeing it only as it were.[5]

Someone may want to object that talking of mental I-displacement is ather mysterious and that there is a much simpler and robust account of the henomenon in terms of a memory (or mental) image that I now actually have f the Caffè, instead of having a perception of the Caffè itself there and then. hat sounds familiar, after all; not only is there a lot of current work on mental nagery — think of, e. g., St. M. Kosslyn's (1980, 1994) major contributions the psychological and neuroscientific study of imagery — , there is also avid Hume to be recalled in this context, when he writes the following in the hapter "Of personal identity" in his *A Treatise of Human Nature* (1967: 260/ 1):

> For what is the memory but a faculty, by which we raise up the images of past perceptions? And as an image necessarily resembles its object, must not the frequent placing of these resembling perceptions in the chain of thought, convey the imagination more easily from one link to another, and make the whole seem like the continuance of one object? In this particular, then, the memory not only discovers the identity, but also contributes to its production, by producing the relation of resemblance among the perceptions. The case is the same whether we consider ourselves or others.

Back to Husserlian phenomenology where things present themselves ver differently and where it is shown, in particular, that the case is precisely *nc the same* whether we consider ourselves or others! As reflection makes clea in my conscious experience of rememberingly thinking of the Caffè etc., I d *not* have a conscious experience of seeing an *image* of the Caffè rather tha the Caffè itself, for I do *not* have an awareness of a *depiction* of the Caffè, bu clearly one of the Caffè itself, *as it were*. My rememberingly intentionall referring (as a so-and-so structured conscious event) is altogether different i its 'what-it-is-likeness' from my intentionally referring to the Caffè itself i actual perception; but the object itself (the Caffè etc. out there in the world that I intend, or intentionally refer to, is still *just the object itself* for m consciousness. There is no second object like an image resembling the Caffè Ontologically speaking, there cannot be an image without a vehicle of i carrying its appearing, and since I am in no way conscious of such a carrie when I rememberingly refer to the Caffè, but am conscious only of the Caff itself, it would seem clear that recourse to a mental image of the Caffè supposedly present in the mind, cannot be accepted as an account of th phenomenon of re-presenting the event to be preferred to the descriptiv account in terms of I-displacement.

Let me now turn to the re-presentational consciousness of *imaginin* something. This will be done much more briefly but in the interest of widenin the scope of the kinds of conscious experiences that involve re-presentation of experiences of my own, not unlike what we have just seen in the example c remembering something. With imagination, it would seem that I, as th contingent empirical self that I am, i.e., with this or that human body, these o those personal traits etc., do not belong to the re-presented imaginary worl To be sure, I, the empirical person which I am, living in the factually give world with my factually given body etc., am co-present, I am the one doing th imagining, just like I am the one doing the remembering. And, living in m imaginings, I can, if I wish so, imagine myself into the imaginary world — m s the empirical self with my body etc. — , but I need not do so. I can imagine ıe things and events of the imaginary world without co-imagining myself (the mpirical I) as observer or, more generally, as a member of the imaginary vorld, living and acting in it, etc. So, it would seem that the imaginary world ould exist without me.

On the other hand, however, consider that in the imagination I have the orresponding thingly appearances, not unlike what we found in the case of emembering, the things are quasi-perceived in certain orientations and in no thers. Moreover, what is necessarily required when I engage in imaginings, s Husserl has emphasized, are the kinaesthetic systems and the systems of ppearing that depend on them in motivated and not just arbitrary ways, that s, visually, tactually etc. These systems are bound up for me to my typically uch and so determined representation of the body. The things appearing in the nagination, again not unlike what is the case in remembering, point to a here, o a zeropoint of orientation. In his analyses of imagining, Husserl therefore oncluded, convincingly, I think, that in an act of imagining *I* am necessarily o-present after all, as center of the orientation, as subject, to which the ppearances are related. I am thus not only co-present as the one who actually nagines something (cf. Husserl 1973a: 291).

According to Husserl — and I think he is right about this — each point of ıe world could become my here. Out of each here, there must exist aspects, etermined and orderly ones, as perceptual possibilities (Husserl 1973a: 294). f so, however, it is evident that I cannot always be co-present with my body, .g., on the sun. Ideally, I can move everywhere or I can think of being moved verywhere, not really though. Importantly, for the present purpose, it would eem that the I-subject that is re-presented in the re-presentational imaginations nd that necessarily belongs to the imagined world as the correlate of the magined appearances is to be understood as *the same* I as the actually imagining ne. It is however not a question of the body and of the empirical person, but ather of what Husserl and others term the pure I.

Husserl argues along the following line. If the pure imagination were ransformed into a positing act, would we then not have 'our' I, which, to be ure, displaces itself in an indeterminate bodiliness (*Leiblichkeit*) and in an ndeterminate personality, or as pure I, into the function of correlate? After all, am running through the possibility of actual existence, the manifolds of spects from the 'there' to 'here', and vice versa, when I clarify the possibility f the assumed fictional object or event. The crucial point, according to

Husserl's analysis, is that the fictional I would not seem to be a second I. For the transformation of the qualitative modification (the quasi) of the positing act into the positing act itself leads the fictional I over to the I of the imagining to the actual I, and then the fiction turns into a memory or an anticipation.

4. A closer look at the I-involvement in re-presentational consciousness — the contrast to my re-presenting conscious experiences of other minds

Let me now focus on the question of the 'I' — or 'self' — involvement more specifically, leading us rather naturally to a few lose ends or unanswered questions concerning the place for an Ego or I. I want to suggest that when the question of the Ego or I arises we should always talk of I-*consciousness* or I-*awareness*, or lack thereof. What I have in mind is that there is something consciously, experientially given that we denote with the word 'I', something first of all given in re-presentational consciousness. As I see it, it is, however, not the case that an Ego or an I — even, perhaps, considered as some kind of object taken in isolation — would have consciousness of re-presenting, e.g. now of remembering, now of imagining, etc. The point I would like to emphasize is, rather, that in an act of re-presentational consciousness, as I have tried to show by analyzing an example of remembering in detail, there obtains a multiplicity of non-independent moments in the very act of performing the re-presenting. These moments — pace Hume — are not "successive perceptions only" (see above), but are, rather, all simultaneously, or in parallel, involved in the very intentionality of acts of re-presenting something. And these moments are, precisely, unified in the *consciousness* of *I being co-present* (*Dabeisein des Ich*, as Husserl used to say). It is this experientially subjectively unified consciousness that is alive in performing acts of re-presenting something that gets marked with the little word 'I'.[6]

But now, is this not a very idealized view of a place for an I? What about all the uncertainties and possibilities of error, the superpositions of later memories upon earlier ones, etc. that are liable to jeopardize one's I-consciousness? I am prepared to concede all this; for us human beings it is *de facto* the case that we are very often wrong even about our own experiences. Nonetheless, to me it seems also to be true that I, now remembering an episode belonging to past experiences of mine, have a consciousness of my having een co-present there and then, in this or that spatial-temporal position relative the recalled object (thing, event, etc.), perhaps with much indeterminacy as gards my own bodily being and its precise position in space and time. At any te, that which I now remember consciously appears, as it were, relative to a oint of view of *mine* that does not coincide with the presently, actually ccupied point of view.

But what does it mean to say that I have such I-consciousness relative to me experiencing that is taken to be experiencing concerning myself, even if, it could turn out, everything in the experience was wrong? Consider, for xample, the (admittedly contrived) case where it might have turned out that ot I but someone else was actually present there, and what had taken place as not a seeing of the object or event *x* but rather of the object or event *y*, and ore precisely, it was actually not a simple perceptual act of seeing the object event *y* but rather of seeing the object or event *y* as it appeared in a picture, c.! I suggest to say the following: While I had been remembering the object event, in spite of the, as it turned out, cognitively thoroughly false claim of y remembering, *I-consciousness* had occurred, nonetheless; and it had occurred because a situation had experientially been given, in which in the onscious experiencing itself some other consciousness, re-presented as past, ad been implied in the very establishment of the intentional reference to the ast object or event; and such an experientially complex situation presents self with I-consciousness (I being co-present) just if the re-presented consciousness is re-presented as having been (or as possibly being) *originally* xperienced (see Kern 2000) — even though, as I said, it may falsely be meant ich that it was originally experienced by me.

The point of the occurrence of *I-consciousness* in certain forms of re-resentational mental acts becomes, perhaps, still clearer if we finally contrast ich forms with the form of re-presenting another mind's conscious experinces. When I am re-presenting conscious experiences with the understanding at they belong to other, alien creatures, my intentionally complex experience distinctly not given with the I-consciousness found in the previously examed cases of re-presentational consciousness; for, in the case involving other inds, I experience the re-presented consciousness just not as being (or as aving been or as possibly being) *originally* given, whether or not veridically only seemingly but falsely, as later evidence shows. Instead, I experience e re-presented consciousness with an understanding of its being originally xperienced by another creature that is (or has been or would be) simultaeously bodily present with me.

Consider a very simple example of such re-presentational consciousnes
of someone else's experience in the mental act of empathy (*Einfühlung*
Suppose I am re-presenting the perception that someone else has of a windo
that I currently do not see. In such a case, as Husserl described the situation,
have the representation (*Vorstellung*) of the aspect that is *his* or *her* impres
sion. As far as I am concerned, it is a merely imaginary re-presentation. Thi
re-presentation of the aspect *in itself* does not differ from any other re
presentation of the aspect. It is the same that *I* would have if I were to mov
over there, i.e., to the alien here, and were suitably to turn my head and facin
the window; thus I imaginatively posit experiences of my own. By contrast t
a case of merely imagining the view of the window, however, the case of a re
presentation by way of empathy of a not-given experiential present is suc
that, bound up to the positing of the body over there, there is the requireme
of an actually present experiencing that is not mine. As Husserl (1973a: 29
succinctly put it: "When I posit other minds (Andere), I posit actual appea
ances that I do not have, and a subject of these appearances who has the
while I am having other appearances."

In some sense, Husserl argues, I am also co-present in the understandin
of the other mind, crucially, however, the superposition of identity betwee
the I as actually re-presenting the experience of the other and the re-presente
I of the displacement 'there' is no longer required as regards the I there who i
a subject of originally experiencing something. Husserl (1973a: 319f.) write

> Just as I am co-present in my past or in a fiction, just so in the mental life of another mind which I am re-presenting in the empathy. This being co-present is however not connected with the requirement of identification as it is in the remembering of the past (and in every remembering). … That which I posit in the other mind, that is I as subject of these and these re-presented cogitationes, and the I itself is re-presented I, it is I, I feel myself in it, and yet <it is> alien I (fremdes Ich), just like the re-presented and validly posited cogito stands outside of the stream of the actual time-consciousness and makes up a 'novel', 'another' stream.

Before touching, in conclusion, on a very deep problem concerning th
question of the unity of consciousness in relation with the I-unity, let me add
few remarks on the puzzling question of the I as something numericall
identical in one stream of consciousness. When I developed the analysis of re
presenting something with examples of remembering and of imagining some
thing, there was constantly talk of 'I'. Let me once more stress that
understand this I always as I of experiences (Erlebnisse). Experiences a

nalyzed, in phenomenology, as structures or forms that are manifolds in the nity of an experience (see Kern 1975), more precisely, in the unity of an I-erformance (Ich-Vollzug) or a possible I-performance. Now, perhaps close process metaphysicians, I am inclined to say with regard to the I that "what thing is consists in what it does or can do" (e.g., Rescher 1995: 417). In such perspective, I would say that in this doing (experiencing) and possibly doing, espite all the changes over time which I undergo as this and this developing erson, *I* experience myself as *identical*, as *one*, in so far as *I* have become ifferent and am continually becoming different. Put another way: I myself ave become a different one (a different person), but not: I have become nother one (another mind, another human being). This is to say that the ossibility of I being co-present is still guaranteed because something origi-ally experienced is at stake that I subsume or can subsume under the unitary orm 'I' (I can, I do, I suffer, etc.), as opposed to something not-originally xperienced in the case of another one.

But how is it, once again, with all the uncertain cases, say, with experiences vay back into early childhood, etc.? How can I possibly still distinguish etween genuine experiences of mine and experiences of others that I have sort f assimilated as 'mine'? And, after all, I can also genuinely remember another nind's experiences, not only my own. The phenomenon of I being co-present s the I of re-presented originally experienced experiences would itself seem to e just this, a phenomenon. There is this phenomenological difference between eeming to have been originally experienced as opposed to seeming not to have een lived through originally by me. But then, how is it with my possibly ecoming more and more unsettled, my continued doubting perhaps, whether omething has been originally experienced by me or not? Are such cases to be ound in real life? Experts of pathological cases, present among you, have to tell ne.... As I see the predicament, I would rather want to acknowledge no longer o know or to be able to decide (because the criteria had become unclear) vhether something had been experienced by me or not. Thus I would accept aps in my life instead of (pathologically?) dwelling upon indecision and doubts o the point of even having doubts (zu zweifeln) about my I-identity and, erhaps, reducing myself to despair (zu verzweifeln)... But how far can all this o? And what would the underlying physiological mechanisms be like?

There are, however, also clear cases of more or less "normal" experiences. And we have to start from there in the endeavor of understanding "normal" as vell as pathological human life and the place for an I in it. Can we say so? I think so. With the help of such examples, as I have tried to do in this paper, structure of re-presentational consciousness with their I-unity can be explored, and the provide a solid basis for a healthy sense of self or I, one that is fit biologicall speaking, but also culturally, socially etc., to be a member of a group.

The deep problem I alluded to above and which has implicitly bee present almost throughout my discussion is the following: Is it really th relationship to the I as it is given in the I-awareness that is alive pre-reflec tively in mental acts of re-presentational consciousness (e.g., in remembering imagining etc.), is it really this I-identification that founds or grounds the unit of consciousness and its self-containedness in relation to the unities of con sciousness of other minds, or is it, rather, the character of being experienced i the mode of originality that grounds the difference between that which is min as opposed to that which is not mine, but alien (Fremdes)? In Iso Kern (2000 there is a profound discussion of this question, and as far as I see, Husser himself had already been struggling with these two principles of the unity an self-containedness of one temporal stream of consciousness over agains others. Thus, and with these quotations I would like to conclude, we find hin writing on the one hand (Husserl 1973b: 429):

> The most originally mine is my life, my 'consciousness', my 'I do and suffer', the being of which consists in its being pregiven to me as functioning I, i.e. to be accessible, experientiable, intuitable in the mode of originality, of it-itself.

And on the other hand, Husserl (1973c: 351) observes:

> My I and all that which is my own — my ways of consciousness, my acts, my objects of consciousness — that which is mine has its mineness in this I-centering by way of coincidence (Deckung) steadily actualizing itself in each occurring re-presentation.

Notes

1. See, e. g., Husserl (1997), § 1 and § 40.
2. For a short presentation of the essential tenets of such a methodology, see Marbach, 1999
3. Compare W. James' "real ties, realized in the judging Thought of every moment" 1950: 360, et passim.
4. For a systematic discussion of phenomena of "intentional implication and modification" along Husserl's lines, see Kern 1975, and more recently Marbach 1993, introducing a phenomenological notation for capturing the internal structures of conscious experi ences.

See also, e. g., the very thoughtful paper by Sokolowski 1990.

Perhaps, the pronoun 'I' is "idle, superfluous" in soliloquy, as Peter Geach has put it (see Lynne Rudder Baker 1998: 336), precisely because, within the person, unifying I-consciousness is pre-reflectively *alive* with regard to the manifold mental activities she is engaged in as her own at any moment in time. But I do not think it is sufficient for capturing the meaning of the word 'I' in communicative situations to say, with Geach, that the pronoun 'I' serves to call attention to the speaker (ibid.), for then the whole point of the I-*consciousness* in the sense of a unifying consciousness of a manifold of experiences is missed (see also Kern 2000).

References

Hume, D. (1967). *A Treatise of Human Nature* (originally published in 1739). Oxford: Clarendon Press.

Husserl, E. (1973a). *Zur Phänomenologie der Intersubjektivität: Texte aus dem Nachlass. Erster Teil: 1905–1920, Husserliana*, vol. XIII, edited by Iso Kern.The Hague: M. Nijhoff.

Husserl, E. (1973b). *Zur Phänomenologie der Intersubjektivität: Texte aus dem Nachlass. Zweiter Teil: 1921–1928, Husserliana*, vol. XIV, edited by Iso Kern. The Hague: M. Nijhoff.

Husserl, E. (1973c). *Zur Phänomenologie der Intersubjektivität: Texte aus dem Nachlass. Dritter Teil: 1929–1935, Husserliana*, vol. XV, edited by Iso Kern. The Hague: M. Nijhoff.

Husserl, E. (1977). *Phenomenological Psychology: Lectures, Summer Semester, 1925*. Translated by J. Scanlon (originally published in German 1962). The Hague: M. Nijhoff.

Husserl, E. (1980). *Phantasie, Bildbewusstsein, Erinnerung: Zur Phänomenologie der anschaulichen Vergegenwärtigungen. Texte aus dem Nachlass (1898–1925), Husserliana*, vol. XXIII, edited by E. Marbach. The Hague: M. Nijhoff.

Husserl, E. (1982). *Ideas pertaining to a pure phenomenology and to a phenomenological philosophy: First Book, General introduction to a pure phenomenology*. Translated by F. Kersten (originally published in German 1913). The Hague: M. Nijhoff.

Husserl, E. (1997). *Thing and Space: Lectures of 1907*. Translated by R. Rojcewicz (originally published in German 1973). Dordrecht/Boston/London: Kluwer Academic Publishers.

James, W. (1950). *Principles of Psychology,* vol. one (originally published 1890). New York: Dover Publications.

Kern, I. (1975). *Idee und Methode der Philosophie: Leitgedanken für eine Theorie der Vernunft*. Berlin: de Gruyter.

Kern, I. (1989). Selbstbewusstsein und Ich bei Husserl. In G. Funke (ed.), *Husserl-Symposium Mainz 27.6./4.7.1988. Akademie der Wissenschaften und der Literatur, Mainz*. Stuttgart: Franz Steiner, 51–63.

Kern, I. (2000). Zwei Prinzipien der Bewusstseinseinheit: Erlebtsein und Zusammenhang der Erlebnisse. *Facta Philosophica* 2.

Kim, J. (1998). *Mind in a Physical World: An Essay on the Mind-Body Problem and Menta* *Causation.* Cambridge, Massachusetts: The MIT Press.
Kosslyn, St. M. (1980). *Image and Mind.* Cambridge, Massachusetts: Harvard Universit Press.
Kosslyn, St. M. (1994). *Image and Brain.* Cambridge, Massachusetts: The MIT Press.
Marbach, E. (1974). *Das Problem des Ich in der Phänomenologie Husserls.* Den Haag: M Nijhoff.
Marbach, E. (1993). *Mental Representation and Consciousness: Towards a Phenomeno logical Theory of Representation and Reference.* Dordrecht: Kluwer Academic Publish ers.
Marbach, E. (1999). Building materials for the explanatory bridge. In F. Varela & J. Shea (Eds.), *The View from Within: First-person approaches to the study of consciousness* Thorverton Exeter: Imprint Academic, 252–257.
Rescher, N. (1995). Process philosophy. In J. Kim & E. Sosa (Eds.), *A Companion t* *Metaphysics.* Oxford: Blackwell, 417–419.
Rudder Baker, L. (1998). The first-person perspective: a test for naturalism. *America* *Philosophical Quarterly* 35, Number 4: 327–348.
Sokolowski, R. (1990). Displacement and Identity in Husserl's Phenomenology. In S IJsseling (Ed.), *Husserl-Ausgabe und Husserl-Forschung.* Dordrecht: Kluwer Academi Publishers, 173–184.
Strawson, G. (1999). The Self and the SESMET. In S. Gallagher & J. Shear (Eds.), *Model* *of the Self.* Thorverton Exeter: Imprint Academic, 483–518.

PART II

On Understanding Schizophrenia

Naomi Eilan
University of Warwick

Karl Jaspers held, famously, that schizophrenic phenomena are ununderstandable. As he put it: "The most profound distinction in psychic life seems to be between that which is meaningful and *allows empathy* and what in its particular way is *ununderstandable*, 'mad' in the literal sense, schizophrenic psychic life..." (Jaspers 1913/97: 579). His prime examples of the latter are what he calls 'made' phenomena in which subjects appear to be denying immediate ownership of their thoughts and actions. These are radically ununderstandable because "...we are not able to have any clear sight of any psychic event without our self awareness being involved." (Jaspers 1913/97: 578)

Now, I take it that there is something wrong about a brute denial of *any* understandability. But it is not easy to get right the kind of understanding that might be brought to bear on such phenomena while at the same time doing justice to Jaspers' warranted sense of the deep and baffling otherness of the schizophrenic's sense of the self and the world. My central aim in what follows is to give an indication of the difficulties we encounter when trying to solve simultaneously for understanding and utter strangeness. My procedure will be as follows: I begin with some of Jaspers' own claims about the nature of understanding in general. I then raise a question about his application of these claims to schizophrenia which will be used to generate a crude paradox inherent in Jasper's views. I then go on to consider three ways of trying to dissolve the paradox, where the debate between them captures much of the dialectic that informs current debates about the relative strangeness and understandability of schizophrenic phenomena. I will suggest that none of these routes is successful; they either falsify the data or are too philosophically suspect to be taken seriously. I end with a brief look at some recent work which can be regarded as providing a fourth route out of the paradox, and which points, in my view, in the right direction.

To concentrate the mind on the kind of strangeness at issue here we should have before us one of Jaspers' very many examples. His concern, in the passage I will be quoting, is with 'thought disorders'(delusions) that accompany what he calls 'passivity phenomena'. The latter include 'thought insertion' (when subjects say their thoughts are not their own, are forced on them), 'thought withdrawal' (when subjects say their thoughts are taken from them), 'thought broadcasting' (when subjects say others can read their thoughts) and 'alien control' (where subjects say their own will and actions are replaced by the intentions of some other force or agency). He writes:

> The following is an example of the elaborating thought-performance which takes place in delusion: a schizophrenic patient (a factory-hand, who later became a policeman) experiences typical 'passivity' phenomena; there are movements of his limbs and he hears voices. He thinks of remote hypnosis and telepathy. He suspects and reports someone to the police. He arranges for a private detective to make enquiries and finally convinces himself that his suspicions are unfounded. He writes: "Since no one can have been influencing me and I am sure I am not suffering from any false-perception, I have to ask who can it be? The way in which I am plagued and tortured and the hidden meaning in all these conversations and bodily movements suggest that there is some malicious supernatural being at work. He influences and plagues me continually and hopes to destroy me. Are my experiences of the same order as those of mental patients or are they unique? For humanity's sake I feel I should state my conviction that if they are of the same order, then the doctor must be wrong in thinking that the voices which patients hear are hallucinations. Whatever it is in my own case, whether it is the same experience as that of a mental patient or something exceptional, the conclusion is in either case that life goes on after death". (Jaspers 1913/97: 195)

1. Jaspers on Understanding

Jaspers' general characterisation of understanding is somewhat minimal. The two central stipulative claims he makes are the following. First, understanding is a mode of comprehension which we apply to psychic events only, where the distinguishing feature of such events is that they have meaning. The kinds of connections between mental states that understanding seeks to make manifest depend essentially and exclusively on their meaning. Second, exercising understanding is a matter of exercising empathy whereby, as he puts it, 'We sink ourselves in the situation and grasp its significance from the inside.' (Jaspers 1913/97: 301).

Two subsequent distinctions that Jaspers makes introduce some substance and bite into these stipulations about his use of 'understanding'. One is the distinction between understanding and explaining. Another is the distinction between static and genetic understanding. Our focus for generating the paradox will be the second distinction; but in the course of unpacking it I will make some comments about the first.

Static understanding, for Jaspers, is what we employ when we listen to subjects' own accounts of their experience and record these accounts as such, without imposing any pre-conceived theory on them. Such careful listening and listing were taken to be the hallmark of the phenomenological approach to schizophrenia which Jaspers initiated. We are dealing here, essentially, with 'fragments' as Jaspers puts it, and it is such theory-free recording of fragments that Jaspers calls doing phenomenology. The first 300 or so pages of *General Psychopathology* are devoted to it.

In *genetic* understanding, in contrast, as Jaspers defined it, we are concerned with comprehending how one mental state 'emerges' from the other, and in making sense, from the subject's point of view, of the occurrence of a mental event in terms of others it emerges from and generates. An example would be explaining why someone believes it is raining by appealing to her perception of the rain, or why someone feels dejected by appealing to his failure to stop drinking (Jaspers 1913/97: 27, 307).

2. The Paradox

The crude paradox implicit in Jaspers' approach to schizophrenia emerges when we focus on the relation between static and genetic understanding, and the application of this relation to schizophrenia. Jaspers appears to have been committed, in varying degrees of strength, to the following three claims:

(1) Schizophrenic states and events are genuine mental events with intentional content. This means that they have significance for the subject. It is such significance and phenomenology that static understanding records.
(2) It is constitutive of events and states that have intentional mental content that they are genetically understandable.

(3) Schizophrenic states and events are not genetically understandable.

If static and genetic understanding are treated unambiguously, as so far defined, then it is not possible to hold on to all three claims. And, I suggest, a substantial chunk of positions in 20th century debates about schizophrenia can be crudely delineated in terms of which of these three incompatible claims they reject, as a means of avoiding the paradox. What I want to do next is give a brief illustration of attempts to deny each one of these paradox-generating claims, and indicate why none of them are acceptable.

Of all the claims, claim (2) is the one to which Jaspers may seem to have been the least committed, and certainly not one he explicitly formulated in this particular way. Moreover it is not in the forefront of many psychiatric discussions of schizophrenia. All of this may make it tempting to drop it, and to proceed unproblematically with (1) and (3) in place. However, though not often made explicit by Jaspers, everything he does say on the matter suggests some form of commitment to (2). Moreover, Jaspers aside, rejection of (2) is philosophically untenable, and I regard it as the least negotiable of all three claims.

The ideas behind (2) are, roughly put, as follows. Suppose you want to ascribe to Martha a deep anger at her father for having left home when she was a child. The first idea is that any such ascription depends for its truth on a host of other ascriptions of mental states also being true. Trivially one is committed to its being true that Martha believes that her father did leave home; and less trivially that some kind of harm resulted from this. Each one of these beliefs, in turn, implies the ascription of many others, forming, as Jaspers himself puts it, a 'hermeneutic round' in which '… we achieve understanding within a circular movement from particular facts to the whole that includes them and back again from the whole thus reached to the particular significant facts' (Jaspers 1913/97: 357).

The second idea is that it is constitutive of mental phenomena with meaning, or intentional content, that they are interconnected in this way. As Jaspers puts it: 'What is meaningful cannot in fact be isolated …. understanding will therefore push on from the isolated particular to the whole and it is only in the light of the whole that the particular reveals its wealth of concrete implications'. (Jaspers 1913/97: 357).

The final point is one which Jaspers did not make explicit, but which is none-the-less central. The kind of essential interconnections between mental states which he is here alluding to are precisely the kind revealed by genetic understanding. The point in citing other beliefs, desires, emotions and experiences in ascribing a particular state is that the current state is made sense of in terms of its 'emergence' from the other states. There would be no point in citing Martha's belief that her father leaving home caused much harm unless her anger emerged, among other things, from this belief. The connected mental states that we cite are precisely the kind that make sense of current states, from the inside, by showing the current ones to have emerged from those other states.

I will take wholesale rejection of these three claims as tantamount to the adoption of some form of unacceptable atomism, and, as such, not to be taken as a serious philosophical proposition. Moreover I am not aware of any writings in the psychiatric and psychological literature that advocate global atomism. So I suggest we simply drop the idea of rejecting claim (2).

3. Meaning and Belief

Let us move, then, to a consideration of claim (1). To deny (1) is to deny that states and events labelled 'schizophrenic' should be treated as mental states at all. This is a dramatic claim, and not immediately appealing, but one which Jaspers himself, on occasion, seemingly half endorses when he refers approvingly to the 'lay person's' treatment of schizophrenic utterances as 'senseless ravings' (Jaspers 1913/97: 577). He goes even further and suggests in one place that many schizophrenic events, in particular those which seem to involve denial of ownership of thoughts and actions, should not count as 'statically understandable'. (Jaspers 1913/97: 577). Jaspers apart, denial of content is a coherent response to the paradox, and worth spelling out if only because it highlights crucial assumptions that constrain the debate we are concerned with.

Suppose you are an anthropologist who has carefully constructed a translation manual for an alien tribe whose language you are learning. And suppose that having constructed it on the basis of long and patient observation you find many people producing utterances that your manual translates as 'Twins are birds', as the Nuer are reported by Evans-Pritchard to have said. You have two semantic options. You may assign a literal interpretation to their words, or you may opt for a metaphorical one. Opting for the latter is a way of rationalising the beliefs the utterances express, and, thereby, the subjects who express them. If we insist on sticking to the literal interpretation we assign beliefs which are, as we say, mad.

As anthropologists we may feel that the sanity-saving option is to be preferred. The view we are now considering says, first, that this is precisely not the option we should adopt for schizophrenics when we encounter statements to the effect that they are thinking other people's thoughts, or that their thoughts are being broadcast and so forth. The metaphorical rendering is, in essence, the one chosen for example by R. D. Laing, as a result of which schizophrenic states were treated merely as heightened versions of states we are familiar with. (Laing 1969). But such normalising, the first claim is, which places schizophrenia on a continuum that begins with common or garden beliefs and ends with mystical states is wholly inappropriate, fails to capture the qualitative difference which cuts schizophrenic states off from any such continuum.

So suppose we opt for literal interpretations of the problematic utterances. We say such beliefs are mad. But what does this mean? The second claim is that this just means they cannot be genetically understood. But given claim (2) this in turn means that the utterances are not expressive of anything that could count as a state with intentional content. Both what is said and what such utterances purport to express is mere noise. As Berrios, for example, puts it, delusions are 'empty speech acts that disguise themselves as beliefs' (Berrios 1991: 8).

Such a claim rests, crucially, among other things, on the ununderstandability claim. How might it be justified? In Wittgenstein's *On Certainty* we find the idea that purported beliefs are not understandable (and therefore count as 'mad') if there is nothing that could count as evidence for or against them, nothing, in particular, that could count as making a mistake here. When we reach such 'beliefs' then nothing could count as emergence, and so we do not have a belief with content at all. (See, e.g., Wittgenstein 1979: §70–74). In such cases we switch from looking for reasons for the state to causes, an idea we find in Jaspers too (Jaspers 1913/97: 28), and to which we return in the next section. However, finding examples of claims with purported empirical content which would meet these criteria is none too easy a thing to do. One of Wittgenstein's more poignant examples of claims which are such that nothing could count as evidence for or against them illustrates the hazards here. He says that if someone were to say that he had just come back from a visit to the moon we would not understand him — which must have seemed as good an example as any in the 1950's of a claim such that no evidence for or against it were conceivable. (See e.g., Wittgenstein 1979: §117, §226, §660–61). Even today we would, in most cases, regard such a claim as mad, as Wittgenstein claimed, but not ununderstandable in a content-depriving way.

More generally, barring, arguably, negations of the laws of logic, it is hard to find examples of claims which are such that we can *a priori* rule out the conceivability of a world in which evidence for or against them exists. The same holds, at least *prima facie*, for the most baffling claims schizophrenics might make — about thinking other people's thoughts, and so forth. One would have to show that the bafflingness here just comes down to the inconceivability of a world in which it might be the case that one does have evidence for such a claim. I am not saying this is a doomed enterprise but only that it is probably more demanding, philosophically, than those who find the 'noise' option attractive bargained for.

In fact, I suspect that something much weaker is usually meant here. The weaker claim is that what the schizophrenic says cannot be treated as revealing what is *really* going on in her mind and is therefore useless for therapeutic purposes. And as we have no other access to her states, one may as well, for practical therapeutic purposes, assume there *are* no states with content. On this view 'static phenomenology', if it has any use at all, is good only for diagnostic purposes. Once we have located our classic symptoms we need no longer worry about what, if anything, the subject means.

The trouble with this pragmatic version of the 'no content' claim is that it is not a stable resting point. The phenomenologist believes there is a value to listening, to 'static understanding', which goes beyond more listing of symptoms. The noise advocate disagrees. To justify his claim he must say *why* there is no value — and this would suggest having to back up his claim with a philosophically more problematic one about the inconceivability of such statements being expressions of belief.

This dispute apart, the main difficulty with the noise option is that is seems to falsify the data. It simply does not seem to be true that when we read the first 300 pages of Jaspers, or listen to a person in a delusionary state, the words fail to convey any sense at all of the state of mind the schizophrenic is trying to express. There is *some* kind of understanding we bring to bear here, some glimmer of insight the words afford us. It is all very well for Jaspers to suggest 'made' phenomena are statically ununderstandable. But he also claims, virtually in the same breath, that "..the entire complex [of made phenomena] presents itself vividly to us from the self description of patients" (Jaspers 1913/97: 579). The question is, precisely, what does this making vivid consists in if it is not a matter of engaging normal empathy. Unless one is prepared to take Berrios' hard-nosed line here, the claim that there is no state of mind the words express seems like no more than a throwing up of hands at the difficulty of first describing, and then explaining, the form of understanding that *is* brought to bear.

Given these difficulties it would appear, and, indeed, does appear to an increasingly large number of psychologists and psychiatrists, that the guilty party here, the constraining assumption to be jettisoned, is claim (3) — the claim Jaspers is famous for, namely that schizophrenic phenomena are ununderstandable. And it is to this third way of dissolving that paradox that I now turn.

4. Understanding and Explaining

So far, the options have been as follows (assuming some kind of genetic understandability is constitutively applicable to intentional states). We either say the phenomena revealed by static phenomenology are understandable by treating what is said metaphorically, and thereby rendering these states familiar. Or we treat what is said literally and claim ununderstandability, and absence of states with intentional contents (in theory or practice).

The option I want to have before us now agrees that metaphorical normalising is inappropriate and so insists on treating what is said literally. But it also insists that thus treated we should take what is said as an expression of a rational belief. To do so, the claim will be, what we have to jettison is Jaspers' sharp and unjustifiable dichotomy between explaining and understanding.

Roughly, understanding and explaining are distinguished by Jaspers along the following three dimensions. (1) In understanding, we immerse ourselves in the situation and see things from the subject's point of view, from the inside. In explaining, in contrast, we give an account 'from the outside'. (2) In understanding, we are dealing with relations of emergence, which are not causal. In explaining we are dealing with causal relations only. (3) In understanding we seek constantly revisable generalisations. In explaining we seek strict deterministic laws. Jaspers further maintains that only when we are engaged in understanding are we in the domain of the psychological proper. Explaining, in contrast, is the province of the natural sciences only. (Jaspers 1913/97: 301–314)

The issues raised here are many and complex. To narrow them down to the ones relevant to our concerns I first very briefly present an account of the Capgras delusion which provides an example of understanding which challenges this sharp dichotomy and which, in so doing, serves as an instance of the rationalising move I want to have before us.

Subjects suffering from the Capgras delusion believe their nearest and dearest have been replaced by impostors. Such beliefs can have powerful effects on action, as in the case of the subject who decapitated his stepfather, who he believed was a robot impostor, in order to find the batteries and microfilm in his head. Tony Stone and Andrew Young have proposed the following account of these beliefs. (Stone and Young 1997). First, what is lacking, due to brain damage, is the affective ingredient which accompanies face recognition, in virtue of which people feel familiar. So the Capgras subject's spatial recognition of faces is in order but all such recognitions are accompanied by a feeling of utter unfamiliarity and strangeness due to the absence of the normal emotional responses. This is particularly distressing in the case of close relations. In the latter case, the belief system then steps in to make sense of these bewildering experiences by postulating beliefs in impostors. Stone and Young recognize that something is lacking if we leave it at that, for "why does the patient form such a bizarre belief system to explain the anomalous experiences and not adopt what Maher (1988) called 'the more natural explanation' and simply say that things seem strange and stop at that?" (Stone and Young 1997: 341) The impostor conclusion does not seem to be explicable purely as a rational response to disturbing experiences. They therefore suggest that in addition such patients display various general biases in their reasoning which lead them, as we say, to jump to conclusions without serious subjection to counter evidence. The strangeness of the experience coupled with the reasoning biases explains and rationally justifies the beliefs they have.

Independently of whether or not this is the correct account of, specifically, the Capgras delusion, note the following points about the style of explanation it provides. (a) The account is, in part at least, a causal one. It explains the occurrence of the relevant beliefs by postulating abnormal perceptual experiences as their (partial) causes. (b) We cannot 'sink ourselves in the situation' because, our brain working normally, spatial and affective ingredients come together. We could no more have experiences with the quality of strangeness proposed than a colour-blind person can have colour experiences. (c) None-the-less, the account is one that seeks to rationalise the subject's beliefs, make sense of them from her point of view, and as such, relies essentially on the content of these states.

Taking (a) and (b) seriously should, on Jaspers' account, remove these states from the realm of the psychological proper, and the explanation offered from the realm of understanding. Taking (c) seriously places the account firmly within the realm of understanding, and the phenomena within the realm of the psychological. Such cutting across the boundaries Jaspers proposes is certainly not unique to this kind of account, and with this in mind the general points against Jaspers may now be put as follows.

First, with respect to the dual instantiation of (a) and (c), the claim will be that it is not unique to pathologies, but is generally true. Rationalising explanations of a subject's beliefs and action work only *because* we assume that particular experiences cause beliefs and actions. (See e.g. Davidson 1963/80). So, to claim that schizophrenic states are ununderstandable simply because we ask about their causes does not suffice to exclude such states from the realm of the psychologically understandable.

Second, with respect to (b): what the Capgras account serves to bring out is an ambiguity in Jaspers' notion of 'inside understanding'. Often he means what is now referred to as 'simulation': one imagines an experience and then lets one's reasoning run 'off-line' in order to predict what the other will make of it (given other beliefs, desires and so forth). At other times he talks only of rationalising accounts from the subject's perspective, which draw essentially on the contents of the states ascribed to the subject. Now it may well be that, in fact, we often use simulation to engage in the latter activity. But it is a substantive and much debated claim that there is some kind of constitutive connection between them. What the Capgras delusion brings out is that even if there is a constitutive connection on some general level, there are in fact many cases in which we cannot simulate fully another's experiences but can, none-theless, offer rationalising inside explanations. So the fact that a schizophrenic state of mind is not simulable does not exclude it from the realm of the psychological any more than the feeling of seasickness is thus excluded for someone who cannot simulate it.

With these points in place, once we reject Jaspers' dichotomy between explaining and understanding, as we should, the claim will be that what is revealed is a style of explanation which has, in fact, a long history in attempts to account for schizophrenia. (Stone and Young themselves, it should be noted, caution against a simple extension of their account to schizophrenia, in Stone and Young 1997: 329–30). The formula is simple. What is strange and other about schizophrenic phenomena, on this view, are the experiences that provide the input to beliefs (e.g., hallucinations). Our sense of distance comes from our inability to have such experiences. But, barring that, we can understand the schizophrenic's beliefs, in exactly the same way we understand all other beliefs, as rationally caused by these experiences, plus other beliefs, desires etc. (See, e.g. Maher 1974; Frith 1979). So, unlike the metaphor option, on this account, we allow for radical difference, but unlike the noise option, we allow for understanding. Thus, we solve simultaneously for strangeness and understanding. And the question I want to end with is whether this third way of avoiding the paradox gets it right, gets right both where the otherness lies, and the kind of understanding we in fact bring to bear here.

5. A Fourth Route

It is not at all clear to me that Jaspers would necessarily have rejected the Stone and Young style of explanation for at least some specific phenomena we label schizophrenic. But he would certainly have rejected the idea that the strange otherness of the schizophrenic state of mind can be exhaustively located in the strangeness of particular experiences in the manner proposed (See e.g. Jaspers 1913/97: 196). One rationale for such a rejection can be brought out if we compare our reaction to cases of 'visual disorientation', as Holmes called them, to our reaction to schizophrenic phenomena. (See McCarthy 1993/99: 383–4)

In visual disorientation subjects identify visually presented objects while simultaneously maintaining that they have no location in visual space. Now there is something immensely baffling and other about such experiences. The idea that an experience may be visual but not present its objects as being somewhere in space is hard, if not impossible, to get one's mind around. But I suggest that Jaspers' correct intuition was that the kind of strangeness and otherness schizophrenia phenomena present is of a different order. We come closer to it if we try and imagine a subject who not merely maintains that her visual experiences do not present objects as in space, but also maintains that she does not believe that physical objects in fact have location in space. There is a difficulty in comprehending such a claim which goes far deeper than the visual disorientation bafflement. For what seems to be under threat here is a fundamental feature of the very structure of our thought about a mind-independent world and our own places in it.

Now if I am right in thinking that Jaspers thought that many schizophrenic phenomena are strange in this way we can see why it was natural to go on and claim that they are not genetically understandable. If features of thought that we take to be constitutive of our subjective take on an objective world appear to be threatened, then how can genetic understanding, which presupposes them, so much as get going? However, as we have seen, we must allow some kind of understanding which is at least a relative of genetic understanding to occur in these cases, if we both want to say that static phenomenology reveals something about schizophrenic states of mind, and that intentional states are constitutively genetically understandable. What is needed is an account of the kind of understanding that is brought to bear here which makes the borderline nature of these states, the way in which they threaten genetic understanding, integral to the nature of this peculiar understanding. Two recent approaches to some schizophrenic phenomena point, as I understand them, in this direction.

John Campbell has recently proposed that we should treat primary beliefs in paranoid delusions as taking on the role of framework beliefs (Campbell 1999). Our framework beliefs are those fundamental beliefs we do not question, and which globally constrain our inferences and our interpretation of our experiences. These include general beliefs, such as the belief that our environment is spatial and contains physical objects, and more specific manifestations of such beliefs, such as the belief that when I next put my foot down, when walking, it will encounter the ground. The suggestion is that primary paranoid beliefs, such as that the IRA is out to get one, should be treated as constraining one's reasoning and interpretation of one's experience in an analogous manner. They are resistant to counter-evidence because of their fundamental framing role. (But contra the noise option, this does not render their expression senseless). The main difference between this proposal and the 'strange experience plus rational response' proposal, from our perspective, is not that it focuses the strangeness in beliefs rather than in experience. Rather it is that it ocuses on a structural feature which could indeed capture at least one sense in vhich one might want to say, with Jaspers that the schizophrenic's *worlds* are ifferent.

Suppose we accept Campbell's proposal, at least with respect to some inds of paranoid schizophrenic delusions. What bearing does it have on the ind of understandability we have here? In my view it captures beautifully at east part of what we try to do when we do understand expressions of elusions, and the inherent limitations on such understanding. We can, as we ay, fall in, to an extent, with a deluded subject's reasoning. In doing this we ttempt, precisely, to let a primary belief function as a framework belief. But his is something we cannot actually sustain precisely because we cannot treat t as more than a restricted hypothesis. We cannot put it on a level with all our eal framework beliefs, and adjust the latter and our specific beliefs and easoning accordingly. Hence the sense of wild unpredictability for us of the vay in which, for the schizophrenic, other claims gets absorbed in the new ramework.

Campbell's proposal is not intended to capture any particular distinctive *ontent* of schizophrenic delusions. Louis Sass's proposal in *The Paradoxes of Delusion* is intended to do just that, in a spirit consistent, as far as I can tell, vith Campbell's structural proposal. Based on a close analysis of Schreber's nemoirs, Sass's idea is intended to capture the peculiar self-directedness that eople have noted as a distinctive feature of many schizophrenic states. His roposal for how we should understand utterances that have this property is in wo parts. First, we should get ourselves into the frame of mind typical of the hilosophical solipsist, the solipsist who is impressed with the sense in which ll that is really given to him directly are his own experiences, and tries to uggest that the existence of everything over than himself is, therefore, to be loubted. Second, we should step back from such thoughts, and, with the Vittgenstein of the *Tractatus*, for example, give an account of the inherently loomed paradoxical nature of attempts to formulate such solipsism coherntly. For example, one fundamental problem is this. If I want to say that the vorld is mine I must introduce some restrictive empirical force into the mine'. This would suggest I must identify myself, treat myself as an object nd say everything that exists is due to, belongs to, this object. But to do so I nust arguably introduce criteria of identity which distinguish me from other bjects, which is, precisely, to treat myself as one object among others, thus ndermining my central solipsistic claim. Sass suggests that many schizophrenic oscillations between claiming one is nothing, doesn't exist, on the one hand, and claiming that one is God, and that the world is one's own, on the other, should be seen as reflections of the kinds of oscillation that result from the inherent instability of the philosophical solipsist's claims.(See especially Chapter 2: 'Enslaved Sovereign, Observed Spectator', Sass 1994: 31–85)

Here too we have, as in Campbell's case, an account of the understanding we bring to bear which has, built into it, the fundamental difference between schizophrenic states of mind and normal ones. In attempting to immerse ourselves in a solipsistic frame of mind we are engaging in a form of thought which struggles incoherently to be both within and without itself. Certainly not the usual form of empathy. And when we step back to try to understand what is going on as a reflection of the instability of solipsism, it is the very structure of thought that is our concern, and the philosophical understanding we bring to bear on such issues, however explained and defined, is not the normal psychological understanding that Jaspers is concerned with under the heading of 'genetic understanding'.

6. Emotion

Jaspers' primary targets in urging the ununderstandability of schizophrenic phenomena were psychoanalytic and other attempts to explain schizophrenia as an emotional disorder. The following two passages will give a sense of the way he contrasted schizophrenia and such disorders.

> Language has always differentiated affective illness from madness proper. For lay persons madness means senseless ravings, affectless confusion, delusion, incongruous affects, a 'crazy' personality and they think this all the more the more sensible and oriented the individual remains. Should this not be so the lay person rightly tends not to count these states of clouded consciousness as madness proper. Affective illness he indeed calls unmotivated but profound emotional disturbances for which after their own fashion one can have empathy, as for instance those of melancholia. Holding these views the lay person has hit upon a basic difference within morbid psychic life which even today we cannot formulate clearly and precisely….(Jaspers 1913/97: 578)

> Much has been explained as meaningful which in fact was nothing of the kind. Thus attempts have been made to make feelings the explanation of all abnormal phenomena. If we use the term 'feeling' to denote everything for which common usage permits us to use the word, there is always some truth in

> this, but then it comes to very little if we go on to derive delusions, for instance, from feelings. Ideas of senselessness, sinfulness, impoverishment, can understandably said to arise from depressive affects and it was generally supposed that the depressed patient concluded there must be something which made him so miserable. People also wanted to explain delusions of persecution by the affect of distrust, and delusions of grandeur by euphoric moods, but they did not realise that though one may understand ordinary mistakes and overvalued ideas in this way, on can never do this with delusions. Frightening hallucinations in sleep during fever or a psychosis have been attributed to some kind of anxiety, otherwise conditioned. In all these cases we can, it is true, find meaningful connections, and they teach us something about the relationship of delusion contents and previous experiences but nothing at all of how the delusions and false perceptions can have come about in the first place. (Jaspers 1913/97: 409)

As these passage make clear what Jaspers is ruling out is genetic understanding of the occurrence of the phenomena by appeal to a general emotional disturbance in psychic life. But even if one accepts such a restriction, there is still the question of whether and how we should appeal to emotion in accounting both for the utter strangeness of the phenomena themselves, and for their resistance to explanation or understanding. I end with some tentative programmatic remarks about the role emotion might have here in relation to both Campbell's and Sass's suggestions.

I recently heard a woman, now in remission, describing some of her past schizophrenic delusions. Among them was the delusion, during the Gulf War, that Iraqi bombs would be raining down on the streets of London, which made her petrified of going out. In speaking to us she noted a peculiarity of this delusion that was subsequently brought to her attention, namely that it never occurred to her that the bombs would fall on anyone but herself. And this was not because other people seemed not to exist. On questioning she said that had she been in a room with her children, though she would have protected them from normal everyday harms, it would not have occurred to her to try and protect them from the bombs in the street — which existed for her only.

Perhaps the most powerful aspect of the delusion that this woman managed to convey was the sheer, utter terror she felt — where the nature of the terror was precisely constituted by the deep unbridgeable isolation she experienced. The bombs were directed at her in a way that made the rest of the world, her family and friends, wholly irrelevant. What brought home the awfulness of this fear, its other-worldliness, was her response to the question of whether her past delusions felt continuous with her current life, with her autobiographical sense of who she is. The answer was that they were com pletely continuous, and what was clear was that the connection with th present was through the live horror the delusions embodied.

One kind of connection between Campbell's proposal and the role c emotion might be that emotion has a critical casual role in giving the primar paranoid belief its framing role. That is, to understand both what serves t lodge the belief in its powerful framing role, and which particular furthe beliefs get generated with the framework we need to take their emotion significance into account. But implicit here is the suggestion of an eve stronger role for emotion, which can be brought out in connection with Sass' proposal. A clearly unsatisfactory account of the relation between the solipsis tic content Sass ascribes to some schizophrenic phenomena, and the fear, say that the subject feels when thinking thoughts with such contents would be tha the subject first engages in philosophical reflection which leads to solipsisr and then finds the consequences frightening (elating, or whatever). Rather, seems that it is integral to the kind of self directness in play here that it is th contents of a deadening, isolating fear. It is true that on reflection we see tha the contents of the fear have a solipsistic content, and we can use this in partia analysis of the oscillations Sass notes. But the fact that we are dealing with a unutterable fear, say, would seem to be integral to the self directed content o the thoughts. (Incidentally, all of this is consistent with claiming, with Jaspers that a general emotional disturbance is not the cause of the delusion.)

These are, as noted, extremely tentative comments, and clearly nee much development. But even in this primitive stage they suggest another wa in which understanding of some schizophrenic phenomena is simultaneousl available and elusive. As I have presented both Campbell's and Sass's propos als, the difference between normal and schizophrenic states is cognitive, as i the difference in understanding. Taking the emotional significance of suc states into account suggests another component in the kind of understandin that can be play here. There is a way of understanding the self-directed natur of at least some schizophrenic states that involves not a semi-detached immer sion in philosophical solipsism, but, rather, a semi-engaged glimpse of a terro which is constituted, in part, by a sense of utter isolation from the worl everyone else inhabits. The nature of such glimpses into the emotional ingre dient in schizophrenia needs an explanation, and I do not have one to hand What we can say, however, is that they are the closest among the kinds o understanding we have considered to 'inside understanding', but, precisely fo ıat reason, the kind we are least likely to allow ourselves to exercise. That is, ıe reason we find normal empathy psychologically impossible is not (only) ıe cognitive distance from everyday beliefs, but, rather, our very deep esistance to allowing ourselves to engage fully, by simulation, with the kinds f world- and self-losing emotions embodied in these states.

eferences

errios, G. E. (1991). Delusions as 'Wrong Beliefs': A Conceptual History. *British Journal of Psychiatry* 159: 6–13.

ampbell, J. (1999). Delusions. In preparation

avidson, D. (1963/80). Actions, Reasons and Causes. In Donald Davidson: *Essays on Actions and Events*. Oxford: Clarendon Press.

rith, C. D. (1979). Consciousness, Information Processing and Schizophrenia. *British Journal of Psychiatry* 134: 225–235

ıspers, K. (1913/97). *General Psychopathology*. Baltimore and London: John Hopkins University Press.

aing, R. D. (1969). *The Divided Self*. London: Pelican.

IcCarthy, R. (1993/99). Assembling Routines and Addressing Representations: An Alternative Conceptualisation of 'What and 'Where' in the Human Brain. In Naomi Eilan, Rosaleen McCarthy and Bill Brewer (Eds.), 1993/99: *Spatial Representation*. Oxford: Oxford University Press.

Iaher, B. A. (1974). Delusional Thinking and Perceptual Disorder. *Journal of Individual Psychology* 30: 98–113.

Iaher, B. A. (1988). Anomalous Experience and Delusional Thinking: The Logic of Explanations. In T. F. Ottomanns and B. A. Maher (Eds.) : *Delusional Beliefs*. Chichester: Wiley.

ass, L. (1994). *The Paradoxes of Delusion*. Ithaca and London: Cornell University Press.

tone, T. and Young, A. (1997). Delusions and Brain Injury: The Philosophy and Psychology of Belief. *Mind and Language* 12/3–4: 327–364

/ittgenstein, L. (1979). *On Certainty*. Oxford: Basil Blackwell.

The Self and Intentionality in the Pre-Psychotic Stages of Schizophrenia

A Phenomenological Study*

Josef Parnas
Copenhagen University

. Introduction

lthough the notion of Self is absent from the current diagnostic list of ymptoms and signs of schizophrenia, varieties of self-disorders in schizo-hrenia have always been recognized, at least implicitly, as an important omponent of the clinical picture. The apparent lack of a direct reference to the isorders of Self is frequently a merely terminological absence, because the elevant psychopathological phenomena are addressed in other terms and/or in nother theoretical framework.[1] Self-disorders were usually described on the ame nosographic plane as other symptoms and signs, e.g. delusions, halluci-ations, disorder of thinking and affect etc.; i.e. the domain of Self was not ssigned any particular prominence or priority (e.g. Bleuler 1911; Kraepelin 896). However, some German-speaking psychiatrists have emphasized the nportance of this domain shortly after the term "schizophrenia" was coined 1911. Jaspers introduced the concept of "Ichstörungen" (which is here anslated as "self-disorders" rather than "I-disorders")[2] and attempted a clas-ification as early as in 1913. In a very influential textbook of psychiatry from 932 (Bumke 1932), Ichstörungen were thoroughly described and assigned a rucial status (only second to the formal thought disorder) for diagnosing

This contribution is a part of a collaborative effort with Dr. Louis Sass (see also Sass this volume) on the phenomenological aspects of schizophrenia.

schizophrenia. This concept was taken up by Kurt Schneider (1959) and mor recently by Scharfetter (1980, 1990, 1996). But what all these attempts have i common is the fact that they do not provide any unified frame of referenc there is no explication of *what* a Self *is* and what it is that is disturbed (Spitze 1988; Spitzer 1990: 51)

A more central pathogenetic status of the self-disturbances is suggested i the phenomenologically oriented work (e.g. Laing 1959; Blankenburg 196 1971, 1988; Tatossian 1978, 1994; Bin 1997). Unfortunately, most of thes contributions are practically unknown to the English-speaking audience an many are phrased with a very difficult terminology and/or are presented on level of abstraction, which is quite remote from the clinician's perspectiv (with notable exceptions of Blankenburg and Laing).

In conclusion, claiming pathogenetic importance of self-disorders is nc enough. An exposition is needed which is primarily *clinically anchored*, i.e demonstrating such importance through clinical observations, and, which als offers a theoretical account of normal self-constitution, that may help situatin the schizophrenic difficulties.

The purpose of this paper is therefore to address the self-experience in th initial stages of schizophrenia by integrating philosophical, clinical and phe nomenological aspects.[3] In particular, I wish to emphasize the manifestation of self-disorders which are detectable at the so-called first (initial) prodromal stages, i.e. stages immediately preceding and leading to the onset of a schizo phrenic psychosis (the latter happens typically around the age of 20–27 years and perhaps at even earlier, more antecedent, the so-called premorbid phases This specific accent on the early stages of schizophrenia is motivated by premise, claiming that studying advanced stages of schizophrenia is of limite value for the understanding of the etiologic and pathogenetic processes (Parna and Bovet 1995). The psychopathological pictures of these advanced stages c schizophrenia reflect sediments of longstanding interactions between primar pathogenic factors, variety of stress factors, secondary illness adversities (e.g isolation, stigma, poverty), treatment effects, and the patient's attempts to cop and adapt. The original pathogenetic factors may simply vanish in the com plexities of chronic illness.

Self-disorders in the early, prodromal stages may be ascribed a generating pathogenic role as at *the illness core*, i.e., defining its essence ("troubl générateur", see below): they underlie and shape the emergence of later an psychotic pathology and may thus unify what, from a purely descriptiv sychiatric standpoint, may seem to be unrelated or even antithetical syn- romes and symptoms. Two recent independent empirical studies (Parnas et al. 998; Möller and Husby 2000) seem to corroborate the view expressed above.

In a previous work of this author concerning phenomenology of schizo- hrenia, the disorder was essentially characterized as a deficient *pre-reflec- ive, context sensitive attunement* to the world and the Other (Parnas and ovet 1991) with a correlated dissolution of the Self (Bovet and Parnas 1993). t was suggested that psychotic symptoms, such as delusions or hallucinations, nly attain a diagnostic specificity for schizophrenia, in so far as they reflect his initial, morbid self-world transformation (Bovet and Parnas 1993; Parnas 999 a, b). The present contribution is therefore best to be considered as a ontinuation of this earlier work, but now with a specific focus on the onfigurations of the Self and intentionality in the pre-psychotic phases of chizophrenia.

But it is first necessary to survey some philosophical treatments of the elf and clarify the reasons for choosing the phenomenological approach as ne most relevant for studying schizophrenia.

. The structure of self-experience

here are different levels at which the referent of an "I" may be examined and iscussed[5] (see also Zahavi, this volume). For the purpose of simplicity of our xposition we can distinguish here between 1) the level of personhood, 2) the vel of I-experience, and 3) the level of the basic, prereflective selfhood.

(1) At the most sophisticated level, the "I" refers to the *person* of whoever tters it as a speaker (for Strawson 1959, the person is a "basic term", which is lso to some degree a common sense view). The object of this type of self- ference is phenomenologically speaking, quite complex, mainly marked by ne problematic of *sameness* in the temporal change. Personal identity, as roposed by Paul Ricoeur, is constituted in a narrative-mediated and hence ntersubjectively embedded, *dialectic* between indexicality of mutable, yet ersisting sameness (idem-identity) and the experiential self-hood (ipse-iden- ty) (Ricoeur 1990). This type of self-identity and self-awareness involves the ody, marks, habits-dispositions, and socio-cultural contexts. Social Self, a najor topic in the study of abnormal personality, can be very much construed t this level.

(2) The object of a more direct and elementary phenomenological interes is the *first-personal aspect of experience*, i.e., the referring function of an "I *in experience*, described as "I"-consciousness. The most fundamental aspec of such self-experience is a sense of possession of one's own experiences an actions (see Strawson, this volume). But what *is*, precisely, this entity en dowed with such powers?

One way to answer evokes the *transcendental subject*, a construct im plied in the structure of awareness, neither as purely abstract, nor independer of experience, nor simply present as one of its components. We will not pursu here the transcendental-empirical distinction, because it is not necessary fc the purpose of this exposition.

The "I" seems to be elusive to any standard type of analysis and i therefore frequently *aporetically construed* (especially outside phenomenol ogy): either as an active subject *behind* the acts of consciousness and henc invisible and out of grip (always receding a step further away at each attem of grasping it) or as a *something*, which *can* be captured in an introspectiv reflection, but which then becomes inert and deprived of subjecthood. Thi apparent tension is perceptible in the major theoretical treatments of the Sel

Thus, one solution to the problematic of the Self is to deny its existenc Hume (1888), in his attempts to locate the Self, only found "bundles c sensations". William James was not more successful; his search demonstrate proprioceptive sensations from the head (James 1981). Contemporary ve sions of this "no-self doctrine" are put forth by those who assert that the self i a post-hoc "logical subject" (a certain Kantian-styled interpretation), materia ist-eliminativist philosophers, who consider the entire phenomenal realm a epistemologically misleading and ontologically ephemeral, and by continent post-structuralists who claim that the "I" is only a language-generated devic

By contrast, the most common way of conceiving the reality of the sel especially in the information-processing approaches of psychology and cogni tive science, is to treat the self as an object or potential object of awareness-- "concept about oneself" or "*mental representation*" (or even a meta-represer tation).[6] Two influential scholars, the philosophers D. M Armstrong (199 and D. Rosenthal (1997) assert a close analogy between *perception* an *introspection*: only by becoming the *object* of an introspective act can a ment state be self-aware. Their approach seems to be weak on two points: First, ho can the subject recognize that his representation of Self is indeed a represent tion of *his* own Self unless there is *already* some kind of prior self-acquai ance? (Zahavi and Parnas 1998; Zahavi 1999). Second, the self as a repre-ented object would be deprived of the witnessing and constitutive role that is o distinctive of human self-awareness.

In the clinical investigation of pathologic self-experience, neither a "no-elf" doctrine nor a mental-representation variant appears as potentially use-ul. A patient, living through a painful self-transformation, and a doctor, onfronted with the patient's complaints, are both forced to acknowledge the ubjective reality of a Self, whose constituting power is vanishing and dissolv-ng. Subjective experience should therefore merit a major share in the psycho-athological investigation (this is far from being the case, due to the prevailing bjectivistic/neo-behavioristic models [Parnas and Bovet 1995]).[7] The need or a reappraisal of subjective experience in psychopathology is the major eason to choose a phenomenological approach. Only continental phenom-nology, despite its internal divisions and terminological difficulties, offers a vell-developed methodology for studying first-person experience (Mishara, r al. 1998; see also below).

(3) The most basic phenomenological level, i.e., the most simple level at vhich we can still talk about conscious experience, is the domain of the pre-eflective. The pre-reflective denotes the experiential non-thematic pre-ivenness, tacitly present and thus co-constitutive of the structure of the field f awareness. It is important not to confuse the pre-reflective with "fringes" of he field of awareness (James 1981) nor with peripheral attention (Gurwitch 964). It is on this level that we encounter the most basic self-hood, which is *resupposed* by the reflective consciousness of an "I". This most basic or lementary self-awareness is not an awareness of a Self (or "I"-consciousness f a central agency/will or experiencing/constituting "Ich-Pol") but the inten-onal act's awareness of *itself*. On this level the "*Who*" of an experience is nplicitly and *pre-reflectively* present in the field of awareness and is crucial ɔ its structure. The I-pole is properly speaking not yet a pole but more a field r a dimension and the "I", in its full egological structure, does not yet exist. 'his basic self-awareness does not arise from any inferential reflection or ntrospection because it is not a relation at all. It is a direct *self-manifestation f experience*. When *I* have a perception of a red rose, this perception *is imultaneously a tacit self-awareness*, because my act of perception is given ɔ me in the first person perspective, from my point of view and in my field of wareness. This basic dimension of subjecthood, technically called *ipseity* from Latin, ipse=self, itself) is more like a medium or a ground in which

experience, including more explicit and thematic reflection, is rendered possible and takes place.[8] It is a *primary presence*, a transparent first persona perspective, bereft of standard ontological predicates (Klawonn 1991). Radically and metaphorically speaking, specific modalities of intentional experience, such as perception or judgement, are simply object- and meaning *modifications* of this medium of self-presence or ipseity (Klawonn 1991 Henry 1963). On this account, the concept of qualia is nothing else than self awareness of intentional acts.

The work of the contemporary French philosopher Michel Henry (1963 1965, 1993) on the role of affectivity in the constitution of ipseity seems ver relevant for this project; his writings make Klawonn's statement on the absenc of predicates for the primary presence a little less dogmatic.[9] Henry (a Klawonn) also insists on the foundational role of ipseity, as a logically an phenomenologically prior, necessary condition for intentional directedness. H uses the term "auto-affection" to emphasize the direct, *non*-relational and pre reflective presence to itself of the first-personal mode of experience. Auto affection, says Henry, the "self-feeling of self," is something pre-given unmediated by transcendent, foreign elements (e.g. a concept, classificator criterion, or a perceptual object). It is not something which we can choose to do but something that happens, a feeling, passion, or sense of aliveness "*L'affectivité est l'essence de l'ipseité*" says Henry (1963) and this means tha the affectivity of auto-affection is not *a merely particular quality* or an extrinsi feature of the intentional acts, nor is it a typologically specific feeling-tone. Th self-awareness of intentional acts is *already an affection or being affected.* Thi is so because intentional acts *are not primarily sensed but lived.* Thus we ma be sad, happy, bored, apprehensive, tired, etc. This is our non-reflexive self awareness: *the way we are affectively is the way we are self-conscious* and self affecting (Hart 1999). It is the *affective tonality* of auto-affection, in Henry' words "the being-affected by self", that is the foundation or condition both fo "the Being and the possibility of Self" and for our encountering of the world "Sensing of a sensible content (…) is possible in principle only on th foundation in it of the self-feeling of self"(479). This sense of aliveness i autoaffection cannot be thought of in "mechanical" terms — e.g., as a kind c stored energy (nor as an "instinct" or a "disposition") which is at the subject' disposal — for it has a far more foundational status and role. There is no interna distance here, and no relation, because there are no relata: the Self is th substance or medium constitutive of affectivity. Autoaffection (or "life") is a nduring, microgenetic articulation of *immanent* phenomenality, in which *ppearing* (as appearing *of*) and *manifestation* (as manifestation *for*) are but one oment, identical with itself. This *primordial phenomenality* is the condition f *object intentionality,* in which an object appears for a subject. The subject can nly be intentionally affected in so far as phenomenality of self-affection ndows him/her with a sensitivity to hetero-affection.

Henry's very detailed analyses permit us to grasp that perception, cogni-on, the acts of understanding and motivation, are *founded* on the affective nalities of ipseity, which is the medium of their formation or constitution.

But a central tenet of phenomenology is also that the Self is intimately ssociated with *otherness* (alterity). Consciousness is directed towards an bject other than itself, and this subject-object configuration is *intentionality.* elf-awareness and object-awareness are interdependent and intrinsically con-ected. Henry disagrees with the vast majority of phenomenologists. On his ccount, the subjectivity's *intentional* directedness to the transcendent object is econdary and not definitive of the essence of the former. Intentionality is *unded,* and so dependent, on the immanent self-manifestation. This disagree-ient, however, is not consequential for this exposition, because we are more oncerned here with the structure of experience (mainly that of the pre-eflective type) than with the ontological segmentation of subjectivity. For lenry too, object-awareness and self-awareness go hand in hand in experience. Pure phenomenality has the structure and division according to the co-original imensions of representation [intentionality] and life" (quoted in Hart 999: 187). What is primarily given in intentional experience,[10] is, in the words f Merleau-Ponty, a *presence,* of which the subject and the object are correlative nd abstract moments of phenomenal clarity (Merleau-Ponty 1945).

Merleau-Ponty further describes the fundamental structure of our relation ith the world as an "intentional arc", a "mobile vector, active in all directions ...) through which we can orient ourselves towards anything *outside and inside* s, and have an attitude to that object". Biologist-philosopher M. Polanyi (1964) omplements this description of intentionality, especially in its epistemic spects, as a dialectic interplay between the distal pole (thematic, explicit or cal object of awareness) and the proximal pole, which exists more in the "tacit imension". The proximal is known in a *subsidiary* and implicit and pre-eflective manner; it includes the background or context as well as the structures nd processes of the embodied, knowing self. A similar point emerges in the so-alled ecological approach to perception: perception always involves a preconceptual awareness of one's relationship *to* the world (Gibson 1986). Th world appears always originally structured through the interaction with th body-subject: The world is seen as an option or as a potential field for subjectiv possibilities and inclinations; the world is a field of "affordances" — fc instance, whether a surface allows for, or affords, walking on it (see Sanders [1999] on affordances as "ontological primitives"). This prereflective bodil intentionality, or, in Husserlian terms, operative intentionality (fungierend Intentionalität), is, according to Merleau-Ponty, "a third term", in addition t subject and object terms, needed for *figure-ground differentiation*. This "thir term " is neither the figure nor the ground of Gestalt psychology. It encompasse all the implicitly felt, tacitly constitutive and subjective correlates of th Gibsonian affordances. Object-directedness of intentionality and subjectiv self-affection are closely interdependent moments of the intentional arc. Fc both Merleau-Ponty and Polanyi intentional relation has a dimensional an multi-layered structure with changing gradients from one end to another.

In the founding layer, the infrastructure is implicit, pre-reflective, sel given, but is also linked to perception and to holistic sensori-motor equiva lences; this is the realm of the tacit pre-reflective self-awareness (ipseity) an normally occurring in conjunction with a focal or explicit positing of an objec of awareness.

Tacitness is crucial; it is, in a sense, the very medium or the very being o auto-affection, of the pre-reflective subjecthood, ipseity, or self-awareness tha is in turn the medium through which all intentional activity is realized. An disturbance of this tacit-focal structure, or of the ipseity it implies, is likely t have subtle but broadly reverberating effects; such disturbances must necessa ily upset the balance and shake the foundations of both self and world.

3. Clinical aspects of early schizophrenia

3.1. *Data sources*

The descriptions and analyses presented below are based on clinical work an psychopathological research. In the ascending degree of systematicity, th psychopathological data have been collected during many years of clinica hospital experience with the schizophrenia spectrum patients, especially wit the first-episode patients (patients admitted for the first time because o sychotic decompensation) and with the diagnostically unclear cases. More ystematic data have been collected over the course of several research nvestigations relevant to our topic. In a prospective study of 207 offspring of chizophrenic mothers (Parnas et al. 1993) the focus was specifically the ehavioral and experiential *antecedents* of psychosis (Parnas et al. 1982; arnas and Jørgensen 1989). In an ongoing multidisciplinary investigation of xtended families with several schizophrenic members, subtle qualitative hanges of experience and self-experience are being thoroughly assessed. In ddition, clinical studies have been conducted, specifically targeting self-xperience in the early phases of schizophrenia. In this latter group, a very areful, in-depth psychopathological examination has been performed of 18 atients with symptoms of beginning schizophrenia and admitted to a special-zed unit for the first episode schizophrenic patients (Parnas et al. 1998). urrently, a standardized psychiatric evaluation of 80 consecutive first epi-ode schizophrenic or schizotypal[11] patients is being analysed.

.2. *Self-disorders: frequency and reporting*

elf-disorders in the prodromal, pre-psychotic phases occur in the vast majority f patients. In a uniquely detailed Norwegian phenomenological study (Möller nd Husby 2000) they were observable in the history of all twenty, in-depth xamined, first-episode schizophrenic patients. In the Copenhagen series these isorders were clearly present in more than two thirds of the patients.

Naturally, the patient uses ordinary lay psychiatric cliché vocabulary to eport the nearly ineffable experiences of self-disorders and usually in non-pecific terms such as depression, fatigue, or anxiety, complaints which bring im into contact with treatment facilities. The self-disorders reveal themselves nly after some attempt to penetrate beyond the “surface level” of such omplaints. Blankenburg (1971) speaks of a “specific non-specificity” of such surface complaints”. As an example, a trivial complaint of fatigue (a non-pecific complaint), turns out on a more close evaluation, to be linked to a ervasive inability to grasp the everyday significations of the world and a orrelated paralyzing and exhausting perplexity (a condition highly suggestive f schizophrenia, hence “specificity”). The difficulty which the patients have in escribing their experiences is multidetermined. The linguistic resources for haracterizing dimensions of human subjectivity, especially of the non-propo-itional type, are not readily available and often require specialized knowledge or special verbal talent. This is doubly true of the pre-reflective experiences that have taken on an unusual and thus unfamiliar quality, and which, as it is more specifically the case with the self-disorders, affect the very conditions of experience and its verbalization. Adding to these difficulties is the fragility of the forms of consciousness in question, with their unstable wavering of implicit into explicit modalities. This point is crucial: in order *to obtain a description* of these experiences, it is necessary to create an appropriate rapport, which enables the patient to reflect on the qualities of his experience and to search for suitable expressive metaphors.[12] The subtle abnormalities of self-experience reported here are, in general, only observable in the early illness stages. They cannot be recollected or described by chronic patients. It seems that apart from a continuous presence in few patients, they become incorporated in and transformed by the emergence of the psychotic forms of conscious organization.

3.3. *A case example of the prodromal experience*

The following (anonymized) vignette, already published elsewhere (Parnas et al. 1998), is selected from a series of first admission cases as a paradigmatic example of early schizophrenic experiences. It will serve us as *a point of departure* for a more general description of the self-disorders in early schizophrenia, a description that is not exhaustive from the clinical point of view, but sufficient in detail to highlight the major aspects of the transformation of the intentional arc.

> Robert, a 21 year-old unskilled worker, complained that for more than a year, he had been feeling painfully cut-off from the world and had a feeling of some sort of undescribable inner change, prohibiting him from normal life. Moreover, he lost his initiative and energy, and had a tendency to an inverse sleep pattern. He was troubled by a strange, quite pervasive and a very distressing feeling of not being really *present*, or fully alive, of not participating in interaction with his surroundings. He was never entirely *involved in the world,* in the sense of engaged absorption in daily activities and daily life. This experience of disengagement, isolation, or ineffable distance from the world, was accompanied by a tendency to observe or monitor his inner life. He summarized his affliction in one exclamation: "my first personal life is lost and replaced by a third person perspective" (He was not at all philosophically read). In order to exemplify this statement more concretely, he said that, for instance, listening to music on his stereo would give him an impression that the musical tune somehow lacked its natural fullness; "as if something was wrong with the sound itself," and he tried to regulate the sound parameters on his stereo equipment, to no avail and only to finally realize that he was somehow

> "internally watching" his own receptivity to the music, his own mind receiving or registering of musical tunes. He so to speak witnessed his own sensory processes rather than living them. It applied to most of his experiences that, instead of living them, he experienced his own experiencing.
> He reflected on self-evident daily matters and had difficulties "in letting things and matters pass by" and linked it to a long-lasting attitude of "adopting multiple perspectives," a tendency to regard any matter from all possible points of view. When younger he considered this ability as a gift, a source of creativity, despite the fundamental indecisiveness it caused. Now it had become more like an affliction, associated with a feeling of floating around, social withdrawal and abstention from action. Periodically he experienced his own movements as reflected upon and de-automatized. His thinking processes could acquire an acoustic quality, becoming a sort of loud monologue confined to his skull. He considered all these experiences to be morbid, or at least, unusual and certainly very distressing, preventing him from normal life. However, he also claimed that, perhaps due to such experiences, he was sometimes brought for fleeting moments face-to-face with other, non-physical, and normally hidden dimensions of reality.

According to a standard psychopathological description, we could designate nearly all of Robert's complaints as symptoms with specific names (e.g. depersonalization, perceptual anomalies) and perhaps make a grouping between the so-called deficit- or "negative symptoms", such as lack of energy and "positive"- or excess symptoms, such as "hearing thoughts aloud" (see Sass, this volume on the distinction between the positive and negative symptoms). Almost all of these experiences are classifiable as the so-called "basic symptoms" (Klosterkötter 1988; Huber 1983), i.e., as non-psychotic, qualitative and quantitative changes of experience, in perceptual, cognitive, emotional, motor, and corporeal domains.

3.4. *Phenomenology of the self-disorders in the early stages*

From a phenomenological perspective, the diminished sense of presence, altered perception, increased distance to the world, and incipient fragmentation of meaning can all be seen as *aspects* of a profound transformation of the intentional arc: a deformation of ipseity and predominance of hyper-reflexive forms of consciousness. It is important to realize already now, that this particular domain of psychopathology does not lend itself to a neat classification. As it has already been pointed out, the primary presence-ipseity is so fundamental and intrinsic to the life of consciousness, that it is bereft of predicates (Klawonn 1991). The descriptive effort can only consist of a phenomenological examination of typical clinical complaints in order to articulate their phenomenological structure and internal relations.

The most prominent feature is the altered sense of the groundedness fullness or reality of the self and an intimately correlated feeling of alienation from the world. The patients feel that a profound change is *afflicting* them, but they cannot verbalize and pinpoint *what exactly is changing*. It is clearly not a *something* that can easily be thematized. What seems to become affected is the pregiven, pervasive, and normally unnoticed medium or foundation of being. The patient appears to be saying that he feels being bereft of the foundation of his existence. The phrasing may range from a trivial "I don't feel myself" or "I am not myself" to "I am turning inhuman" or "I am becoming perverse, a monster" etc. The patient may sense an inner void, a lack of an undefinable "inner nucleus". Such complaints allude to experiential pre-reflective level which is far more basic than that of the self-image and self-awareness associated with inferiority feelings, insecurity, and unstable identity, seen in the personality disorders outside the schizophrenic spectrum. In the former case we are dealing with a diminishment of the *body schema's* constitutive functions (Merleau-Ponty 1945; Gallagher, this issue). In the latter disorders, the issue is of the *self-image*, and linked to the problematic of personal-social identity, self-assertiveness, self-esteem and autonomy, and is especially manifest in the interpersonal contexts.[13] In the case of schizophrenia, the patient describes a lack of a vital core, which is normally constitutive of his field of awareness and *crucial to its very subsistence*. Sometimes these complaints take a clearly existential turn: The patient does not feel being fully existing or alive, fully awake or alert, or as Robert phrased it, fully *present and affected*. We should note here that psychiatrists frequently describe such patients as being "an-hedonic" (deficient in feeling pleasure), but anhedonia is just one particular aspect of the diminishment of the primordial affectability (founding a hedonic experience) and sense of aliveness.

The essential aspect of these complaints can be captured as a distortion of ipseity: tonality of auto-affection, as a source of pregiven, tacit sense of myness, is failing, leading to an inexplicable inner fissure or void. In these stages, *perplexity*, a feeling of a need to grasp the meaning of the situation, may dominate the picture and may become thematized through hypochondriacal preoccupations.

This shrinkage of ipseity is often, as in the case of Robert, described as diminished *presence*.[14] Lack of immersion, diminished existential feeling one, and increasing "phenomenological distance" within perception and action. In a normal perceptual experience, the object perceived is given directly, n the flesh so to say, but for Robert it appears somehow filtered, deprived of ts fullness, mainly because the *sensory process lacks its medium of tonality of uto-affection*. Perception is not lived but is now more like a mechanic, purely eceptive sensory process, unaccompanied by its affective feeling-tone.[15] In ddition, perception becomes deformed by the now-intrusive processes of nowing.

Hyperreflexivity (Sass 1992; Sass, this volume), which is an excessive endency to take a self or its part as an object of awareness, is certainly prominent n the case of Robert — perhaps most obviously in the symptoms involving houghts-aloud, ruminations on meaning and metaphysical preoccupations.

Thus, Robert reports increasing objectification of introspective experience. Inner speech is transformed from *a medium of thinking* into an objectike entity with quasi-perceptual characteristics. Other patients may exhibit a nore subtle *spatialization* of inner experience. E.g., they may describe their houghts or feelings in physical terms, as having object-like qualities ("my houghts are dense and encapsulated"), or may even locate them spatially "my thoughts feel mainly in the right side of the brain").

There is yet another aspect of ipseity-disturbance. It seems that shrinking of ipseity exposes the experience as stripped off its lived context, immobilized nd inviting introspective, hyperreflexive awareness. In this process, normally oundational and constituting processes become available for objectification. Thus Robert's musical experience reveals an introspective access to passive, fferent, sensory input, *which is normally never discernible in the acts of ngaged perception.* We may suspect that such a hyperreflexive mode of aving an ongoing "experience of experiencing" leads to an access (or an llusion of access) to the subjectivity's own constituting role. In effect there is peculiar *splitting or a doubling of the Self* ("Ich-Spaltung") into an observing nd observed (represented) ego, neither of each assuring ipseity function. This xperience of doubling of the ego becomes especially prominent immediately rior to the onset of a frank psychotic episode. It may be felt as a form of inner truggle or an oscillation between the good and the evil "parts" or between lifferent selves (which themselves may be described in spatialized terms). This is, at least initially, felt and communicated on the so-called "as if" netaphorical level.[16] Normal processes of reflection and imagination always nvolve an ego-split, but they possess a natural flexibility and happen in a unified field of experience in which the sense of myness/autoaffection never questions itself.

I believe that it is such a direct experiential access to the constituting, and hence normally unnoticed conditions of experience, that facilitates a shift towards a solipsistic position in schizophrenia. Thus a young patient reported that he had, in brief moments, a feeling that only the objects in his current field of vision were real, "as if" the rest of the world, including most familiar places and persons, did not really exist.[17] Another patient, probed about harboring suicidal intentions, replied: "No, I could never kill myself. I can't imagine the world not being represented !! [by me, presumably]". It is this solipsistic sentiment which guides the patient to suspect an existence of a hidden ontological domain, only accessible to himself. This is the source of a certain and quite specific type of grandiosity observable in the schizophrenia spectrum patients: The patient may regard other people as pitiable, ontologically ignorant morons, solely preoccupied by chasing the material aspects of their life. In later, more chronic stages of the disease, the entire ontological-epistemological framework of experience, normally revolving around "naïve realism" (in the Western world) is dramatically transformed, leading to "beliefs", which, on a purely contentual basis, are classified as the so-called bizarre delusions (defined as "physically impossible"; APA 1994).

The patient and his family may agree that the current condition is only an exacerbation of certain tendencies datable to quite early childhood ("always felt being different from the others"). This exacerbation may take an alarming intensity, accompanied by a panic of literal dissolution, of "going into pieces", where the psycho-corporeal unity seems to lose coherence and dissolve into parts. One patient reported a feeling "as if" his consciousness consisted of multiple points of emanation, disconnected from each other and each pulsating at its own pace (see below on the "as if" experiential mode).

In Robert's case, the incertitude, a sort of polyvalence (rather than ambivalence) is linked to a more global fragmentation of meaning, a loss of "natural evidence", which is the hallmark of the schizophrenic autism (Parnas and Bovet 1991). Robert resembles Anne, the patient described by Blankenburg (1971), whose main and monotonous complaint was her inability to prereflectively grasp the world's natural significance and appeal. Nothing was self-evident and Anne had a distressing difficulty in the automatic understanding of people and situations. As she once put it: "it is not the question of knowledge; it is *prior to* knowledge (…); it is so small, so trivial; every child has it !!". Anne engaged in endless ruminations on everyday matters. The experience of fragmentation of meaning is quite often associated with a lack of a stable, middle perspective, normally imposing the "perspectival abridgement" which is necessary for the fluid attunement to the world. Such abridgement can only happen in the medium of ipseity (i.e., in the experiential medium of reliable selfness) and on the condition of a smooth interplay between the tacit and explicit (framework/focus) intentional moments. As Robert's case illustrates, fragmentation of meaning is associated with hyperreflexive forms of awareness, which are discernible in the emotional life, perception, cognition, and action.

Important symptomatological aspects of the prodromal stage comprise a-nergia and a-volition. These features cannot be entirely reduced to simple, mechanic shortages of energy and initiative, as it is portrayed in the standard texts on schizophrenia and described as the so-called deficit- or "negative"-symptoms (what the deprivative α is suggesting).[18] Rather, as it seems to be the case with Robert, they follow from a more fundamental but also more complex dissolution of the structure of the intentional arc. To be moved and inspired to action, in other words to be *affected* by an object (hetero-affection) presupposes self-affectability and self-affection of ipseity. Prior to the volitional self-awareness of an I as an agent, there is a *more elemental non-reflexive experience of self-affection*, in which I am the one who is both the affected as well as the affecting: *I have a capacity that I have not created.* The "I-can" structure of agency arises from this self-affection as its emergent moment. This moment is the *constitutive core* around which the complex whole of willed action crystallizes itself by entraining, and clustering in a smooth, self-organizing way, affectivity-affection, desire-motive, cognition and perceptuo-motor response. Successful realization or completion of acting requires a steady support or embededness in the tacit medium of ipseity.[19] The disturbed dynamics of tacit/explicit-framework/focus and failing phenomenality of ipseity contribute to the distortions in the flow of affective and conative processes and result in *varieties of disjunction* in this domain. Action may be inhibited, inconsequential, intersubjectively inappropriate (described by Minkowski as "autistic activity") or having a paradoxical, internally contradictory or ambiguous structure. It is usually no longer spontaneous because it is *not lived*, and this applies both to the non-reflexive acting as well as to an acting organized by a focal, thematic core. Almost complete stupor in early schizophrenia may be associated with intense hyperreflexive ruminations, which further impede emerging of a dominant, leading theme, capable of initiating and sustaining action.

3.5. *Progression into psychosis*

In the more advanced stages of schizophrenia, the self-disorders are reported on a more thematic level, linked to the phenomenological features of the reflective "I" consciousness.[20] These are primarily disturbances in I-activity (agency), ego-demarcation (transitivism), diachronic identity and synchronic coherence, originally described by Jaspers (1923) and elaborated in rich detail by Scharfetter (1990, 1996).[21]

The patient may have overwhelming experiences of falling apart and disintegrating, leading to anxiety and feelings of imminent disaster. Pervasive sentiment of centrality and self-reference (to the point of a "co-vibration" between the immanent experience and the transcendent world-events) precedes the emergence of delusions, hallucinations and other psychotic phenomena (Conrad 1958). Many of these (so-called Schneiderian) symptoms involve a fundamental alteration of the sense of possession and control of one's own thought, action, sensation, emotion or bodily experience. These self-disorders (either explicitly recognized as such or implicit in the symptoms) are linked to the more original ipseity transformations described above, because, as it was mentioned above, ipseity is the condition for the constitution of phenomenal features of "I"-consciousness. It is therefore quite common that the emergence of transitivistic psychotic phenomena (e.g. experiences of being influenced from outside) is preceded by a vague feeling of losing one's sense of myness (ipseity). The patient feels changing, losing autonomy and has an impression of being "at the mercy" of the world ("Beeinflussungsstimmung").

The following, quite unique (but strongly abbreviated) vignette from a Norwegian phenomenologic study (Möller, in press) illustrates the temporal symptom evolution of the illness from the prodrome into a frank psychosis.

Peter, history of illness:

January 1985:	"strange change is affecting him", diminished self-presence, feels "self-disgust", has "lost contact to himself".
August 1985:	increasingly preoccupied by existential themes and Indian philosophy; "perhaps meditation could help". Increasingly isolated.
January 1987:	feels fundamentally transformed, "something in me has become inhuman", "no contact to his body", "feels empty", has to "find a new path in his life".

January 1988:	is of the opinion that Indians are superior compared to other human races; they perhaps have a mission to save our planet.
September 1992:	preoccupied by recurring thoughts about extraterrestrials.
January 1993:	is convinced that Indians are reincarnated extraterrestrials.
April 1994:	feels that he is being brought here each day from another planet in order to assist Indians in their salvatory mission. Feelings of being influenced from the outside.
June 1994:	first admission to a psychiatric ward, as 24 yrs old.

We notice here the initial ineffable self-transformation, comparable to the experiences of Robert, and a subsequent increasing thematization of this change: new interest in existentialism and Buddhist philosophy and a progressive articulation of charismatic and eschatological contents. The more conspicuous psychiatric symptoms evolve through a stage of "odd or overvalued" ideas only to culminate in the emergence of "bizarre delusions" (APA, 1994).

4. Phenomenology and "psychopathological explanation"

We need to address, at least briefly, a few general theoretical questions which signal their relevance at this point. How can we situate the phenomenological approach in the context of current philosophy of mind and its accounts of mental causation? What understanding of mental states is achieved by phenomenological approach? And in what sense can the described psychiatric approach be considered as being phenomenological at all?

One may concede that the issue of mental causation, despite its pragmatic import (clinicians are confronted with this type of question on a daily basis) has not been studied systematically in psychiatry neither on a theoretical nor empirical level since Jaspers' "General Psychopathology" first appeared in 1913. In the current psychopathological approaches (APA 1994) the entire issue is more or less officially non-existent, eradicated by the neo-behavioristic reductionism (Parnas and Bovet 1995). Jaspers (1923) imported Schleiermacher's and Dilthey's original distinction between "explanation" and "understanding" (Palmer 1969). The former is said to pertain to physical processes and the latter is considered to be appropriate for the empathic comprehension of human experience, action, and expression (see Eilan, this volume). Thus explanation, according to Jaspers, was appropriate for mental disorders of organic nature (e.g. Huntington's chorea) whereas understanding was applicable to certain abnormal developments of personality and to the so-called psychogenic psychoses, i.e., psychoses consequential to a "psychologically traumatic" event, affecting Achilles' tendon-spot in a vulnerable person. A necessary criterion for the presence of psychogenesis was a *contentual coherence* between the content of the traumatic event and the content of the ensuing psychotic symptoms (Jaspers 1923).[22] Schizophrenia and manic-depressive illness had and have a more ambiguous place. They were considered as hereditarily determined but without a clear-cut and a specific cerebral lesion and this continues to pose nosographic problems.

For Jaspers, the crucial criterion of understandability of a morbid experience is that it is essentially *normal*–either differing only quantitatively from normal states (e.g. depressed mood) or involving some combination of normal experiences (e.g. "secondary delusions" in morbid jealousy, grounded in the more primary feelings of inferiority). In other words, Jaspers' notion of understandability requires that the experience is *accessible to an empathic act of a normal, lay person.* It must conform to the common sensical, folk psychological perspective and be imaginable, either emotionally or rationally, within this framework.

In schizophrenia, however, there are experiences that are simply incomprehensible: either they are too strange to allow empathy or their evolution from antecedent states does not make sense. In Jaspers' view, they must be seen as direct morbid eruptions from an underlying process of an organic nature.[23] Such assumptions continue to be widely held in contemporary psychiatry, where the ideas of Donald Davidson and other analytic philosophers have recently been used to defend a position on schizophrenia reminiscent of Jaspers (Bolton and Hill 1996). In the analytic philosophy (Evnine 1991) mental causality is construed as a triangulation of desire, belief and a dispositional belief system. But a desire, motive, or reason is redescribable as something that has causal efficacy, on the condition that *overall rationality of the person being understood is intact,* which naturally precludes the possibility of understanding schizophrenia.

The status of rationality as a key-concept in mental causation is partly due to the fact that analytic philosophy has focused almost entirely on the question of the rational coherence and potential explanatory significance of individual mental *contents* (not unlike Jaspers).[24] This focus on mental content is likewise present in the standard preoccupations of psychoanalysis and in the contemporary operational psychopathology (e.g., the concept of delusion is solely defined from the content perspective, denying any qualitative change in the field of the patient's experience [e.g. Sims 1988]).

In my opinion, this sterile and narrow preoccupation with mental content (preferably of the propositional type only) has been quite harmful for psychiatry. Mental content, considered apart from its experiential mode, may easily manifest itself either as "statically" incomprehensible (e.g., delusion of external control) and therefore seductive to an organic interpretation, or as being vacuously trivial (e.g., emotional ambivalence towards a parental figure) and hence deprived of any explanatory value.

It is on that point that a certain shift of the focus of interest appears in phenomenology. A shift, because for phenomenology, propositional attitudes and their contents do not exhaust the nature of consciousness. Studying *formal* or structural aspects of human experience has been an equally important theme of descriptive effort. These pervasive, formal aspects, which may be called *experiential infrastructures*, have more in common with the phenomenon of cognitive style or mood than they do with particular beliefs, perceptual contents, or wishes whose significance can be captured propositionally. These infrastructures are *configurations of consciousness* in its intentional articulations, e.g., the structures of self- and object awareness, temporality and embodiment. Consciousness is not seen by phenomenology as just another (physical or psychical) object in the world but as the constitutive dimension or medium that *allows for phenomenal manifestation*, as the "locus" "in" which the world reveals and articulates itself. Therefore the aim of phenomenology is not to account for how a physical world gives rise to a first-person perspective but rather the obverse: how phenomena, including the objective world, emerge in the first-person perspective. Phenomenological investigation of the *noematic*[25] type aims at the essential articulation of the structure of phenomenon (eidetic variation; this is an imaginative technique extracting essential features of the phenomenon under investigation). Another type of questioning concerns the *conditions of possibility* of a given experience, i.e. *how consciousness must be* in order to allow for a given phenomenon to manifest itself. And this *noetic* analysis may be extended into a study of generative moments of a given experience ("genetic" analyses). Thus phenomenology arrives at a description, which is already an understanding, but it is an understanding that cannot be reduced to a folk psychological account.

What can then be said specifically about phenomenological-*psychiatric* approach? Basically, the phenomenological psychiatrist adheres to the steps of phenomenological investigation in his attempt to articulate the essence of the patient's experience (Kraus 1999). The symptom is not seen as merely an indicator of something else (e.g., a focal neural defect) but as *a phenomenon* in its own right, possessing a certain wholeness and intrinsic structure reflected in its facets. The psychiatrist performs an epochè (suspending common sense assumptions about experience) (Naudin et al. 1999; Depraz 1999) or the epochè is already performed for him: the lifeworld of the schizophrenic patients reveals itself after a certain suspension of common sense assumptions about existence and experience. The psychiatrist does not start each time entirely *de novo*, from scratch: he has a *skill* and performs thematic (and pre-reflective) *typifications* which facilitate his attempts of eidetic reduction. His typifications are moulded by the accumulated experience and familiarity with previous patients, their experiential contents, ways of experiencing and ways of expression (Schwartz and Wiggins 1987).

Psychiatric phenomenology is, however, not a hetero-phenomenology in the sense proposed by Daniel Dennett, i.e., a collection and averaging of third- and second-person data, followed by inferential construction of explanatory models (based on analytic procedure presupposing overall rationality of the examined subjects), models which ultimately may serve for the third-person scientific use (Dennett 1991). Dennett's data-collector is never really situated and, faithful to his behavioristic heritage, he relies on "external traces" of intentionality for his model-construction. The phenomenological psychiatrist on the other hand, in every single clinical situation of the second-person data collection, is penetrating afresh, through his methodical efforts, a new and unique first-personal realm.

In what sense can phenomenology be helpful for the purpose of explaining experience and behavior, i.e., what is its contribution to the clarification of the realm of "mental causation"? The answer to this question follows several interrelated tracks.

As we have already noted, phenomenology does not look at consciousness as an object but as a medium of phenomenality. This implies, in Husserl's words (Marbach 1993, 28), that the essence of conscious life is not to consist of clearly separable, substantial (reified) elements, exerting a spatial-mechanical-efficient causality on each other. Rather, the concepts of consciousness and intentionality imply a *meaningful* network of interdependent connections, founded on intertwining, motivation and mutual implication (more like the

Aristotelian formal cause); a network which, we may add, in some sense also encompasses and is framed by the intersubjective matrix in which it emerges. Phenomenological investigation provides us with a description pregnant with dynamics, because the examined aspects are not static and isolated from each other. They point to the constitutive, noetic fabric and reveal the essential noematic articulation of the field of experience. Noetic and genetic analyses clarify the origins of phenomena, which on a purely contentual level of description may appear, in Jaspersian terms, as incomprehensible. Thus the notion of understanding in the process of phenomenological investigation extends beyond Jaspersian definition: it points more to a comprehension of a *certain coherence in the patient's experience as a dialectic of its form and content*. The form and the content of experience are interdependent (Bovet and Parnas 1993): specific experiential modes frequently entail specific contents and, vice versa, certain contents point towards certain modes of experience. The notion of form refers here to the structural configuration of consciousness, and not merely to the mode of intentionality being described. These experiential infrastructures constrain or shape the nature of particular symptoms (e.g., specific delusional beliefs may reflect, emerge from, or serve making subjective sense of the infrastructures). The infrastructures channel, often in psychologically accessible ways, longer-term developmental transitions involving shifts into different but related types of infrastructures.

Thus, as illustrated by the case of Peter, fantastic delusions, experiences of external control and the general messianistic content, *prima facie* incomprehensible in the Jaspersian scheme, become more comprehensible when seen as a progressive thematization of self-dissolution, transitivism and solipsism of the initial prodromal stages.

However, the moment we extend the notion of mental causation to include long-term transitions between successive mental states and forms of organization of consciousness and long-term evolution of psychopathology, we move outside pure phenomenology in order to engage in a hermeneutic endeavor. To use Ricoeur's (1991) expression, we work within a "hermeneutic arc", which, in its clinically pragmatic-eclectic version, relies on a combination (and mutual interdependence) of phenomenological, empathic-hermeneutic, idiographic and causal-biological considerations. The secret of good clinical work consists of being aware of which framework (and why) one is using at a given moment.

5. Dissolution of "operative" intentionality as "trouble générateur"

Two fundamental aspects of the intentional-arc disturbance in schizophreni were emphasized: first, a profound transformation of ipseity; second, exagger ated self-consciousness or "hyperreflexivity". The third component, the loss o meaning, is a corollary of this distortion of the intentional arc. This transforma tion of intentionality, this complex of ipseity disturbance-hyperreflexivity-los of meaning, is therefore the essential disorder of schizophrenia; its "troubl générateur" upon which the clinical picture and its transformations are to b comprehended.

It is, however, important to realize that hyperreflexivity is not a homog enous phenomenon nor a *new species of intentionality*, somehow added to th habitual equipment of consciousness. In a similar vein, ipseity-disturbanc cannot be considered in isolation from the pathological experience in which i enters as its constitutive moment and through which it manifests itself. Th clinical complaints of diminished presence and hyperreflexive awareness ar of course all constituted, noematic phenomena. In the analysis of Robert' case an effort was made to identify certain constitutive noetic moments of thi compound of morbid self-experience and hyperreflexivity. Can one say some thing more general on this noetic source?

As it was noted in the theoretical discussion of selfhood, intentionality i "multilayered". Its founding level was called "operative" or bodily intentional ity with its selfhood dimension of ipseity/autoaffection. Operative intentional ity designates a *prereflective experience* that is functional without bein thematic or engaged in any explicit epistemic acquisition. The active-explicit thematic-focal intentionality (e.g. the acts of object perception, recognition o judgement), on the other hand, is embedded in, dependent or *founded on* thi prereflective operative intentionality. It is a *founding* in a twofold but connecte sense: a) as that upon which active, thematic intentionality has to build, and b as that which makes the intentional acts *acts of consciousness*, i.e., acts o phenomenal disclosure and presentation, making *phenomenal appearing* pos sible. It is at this intentional level, closely linked to or grounded in the primordia phenomenality of auto-affection, that the primary *presence to the world* i constituted, which is the *condition of intentional phenomenality* (i.e., the fac that something appears for us rather than not) (Hart 1998). Ipseity, o prereflective self-awareness is therefore the proximal moment of operativ intentionality. Operative intentionality is a "primal phenomenon" or a prima sensibility (it is *at* its object rather than *positing it* [Merleau-Ponty 1945]). It procures a basic texture or organization, and hence a certain unity and familiarity, to the field of experience. It is upon that texture that the active, synthetic, thematic intentionality configures its categorial, recognizing or judgmental disclosures. Operative intentionality happens, phenomenologically speaking, in a passive, "non-willed", automatic mode, described by Husserl (1952) as "passive synthesis" and linked to "inner time consciousness". It is here that Henry's claim on the intra-subjective autonomy of ipseity from temporality and embodiment must be questioned (see Gallagher, this volume). Operative intentionality is presumably dependent on sensory and sensori-motor ("kinesthetic" [Husserl, Merleau-Ponty]) associations and equivalencies across sensory fields, realized in the series of spatio-temporal moments or perspectives, instigated by bodily movements (Dodd 1997). An optimal conceptual or perceptual "grip" on the object, an optimal proportion of "inversely related richness and distinctness", is achieved in an adequate balance of tacit/explicit intentional acts (Merleau-Ponty 1945). It is in the mode of operative intentionality that habits and dispositions become sedimented. In this mode, the call for action does not come from a thematic, propositional content in the mind, i.e., from a represented goal, but rather from a thing itself, perceived as a certain tension created by a deviation from the optimal Gestalt, and leading to a globally attuned response (Dreyfus and Dreyfus 1999). Operative intentionality is therefore a prerequisite of a non-reflexive *attunement*, which is severed in the schizophrenic autism (Parnas and Bovet 1991).

It is in the shift in the structure of intentionality from tacit to explicit, due to a disturbance in its operative mode and its founding ipseity dimension, that the experiential self-pathology and hyperreflexivity unfold, with a correlated loss of meaning (see also Gallagher, this volume). On this view, the dissolution of operative intentionality is the primary constitutive, noetic aspect of the "trouble générateur".

The notion of hyperreflexivity (Sass 1992), used throughout this text, deserves now a more detailed clarification. Disturbed ipseity and hyperreflexivity seem to be mutually dependent, implicative aspects of the same whole. Whereas hyperreflexivity denotes the way in which something normally tacit (awareness of one's own subjectivity) becomes focal and explicit, the notion of disturbed ipseity emphasizes a complementary aspect of this process, the fact that what was once tacit is no longer inhabited as a medium of taken-for-granted selfhood.

The most elementary, basal type of hyperreflexivity (Parnas et al. 1998) denotes a process in which the normally transparent experiential texture (a primary field of presence) fades or dissolves and so yields to popping up of unusual sensations, feelings or thoughts which have an object-like quality (spatialization of experience).[26] It is a *passive process*, an affliction, with typical examples to be found in the loss of automaticity of movement, cenesthesias (unusual bodily sensations) and in certain cognitive and perceptual disturbances (Klosterkötter 1988; Huber et al 1979; Huber 1983). The same process manifests itself in the proximal intentional moments as a fundamentally diminished or altered sense of self-presence and presence to the world. *Another type* of hyperreflexivity consists in *active* (synthetic) perceptual or conceptual intentionality. The adjective "active" refers to *intentionality* (as contrasted with the passive syntheses of operative intentionality) and should not be confused with a voluntary process. This is the most frequent and the most important type of hyperreflexivity. It is also consequential to the dissolution of the tacit operative foundations, but it takes its own autonomous course: the initial experiences of loss of natural evidence, perplexity and ineffable self-transformation become associated with and replaced by the processes of morbid spatialization and objectification. The patient engages in ruminations to the point of a loss of meaning, attention becomes devoted to detail, with a consequential destruction of Gestalt and the emergence of perceptual disturbances. Inner life becomes overly and painfully self-conscious.

Active hyperreflexivity has, in a *diachronic perspective*, a progressive detrimental impact, leading to increasing experiential dissolution and a centrifuging of the Self: mental contents become progressively externalized, spatialized and endowed with autonomy, as illustrated by the longitudinal work of Huber's group in Germany (Klosterkötter 1988; Huber et al. 1979). Finally, hyperreflexivity can be *compensatory*, as in the pseudo-obsessive ruminative efforts of a schizophrenic patient who tries *to make up* for the more primary slippery sense of self and feelings of unnaturalness and perplexity (Blankenburg 1971). We may guess that the long-term progression of psychotic symptoms in schizophrenia reflects, to a large but unknown extent, punctuated cascadings of auto-catalytic spirals of self-disturbances and various types of hyperreflexivity.

6. Empirical implications

Schizophrenia, contrary to the classical view, is seen here as a disorder of consciousness, although certainly of a different kind than the pathology observed in the organic delirious conditions. These essential phenomenological features are already present in the very initial stages of the illness. The development of frankly psychotic schizophrenic symptoms needs not be considered as a contingent, unexpected popping up into consciousness of "primary" (modular) eruptions from a malfunctioning organic substrate (as proposed by Jaspers), but more as complex temporal vissicitudes of the unstable structure of intentionality. The concept of operative intentionality refers to a quite basic and foundational configuration of the self-world relation, linking this concept very closely to early phases of perceptual processes. Accordingly, the primary, generative disorder in schizophrenia is more likely to be of the "bottom-up" type, and not of the "top-down" type, as proposed in the cognitivist models currently in vogue (Frith 1992).[27]

Psychotic developments can be grasped as coherent reorganizations of awareness in accordance with patterns dictated by definable transformations of the intentional arc. They take place both as progressive adaptive processes and as non-linear self-organizing sequences of novel coherence patterns with various degrees of stability and hence of temporal constancy (Parnas and Bovet 1995; Parnas 1999a).

The claim of specificity and causal efficiency of intentional disturbance gives the perspective on schizophrenia another turf: The schizophrenia spectrum disorders need no longer be defined as contingent agglomerations of essentially disconnected symptoms, held together by a convention. Rather, these disorders constitute a unitary group, qualitatively distinct from the bipolar and organic disorders, and organized around the *self-disorder-hyperreflexivity-autism* complex (Parnas 1999b). This organizing axis becomes a measure of the validity of the schizophrenia spectrum concept. This unitary view is, of course, not new. It was behind many previous attempts to extract a specific, unifying Gestalt from the polymorphic picture of schizophrenia, although, as aptly commented by Bleuler, this Gestalt is quite elusive: "the disease is characterized by a peculiar transformation of feeling, thinking and perceiving, found nowhere else in this particular fashion" (Bleuler 1911).

Empirical pathogenetic research, guided by phenomenological considerations, should focus on the early illness stages and even on its earlier, infantile antecedents. Data are accumulating which show that the pre-psychotic abnor-malities are traceable to the neonatal period (e.g., impeded automation of newly acquired skills; Asarnow et al. 1995; Waddington et al. 1995; Murray and Lewis 1987; Parnas 1999a). Neurodevelopmental difficulties may be reflective of early instability of the configurations of consciousness and a precursor of subsequent dissolution of the operative intentionality. Develop-mental patterns in infants and children at increased risk for schizophrenia should be studied in conjunction with studies of normal ontogenesis of Self and perception. A multidisciplinary framework, e.g. outlined in Rocha (1995), with focus on the infantile selfhood (Neisser 1995; Stern 1985), might be an appropriate point of departure for such a research program.[28]

Notes

1. Grouping authors on that issue is neither quite fair nor simple. An illustrative example of this problematic is the work of the French psychiatrist Eugéne Minkowski (1927, 1933). Minkowski does not utilize the concept of "Self" at all (apart from a colloquial use) in his descriptions and analyses of schizophrenia. Nonetheless, the primary schizophrenic disorder, according to Minkowski, consists of *a loss of "élan personnel"*, which is a *structural* change of the total personality configuration. It signifies the cease of the Self's intentional unfolding towards the future, with insufficient dialectic between lived time (Bergson's "durée") and lived space, and hence an inadequate attunement to the world and the Other. On one occasion, however, the following statement appears: "(…) la folie (…) ne consiste pas ni dans un trouble du jugement, ni de la perception, ni de la volonté mais dans une perturbation de la structure intime du moi (…)" (1997: 114). See note 14 for additional comments on Minkowski.
The American psychiatrist, Sandor Rado (1960) also offers an interesting and a clinically highly significant hypothesis, likewise without using the term "Self". According to Rado the organizing nucleus of schizophrenia consists of a profound pleasure deficiency (anhedonia) and disturbed bodily awareness (see also Meehl 1962, on a further elabora-tion of this hypothesis).

2. The German "Ich" has a much more direct philosophical resonance, which the English "I" does not have.

3. Integration does not imply here a reduction of one level of description to another, but more of a parallel exposition, suggesting points of intersection.

4. The notion of a prodrome, refers to a *pre-psychotic* phase (which is on average of four years' duration), in which signs of the approaching disease become observable by the patient and his relatives. Here we are concerned with the prodromes preceding first episode, but the term is also used to designate antecedents of a psychotic *relapse*. The prodrome consists in a *change* from the habitual way of experience and behavior. Premorbid phase refers to a habitual, non-psychotic behavioral abnormality, usually present since early childhood (see Parnas 1999a, for a detailed conceptual discussion)

. I will not distinguish between an "I" and a "Self". Such distinction, although scholastically appropriate, will unnecessarily complicate this exposition.

. Typically, the term "re-presentation" signifies a mental picture which mirrors its object; see Shanon (1993) for a very extensive and critical analysis of this concept.

. Subjective experience *is*, in fact, being currently resurrected by few analytic philosophers (e.g. Searle 1992; Strawson 1994; Chalmers 1995; Strawson, this volume), who consider the mainstream view, i.e. neo-behavioristic functionalism, as being insufficient for our understanding of the mind. They argue in favor of including the first-personal, experiential domain; we need "phenomenological considerations". But this analytic version of 'phenomenology' amounts to an a-theoretical and pre-scientific account of how things seem to be at a perceptual or introspective glance. Phenomenology and folk psychology are tacitly equated, but such equation is seriously inexact. The so-called natural, folk-psychological attitude is saturated with ontological presuppositions and theoretical prejudices, and it is a mistake to assume that the raw (atheoretical) data serving as constraints for the theoretical models can be collected on the basis of such common-sense assumptions (Zahavi and Parnas 1998).

. The reflective I-consciousness (our level 2 of self-reference) is derivative and dependent on the more simple elementary level of ipseity. Phenomena such as feelings of agency, coherence, unity and demarcation presuppose ipseity in order to be articulated. Two examples: First, if a memory of a past event is to contribute to my sense of temporal identity (a claim widely held in cognitive science), it can only do this job in so far as the past event is being remembered *as haven taken place in my field of awareness*, as something which was originally experienced from my first-personal perspective. Second, the border me/not me (deficient in transitivistic experiences in schizophrenia) is automatically constituted in the pre-reflective self-awareness of the experience in question; this border is but merely an aspect of the non-reflexive self-awareness.

. Klawonn and Henry developed their ideas independently of each other, with no mutual influence.

0. We can not engage here in a detailed enumeration of possible experiences, like those from Buddhist meditation, of a contentless or pure Self, and its apparent opposite, a total immersion in the world. It is also beyond the scope of this article to address Henry´s claim of ontological intra-subjective homogeneity of ipseity, as independent from fractures of temporality and embodiment.

1. The term "schizotypal" refers to the so-called schizophrenia spectrum conditions; i.e. disorders genetically linked to schizophrenia (aggregating in the same families) and exhibiting similar basic symptomatic features but without overt psychosis.

2. This fact bears upon epistemological and methodological questions concerning psychiatric interview methods for the first person data. It is beyond the scope of this article to discuss these questions, except for noting that the structured form of conducting an interview (a method dominating psychiatric research today) is not suited for studying the pathologies of self-experience.

3. It is, on the other hand, quite common, that interpersonal difficulties, unstable relationships, apparent autonomy problems, are, on a closer inspection, reflective of quite basic self-disorders.

14. Just before turning this paper for press, I came into possession of a previously unavailabl "Traité de Psychopathologie" by Minkowki, just reprinted (1999). Minkowki present (pp. 232–248) a case, less symptomatic than Robert's (the diagnosis in current terms i schizotypal personal disorder), but otherwise remarkably resembling Robert: the patier never felt present, even at the climax of his overt engagement with the world; all th things he does, he does not do *really*, he senses a permanent inner void. This state according to Minkowski, is quite essential for the understanding of the basic mechanism in schizophrenia. The disturbance consists of a diminished affectability of "le vècu" ("th lived", as a substantive), conceived of as the very core of Self, a region of affectiv spontaneity, on which intentional life is founded. A close parallel to Henry's view on sel awareness.

15. Apart from this disjunction of perception, Robert is spared for perceptual anomalie which are nevertheless quite common at this stage (especially in the visual modality instability or deformation of the perceptual object, sometimes associated with instabilit of perspective (e.g. the patient feels "as if" he was looking from the position of hi shoulder), dissolution of Gestalt, physiognomization of the world, and changing (increas ing or decreasing) perceptual intensity and clarity.

16. "As if" (als ob) experience designates an experience in which the patient qualifies it doxic aspect, by saying that he feels "*as if* he was split in two"; i.e., *he knows that he i not*. The "as if" mode occurs in connection with many morbid experiences in schizophre nia

17. Sass (1994) has made a very important contribution to the description of solipsism i schizophrenia.

18. A good and detailed analysis of the complexity of these states can be found in Munc (1985).

19. A somewhat similar view is formulated by the French psychiatrist Maurice Dide (Did and Guiraud 1926), who considered *athymia* (lack of vital feelings) as being associate with a more complex pathology affecting action, the so-called *an-hormia* (weakening c vital dynamism). The latter was seen as the essential feature in schizophrenia. Th concept of an-hormia is influenced by the teachings of von Monakow, a famous biologis who, quite ahead of his time, regarded *horme* (a *self-organizing tendency* of comple systems) as a fundamental principle of biology.

20. The exact transition or distinction between a pre-reflective and a reflective level of th self-disorder may not be easy to specify and to pinpoint clinically. Nevertheless, th distinction is of a fundamental importance for the theory of schizophrenia and, i practical terms, the clinician's mindfulness of the prereflective level of self-experience i a necessary condition for the very detection of the disorders at that experiential level.

21. Scharfetter, following Jaspers, also speaks about the disturbances in vitality and activit of an "I". These correspond roughly to what has been already described as the distur bances of ipseity.

22. The category of "psychogenic psychosis" has been eliminated in the modern diagnosti criteria, due to a lack of reliability and due to empirical studies showing that many of suc patients later developed typical schizophrenia (Færgeman 1963).

3. It should be noted here, because it is rarely realized, that Jaspers' claims were based on (and therefore biased by) studies of chronic stages of schizophrenia, in which incomprehensibility and inaccessibility are almost caricatured. By contrast, studying first episode patients has lead Klaus Conrad (1958) to quite different conclusions, very similar to my own (see Bovet and Parnas 1993).

4. Jaspers, in his phenomenology, stressed the importance of form, especially for diagnostic evaluation. However, his own contribution on what is a form, is quite weak.

5. Noesis (noetic as adjective) refers to the constituting stream of intentionality; noema (noematic as adjective) refers to the constituted object of consciousness.

6. The British (and atypical) psychoanalyst, Wilfred Bion, is one of the few psychiatrists who strongly emphasized that the experiential spatialization of mental contents (e.g. thoughts, sensory fragments; the so-called β-thinking) is quite characteristic of schizophrenia (Symington and Symington 1996).

7. Such discussion presupposes, of course, that "bottom-up"/"top-down" distinction is meaningful. In the functioning brain, even a quite simple perceptual operation, like detecting a triangle, involves a quite widespread cortical participation, including the frontal lobes.

8. A proposal was made suggesting a faulty development of cortico-cortical connectivity in schizophrenia (Parnas et al. 1996). Proto-intentionality (operative intentionality) is, on a biological level, heavily dependent on the evolution of capacities for intra-modal binding of disparate Gestalt features, as well as on the capacities for inter-modal sensory and sensori-motor integrations. Intact intracortical and cortico-cortical connectivity is a necessary condition for such developments.

References

American Psychiatric Association. (1994). *Diagnostic and Statistical Manual of Mental Disorders*. 4-th ed., revised (DSM-IV). Washington: The American Psychiatric Association.

Armstrong, D.M. (1993). *A Materialist Theory of the Mind.* London: Routledge.

Asarnow, R.F., Caplan, R., Asarnow, J.R. (1995). Neurobehavioral studies of schizophrenic children: A developmental perspective on schizophrenic disorders. In Häfner, H., Gattaz, W.F. (eds) *Search for the Causes of Schizophrenia*. Vol. III. Berlin: Springer, 87–113.

Blankenburg, W. (1969). Ansätze zu einer Psychopathologie des "common sense". *Confinia Psychiatrica*, 12: 144–163.

Blankenburg, W. (1971). *Der Verlust der natürlichen Selbstverständlichkeit. Ein Beitrag zur Psychopathologie symptomarmer Schizophrenien.* Stuttgart: Enke.

Blankenburg, W. (1988). Zur Psychopathologie des Ich-Erlebens Schizophrener. In Spitzer, M., Uehlein, F.A., Oepen, G. (eds) *Psychopathology and Philosophy*. Berlin: Springer, 184–197.

Bleuler, E. (1911). Dementia Praecox oder Gruppe der Schizophrenien. In: Aschaffenburg,

G., ed. *Handbuch der Psychiatrie*. Spezieller Teil, 4. Abteilung, 1. Hälfte. Leipzi Deuticke. Translated by J. Zinkin and N.D.C. Lewis Dementia Praecox or the Group Schizophrenias. New York: International University Press, 1950.

Bolton, D., Hill, J. (1996). *Mind, Meaning and Mental Disorder*. The Nature of Caus Explanation in Psychology and Psychiatry. Oxford: Oxford University Press.

Bovet, P., Parnas, J. (1993). Schizophrenic delusions: a phenomenological approac *Schizophr Bull* 19: 579–597.

Bumke, O. (1932). *Handbuch der Geisteskrankheiten*. (ed. O. Bumke). Vol. IX (D Schizophrenie). Berlin: Springer.

Chalmers, D. (1995). 'Facing up the problem of consciousness,' *Journal of Consciousne Studies* 2: 200–219.

Conrad, K. (1958). *Die beginnende Schizophrenie. Versuch einer Gestaltanalyse d Wahns*. Stuttgart: Thieme.

Dennet, D.C. (1991). *Consciousness Explained*. New York: Little, Brown.

Depraz, N. (1999). The phenomenological reduction as praxis. *J Consc Studies*. 6: 95–11

Dide, M., Guiraud, P. (1926). *Psychiatrie du médecin praticien*. Paris: Masson.

Dodd, J. (1997). *Idealism and Corporeity. An Essay on the Problem of the Body Husserl's Phenomenology*. Dordrecht: Kluwer Academic Publishers.

Dreyfus, H.L., Dreyfus, S.E. (1999). The challenge of Merleau-Ponty's phenomenology embodiment for cognitive science. In G. Weiss, H.F. Haber (eds): *Perspectives Embodiment. The Intersection of Nature and Culture*. London: Routledge, 103–120.

Evnine, S. (1991). *Donald Davidson*. Stanford: Stanford University Press.

Frith, C.D. (1992). *The Cognitive Neuropsychology of Schizophrenia*. Erlbaum: Hove.

Færgeman, P.M. (1963). *Psychogenic Psychoses Following Psychological Stress*. Londo Butterworths.

Gibson, J.J. (1986). *The Ecological Approach to Visual Perception*. Hillsdale, N Lawrence Erlbaum Associates.

Gross, G., Huber, G. (1972). Sensorische Störungen bei Schizophrenien. *Arch Psychia Nervenkr* 216: 119–130.

Gurwitch, A. (1964). *The Field of Consciousness*. Pittsburgh PA: Duquesne Universi Press.

Hart, J.G. (1998). Intentionality, phenomenality, and light. In D. Zahavi (ed) *Self-Aware ness, Temporality, and Alterity*. Dordrecht: Kluwer Academic Publishers, 59–83.

Hart, J.G. (1999). Michel Henry's phenomenological theology of life: A Husserlian readin of C'est moi, la vérité. *Husserl Studies* 15: 183–230.

Henry, M. (1993). *The Genealogy of Psychoanalysis*, tr. D. Brick (Gènèalogie de Psychanalyse: Le commencement perdu, 1985, PUF) Stanford: Stanford Universi Press.

Henry, M. (1963). *L'essence de la manifestation*. Paris: PUF.

Henry, M. (1965). *Philosophie et phénoménologie du corps*. Paris: PUF.

Huber, G., Gross, G., Schüttler, R. (1979). *Schizophrenie. Eine Verlaufs- und sozia psychiatrische Langzeitstudie*. Berlin: Springer.

Huber, G. (1983). Das Konzept substratnaher Basissymptome und seine Bedeutung f Theorie und Therapie schizophrener Erkrankungen. *Nervenarzt* 54: 23–32.

Hume, D. (1888). *The Treatise of Human Nature*. Oxford: Clarendon Press.

usserl, E. (1952). *Ideen zu einer reinen Phänomenologie und phänomenologischen Philosophie II*, Husserliana IV. Den Haag: Martinus Nijhoff.

mes, W. (1981). *The Principles of Psychology*. Cambridge: Harvard University Press.

spers, K. (1923). *Allgemeine Psychopathologie*. 3rd ed. Berlin: Springer.

imura, B. (1997). Cogito et le Je. *L'Évolution Psychiatrique* 62: 335–348.

lawonn, E. (1991). *Jeg'ets ontologi*. Odense: Odense Universitetsforlag.

losterkötter, J. (1988). *Basissymptome und Endphänomene der Schizophrenie. Eine empirische Untersuchung der psychopathologischen Übergangsreihen zwischen defizitären und produktiven Schizophreniesymptomen*. Berlin: Springer.

raepelin, E. (1896). *Psychiatrie*. 4th Edition. Leipzig: J.A. Bath.

raus, A. (1999). Phänomenologisch-anthropologische Psychiatrie. In H. Helmchen, F. Henn, H. Lauter, N. Sartorius (eds) *Grundlagen der Psychiatrie*. Berlin: Springer, 577–603.

aing, R.D. (1959). *The divided Self*. London: Tavistock.

larbach, E. (1993). *Mental Representation and Consciousness. Towards a Phenomenological Theory of Representation and Reference*. Dordrecht, Kluwer Academic Publishers.

leehl, P.E. (1962). Schizotaxia, schizotypy, schizophrenia. *American Psychologist* 17: 827–838.

lerleau-Ponty, M. (1945). *Phénoménologie de la perception*. Paris: Gallimard. Translated by C. Smith *Phenomenology of Perception*. London: Routledge & Kegan Paul, 1962.

linkowski, E. (1927). *La schizophrènie*. Psychopathologie des schizoïdes et des schizophrènes. Paris: Payot, 1927.

linkowski, E. (1933). *Le Temps vècu. Etudes phénoménologiques et psychopathologiques*. Paris: Collection de l'Evolution Psychiatrique. Translated by N. Metzel *Lived Time*. Phenomenological and Psychopathological Studies. Evanston: Northwestern University Press, 1970.

linkowski, E. (1997). Du symptome au trouble générateur. (originally published in *Archives suisses de neurologie et de psychiatrie*, 1928; 22). In *Au-delà du rationalisme morbide*. Paris: Éditions L'Harmattan.

linkowski, E. (1999). Traité de psychopathologie (original publication in 1946). Le Plessis Robinson (France), Institut Synthélabo pour le progrès de connaisssance, 301–332.

lishara, A.L., Parnas, J., Naudin, J. (1998). Forging the links between phenomenology, cognitive neuroscience, and psychopathology: the emergence of a new discipline. *Current Opinion in Psychiatry* 11: 567–573.

lundt, C. (1985). *Das Apathiesyndrom der Schizophrenen. Eine psychopathologische und computertomographische Untersuchung*. Berlin: Springer Verlag.

lurray, R.M., Lewis, S.W. (1987). Is schizophrenia a neurodevelopmental disorder? *Br Med J* 295: 681–682.

löller, P., Husby, R. (2000). The initial prodrome in schizophrenia: searching for naturalistic core dimensions of experience and behavior. An exploratory case study beyond prestructured symptom lists. *Schizophrenia Bulletin* 26: 217–232.

löller, P. Duration of untreated psychosis in schizophrenia; are we ignoring mode of initial development? An exploratory naturalistic case study of phenomenal continuity. *Psychopathology*, in press.

Naudin, J., Gros-Azorin, C., Mishara, A., Wiggin, O.P., Schwartz, M.A., and J.M. Azori (1999). The use of the Husserlian reduction as a method of investigation in psychiatry. *Consc Studies* 6: 155–171.
Neisser, U. (1995). Criteria for an ecological self. In Rochat, P. (ed) *The Self in Infancy Theory and Research*. Amsterdam: Elsevier, 17–34.
Palmer, R.E. (1969). *Hermeneutics: Interpretation Theory in Schleiermacher, Dilthey Heidegger, and Gadamer*. Evanston: Northwestern University Press.
Parnas, J. (1999a). From predisposition to psychosis: Progression of symptoms in schizophrenia. *Acta Psychiatrica Scandinavica* (Suppl. 395), 99: 20–29.
Parnas, J. (1999b). On defining schizophrenia. In M. Maj, N. Sartorius (eds) *Evidence & Experience in Psychiatry*. Volume II: Schizophrenia. New York: Wiley and Sons, 43–4
Parnas, J., Bovet, P. (1991). Autism in schizophrenia revisited. *Compr Psychiatry* 32: 7–2
Parnas, J., Bovet, P. (1995). Research in psychopathology: epistemologic issues. *Compr Psychiatry* 36: 167–181.
Parnas, J., Cannon, T.D., Jacobsen, B., Schulsinger, H., Schulsinger, F., Mednick, S.A (1993). Lifetime DSM-III-R diagnostic outcomes in the offspring of schizophrenic mothers. Results from the Copenhagen High-Risk Study. *Arch Gen Psychiatry* 50: 707 714.
Parnas, J., Jørgensen, Å. (1989). Premorbid psychopathology in schizophrenia spectrum *Br J Psychiatry* 155: 623–627.
Parnas, J., Schulsinger, F., Schulsinger, H., Teasdale, T.W., Mednick, S.A. (1982). Behavioral precursors of the schizophrenia spectrum. *Arch Gen Psychiatry* 39: 658–664.
Polanyi, M. (1964). *Personal Knowledge. Towards a post-critical philosophy*. Chicago Chicago University Press.
Rado, S. (1960). Theory and therapy: The theory of schizotypal organization and it application to the treatment of decompensated behavior. In Scher, S.C, Davis, H.R (eds) *The Out-patient Treatment of Schizophrenia*. New York: Grune & Stratton, 87 101.
Ricoeur, P. (1990). *Soi-même comme un autre*. Paris: Les Editions Seuil.
Ricoeur, P. (1991). A *Ricoeur Reader: Reflection and Imagination*. M.J. Valdés (ed Toronto: University of Toronto Press.
Rochat, P. (ed) (1995). *The Self in Infancy: Theory and Research*. Amsterdam: Elsevier.
Rosenthal, D.M. (1997). 'A Theory of Consciousness', in *The Nature of Consciousness* eds. N. Block, O. Flanagan & G. Güzeldere. Cambridge, MA: MIT Press, 729–753.
Sanders, J.T. (1999). Affordances: An ecological approach to first philosophy. In G. Weiss H.F. Haber (eds): *Perspectives on Embodiment. The Intersection of Nature and Culture* London: Routledge, 121–142.
Sass, L.A. (1992). *Madness and Modernism. Insanity in the Light of Modern Art, Literature, and Thought*. New York: Basic Books.
Sass, L.A. (1994). *The Paradoxes of Delusion. Wittgenstein, Schreber, and the Schizophrenic Mind*. Ithaca: Cornell University Press.
Scharfetter, C. (1980). *General Psychopathology: An Introduction*. Tr.H. Marshall. (Allgemeine Psychopathologie, 1976, Georg Thieme Verlag, Stuttgart). Cambridge: Cambridge University Press.

charfetter, C. (1990). *Schizophrene Menschen.* Dritte Auflage. München: Psychologie Verlags Union, Urban & Schwarzenberg.

charfetter, C. (1996). *The Self-Experience of Schizophrenics. Empirical studies of the ego/self in schizophrenia, borderline disorders and depression.* 2-nd edition. Zürich: Private Publication.

chneider, K. (1959). *Clinical Psychopathology.* Tr MW Hamilton. New York: Grune and Stratton.

chwartz, M.A., Wiggins, O.P. (1987). Diagnosis and ideal types: a contribution to psychiatric classification. *Comp Psychiatry* 28: 277–299.

earle, J.R. (1992). *The Rediscovery of the Mind.* Cambridge: MIT Press.

hanon, B. (1993). *The Representational and the Presentational. An Essay on Cognition and the Study of Mind.* New York: Harvester.

ims, A.C.P. (1988). *Symptoms in the Mind: an Introduction to Descriptive Psychopathology.* London: Ballière Tindall.

pitzer, M. (1988). Ichstörungen: In Search of a Theory. In: Spitzer, M., Uehlein, F.A. and Oepen, G., eds. *Psychopathology and Philosophy.* Berlin: Springer, 1988, 167–183.

pitzer, M. (1990). Kant on schizophrenia. In M. Spitzer and B.A. Maher (eds). *Philosophy and Psychopathology.* Berlin: Springer, 44–58.

tern, D.N. (1985). *The Interpersonal World of the Infant. A View from Psychoanalysis and Developmental Psychology.* New York, Basic Books.

trawson, G. (1994). *Mental Reality.* Cambridge, MA: MIT Press.

trawson, P.F. (1959). *Individuals.* London: Methuen.

ymington, J., Symington, N. (1996). *The Clinical Thinking of Wilfred Bion.* London: Routledge.

atossian, A. (1994). La subjectivité. In D. Widlöcher (ed.) *Traité de psychopathologie.* Paris: PUF, 253–318.

atossian, A. (1979). *Phénoménologie des psychoses.* Paris: Masson.

yrka, A.R., Cannon, T.D., Mednick, S.A., Haslam, N., Schulsinger, F., Schulsinger, H., Parnas, J. (1995). The latent structure of schizotypy: I. Premorbid indicators of a taxon of individuals at risk for schizophrenia spectrum disorders. *J Abnorm Psychol* 104: 173–183.

'addington, J.L., O'Callaghan, E., Youssef, H.A., Buckley, P., Lane, A., Cotter, D., Larkin, C. (1995). The neurodevelopmental basis to schizophrenia: beyond a hypothesis? In Fog, R., Gerlach, J., Hemmingsen, R. (eds) *Schizophrenia: An Integrated View.* Alfred Benzon Symposium # 38. Copenhagen: Munskgaard, pp 43–53.

ahavi, D. (1999). *Self-Awareness and Alterity. A Phenomenological Investigation.* Evanston Il: Northwestern University Press.

ahavi, D., Parnas, J. (1998). Phenomenal consciousness and self-awareness: A Phenomenological Critique of Representational Theory. *J Consc Studies* 5: 687–705.

Schizophrenia, Self-Experience, and the So-Called "Negative Symptoms"

Reflections on Hyperreflexivity

Louis Sass
Rutgers University

1. Introduction

For nearly two decades, the most prominent ways of subtyping or otherwise characterizing the diverse manifestations of schizophrenia, at least in Britain and North America, have been based on the distinction between "positive" and "negative" symptoms.[1] Whereas positive symptoms, mainly hallucinations and delusions, are said to involve the *presence* of experiences that would normally be *absent,* the negative symptoms — including poverty of speech (alogia), affective flattening, avolition, apathy, anhedonia, anergia, and inattentiveness — are defined by an apparent *diminution* of what would normally be *present* (Marneros, Andreasen, Tsuang 1991).[2] These two categories are often supplemented by a third group of "disorganization" symptoms: consisting mainly of aspects of formal thought disorder, these latter are generally conceptualized in quantitative terms — as a diminishment of the degree of structure or organization inherent in an individual's thought and language (Liddle 1987).

The empirical evidence for the distinctness of these syndromes is far from definitive and has been hotly debated (see, e.g., McGlashan and Fenton 1992; Häfner et al. 1998). But the distinction itself — quite independently of its actual empirical validation — clearly has great intuitive appeal in Anglophone psychiatry; and it is worth considering why this should be the case.

One source of appeal is the way this distinction promises to satisfy certain positivistic or empiricist criteria. The very notion of positive-versus-negative or more-versus-less, suggests the possibility of a straightforward, non-inter pretative assessment of signs and symptoms — an assessment not of *what* one may be observing but merely of whether, or to what extent, something i present; this seems to hold out the promise both of quantification and of hig reliability. Also important is the way the positive-negative distinction reso nates with mechanistic and often reductionistic propensities that have bee dominant in biological psychiatry for more than a century. It is congruent wit the deeply ingrained assumption that the central clinical features of schizo phrenia are manifestations or consequences of a defective cognitive mecha nism or "broken brain" (Andreasen 1984), and largely involve a decline of th higher or more quintessentially human faculties of the mind.

These latter, mechanistic assumptions were explicit in the work of th neurologist who popularized and defined the negative-versus-positive distinc tion at the end of the nineteenth century. In J. Hughlings Jackson's influenti view, all mental illnesses are, in essence, consequences of a disintegration o the higher or more conscious and volitional mental processes. The effects o this disintegration can show up directly, as "negative" mental symptom involving deficiencies of higher mental processes, or else indirectly, as "pos tive" symptoms (including hallucinations, delusions, and impulsive behavio patterns) that are supposedly released by the failure of higher levels to exer their normal inhibitory control (Stengel 1963; Clark 1981). This conceptio has tended to discourage a search for meaning or intentionality in psycho pathological experience and expression, or even a close examination of th subjective or phenomenological dimension; for it has been taken to imply tha the key feature is a defect or deficiency that basically reflects an abnormalit of brain structure or function.[3] Jackson himself did not consider abnorma states of consciousness to be legitimate objects of study in their own righ "strictly speaking," he wrote, these "mental symptoms" are "only signs t physicians of what is not going on or what is going on wrongly in part of patient's material organization" (quoted in Clark 1981: 271).

Those who hold such views have generally considered the experienc and expression of the insane to be either unintelligible or else fairly uninteres ing and unimportant — either beyond the pale of empathic understanding o rational grasp, or else lacking in the complexity and subtlety typical of norma mental functioning. Thus Charles Mercier, one of Jackson's disciples, con cluded that "we cannot dive into the illogical processes of the insane," and th

British psychiatrist Henry Maudsley spoke of the surprising "mindlessness" hat, he believed, exists even "at the back of what looks like very partial nental disorder" (quoted in Clark 1981: 286, 284).

It would be misleading simply to equate contemporary notions of posi-ive-versus-negative symptoms with Jackson's original conception (Berrios 985). In recent years, positive and negative syndromes are commonly viewed s manifestations of fairly independent processes that need not be in the sort of lose reciprocal relationship that Jackson postulated.[4] But there are other eatures of the traditional perspective that seem to have remained fully intact. n the neo-Kraepelinian climate of present-day psychiatry, schizophrenia is ncreasingly identified with the negative symptoms, which, in turn, are largely nderstood as defect states reflecting malfunctions of the brain.[5] It is perhaps ot surprising that there has been so little attempt, at least until quite recently Kring et al. 1993; Selten et al. 1993; Selten, Bosch, Sijben 1998), to study the ubjective dimension of what might better be termed the negative *signs,* or to onsider whether, on the subjective level, these might involve not mere eficits but processes of a more subtle or complex sort.

The empirical evidence, largely correlational, that bears upon the validity f the two- or three-syndrome distinction has been extensively reviewed by thers (e.g., Marneros, Andreasen, Tsuang 1991; Liddle, Carpenter, Crow 994; Andreasen, Nopoulos, Schultz, et al. 1994). Here I concentrate on ertain theoretical issues and, in particular, on the ways in which the so-called negative symptoms" are experienced by the patients themselves. In the first ection below, I offer some general, critical remarks on the positive-negative istinction, and then on the so-called negative syndrome in particular. In the ollowing two sections, I summarize and discuss two lines of German psycho-athological research that bear upon the nature of the "negative" syndrome. In he next section, I turn to the writings of Antonin Artaud — recently acknowl-dged as one of the very few schizophrenic individuals who has recorded his negative" experiences in elaborate phenomenological detail (Selten et al. 998; see also Sass 1992, 1996). After a brief interlude to introduce some elevant philosophical ideas from Michael Polanyi and others, I return to iscuss Artaud in the final two sections. As we shall see, these so-called egative symptoms cannot be understood on a simple deficit model; they nvolve various "positive" phenomena as well. A close phenomenological nalysis suggests, in fact, that the characteristically schizophrenic abnormali-es of experience defy any simple quantitative description and demand a richer and more qualitative set of concepts.

I shall argue that schizophrenia involves alterations or mutations in two mutually interdependent aspects or facets of the act of consciousness — what can be termed "hyperreflexivity" and "altered ipseity." The term "reflexive" refers to situations or processes whereby some being, especially an agent or self, takes itself or some aspect of itself as its own object of awareness; the exaggerated way in which this occurs in schizophrenia can be described as a "hyperreflexive" tendency (Sass 1992). "Ipseity" (from the Latin, *ipse*, which means 'self' or 'itself') refers to a basic sense of self-coinciding, sometimes called 'autoaffection" — that is, to the implicit sense of being a center of consciousness and source of intentionality. Schizophrenia, in my view, can best be understood as a self-disorder in which phenomena that would normally be inhabited, and in this sense experienced as part of the self, come instead to be taken as objects of focal or objectifying awareness. Intimately connected with — indeed implicit in — this development is a profound weakening of the sense of existing as a subject of awareness, as a presence for oneself and before the world (see Parnas, this volume).[6]

It may sound as if the distinction between, on the one hand, an exaggerated reflexive awareness, and, on the other, a diminished sense of self, parallels the positive-negative distinction. Actually, this is not the case. Positive and negative symptoms are usually treated as separate processes that may nevertheless interact; by contrast, I prefer to see hyperreflexivity and altered ipseity, and their various manifestations, as aspects of a single whole. Although one or another of these aspects may be more prominent or obvious at a given moment, these features (as the term "aspect" indicates) are equally important — equiprimordial, one might say (borrowing a term from Heidegger 1962). Indeed, their relationship is of the most intimate kind, involving something more like mutual phenomenological implication than causal interaction; they are, in a sense, different aspects of the very same phenomenon, but described from two different standpoints. The focus of the present paper, however, will be primarily on the hyperreflexive aspect. As we shall see, hyperreflexive qualities can be manifest on a number of distinct levels or in a variety of different ways — involving different degrees of sophistication and intellectual self-consciousness and not necessarily implying a significant amount of volition, intellectual activity, or reflective self-control.

It is useful to recall the phenomenological philosopher Maurice Merleau-Ponty's description of the "intentional arc" — a term he uses to refer to th ındamental dynamic structuring of our field of awareness and lived world, ıd which he describes as a "mobile vector, active in all directions ... through 'hich we can orient ourselves towards anything *outside and inside us*" and hich "endows experience with its degree of vitality and fruitfulness" 1945: 158, 184; 1962: 135–136, 157, translation altered). This arc or vector is very general feature of consciousness which, at the most fundamental level, ways involves a relatively passive, automatic, or unreflective dimension of peration — what Merleau-Ponty (1962), following Husserl, called "opera-ve intentionality" (*fungierende Intentionalität*). But it can also be imbued, at igher levels, with a sense of activity and volition — with the "reflective ıtentionality" that is characteristic of our explicit judgments and of "those ccasions when we voluntarily take up a position" (xviii). Here I shall distin-uish between "reflective" and "operative" forms of hyperreflexivity. I shall so distinguish according to whether the reflexivity is *compensatory, conse-uential*, or *basal*–that is, whether it occurs in some kind of defensive com-ensation *for* or as a consequence *of* some more basic defect or abnormality, or se as a facet of the basic defect itself.[7]

. Positive versus negative: Critical remarks

is now well established that most patients show symptoms from both the ositive and the negative (and probably also the disorganization) syndromes at me time in the course of their illness, and that most patients will, at some me, simultaneously manifest symptoms from two or even all three groupings iddle 1987: 150; Maurer and Häfner 1991).[8] It is also true, however, that the mptoms called positive, negative, and disorganized do indeed cluster to-ether to some extent, at least in certain phases or in certain patients. Patients ın indeed be more or less active and expressive, more or less alert or shut own, more or less coherent and controlled. One must acknowledge as well at the progression of a schizophrenic illness often includes periods of mental yperactivity as well as more inert phases in which the patient seems "burnt-ıt," exhausted, or defensively "shut down." But to understand the *signifi-ınce* of these apparent clusterings, one must take a more careful and a more itical look at the nature of signs and symptoms at issue.

The distinction of positive-versus-negative symptoms, as typically used the Anglophone literature, is based on the commonsensical assumption that positive and negative symptoms reflect, respectively, an *excess* and a *lac* with the deprivative *a* preceding each function that is supposedly lackin (anergia, avolition, etc.).[9] Thought blocking or deprivation is usually consic ered to be a straightforward instance of a negative symptom (a thought i lacking or removed), thought insertion a straightforward example of a positiv symptom (a new thought is added). Although the rationale of this distinctio may seem straightforward enough, its logic as well as its clinical accuracy ar actually quite problematic.

One issue concerns a certain arbitrariness that seems inherent in classify ing something as positive or negative. The absence of one thing will, after al inevitably allow for, indeed necessitate, the presence of something else — only of the state, whatever it may be, that must necessarily supervene. Thu Schneiderian first rank symptoms (Mellor 1970) are generally considere positive symptoms since they involve the presence of experiences normall absent — hallucinations and delusions; however, the symptoms in questio necessarily imply the simultaneous *absence* of something that is normall *present* — the sense of ownership or intentional control. Although flat affect supposedly a quintessential negative sign, it is frequently accompanied by th presence of something abnormal and anomalous: mask-like facies or inco gruous facial expression. And asociality, the absence of other-directed, so cially oriented behavior, is often accompanied by the presence of strange socially inappropriate, self-directed behavior.[10]

We have been considering discrepancies existing on the same plane – either with*in* the realm of experience or with*in* that of observable behavio Perhaps even more important, however, are contrasts *between* the behavior and the experiential planes, i.e., between the observable sign and the subje tive symptom. Here I shall focus exclusively on the case of the so-calle negative symptoms.[11]

The concept of "negative" symptomatology is often said to be perfectly theoretical, merely a behavioral description. Actually, the overt behavior lack in question is often taken to indicate a paucity of psychological activity subjective life, or else some underlying and fundamental deficit or diminis ment of an "inferred function one normally expects to be present" (Somme 1985) — perhaps especially of higher mental processes involving volitio self-awareness, reasoning, abstraction, and complex emotional respons (DSM IV, e.g., refers to "diminution or absence of affect" and to an appare "diminution of thoughts"; American Psychiatric Association 1994: 276–277

Recent research on subjective reports suggests, however, that the underlying experiences may not, in fact, be direct equivalents or analogues of what is observed at the behavioral level. Patients who, from the observer's standpoint, seem to demonstrate absence of thoughts, lack of motivation or energy, anhedonia, asociality, or the inability to feel intimacy and closeness, do not seem to have (or at least do not report) the subjective experiences one might expect (Selten 1995: 212; Selten, Bosch, Sijben 1998).[12] There seems, for example, to be no correlation between negative symptoms and the subjective experience of reduced cognitive efficacy (Bosch, Rombouts, van Asma 1993). And a study of subjectively experienced changes in early and prodromal phases of illness shows that, whereas depressive patients generally report a quantitative decline in the intensity and efficiency of mental functions, schizophrenics recalling their prodromal experiences are more likely to emphasize *qualitative* alterations of thought and perception that are far more difficult to describe (Cutting and Dunne 1989).

It is true that "negative-symptom" patients sometimes do have an inner sense of lacking thoughts. Just as often, however, they deny such experiences (Selten 1995: 135, 138, 139), and may even report a speeding-up or proliferation of thought processes (see Artaud's account below); indeed, many patients with a negative-symptom profile have no prominent subjective complaints at all (Andreasen 1982). Earlier reports had already indicated that patients displaying catatonic withdrawal are usually acutely aware of surrounding events and can be afflicted with hyperconsciousness (Arieti 1978), and that asocial behavior is often accompanied by an underlying yet fearful yearning for contact (McGlashan 1982). Recently it has also been demonstrated that patients who display flat affect actually report an intense emotional reactivity that contradicts their lack of overt affective expression (Kring et al. 1993; Bouricius 1989; Berenbaum and Oltmanns 1992) — a claim corroborated by electrodermal measurements showing higher reactivity than for normal subjects (Kring and Neale 1996). Below we shall consider some autobiographical reports showing that the so-called negative symptoms may involve positive aberrancies of all kinds.

A straightforward linear or quantitative model — a model of positive-versus-negative or more-versus-less — is clearly inadequate for capturing the complex, even contradictory combinations of experiential phenomena that often occur in the so-called negative syndrome. So far, however, there is virtually no work in the English-language literature that offers any kind of detailed or theoretically informed understanding of the patient's experience of what should really be called the negative *signs.*[13]

3. Loss of natural self-evidence

The richest account of the subjective side of the negative or predominantly "deficit" syndrome is provided in Wolfgang Blankenburg's book of 1971, *Der Verlust der Natürlichen Selbstverständlichkeit* (*The Loss of Natural Self-Evidence: A Contribution to the Study of Symptom-Poor Schizophrenics*), which has not yet been translated into English. (Unless otherwise noted, the page references below are from the French translation: Blankenburg 1991; 1971 indicates the German edition)[14] In Blankenburg's view, the central defect or abnormality in schizophrenia is best described as a "loss of natural self-evidence." This term — which he borrows from a patient named "Anne" — refers to a loss of the usual common-sense orientation to reality, that is, of the unquestioned sense of obviousness and of the unproblematic background quality that normally enables a person to take for granted so many of the elements and dimensions of the social and practical world. This distinctive but subtle abnormality appears in its purest and most easily discernable form in patients with the negative syndrome. Blankenburg believes, however, that such a loss underlies many of what would be called the positive and disorganization symptoms as well; it is the "nonspecific specificity" (30, 97) that defines the essence of schizophrenic illness and helps to account for many of its characteristic features. Blankenburg's approach is consistent with empirical studies which show that, although schizophrenics can often do surprisingly well on many intellectual tasks requiring abstract or logical thought, they have particular difficulties with more practical or common-sensical problems, perhaps especially when these relate to the social world (Cutting and Murphy 1988, 1990).

A loss of the feeling of natural self-evidence necessarily undermines the ease and smooth flow of normal experience and everyday practical activity and may therefore help to account for the withdrawal, slowing, and inactivity that is characteristic of the negative syndrome, and perhaps also for the general lack of attunement to the world that is so characteristic of schizophrenia (Parnas and Bovet 1991). Indeed, this loss might itself be taken for a fairly straightforward negative symptom, a privation of something normally present namely, common sense); the patients themselves will often speak of having a deficit or *Defekt* (Blankenburg 1991: 89; 1971: 51). It is important to note, however, that the loss of natural self-evidence in negative-symptom patients is bound up with a characteristically schizophrenic alienation (34, 201) — a sense of being outside the usual customs and concerns of the shared social world and detached from the usual taken-for-granted background of assumptions and practices. "It is as if I watched from somewhere outside the whole bustle of the world," said Blankenburg's patient Anne (113). The loss of self-evidence often seems to be accompanied as well by exaggerated forms of self-conscious awareness in which patients have an acute or explicit awareness of aspects, features, structures, or processes of action and experience that, in normal experience, would simply be presupposed and unnoticed (107–122). They often have a sense of amazement before that which would seem to be *most* self-evident, a reaction that Blankenburg (112) likens to the wonder sought by a phenomenological philosopher who suspends normal assumptions in order to bring them to light.

Blankenburg's central case example, the patient Anne, speaks, for instance, of being "hooked to" or "hung up on" (79–80; *hängen bleiben*–1971: 44) obvious or self-evident problems and questions which healthy people simply take for granted. "It is impossible for me to stop myself from thinking," (82), she says. Anne would find herself ruminating on questions she herself found pointless (91) — asking herself, for instance, why one does something in one way and not another, how one says thank you or washes oneself, or what old age is — or else seeking the rational principles dictating why certain kinds of cloth or of clothing are or are not appropriate for particular occasions (80–81, 130). In such patients there is often a remarkable disproportion between an elevated level of self-reflection and a remarkable inability to confront the demands of everyday life (191); the constant need to think is generally accompanied by a constant inability to understand (11, 72).

According to Blankenburg (94), loss of natural self-evidence is what underlies the characteristically schizophrenic "perplexity" (*Ratlosigkeit*) that is described in classic German psychopathology (Jaspers 1963; Störring 1987). This distinctive form of perplexity involves a self-aware, anguishing, and (to the patient) inexplicable sense of being unable to maintain a consistent grasp on reality, to empathize with others, or to cope with normal situational demands. There is usually a "strange turning in upon one's self," accompanied by a sense that one's activity level is declining and that one is gradually becoming detached from the world of perception (Störring 1987: 80). To understand this perplexity, it is not sufficient, in my opinion, to stress any purely quantitative factor — whether this be the patient's sense of declining vitality and activation or the fact that, with the emergence of the normally tacit, the patient's consciousness is now flooded with *more* input, in a state of cognitive overload. More crucial is a radical *qualitative* shift: namely, that when the tacit dimensions become explicit, they can no longer perform the grounding, orienting, in effect *constituting* function that only what remains in the background can play.

The patient Anne speaks of the "way," "the manner of thinking," or "the framework" (126, 140; *"eine Bahn, eine Denkweise"; der `Rahmen' in dem alles abspiele"* — 1971: 79, 90) that every person needs in order to know how to conduct him or herself. Normally, she says, this is something that develops naturally and over time, and largely unnoticed, like one's character itself. But whereas the normal person has a *natural* relationship to this manner or framework, Anne herself feels at an enormous distance from any such thing. "In my case," she says, "everything is just an *object* of thought" (127; *"Bei mir ist das alles nur angedacht"*–1971: 79). Blankenburg (144–157) describes closely related problems with the constitution of the active 'I', transcendental ego, or prereflective cogito, the functioning of which normally resides on the foundation of a taken-for-granted background. In the absence of such a grounding, the patient will usually suffer a diminished sense of vitality, motivation, or even legitimacy as a perspective on the world. One consequence of the loss of natural self-evidence, of the normal sense of embeddedness in a framework, is that the patient must devote energy and a kind of active, conscious effort and control to processes that would normally take place automatically. The very constitution of self and world — a "transcendental operation" (*"transzendentale Leistung"*–1971: 84) normally arising via preconscious passive syntheses — may require an almost *physical* effort that uses up available resources. This may account, at least in part, for the lack of energy and general sense of exhaustion so common in schizophrenia (the latter being what Blankenburg calls schizophrenic "asthenia" — see 132–133, 153, 155–156).

Blankenburg considers reflexivity to be an important and, in many respects, a distinctive characteristic of schizophrenia (he explains, e.g., how the schizophrenic's doubting and perplexity differ from that of the obsessive-compulsive person — 91). But this does not mean that he views it as being primary in a causal or temporal sense, or as having what he calls a "basal" character (106). Generally he describes it as a secondary process that develops largely by way of compensation for a more fundamental or primary defect or deficit involving the loss of one's spontaneous attunement to common-sense reality — namely, loss of natural self-evidence (93). In addition, he appears to endorse Jaspers' description of how reflexivity can insert itself in an almost automatic or consequential (as opposed to compensatory) fashion once it is no longer excluded by the natural, spontaneous flow of immediate life experience (101; Blankenburg speaks here of *"Einbau der Reflexion in die Unmittelbarkeit"*–1971: 59).

Also, when Blankenburg speaks of "reflexivity" (the German terms he uses include *Reflexivität, Reflexionskrampf, Reflexion, Reflektierheit,* and *reflektierte Alienation*–1971: 53, 54, 59, 121), he is referring primarily to the *reflective* type of reflexivity. This is the sort that has an at least semi-volitional quality and that typically engages processes of understanding or introspection of an intellectual or even hyper-rational sort (it occurs, he says, *"mit Hilfe des Verstandes reflektierten ... Selbstverhältnis"*–1971: 102; 1991: 154). By contrast, what he considers the basal trouble pertains to the person's immediate prereflective or pre-intentional relationship to self and to world (113, 154, 201) — that is, to what Blankenburg, following the later Husserl, refers to as the "fundamental receptivity" inherent in the "passive synthesis" or "passive genesis" of experience (93, 130).

This is not to say, however, that reflexivity need play an entirely secondary or non-causal role in Blankenburg's account. Blankenburg certainly does not stress the point; however, it seems clear that even though reflexive ruminations may develop largely in compensation for a more basic loss, they can also have the effect of *further* distancing the patient from a sense of naturalness or a capacity for spontaneous action, thereby increasing the patient's sense of perplexity and making it more difficult to break out of what can become a vicious circle or even a cascading auto-catalytic spiral. This latter possibility was described by a highly introspective and intellectual young man with schizophrenia who was treated by a colleague of mine. "My downfall was insight," he explained in one therapy session. "Too much insight can be very dangerous, because you can tear your mind apart." "Well, look at the word 'analysis,'" he said on another occasion. "That means to break apart. When it turns in upon itself, the mind would rip itself apart." "Once I started destroying [my mind], I couldn't stop" (quoted in Sass 1992: 337–338).[15]

Blankenburg's (1991) perspective is descriptive, holistic, and somewhat static. He seeks to comprehend the overall tenor, dominant theme, style of existence, or fundamental conditions of possibility of the schizophrenic lifeworld, and he does so largely through the careful examination of a single patient. Although Blankenburg describes "loss of natural self-evidence" as a "*basic* disorder" or "*Grundstörung,*" he does not intend to imply that it has either temporal priority or causal primacy (27; 1971: 4); nor is he especially interested in breaking the phenomenon of loss of self-evidence down into component parts or in tracing causal sequences. Given these limitations, it is interesting to consider a complementary but more nomothetic and longitudinal program of research on "basic symptoms" that has been carried out in Germany over the last 50 years.

4. The "basic symptoms"

Like Blankenburg (28, 229), the psychiatrists Huber, Gross, Klosterkötter, and colleagues focus on symptoms that they see as overlapping with Bleuler's "fundamental" symptoms and the negative symptoms of contemporary psychiatry (Klosterkötter 1992: 31). Using a structured interview technique (Klosterkötter 1992), they have gathered first-person data in different patient samples and mapped subjective experience in the prodromal, active, as well as residual phases of schizophrenia — thereby uncovering a set of relatively mild, nonpsychotic anomalies that would seem to be associated with the loss of natural self-evidence and related developments. Although originally studied as precursors to schizophrenia with first rank symptoms, the "basic symptoms" actually represent the subjective dimension of seeming deficiency states that occur both before and after (and possibly also during) the development of productive, positive symptoms. They are often seen as being the subjective experiences that most closely reflect the basic biological defect that is assumed to be the true core of schizophrenic illness. The basic-symptom research clearly demonstrates that even the most clearly "negative" symptoms, such as apathy or avolition, are accompanied by a panoply of subtle but "positive" experiential disturbances in the domains of cognition, perception, bodily-experience, action, and emotion.

Bringing Blankenburg together with the basic-symptom research enables us to describe the peculiar but characteristic combination of what seem to be hyperconcrete as well as hyperabstract tendencies that can occur in schizophrenic experience and expression (Sass 1992: 164–168, 191–193). Whereas Blankenburg draws our attention to some of the more abstract preoccupations that give to the thought and speech of some schizophrenics a quasi-philosophical or hyperabstract quality (e.g., the patient's detached querying of conventions of social interaction, framework assumptions, and the like), the basic-symptom research documents a concomitant and often simultaneous aspect of schizophrenia: how the larger unities of experience and action can break down due to preoccupation with the sensory particulars — kinesthetic, proprioceptive, and the like — that constitute what Klosterkötter et al. term the forms of "basal irritation".[16]

One cluster of the basic symptoms involves perceptual mutations, of vision in particular. In this hyperalert state of consciousness, sounds, voices, faces, gestures, and patterns of behavior come to look strange or false and to feel irritating and affectively stirring in some peculiar way (Klosterkötter 1992: 33). Other "basic symptoms" involve abnormalities of the core sense of the self as a thinking, feeling, or willing being. To think clearly begins to seem difficult; thoughts seem to disappear or come to a halt; emotions feel unnatural, absent, unsatisfying or somehow inappropriate or out of kilter. There are also various "dynamic deficiencies": both the "direct dynamic deficiencies" of diminished physical energy, resilience, perseverance, or will-power, and also what they call "indirect dynamic deficiencies," involving inner disquiet or tension, sleep disturbances, lack of concentration, and obsessional thought patterns.

Still another cluster of "basic symptoms" are the cenesthesias: sensations of movement or of pulling or pressure inside the body or on its surfaces; electric or migrating sensations; awareness of kinesthetic, vestibular, or thermic sensations; and sensations of diminution or enlargement, of heaviness or lightness, of sinking or emptiness, or of numbness or stiffness of the body or its parts. Generally unpleasant, and frequently accompanied by feelings of decline of vital energy, these experiences are combined with a loss of automatic skills and with various forms of interference with or blockage of the smooth flow of motor activity. They appear to involve hyperreflexive awareness of bodily sensations that would not normally be attended to in any direct or sustained fashion.

These strange bodily sensations are, in fact, remarkably similar to the experiences reported by normal subjects who have been encouraged to adopt a certain kind of detached, introspective stance toward their own bodies — as was amply demonstrated in classic introspectionist experiments carried out by Titchener and others (see Angyal 1936; Hunt 1985: 248; Sass 1994: 90–97, 159–161). If a person sits immobile, closing her eyes and banishing all theoretical knowledge about the body, and any image of how it might look from without, then her somatic and kinesthetic feelings will indeed begin to seem disorganized and oddly labile, with strange sensations of forces, flows, or tension states akin to those reported by schizophrenic individuals (Hunt 1995: 201). (There are also remarkable resemblances between the schizophrenic and the introspectionist experience of language, thought, and meaning; see Hunt 1985; Sass 1994: 90, 94.) In a sense, these now-emergent phenomena are merely the normal bodily sensations that are always present, even though we do not usually attend to them; but, of course, this very attending actually constitutes a radical mutation of the experiential world: We might say, then, that such phenomena represent the perfectly *normal* phenomena of ordinary human experience, but lived in the perfectly *abnormal* condition of hyperreflexive awareness and diminished self-affection.

5. Antonin Artaud

It is obvious that the self-reports of a single individual cannot, by themselves, *prove* anything about schizophrenia in general. They can, however, provide materials for a detailed, idiographic analysis, illustrating general trends as well as illuminating certain kinds of psychopathological and pathogenetic possibilities. But good first-person descriptions of schizophrenic negative symptoms are exceedingly rare, for reasons that are not difficult to understand. Normal everyday language is inherently ill-suited to the description of unusual and "inner" kinds of experience, or of alterations in dimensions of experience that constitute the very conditions or foundation of language itself — such as the assumption of natural self-evidence.[17] Also, the states themselves, with their wavering of implicit into explicit modalities, are likely to undermine the very capacity for continuous and focused thought or discourse on any topic, let alone the most ephemeral or universal ones.

We are therefore extremely fortunate to have the writings of one schizophrenic individual who described his experience of negative symptoms in eloquent detail: Antonin Artaud, a poet, playwright, and actor who showed schizotypal symptoms from an early age and who, after a clear psychotic break, spent a decade in mental asylums. Artaud manifested significant positive symptoms during the last decade of his life, but the period that we will be considering (roughly, the 1920s and early 1930s) was dominated by what would be termed "negative" symptoms and signs. If the negative or defect symptoms are as important as is often claimed (e.g., by Andreasen, Huber, and others), then Artaud's evocative and uncannily precise writings may, in fact, turn out to be the most valuable of all autobiographical accounts of schizophrenia. His eloquence makes him atypical, but Artaud may nevertheless be a particularly exemplary case. As we shall see from his account, hyperreflexivity may not simply be elicited in the ways Blankenburg describes — namely, as a defensive *compensation* for, or perhaps a natural *consequence* of, a prior and a more basic defect such as loss of natural self-evidence. It may also have a *basal* status as an element or aspect of the originary disturbance itself.

Artaud was certainly a highly introspective person — acutely sensitive to and preoccupied with experiences of his body and the often disconcerting movements of his inner life. "I study myself microscopically," he wrote. "I put my finger on the exact place of the fault, the unadmitted sliding" (1965: 37). There are many passages in which he speaks in what seem to be distinctly deficit or negative terms, describing an inability to think, speak, feel, focus his attention, or carry out normal actions: "I am the man who has best charted his inmost self, his most imperceptible slitherings … I am the man who knows the innermost recesses of loss," he writes (1965: 37). "This void possesses me, fills me with anguish and sorrow … expressed in the soul in a coloration of nothingness" (1976: 289–290). "I am an idiot by the suppression of thought, by the malformation of thought; I am vacant by the stupefaction of my tongue" (1976: 83). (Henceforth, all Artaud references not otherwise noted are from Artaud 1976.)

Artaud describes a "central collapse of the mind," what he calls "a kind of erosion, both essential and fleeting, of my thinking." This erosion deprives his thought of its "concentration," "cohesion," "constancy," and "consistency" (1965: 10–11), causing his "incorrigible inability to concentrate upon an object" (1965: 20) and preventing him from being "validly and lastingly aware of who I am … from becoming aware and staying aware of *myself*" (292). "In my case," he states, "this obscuring, this uprooting of the higher levels of consciousness and thought holds true, unfortunately, for all the circumstances of life, … intellectually my brain has become inoperative, can no longer function" (290).

Although Artaud talks incessantly about the erosion, paralysis, or vacuity of his thinking, it is clear that he does not consider his problem to be rooted in cognition alone, but in something closer to the vital core of life itself. "Not merely the thought, but the personality, the life" (294) is afflicted, he says, describing "dispossession of my vital substance" (82), "a fundamental absence of mental fire, a lack of circulation of life" and a feeling of being "Abandoned by my body, / Abandoned by every possible human feeling" (1965: 42–43). His affective expression often struck others as having a stiff and masklike quality (Knapp 1969: 31). He himself states that "apathy" has "taken possession" of his mind, and complains of an inability to feel, or to feel at one with, his emotions: "I have no life, I have no life!!! My inner enthusiasm is dead." Everything lacks "an emotional aroma" (169, 65).

In the first phase of his writing career, the period of the 1920s and early 1930s, Artaud actually identifies health and vitality with a certain kind of reflexive self-awareness. He defines a "living mind" as one that is "still conscious, lucid, capable of observing and measuring its own life, capable, if necessary and at certain moments, of weighing and judging its own thought" (70). One biographer (Knapp 1969: 11) notes Artaud's remarkable ability to analyze his own difficulties with the process of writing, and states that he gives "the impression of a man working at an art and at the same time watching himself work at it through a mirror." It is understandable that, at this stage, Artaud's reaction to his difficulties should include compensatory or defensive forms of hyperreflexivity — that is, the hyperreflective forms of introspective self-awareness that Blankenburg describes as occurring as attempts to compensate for the loss of self-evidence and spontaneity. "This paralysis overtakes me and hinders me more and more from coming back to myself," he writes. "My torment is as subtle and refined as it is bitter. It is necessary for me to make insane efforts of the imagination, multiplied tenfold by the grip of this strangling asphyxia, in order to succeed in *thinking* my disease" (92).

There is a sense, in fact, in which virtually all of Artaud's writings of the 1920s and early 1930s are an attempt to overcome his difficulties through a kind of introspection. He speaks of "this pursuit, … this need to pin down once and for all the state of my suffocation" (92), and writes in a letter of wanting "to illuminate once and for all" what he calls "the notion of this private intellectual vacuum [which] seems to me the dominant characteristic of my condition" (290). It is as if he hoped to cure his illness, or at least distance himself from it, by means of an intellectual and verbal kind of understanding.[18]

But Artaud also describes forms of reflective self-consciousness that seem to have a consequential rather than compensatory status. Consider, e.g., the self-conscious focusing on words described in the following passage, a focusing that seems to come about as a result of some erosion in his thinking, of some prior undermining of the normal sense of the flow of meaning:

> I felt the ground under my thought crumble, and I am *led* to consider the terms I use without the support of their inner meaning, their personal substratum. And even more than that, the point at which this substratum seems to connect with my life suddenly becomes strangely sensitive and potential. (94; emphasis added)

Here we seem to have an example of what Jaspers (Blankenburg 1991: 101) described as the almost automatic popping up or out of reflective awareness once it is no longer suppressed by the natural flow of immediate experience.

In another passage we can see how this kind of reflective focus on words — what Artaud calls a "considering of terms" — has the effect of further alienating him from any natural sense of meaningfulness. We see how acute hyperreflection — in this case, a critical focus on the relationship between a phrase ("it is cold") and the inner sensations that one might expect to accompany it — may serve to exacerbate the sense of the arbitrariness and inadequacy of words. (It is interesting to consider Artaud in light of Wittgenstein's private-language argument; see Sass 1995.)

> …not only must I rack my brain to discover what I think about some point or other … but my confusion is such that I am often rendered incapable of translating the simplest impressions, of expressing my own reaction to the weather, for example, however incredible this may seem. If it is cold I can still say that it is cold, but there are also times when I am incapable of saying it: this is a fact, for there is in me something damaged from the emotional point of view, and if someone asked me why I could not say it, I would answer that my inner feeling on this slight and neutral point did not correspond to the three simple little words I would have to pronounce [--"it is cold"]. And this lack of correspondence, therefore, between a physiological sensation and its emotional response in the first place and next its intellectual response — insofar as it is possible to summarize and synthesize in general terms this series of swift, almost instantaneous operations which give rise to the truism *it is cold* — this lack of correspondence, since it does not select its subjects or spare me in any way, culminates, as it spreads, in the colossal troubles which correspond perfectly, alas, to the loss of personality. (294–295)

Focusing explicit attention on the signifier-signified relationship, which is normally simply taken for granted, seems to increase Artaud's sense of the arbitrariness of the signifier and his alienation from meaning, further undermining his capacity to inhabit his thought or language in a natural way, and ultimately coming to affect even his sense of personality or selfhood. In a postcard written nine years earlier, Artaud (1976b) wrote of this problem. He complained of being deprived of a necessary "minimum of absorption of my thought within my thought," of "that fusion … of the expression with the thought, that instantaneous forgetting which is given to all men and allows them convenience of expression" (210).[19]

There are other passages in which Artaud describes forms of hyperreflexivity that are associated with what, in the basic-symptom research, are termed "secondary" types of "dynamic deficiency." Artaud often describes a basic — and painful — lack of vital energy and directedness that seems to prevent actions from having a natural or spontaneous sort of coherence and flow. This lack, however, also has the effect of bringing on a secondary sort of fatigue, for it forces Artaud to expend effort, and thereby further deplete his energies, in order to achieve forms of bodily and cognitive integration that would normally occur in an effortless and automatic fashion. In a passage from "The Umbilicus of Limbo," Artaud describes:

> … a staggering and central fatigue, a kind of gasping fatigue. Movements must be recomposed, a sort of deathlike fatigue, … mind fatigued at simplest muscular tension like gesture of grasping — unconsciously clinging to something, holding it together by constant will power. A fatigue of cosmic Creation, the sense of having to carry one's body around, a feeling of incredible fragility which becomes a shattering pain, a state of painful numbness, a sort of localized numbness on skin surface which does not hinder a single motion but alters nevertheless that internal feeling in your limbs so that the mere act of standing vertical is achieved only at the price of a victorious struggle. (64–65; also 1965: 28–29)

This effortfulness and exertion of will may well be a consequence of, or perhaps a compensatory response to, something more fundamental; but it seems to contribute, in turn, to a still greater sense of exhaustion.[20]

6. The tacit dimension

I have been speaking of reflective forms of hyperreflexivity that occur in a compensatory or consequential fashion, and also of certain counterproductive effects (alienation from meaningful language, secondary dynamic deficiencies) that these forms of experience can have. But what of the more basic or fundamental defect that Artaud characterizes as the original "fault," "erosion," "dispossession," "malformation," or "collapse"? It is this underlying distortion and weakening that Huber and Klosterkötter refer to with their notion of "*basal* irritation," and that seems most likely to correspond to the basic defect, deficit, or loss postulated by Blankenburg as well as by traditional medical-model psychiatrists in the tradition of Emil Kraepelin. I now want to show that these underlying experiential distortions may also involve forms of hyperreflexivity. In this case, however, the hyperreflexivity in question would be of an operative rather than a reflective kind — affecting what Blankenburg (following Husserl) calls the "fundamental receptivity" of the automatic or "passive syntheses" that structure the basic act of consciousness and constitute a person's most immediate and fundamental relationship to self and to world.[21] In order to understand this possibility of basal hyperreflexivity, it is helpful to recall Merleau-Ponty's notion of the intentional arc, and to consider the accounts offered by two theorists with complementary views: the biologist-philosopher Michael Polanyi and the perceptual psychologist James Gibson.

The nature of the intentional arc or vector of awareness is clarified by Polanyi's (1964, 1967; Grene 1968) notion of a continuum that stretches between the objectified or focally known *object* of awareness and that which exists more in the "tacit dimension," that is, which is known in a more subsidiary, proximal, implicit, or tacit manner. The latter includes the background or context of awareness as well as the structures and processes of the embodied, knowing self. (Tacit knowledge can be profoundly unconscious, but it may also involve a peripheral kind of awareness; Polanyi 1968: 420.) One might exemplify these two ways of knowing — tacit and focal — by distinguishing the body-*image* from what might be called the bodily or corporeal *subject*. Whereas the body image is a representation *of* one's own body that is or could be an *object* of awareness, the notion of corporeal subject refers to the body as a sensori-motor agent and witness that encounters and in some sense actually constitutes the world of our awareness as well as our most basic sense of self (see Gallagher and Meltzoff 1996, and Merleau-Ponty 1962: 99–104, re body image versus body schema).[22]

The self-feeling or ipseity of this bodily subject is based in part on awareness of proprioceptive and kinesthetic sensations. Normally, however, these sensations are not in the objectifying focus of attention; nor do they have their significance "in themselves," but rather as the subjective correlates of other- or object-directed forms of intentionality. Gibson (1979) emphasized the fact that perceptual awareness of the external world always includes a preconceptual awareness of one's relationship *to* the world. Thus we see something as located near or far *from us*, and we see the world primarily in terms of "affordances" — for instance, whether an object allows for (affords) walking on or jumping over. The prereflective "intentionality" of the body subject could be said to encompass all the implicitly felt and tacitly constitutive subjective correlates of these Gibsonian affordances. Any disturbance of this tacit-focal structure, or of the ipseity it implies, is likely to have subtle but broadly reverberating effects; such disturbances must necessarily upset the balance and shake the foundations of both self and world.

It is important to realize that the structuring of this vector of awareness is part of operative intentionality. The determination of which elements of awareness will be focal and which tacit will obviously be affected by the subject's orientation and choice of focal object, which can be under voluntary control. However, the actual structuring of the vector of awareness occurs automatically, as part of the passive synthesis of the act of consciousness.

Polanyi uses the terms "indwelling" and "inhabiting" to capture the intimate manner in which bodily sensations are typically experienced when they serve as the proximal term in the tacit-to-explicit, proximal-to-distal, or from-to structure that is essential to all knowing. Indwelling is not restricted to the body alone, however. Indeed, Polanyi's analysis shows how the boundary between self and world is, in some sense, less a matter of the physical boundary of the body than a function of the experiential orientation of the active subject. This boundary is extended outward when an active subject takes up elements of external reality and employs them as tools. By using a cane in the service of skillfully exploring the world, e.g., its feel against one's hand comes to function as what Polanyi (1967) calls "the proximal term of tacit knowing": "we incorporate [the cane] in our body — or extend our body to include it — so that we come to dwell in it." (16; see also Polanyi 1964: 55–59). Polanyi (1968) generalizes the point: "whenever we experience an object outside us subsidiarily, we feel it in a way similar to that in which we feel our body": "We may be said to interiorize these things or to pour ourselves into them" (405). An obverse point should also be made: namely, that our self-awareness in relating to the world is not merely mental or spiritual but entails a crucial background recognition of our kinship with the natural or physical realm (this is the point of Merleau-Ponty's [1968] notion of "the flesh" or the "fold" in being; see also Evans quoted in Bermudez 1998: 222). Tacitness is crucial; it is, in a sense, the very medium of normal auto-affection — of the pre-reflective sense of subjecthood or self-awareness that is necessary for normal forms of intentional awareness and activity.

Polanyi's analysis shows how the boundary between self and world can be extended outward as parts of external reality are incorporated by an active subject who uses them as tools. Many classic schizophrenic experiences suggest just the opposite movement: A migration backward and inwards whereby the sense of self withdraws from what it had previously inhabited, and what had previous functioned as the very medium of our selfhood, comes to be experienced as external objects or alien objects rather than as the medium of our existence. Many of Artaud's descriptions of his sense of absence, abandonment, and erosion seem to illustrate the possibility of just this kind of distorting mutation of operative intentionality.

7. Artaud: Operative hyperreflexivity

Consider, e.g., a work called "Fragments of a Diary from Hell" of 1925, in which Artaud describes an "absence" and a "standstill" felt "in the limbs and the blood": "A terrible cold,/ An atrocious abstinence,/ The limbo of a nightmare of bone and muscles, with the sensation of stomach functions snapping like a flag in the phosphorescences of the storm./ Larval images that are pushed as if by a finger and have no relation to any material thing." (1965: 44). Here Artaud seems to be describing phenomena that were never meant to be in the focus of attention. It is as if normally implicit, often fleeting, yet grounding experiences of the lived-body have lost their natural, taken-for-granted status as part of a background or medium of awareness and taken on hybrid and (in some ways) contradictory qualities that nearly defy verbal description — qualities of what Laing (1965: 158) aptly termed "a kind of phantom concreteness": in the unnatural light of hyperreflexive awareness, visceral and muscular sensations come to seem distant, dreamlike, unfamiliar, and unreal, but also (and even at the same time) somehow exaggeratedly material, sensorially precise, electric, or hyperreal.

Other passages bring out the sense of vertigo and bewilderment, and the consequent withdrawal, that occurs when bodily appendages and movements have come to seem distant, dislocated, devitalized, and strange. Artaud complains, e.g., of a "state of exhaustion and physical pressure" that is "reinforced by a sensation of physical withdrawal from myself, as if I were about to lose control of my limbs, my reflexes, my most spontaneous motor reactions." In even more precise characterization of what seems likely to be a kind of basal irritation, involving operative hyperreflexivity, he describes an "incoherence of steps, of gestures, of movements. Will power constantly inhibited in even the simplest gestures" — and speaks of something that is

> felt like the radical suppression of a limb, transmitting to the brain no more than images of bloody old cottons pulled out in the shape of arms and legs, images of distant and dislocated members. Sort of inward breakdown of entire nervous system. A shifting vertigo, a sort of oblique bewilderment which accompanies every effort. (64–65; also 1965: 28–29; translations combined)

Here we see, on a brute, bodily level, some of the experiences that can underlie Blankenburg's "loss of natural self-evidence," and that can lead to motoric slowing or even complete withdrawal from action. To distinguish with certainty between the core of an illness and its immediate sequelae (which may be compensatory or consequential) is an impossible task. Still, in reading these descriptions of the nearly indescribable, these accounts of "unconscious incoherence" of movement, of "larval images" and the "limbo of a nightmare of bones and muscle," one has the impression of coming into close contact with the nearly inaccessible, underlying mode of experience or basic defect that so disconcerts Artaud and other persons in the schizophrenia spectrum. The passages themselves are verbal reports, obviously involving reflective forms of self-consciousness, yet the underlying reflexivity, the alienation from the normally inhabited, that they describe does seem to involve a hyperreflexivity of a more basic or operative kind. Here one should note the utter complementarity of hyperreflexivity and ipseity-disturbance. Whereas the notion of hyperreflexivity emphasizes the way in which something normally tacit becomes focal and explicit, the notion of disturbed ipseity or self-affection emphasizes a concomitant aspect of this same whole: the fact that what once was tacit is no longer being inhabited as a medium of taken-for-granted selfhood.

The peculiar nature of this alienated self-awareness — how it can derealize yet also objectify phenomena never meant to be in the focus of attention — is particularly clear in two passages in which Artaud seems to be describing an alienation from what might seem the most intimate of phenomena: the inner experience of his own face. One's own face, not as seen in a mirror but as it is lived from within, might seem the most intimate part of the self — the very nedium of one's pattern of reactions and intentions. But Artaud describes ertain strange transformations of facial awareness that one might imagine ccurring under conditions of prolonged withdrawal and hyperreflexive con- emplation — conditions in which the normally implicit and inner is extruded nto a state of quasi-externality.

In the first passage, from a letter written in 1932, Artaud describes having . sensation of "active emptiness" in the facial nerves and of magnetization efore his face which he finds distressing and vertiginous. "These are not mages and this should be taken almost literally," he writes (289). A person's ace is, in fact, an "active emptiness": for, although invisible to its possessor – therefore, in a sense, "empty" — it is experienced as the locus of one's ntentionality — therefore "active." And since it is also the most acute source f all our knowing of objects, it does, in a way, attract — metaphorically peaking, "magnetize" — all that passes in front of it. It seems, then, that the ensations of which Artaud becomes aware are in one sense perfectly normal nd unremarkable, indeed, utterly universal. It is his focal or explicit aware- ess of them that renders them strange and alien — a source of basal irritation, f vertigo, and of distress.

The nature of this kind of alienating self-awareness and associated distur- ance of self-affection is perhaps more obvious in the following, particularly izarre passage: a description of a lived face that, under conditions of yperreflexive awareness and diminished self-affection, seems to be turned nside out, flattened and extruded — becoming a kind of fluid mask, a fragile ived membrane of squirming sensitivity and kaleidoscopic pattern that seems o lift off from his head to float independently in the air. Artaud describes a

> human face flattened out, deflated, as if sucked up by shriveling leeches. And this lubricating membrane will go on floating in the air, this caustic lubricating membrane, this double membrane of multiple degrees and a million little fissures, this melancholic and vitreous membrane, but so sensitive and also pertinent, so capable of multiplying, splitting apart, turning inside out with glistening little cracks, its dimensions … (1965: 39)

As normally tacit phenomena — the planes and cavities of the face, its sense f solidity or flow, of tension or release — move out of the tacit dimension and merge into hyperreflexive awareness, they take on the hybrid or contradic- ory qualities — phantasmic yet at the same time hyper-specific or quasi- naterial — of "phantom concreteness." Both aspects can be understood as onsequences of a hyperreflexive awareness that derealizes sensations by detaching them from their familiar context (in the normally unnoticed background or medium of awareness), while simultaneously subjecting these sensations to a process of externalization, reification, and spatialization. It is not difficult to imagine how such basic experiences of altered self-affection, or self-alienation rooted in basal irritation, might be conducive to forms of inactivity and social withdrawal and to a sense of effortfulness and associated fatigue; they may also help to account for the distortions of affective experience and expression that characterize the negative-symptom syndrome.

Affective experience generally seems to be rooted in experiences of bodily states — in what might be termed "representations" or "images of the body" that have come to be associated as "somatic markers" with particular contexts or stimulus situations (Damasio 1994). It seems likely, however, that normal emotional experience would involve, in large measure, not representations of the objectified body *image* so much as implicitly felt experiences involving the body *subject*. These would be experiences in which the somatic markers, patterns, or tension-states are experienced as the tacitly inhabited medium of an attitude — such as fear, desire, or disgust — that is directed toward some object in the world. (Such experiences could be described as the subjective correlates of the emotional affordances of the world.) When experiences that normally exist in the tacit dimension come to be the objects of a more focal and objectifying awareness, as happens with Artaud, one would expect profound transformations in the felt quality of the affective life. Rather than serving as an attitude *toward* the world, certain emotional configurations would instead be experienced at a subjective distance, almost as objects in themselves, while others might simply fail to coalesce at all. The normal fluidity and flow of both affective experience and affective expression would be disrupted, leading to a sense of awkwardness, artificiality, and distance both in the patient's experience of emotion and in the expression visible to others (see, e.g., Artaud 1976: 91–92, 169, 308).[23]

The bizarre and profoundly disconcerting potential of hyperreflexive awareness is probably most apparent in a passage from "The Umbilicus of Limbo," a work from 1925 in which Artaud describes the estrangement of something that is normally even more intimate and inner than the lived face. Here Artaud speaks of a "fundamental slackening of my being" that diminishes not his intelligence but his "utilizable intellectuality," and that, he says, "has more to do with my own sense of myself than with the part of myself that I show to others" (61). He describes his soul as an "abyss" and the universe as "wind" that is filled with a "network of veins" or "tiny rootlets" which he ees "trembling at the corners of my mind's eye" (59). While Artaud's eference to an "abyss" suggests diminished self-affection, the "rootlets" emand to be read as a hyperreflexive, phantom-concrete image of his own onsciousness — a consciousness that has somehow managed the seemingly mpossible feat of seeing itself from *within.* In these lines, it does appear that omething inconceivable has actually come to pass. What would normally ake place without awareness or conscious effort of any kind — the very onstituting of the perceived world — is here experienced as an *object* of self-onscious awareness. The supposedly imperceptible epistemic or representing elf — symbolized by the image of rootlets or capillaries of blood at the orners of one's eyes or visual field — seems to become detached; to flow out nto its own field of objects, become visible there, and then to dissolve. And long with this, there occurs a horrifying ontological catastrophe which is a ort of ultimate example of the loss of perceptual hold: the "vegetable mass" f space trembles in response to Artaud's shifting of his consciousness and his aze, followed by the nothingness implied by the homogeneity of objectless arkness and "total frost." The description suggests that this whole process akes place in an automatic rather than a willful or reflective way — as a kind f operative hyperreflexive alienation that distorts or even destroys the pas-ive syntheses necessary for the normal constitution of both self and world:

> Yes, space was yielding its whole mental padding in which no thought was yet clear or had replenished its load of objects. But little by little the mass turned like a slimy and powerful nausea, a sort of vast influx of blood, vegetal and thundering. And the rootlets which were trembling at the corners of my mind's eye detached themselves with vertiginous speed from the wind-contracted mass. And all space trembled .... all profound thinking at this moment formed layers, resolved itself, became transparent and reduced. .... And two or three times more the whole vegetable mass heaved, and each time my eye shifted to a more precise position. The very darkness became profuse and without object. The total frost gained clarity. (60)

'he subjective or knowing self, symbolized in the rootlets at the corners of the nind's eye, has somehow come to take itself as its own object. Such a process rst extrudes, then undermines, and finally dissolves the normally unseen laments that ground the very possibility of a stable self or world.

There is something weirdly contradictory about this uncanny, quintessen-ally schizophrenic image of rootlets at the corners of the mind's eye. It is, at ne same time, a reified object and the transcendental foundation of the world, something that plays a godlike or solipsistic role. This seems highly emblem atic of schizophrenia — a condition in which a person is especially likely t experience himself as a machine, a phantom, or as God, rather than as a huma being who lives among other similar beings of flesh and of blood.[24]

8. Artaud: Conclusion

I shall end by discussing passages that are of particular relevance, for in then Artaud himself offers what can be read as his own spontaneous deconstructio or implicit critique of the conceptual foundations of the positive-negativ dichotomy. The passages, from a letter written in 1932, illustrate not only th inseparability of "positive," "negative," and "disorganization" aspects bu also the need for qualitative concepts such as hyperreflexivity and diminishe self-affection.[25]

In the letter, Artaud speaks of his profound sense of exhaustion an burdensome fatigue, of his feelings of emptiness (what he calls "lack o nervous density"), and especially of his "inability to form or to develo thoughts." He compares the latter inability, a kind of thought-blocking, to "th stammering which possesses my outward elocution almost every time I wan to speak," and explains it in the following way: "it is as if each time m thought tries to manifest itself it contracts, and it is this contraction that shut off my thought from within, makes it rigid as in a spasm." At first these ma appear to be negative symptoms, involving a deficit of both thought an energy. However, in the very next sentence, Artaud seems to contradict this telling us that his stammering and thought-blocking actually result from condition of excess — from too many thoughts at once, competing fo attention: "the thought, the expression stops because the flow is too violen because the brain wants to say too many things which it thinks of all at once ten thoughts instead of one rush toward the exit" (293). But a few lines late Artaud reverses himself again, now stating that, at a more profound level, hi mind really *is* too empty, and alluding to what sound like disorganizatio symptoms. "But if one really analyzes a state of this kind it is not by being to full that consciousness errs at these moments but by being too empty, for thi prolific and above all unstable and shifting juxtaposition is an illusion."

It seems that Artaud experiences his consciousness as both too full *an* too empty. This may appear to be a bald contradiction. One can make sense o

, however, if one pays close attention to Artaud's account of his mental ontents. In doing so, one discovers that the "violent flow" of which Artaud peaks does not involve thoughts, images, or feelings of a normal sort (or, for nat matter, of the kind one would be likely to find in mania, delirium, epression, or borderline conditions). It is really a kind of hyperreflexive ascade — a collapse of meta-levels, of hyperabstract meta-perspectives vhose proliferation suggests a loss of perspectival abridgment and natural elf-evidence, and a tendency to experience one's own mind almost as if it vere being seen from the perspective of an outside observer. "The brain," rtaud writes

> sees the whole thought at once with all its circumstances, and it also sees all the points of view it could take and all the forms with which it could invest them, a vast juxtaposition of concepts, each of which seems more necessary and also more dubious than the others, which all the complexities of syntax would never suffice to express and expound. (293)

Iere we have a hyperreflexive proliferation of viewpoints, a slippage among ossible perspectives as well as among perspectives *on* perspectives that rodes any capacity for conceptual or perceptual hold. But this is the counter-art of an *absence* of something more basic — a decline of the vital reactivity nd outer-directedness that would give bias, direction, and a kind of organiza-on to one's thinking. As Artaud explains with his characteristic precision:

> in every [normal] state of consciousness there is always a dominant theme, and if the mind has not *automatically* decided on a dominant theme it is through weakness and because at that moment nothing dominated, nothing presented itself with enough force or continuity in the field of consciousness to be recorded. The truth is, therefore, that rather than an overflow or an excess there was a deficiency; in the absence of some precise thought that was able to develop, there was slackening, confusion, fragility.
>
> It so happens that this slackening, this confusion, this fragility express themselves in an infinite number of ways and correspond to an infinite number of new impressions and sensations, the most characteristic of which is a kind of disappearance or disintegration or collapse of first assumptions which even causes me to wonder why, for example, red (the color) is considered red and affects me as red, why a judgment affects me as a judgment and not as a pain, why I feel a pain, and why this particular pain, which I feel without understanding it… (293–294)

'he simple quantitative concepts of positive and negative clearly will not uffice: Artaud's mind is too full, it seems, precisely *because* it is also too mpty — void of any sense of directedness and of any anchoring set of concerns. But we could also say that his mind is too empty precisely *because* is too full — too full of the products of a kind of maniacal reflexive sel awareness that serves to undermine his sense of natural self-evidence and t destabilize all foundations. (Thus Artaud describes himself as "losing conta *with*" but, at the same time, becoming focally aware *of* "all those fir assumptions which are at the foundation of thought"; 290.) Hyperreflexivit and disturbance of self-affection are two facets of a fundamental qualitativ transformation of the structure of intentionality. Together they provide wh Artaud calls "the destructive element which demineralizes the mind an deprives it of its first assumptions," thereby making "the ground under m thought crumble" (290, 94).

Notes

1. This article is indebted to collaborative work being carried out with Josef Parnas.

2. The primary negative symptoms of schizophrenia can be listed as follows: 1. *Poverty speech*, sometimes called "alogia" — i.e., a tendency to speak very little or not at all; *Affective flattening or blunting*–manifest in unchanging facial expression, paucity expressive gesture or verbal inflection, poor eye contact, and a general lack of soci responsiveness; 3. *Avolition* and *apathy* — manifest in a lack or slowing of spontaneo activity, poor grooming and hygiene, and an "inability to initiate and persist in goal - directed activities" (American Psychiatric Association 1994, DSM IV: 277); 4. *Anh donia* — an apparent dearth of energy or motivation for work, recreation, socializing, sexual activity, and an apparent inability to feel closeness or intimacy with other peop and 5. A *general inattentiveness* to the social or practical world (Andreasen 1989).

3. Charles Mercier, one of Jackson's most prominent disciples, could not have been mo explicit: "In every case of insanity the essential feature is defect," he wrote. "T affection of function is always in the direction of loss, of deficit, or diminution . degradation of action to a lower plane." Defect, he said, is "the underlying disorder up which the other [symptoms] are superimposed, and around which they are clustere (quoted in Clark 1981: 284).

4. Some researchers and theorists have, however, followed Jackson's lead in viewi positive symptoms as release phenomena secondary to deficits of the "higher" ment functions. See, e.g., Weinberger (1987) re the reciprocal relationship between prefront and limbic functions; also Andreasen (1986); both discussed in Sass (1992: 382).

5. Kraepelin considered what we now call schizophrenia to be a form of precocio dementia: "dementia praecox."

6. The transformations of the experiential world that occur in schizophrenia — the wave ing, slippage, and fragmentation of form and meaning inherent in what might be calle the loss of perceptual and conceptual "hold" — are best understood as consequences

these fundamental mutations in the act of consciousness whereby the world of perception and of thought are constituted. In Husserlian terminology, the loss of hold is a feature of the "*noema*" or *object* of awareness; hyperreflexivity and ipseity disturbance are more closely related to the "*noesis*" or essential, constituting *act* of awareness.

The reflective-operative (or reflective — non-reflective) distinction is meant to refer primarily to the *nature* of the phenomenon in question. The basal-consequential-compensatory distinction pertains to its *causal status*. Whereas compensatory hyperreflexivity tends to be of the reflective sort, basal hyperreflexivity tends to be of the operative kind. Consequential hyperreflexivity seems equally likely to be reflective or operative; in this article, however, I will emphasize the reflective forms.

Given these facts, it is now virtually impossible to maintain that the positive, negative, and disorganization syndromes represent distinct *types* of schizophrenia. It is often assumed, however, that they do reflect "discrete pathological processes occurring within a single disease" (Liddle 1987: 150). This latter, somewhat ambiguous claim is difficult to refute. I would argue, however, that it is generally more appropriate to think of positive, negative, and disorganization symptoms as representing distinguishable aspects of a unitary though not entirely homogeneous process.

"Positive symptoms are behaviors that schizophrenic patients engage in, but normals do not. Negative symptoms, when inverted to their opposites … are behaviors which normals engage in but schizophrenics do not, or only in diminished fashion" (Zubin 1985: 462).

). Other methodological problems include that of illusory correlation. Consider, e.g., that a patient with poverty of speech or poverty of content of speech is, *ipso facto*, less likely to manifest Schneiderian first rank symptoms, since, virtually by definition, the latter *require* some kind of understandable verbal report. To what extent is the negative correlation between positive and negative symptoms an artifact of factors like this? A second kind of illusory correlation (positive, in this case) occurs when the correlated items are simply two aspects of the same phenomenon that could hardly help but co-occur. Consider the negative symptoms "avolition" and "poverty of speech," or the disorganization symptoms "tangentiality," "derailment," and "distractibility": are these really distinct items, as is often implied, or have we simply found more than one way of describing and measuring what is essentially the *same* global phenomenon? For additional criticisms, see Parnas and Bovet (1994).

1. I am grateful to my student Cecilia Dintino for calling my attention to a number of relevant references, and for helpful conversation re negative symptoms.

2. Andreasen (1991: 34) reports that she found a low correlation between objective and subjective ratings of negative symptoms. She attributes this to the patients' "poor insight" into their own illness and deficits.

3. In psychiatry, a distinction is often made between "symptoms" and "signs" — with the former term referring to patient reports of abnormal subjective experiences and the latter to behavioral abnormalities that are observable by another person. But the term "symptom" is also used in a broad sense that can include either kind of abnormality; this is the case with the phrase "negative symptoms."

4. A key article by Blankenburg will appear in English translation in a future issue of *Philosophy, Psychiatry, Psychology*.

15. This patient once spoke of "doing six self-analyses simultaneously" and of how h needed to change his living environment often, because he knew that, once everythin around him had been scrutinized, his mind would then turn inward and begin undoin itself, leading him eventually to the feeling of having no real mind at all.

16. For a related point, concerning breakdown of the sense of self due to loss of "higher-lev action identities," see Hemsley (1998); also Sass (1992: 214–241).

17. Anne felt that anything that could be expressed was *ipso facto* inadequate for capturin the pervasive trouble she experienced.

18. In later periods, Artaud tries to overcome self-alienation through anti-intellectual meth ods: first via Dionysian or primitivist ploys, an escape into instinct and sensual intensi (in the period of his most famous work, *The Theatre and Its Double*); later through paradoxical attempt to achieve the condition of inorganic matter. All three periods a discussed in Sass (1996).

19. My translation. The original: "Ce minimum d'absorption de ma pensée dans ma pensé cette fusion du mot et du terme, de l'expression avec la pensée, cet oubli d'un insta donné à tous les hommes et qui leur fait admettre la convenance de l'expression, voilà c qui m'est refusé."

20. Artaud speaks of being "deprived of life, of the nervous irradiation of existence," ar even felt at times that he had to provide his own sense of aliveness: "I am the Generator my own vitality" (110).

21. Husserl's conception of passive synthesis or genesis is an obscure and somewhat ne glected topic. For discussion, see Mishara 1990; Heinsen 1982: 162–165.

22. Merleau-Ponty's distinction between body image and body schema parallels in som respects the distinction I am making here, although the emphasis of his body-schem notion seems to focus more on the body as a system of motor functions rather than as more general, transcendental condition of all experience. Hence I use the phrase "boc subject" or "corporeal subject" in this article. I am grateful to Shaun Gallagher for helpf conversation on this issue.

23. We now know that emotion-related, spontaneous movement sequences and deliberate voluntary actions are actually triggered in two different parts of the brain (Damas 1994: 140). The facial expressions of a person who relies on deliberation and volition control will therefore look awkward, artificial, and unconvincing — as often seems th case in schizophrenia. As an illustration, consider the strangely off-putting self-portrai by Messerschmidt, a psychotic sculptor of the 18th century (Kris 1964).

24. One might contrast this seemingly self-contradictory image of rootlets at the corners c the mind's eye with the harmonious synthesis of mind and matter and of inner and out that is implied in Merleau-Ponty's (1968) notion of "the flesh" or the "fold" (which wa mentioned above). The notions of the "flesh" and the "fold" are meant to place huma beings in the shared physical and social world — a world composed neither of me matter nor of disembodied spirit, and that a person does not just witness from afar b rather participates in or literally partakes of. The post-Cartesian tendencies towa dualism and solipsism that Merleau-Ponty is attempting to overcome seem to be exace bated in the mode of existence implied by the image of the rootlets. The latter imag

exemplifies Michel Foucault's (1970) notion of the "empirico-transcendental doublet" characteristic of modern thought, discussed in Sass (1992: 327–333; 1994: 80–85).

5. It is worth noting that the usual conception of the so-called "disorganization syndrome" also relies on a deceivingly simple quantitative model: the notion of a diminishment or absence of organization. When one takes a closer look at actual persons with schizophrenia, what one often finds are unconventional or alternative *kinds* of organization — e.g., various types of perspectival shift or drift that dissolve the sustained "perspectival abridgement" necessary for practical action or clear communication (Holzman, Shenton, Solovay 1986) while often encouraging hyperreflexive preoccupations of a hyper-abstract or quasi-philosophical kind (Sass 1992: 119–173).

References

American Psychiatric Association (1994). *Diagnostic and Statistical Manual of Mental Disorders* (DSM IV). Washington D.C.: American Psychiatric Press.

Andreasen, N. (1982). Negative symptoms in schizophrenia. *Archives of General Psychiatry* 39: 784–788.

Andreasen, N. (1984). *The Broken Brain: The Biological Revolution in Psychiatry.* New York: Harper and Row.

Andreasen, N. (1986). Is schizophrenia a temperolimbic disease? In Andreasen (ed.). *Can Schizophrenia be Localized in the Brain?* Washington D.C.: American Psychiatric Press.

Andreasen, N. (1989). Scale of the assessment of negative symptoms (SANS). *British Journal of Psychiatry* 155 (Suppl. 7): 53–58.

Andreasen, N., Nopoulos, P., Schultz, S. et al. (1994). Positive and negative symptoms of schizophrenia: Past, present, and future. *Acta Psychiatrica Scandinavica*, Supplementum 90 (384, Suppl.): 51–59

Angyal, A. (1936). The experience of the body-self in schizophrenia. *Archives of Neurology and Psychiatry* 35: 1029–1053.

Arieti, S. (1978). Volition and value: A study based on catatonic schizophrenia. In Arieti, *On Schizophrenia, Phobias, Depression, Psychotherapy, and the Farther Shores of Psychiatry.* New York: Brunner/Mazel.

Artaud, A. (1965). *Antonin Artaud Anthology*, edited by Jack Hirschman. San Francisco CA: City Lights Books.

Artaud, A. (1976). *Antonin Artaud: Selected Writings*, edited by Susan Sontag, translated by Helen Weaver. New York: Farrar, Straus, and Giroux.

Artaud, A. (1976b). *Oeuvres Completes, Tome I* (Textes Surrealistes, Lettres). Paris: Gallimard.

Berenbaum, H. and Oltmanns, T. F. (1992). Emotional experience and expression in schizophrenia and depression. *Journal of Abnormal Psychology* 101: 37–44.

Bermudez, J. L. (1998). *The Paradox of Self-Consciousness.* Cambridge MA: MIT Press.

Berrios, G. E. (1985). Positive and negative symptoms and Jackson. *Archives of General Psychiatry* 42.

Blankenburg, W. (1971). Der *Verlust der Natürlichen Selbstverständlichkeit: Ein Beitra zur Psychopathologie Symptomarmer Schizophrenien.* Stuttgart: Ferdinand Enk Verlag.

Blankenburg, W. (1991). *La perte de l'evidence naturelle: une contribution à l psychopathologie des schizophrenies pauci-symptomatiques*, translated by J.-M. Azori and Y. Totoyan. Paris: Presses Universitaires de France.

Bosch, R. J. van den, Rombouts, R. P., van Asma, M. J. O. (1993). Subjective cognitiv dysfunction in schizophrenic and depressed patients. *Comprehensive Psychiatry* 34 130–136.

Bouricius, J. (1989). Negative symptoms and emotions in schizophrenia. *Schizophreni Bulletin* 15: 201–208.

Clark, M. J. (1981). The rejection of psychological approaches to mental disorder in lat nineteenth-century British Psychiatry. In A. Scull (ed.), *Madhouses, Mad-Doctors, an Madmen: The Social History of Psychiatry in the Victorian Era.* Philadelphia: Unive sity of Pennsylvania Press, 271–312.

Cutting, J. and Dunne, F. (1989). Subjective experience of schizophrenia. *Schizophreni Bulletin* 15: 217–231.

Cutting, J. and Murphy, D. (1988). Schizophrenic thought disorder: A psychological an organic interpretation. *British Journal of Psychiatry* 152: 310–319.

Cutting, J. and Murphy, D. (1990). Impaired ability of schizophrenics, relative to manics c depressives, to appreciate social knowledge about their culture. *British Journal c Psychiatry* 157: 355–358.

Damasio, A. R. (1994). *Descartes' Error: Emotion, Reason, and the Human Brain.* Ne York: Avon Books.

Foucault, M. (1970). *The Order of Things: An Archaeology of the Human Sciences.* Ne York: Vintage.

Gallagher, S. and Meltzoff, A. (1996). The earliest sense of self and others: Merleau-Pont and recent developmental studies. *Philosophical Psychology* 9: 211–233.

Gibson, J. J. (1979). *The Ecological Approach to Visual Perception.* Boston: Houghto Mifflin.

Grene, M. (1968). Tacit knowing and the pre-reflective cogito. In Langford, T. A. an Poteat, W. H. (eds.), *Intellect and Hope: Essays in the Thought of Michael Polany* Durham NC: Duke University Press, 19–57.

Häfner, H., Maurer, K., Loeffler, W., Heiden, W. an der, Munk-Jørgensen, P., Hambrech M., Riecher-Rossler, A. (1998). The ABC schizophrenia study: A preliminary overvie of the results. *Social Psychiatry and Psychiatric Epidemiology* 33: 380–386.

Heidegger, M. (1962). *Being and Time*, translated by J. Macquarrie and E. Robinson. Ne York: Harper and Row.

Heinsen, D. (1982). Husserl's theory of the pure ego. In H. Dreyfus (ed.), *Husser Intentionality, and Cognitive Science.* Cambridge MA: MIT Press, 147–168.

Hemsley, D. R. (1998). The disruption of the "sense of self" in schizophrenia: potenti links with disturbances of information processing. *British Journal of Medical Psycho ogy* 71: 115–124.

Holzman, P. S., Shenton, M. E., Solovay, M. R. (1986). Quality of thought disorder i differential diagnosis. *Schizophrenia Bulletin* 12: 360–372.

Hunt, H. T. (1985). Cognition and states of consciousness. *Perceptual and Motor Skills* 60: 239–282.

Hunt, H. T. (1995). *On the Nature of Consciousness.* New Haven CN: Yale University Press.

Klosterkötter, J. (1992). The meaning of basic symptoms for the development of schizophrenic psychoses. *Neurology, Psychiatry, and Brain Research* 1: 30–41.

Knapp, B. (1969). *Antonin Artaud: Man of Vision.* New York: David Lewis.

Kring, A. M., Kerr, S. L., Smith, D. A. et al. (1993). Flat affect in schizophrenia does not reflect diminished subjective experience of emotion. *Journal of Abnormal Psychology* 102: 507–517.

Kring, A. M. and Neale, J. (1996). Do schizophrenic patients show a disjunctive relationship among expressive, experiential, and psychophysiological components of emotion? *Journal of Abnormal Psychology* 105: 249–257.

Kris, E. (1964). *Psychoanalytic Explorations in Art.* New York: Schocken.

Laing, R. D. (1965). *The Divided Self.* Harmondsworth UK: Penguin.

Liddle, P. F. (1987). The symptoms of chronic schizophrenia: A re-examination of the positive-negative dichotomy. *British Journal of Psychiatry* 151: 145–151.

Liddle, P. F., Carpenter, W. T., Crow, T. (1994). Syndromes of schizophrenia: Classic Literature. *British Journal of Psychiatry* 165: 721–727.

Marneros, A., Andreasen, N. C., Tsuang, M. T. (eds.) (1991). *Negative versus Positive Schizophrenia.* Berlin: Springer-Verlag.

Maurer, K. and Häfner, H. (1991). Dependence, independence, or interdependence of positive and negative symptoms. In Marneros, A.; Andreasen, N.C.; Tsuang, M. T. (eds.), *Negative versus Positive Schizophrenia.* Berlin: Springer-Verlag, 160–182.

McGlashan, T. H. (1982). Aphanasis: The phenomenon of pseudo-depression in schizophrenia. *Schizophrenia Bulletin* 8: 118–134.

McGlashan, T. H. and Fenton, W. S. (1992). The positive-negative distinction in schizophrenia: Review of natural history indicators. *Archives of General Psychiatry* 49: 63–72.

Mellor, C. S. (1970). First rank symptoms of schizophrenia. *British Journal of Psychiatry* 117: 15–23.

Merleau-Ponty, M. (1945). *Phénoménologie de la Perception.* Paris: Gallimard.

Merleau-Ponty, M. (1962). *The Phenomenology of Perception*, translated by C. Smith. New York: Routledge and Kegan Paul.

Merleau-Ponty, M. (1968). *The Visible and the Invisible,* translated by A. Lingis. Evanston IL: Northwestern University Press.

Mishara, A. L. (1990). Husserl and Freud: Time, memory, and the unconscious. *Husserl Studies* 7: 29–58.

Parnas, J. (2000). The self and intentionality in the pre-psychotic stages of schizophrenia. (this volume).

Parnas, J. and Bovet, P. (1991). Autism in schizophrenia revisited. *Comprehensive Psychiatry* 32: 7–21.

Parnas, J. and Bovet, P. (1994). Negative/positive symptoms of schizophrenia: Clinical and conceptual issues. *Nord. J. Psychiatry* Suppl. 31: 6–14.

Parnas, J., Jansson, L., Sass, L. A., Handest, P. (1998). Self-experience in the prodromal phases of schizophrenia: A pilot study of first admissions. *Neurology, Psychiatry, and*

Brain Research 6: 97–106.
Polanyi, M. (1964). *Personal Knowledge*. New York: Harper Torchbooks.
Polanyi, M. (1967). *The Tacit Dimension*. Garden City, New York: Anchor Books.
Polanyi, M. (1968). Sense-giving and sense-reading. In Langford, T. A. and Poteat, W. H (eds), *Intellect and Hope: Essays in the Thought of Michael Polanyi*. Durham, NC Duke University Press, 402–431.
Sass, L. (1992). *Madness and Modernism: Insanity in the Light of Modern Art, Literature and Thought*. New York: Basic Books. (Harvard Paperback 1994)
Sass, L. (1994). *The Paradoxes of Delusion: Wittgenstein, Schreber, and the Schizophrenic Mind*. Ithaca N.Y.: Cornell University Press.
Sass, L. (1995). Antonin Artaud, modernism, and the yearning for a "private language." In K. S. Johannessen & T. Nordenstam (Eds.), *Culture and Value* (papers from 18th International Wittgenstein Symposium). Kirchberg, Austria: Austrian Ludwig Wittgenstein Society, 255–260.
Sass, L. (1996). "The catastrophes of heaven": Modernism, primitivism, and the madness of Antonin Artaud. *Modernism/Modernity* (special issue: The mind of modernism: Culture, psychology, and medicine) 3: 73–92.
Selten, J.-P. (1995). *The Subjective Experience of Negative Symptoms*. Doctoral dissertation, University of Groningen, Holland.
Selten, J.-P., Sijben, A. E., Bosch, R. J. van den, Omloo-Visser, H. I., Warmerdam, (1993). The subjective experience of negative symptoms: A self-rating scale. *Comprehensive Psychiatry* 34: 1–6.
Selten, J.-P., Bosch, R. J. van den, Sijben, A. E. S. (1998). The subjective experience of negative symptoms. In X. F. Amador and A. S. David (eds), *Insight and Psychosis*. New York: Oxford University Press, 78–90.
Sommers, A. A. (1985). Negative symptoms: Conceptual and methodological problems. *Schizophrenia Bulletin* 11: 364–379.
Stengel, E. (1963). Hughlings Jackson's influence in psychiatry. *British Journal of Psychiatry* 109: 348–355.
Störring, G. (1987). Perplexity. In J. Cutting and M. Shepherd (eds.), *The Clinical Roots of the Schizophrenia Concept*. Cambridge, UK: Cambridge University Press, 79–82 (ori published 1939).
Weinberger, D. R. (1987). Implications of normal brain development for the pathogenesis of schizophrenia. *Archives of General Psychiatry* 44.
Zubin, J. (1985). Negative symptoms: Are they indigenous to schizophrenia? *Schizophrenia Bulletin* 11: 461–469.

PART III

Monitoring the Self in Schizophrenia

The Role of Internal Models

Sarah-Jayne Blakemore
Wellcome Department of Cognitive Neurology

ntroduction

n this paper I will discuss a series of studies that investigate how we recognize ne sensory consequences of our own actions. The studies are based on an stablished model of normal motor learning and control. In the first part of the hapter I shall summarize the components of this model of motor control, and xplain how an impairment of the model could lead to certain positive symp- oms associated with schizophrenia. In the second part I shall describe psycho- hysical and functional neuroimaging experiments investigating the normal ehavioral and physiological basis of the components of the model described n the first part. In the final section, preliminary results of psychophysical xperiment involving patients with auditory hallucinations and passivity phe- omena will be discussed in the context of an impairment of the functioning of ne model.

. An outline of the motor control system

ur sensory systems are constantly bombarded by a multitude of sensory timuli, from which we must extract the few stimuli which correspond to nportant changes within the environment. One class of stimuli that are in nost circumstances of little biological importance are those that arise as a ecessary consequence of our own motor actions. Humans can readily detect whether sensory signals are the result of self-generated actions or othe environmental events. The mechanisms underlying this ability are likely t have adaptive value. The ability to distinguish the source of sensory signal permits both the monitoring of ongoing actions, and information about nev environmental events. It is proposed that knowledge of our intentions or motc commands is used to distinguish the sensory consequences of our own action from externally produced sensory stimuli (Jeannerod 1988; Frith 199 Wolpert et al. 1995; Decety 1996; Jeannerod 1997; Wolpert 1997). In order t achieve this, some kind of central monitor (Frith 1992) or internal "forwar model" (Ito 1970; Wolpert et al. 1995) has been postulated. These model capture the forward or causal relationship between actions, as signaled by a *efference copy* of the motor command (Von Holst 1954), and the sensor outcome. It is proposed that efference copy signals are used to make prediction of the sensory consequences (*corollary discharge*; Sperry 1950) c the motor act, and this prediction is then compared with the actual conse quences of such an act. These mechanisms have been the subject of muc investigation, mainly in the oculomotor domain.

Helmholtz (1867) noted that when making eye movements, the percept c the world remains stable, despite the movement of the retinal image. H suggested that the *effort of will* involved in making eye movements contain information about the sensory consequences of the eye movement, which i sent to the visual areas in order for perceptual compensation to occur. Vo Holst (1954) investigated this hypothesis and, on the basis of empiric findings, suggested that when sending motor commands to move the eyes th motor areas of the brain send a parallel efference copy to the visual areas. Thi predicts the sensory consequences (corollary discharge) of the movement an this prediction allows the visual system to compensate for retinal displaceme during voluntary eye movements (Sperry 1950). Although these mechanism have mainly been studied with reference to eye movements, it appears th sensory predictions produced in conjunction with motor commands are n restricted to eye movements, but also provide perceptual stability in th context of all self-produced actions. Our ability to monitor, and recognize a our own, self-generated limb movements, touch, speech and thoughts sugges the existence of a more general mechanism (Frith 1992).

.1. *Internal models*

t is proposed that this "self-monitoring" mechanism involves an internal epresentation of the motor system. Making movements involves the production of an appropriate sequence of muscle contractions in accordance with the notor command. At the same time, sensory feedback from the movements is ritical for deciding what movements to make and for observing the consequences of those movements. In order to accomplish smooth movements and ecognize them as our own, it is possible to consider internal representations, mplemented by neural circuitry, that mimic aspects of the external transfornations. Such internal transformations are known as *internal models.*

.2. *Forward models*

elf-produced events can be recognized and discounted by using the sensory rediction errors made by an internal forward model (Figure 1). Forward nodels capture the forward or causal relationship between actions and outomes by using an efference copy of the motor command (Ito 1970; Wolpert t al. 1995). Based on the efference copy produced in parallel with the motor ommand, the forward model predicts the sensory consequences of movenent. This prediction is then compared with the actual sensory feedback (refference) from the movement. Self-produced sensations can be correctly redicted on the basis of the motor command, and there will therefore be little r no error from the comparison between predicted and actual sensory feedack. As the error from this comparison increases so does the likelihood that he sensation is externally produced. By using such a system it is possible to ancel out the effects on sensation induced by self-motion and thereby distinuish sensory events due to self-produced motion from the sensory feedback aused by the environment, such as contact with objects.

.3. *Monitoring self-produced actions in schizophrenia*

rith (1992) proposed that a defect in central self-monitoring might underlie uditory hallucinations and passivity phenomena experienced by people with chizophrenia. Auditory hallucinations are common in schizophrenia, and ormally consist of hearing spoken speech or voices (Hoffman 1986). Many atients with schizophrenia describe passivity (delusions of control) experi-

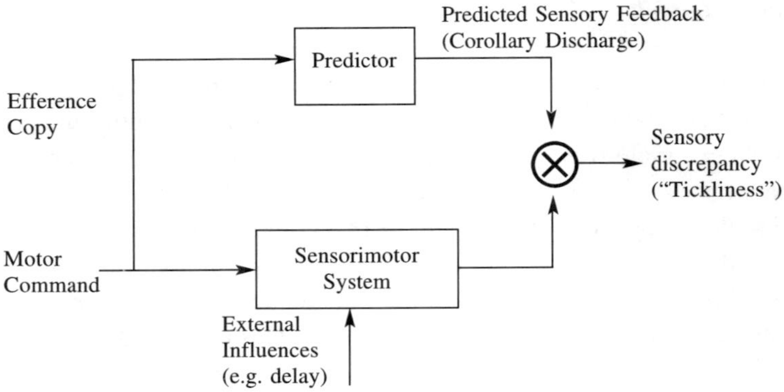

Figure 1: A model for determining the sensory consequences of a movement. An interna forward model makes predictions of the sensory feedback based on the motor command These predictions are then compared to the actual sensory feedback to produce the sensor prediction errors. Self-produced sensations can be correctly predicted on the basis of th motor command, and there will therefore be little or no sensory discrepancy from th comparison between predicted and actual sensory feedback. As the sensory discrepanc from this comparison increases so does the likelihood that the sensation is externall produced. By using such a system it is possible to cancel out the effects on sensatio induced by self-motion and thereby distinguish sensory events due to self-produced motio from the sensory feedback caused by the environment, such as contact with objects.

ences in which their thoughts, speech, actions, feelings and drives have bee replaced or influenced by those of external agents rather than being produce by their own will: "My fingers pick up the pen, but I don't control them. Wha they do is nothing to do with me"; "The force moved my lips. I began to speak The words were made for me"(Mellor 1970). In most cases the actions mad when the patient "feels" that he or she is being controlled by alien forces ar not discrepant with his or her intentions. Thus the patient may be correctl performing the task set by the experimenter (e.g. making random movement of a joystick) at the same time as having the experience of passivity. He/sh does not try to correct these "controlled" actions or prevent them fron occurring. Clearly actions are being correctly selected and irrelevant affor dances are being suppressed.

There is evidence that the auditory hallucinations experienced by schizo phrenic patients are caused by their own inner speech. Originally Goul (1949) amplified the subvocal activity observed in a hallucinating schizo hrenic patient with a microphone. He found that this activity represented vhispered speech that was qualitatively different from the patient's own 'oluntary whispers. Moreover what the whispered voice said corresponded to he report given by the patient of her hallucinations. Green and Preston (1981) ave more recently replicated this result. Further evidence suggesting that allucinations are the consequence of subvocal speech came from studies howing that it is possible to suppress them by occupying the speech muscula-ure by holding the mouth wide open (Bick and Kinsbourne 1987).

Frith (1988) suggested that these abnormal experiences arise through a ack of awareness of intended actions. Such an impairment might cause houghts or actions to become isolated from the sense of will normally ssociated with them. This would result in the interpretation of internally enerated voices or thoughts as external voices (auditory hallucinations and hought insertion), and of one's own movements and speech as externally aused (passivity or delusions of control). We have suggested that the experi-nce of passivity arises from a lack of awareness of the predicted limb position ased on the forward model (Frith et al. 1999). In the absence of such wareness the patient cannot correct errors prior to peripheral feedback and is ot aware of the exact specification of the movement. Thus the patient is ware of the intention to move and of the movement having occurred, but is ot aware of having initiated the movement. It is as if the movement, although ntended, has been initiated by some external force. In a variation on this heme, Spence (1996) has suggested that the problem is to do with the timing f awareness. The awareness of the actual outcome of the movement precedes he awareness of the predicted outcome which is contrary to the normal xperience of our own agency.

There is nothing obviously abnormal in the motor control of these pa-ients. However, there are subtle problems consistent with a lack of awareness f predicted actions. Two experiments, in which subjects had to correct their rrors very rapidly in the absence of visual feedback, found evidence that entral monitoring is faulty in schizophrenia (Frith and Done 1989; Malenka t al. 1982). Normal control subjects were adept at this task, suggesting that hey monitor the response intended (via corollary discharge) and do not need o wait for external feedback about the response that actually occurred. In both xperiments, schizophrenic patients failed to correct their errors in the absence f feedback.

2. Experiments exploring the components of the forward model

2.1. *Perception of the sensory consequences of actions*

"If the action were actually executed, the content of the motor representation would not reach consciousness because it would be cancelled as soon as the corresponding movements were executed (perhaps by the incoming signals generated by the execution itself" (Jeannerod 1994).

Evidence suggests that the sensory consequences of some self-generated movements are perceived differently from identical sensory input when it is externally generated. The attenuation of the perception during self-produced movements is well documented in humans (Angel & Malenka 1982; Chapman et al. 1987; Milne et al. 1988; Collins et al. 1998). An example of such differential perception is the phenomenon that people cannot tickle themselves (e.g. Weiskrantz et al. 1971; Claxton 1975). In Weiskrantz et al.'s (1971) psychophysical study, a tactile stimulus that transversed the sole of the subject's foot was administered by the experimenter, the subject. Subjects rated the self-administered tactile stimulus as less tickly than the externally administered tactile stimulus. When the stimulation was associated with passive arm movements tickle strength was reduced, but not to the level of the self-administered tactile stimulus. The authors attributed the differences in response to the mode of delivery: self-administered tactile stimulation produces both efference copy in accordance with the motor command and re-afference produced by the arm movement; passive arm movement produces only re-afference and externally administered tactile stimulation produces neither efference copy nor re-afference. The authors therefore concluded that although re-afference plays a role, the attenuation signal is based mainly on the efference copy signal produced in concordance with a self-generated movement.

By employing a robotic interface we firstly attempted to replicate Weiskrantz et al.'s findings by investigating whether the perception of the tactile stimulation is modified by a causative self-generated action. In the self-produced tactile stimulus condition 16 normal subjects were required to move an object attached to an optical encoder sinusoidally with their left hand. The motion of this object determined the position of a second robotic motor, on which was mounted a piece of soft foam, which made contact with the subject's right palm. The motion of the left hand therefore determined the tactile stimulus on the right palm. In the externally produced tactile stimulus condition the obotic motor was programmed to produce the sinusoidal tactile stimulus on the ubjects' right palm. Subjects were instructed to rate the sensation on their palm n a scale from 0 (not at all) to 10 (extremely) intense, painful, tickly, pleasant nd irritating. The results showed that they consistently rated a self-produced actile sensation on their palm as being significantly ($P<0.001$) less tickly, ntense and pleasant than an identical stimulus produced by a robot (Figure 2; 3lakemore et al. 1999a).

.2. *The physiological basis of the perceptual modulation of self-produced sensory stimuli*

Neurophysiological data demonstrate that neuronal responses in somatosen-ory cortex are attenuated by self-generated movement. For example, active ouch is "gated" in primary somatosensory cortex of rats (Chapin & Woodward 982) and monkeys (Jiang et al. 1991; Chapman & Ageranioti-Belanger 1991; Chapman 1994) compared to passive and external touch of an identical tactile timulus. For example, neuronal activity in somatosensory areas 3b, 1 and 2 in nonkeys was attenuated when monkeys scanned their hand over a surface exture compared to when their hand was passively moved over the same

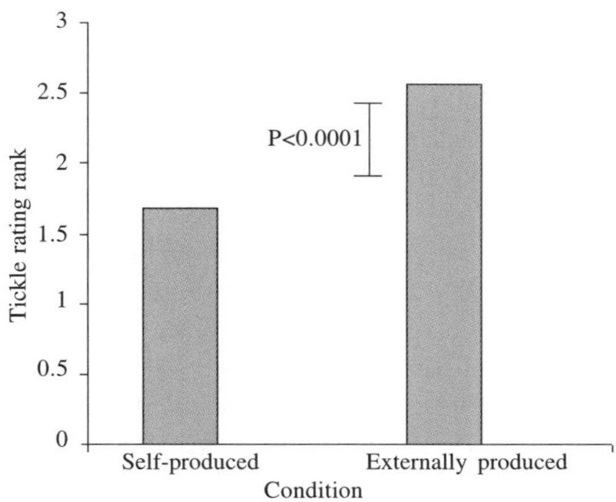

igure 2: Graph to show "tickly" rating ranks for self-produced and externally produced actile stimulation conditions in normal subjects. There was a significant difference between atings for these two conditions.

surface, or when the surface moved underneath their hand (Chapman 1994).

The perceptual attenuation of tactile sensation associated with self-pro duced actions in humans (Weiskrantz et al. 1971; Angel & Malenka 1982 Chapman et al. 1987; Milne et al. 1988; Collins et al. 1998; Blakemore et al 1999) could be due to this movement-related gating of activity in somatosen sory cortex. If this is the case, a further question is how is the modulation o somatosensory responses to self-produced tactile stimuli mediated? In orde for somatosensory cortex activity to be attenuated to self-produced sensory stimuli, these stimuli need to be predicted accurately. The cerebellum is a likely site for a "forward model" of the motor apparatus that provides predic tions of the sensory consequences of motor commands, which are then com pared with the actual sensory feedback from the movement. Evidence for thi supposition comes from computational (Ito 1970; Paulin 1989; Miall et al 1993; Wolpert et al. 1998) and neurophysiological data (Oscarsson 1980 Gellman et al. 1985; Andersson & Armstrong 1985; Andersson & Armstrong 1987; Simpson et al. 1995). The cerebellum is proposed to be a component o the forward model system that provides a precise prediction of the sensory consequences of motor commands that, when congruent with the actua sensory feedback, is used to cancel the percept of a tactile stimulus. The mai input to the cerebellum, the climbing fibres from the inferior olive, has bee proposed to act as a comparator between intended and achieved movement signalling errors in motor performance (Oscarsson 1980). Evidence for thi comes from electrophysiological studies demonstrating that neurons in th inferior olive of cats respond to passively applied cutaneous stimuli but not t similar stimuli produced by a voluntary movement of the cat (except whe stimuli were unexpectedly encountered during movement; Gellman et al 1985). Similarly, Andersson & Armstrong (1985; 1987) demonstrated tha inferior olive neurons fire when a cat walking on a horizontal ladder encoun ters a rung that unexpectedly gives way. Therefore inferior olivary neuron have been proposed to act as somatic "event detectors" responding particu larly reliably to unexpected stimuli (Oscarsson 1980; Simpson et al. 1995).

Using functional Magnetic Resonance Imaging (fMRI) we examined th neural basis of the differential perception of self- and externally produce tactile stimuli in humans (Blakemore et al. 1998). Six normal subjects wer scanned while a tactile stimulation device allowed a sinusoidal tactile stimulu (a piece of soft foam moving at 2 Hz; amplitude 1.5 cm) to be applied to th subject's left palm either by their right hand or by the experimenter. T examine the neural correlates of self-produced tactile stimuli we employed a factorial design with two factors: 1. self-generated movement of the right hand vs. rest; and 2. tactile stimulation on the left hand vs. no stimulation. There were four conditions: self-generated tactile stimulation; self-generated movement without tactile stimulation; externally generated tactile stimulation; and rest. Using this design we were able to assess what brain activity is unique to the self-generated tactile stimulation condition by factoring out activity associated with self-generated movement or tactile stimulation alone. Analysis of the imaging data resulted in the creation of statistical parametric maps (Friston et al. 1990) reflecting the two main effects, movement and tactile stimulation, and the interaction between these two factors.

We found an increase in activity of somatosensory cortex (Figure 3) and the anterior cingulate gyrus (Brodmann Areas 24/32; Figure 4) when subjects experienced an externally produced tactile stimulus on their left palm relative to a self-produced tactile stimulus. The reduction in activity in these areas to self-produced tactile stimuli might be the physiological correlate of the reduced perception associated with this type of stimulation (Weiskrantz et al. 1971; Blakemore et al. 1999). In particular, the activity in the anterior cingulate may have been related to the increased tickliness and pleasantness of externally produced compared to self-produced tactile stimuli. Previous studies have implicated this area in affective behaviour (Vogt et al. 1992; Vogt &

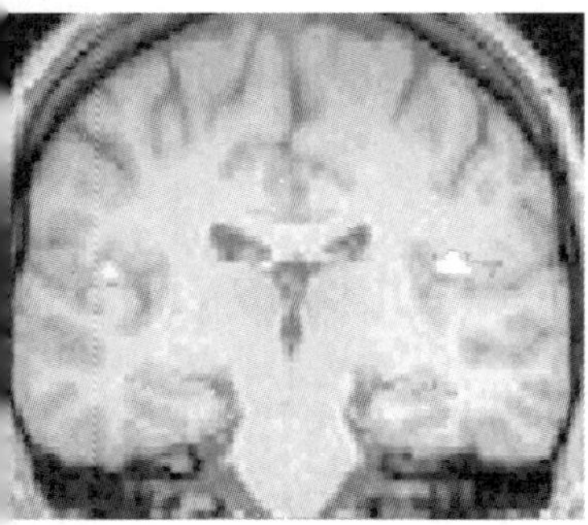

Figure 3: The bilateral secondary somatosensory cortex was significantly more activated by externally produced tactile stimulation than by self-produced tactile stimulation.

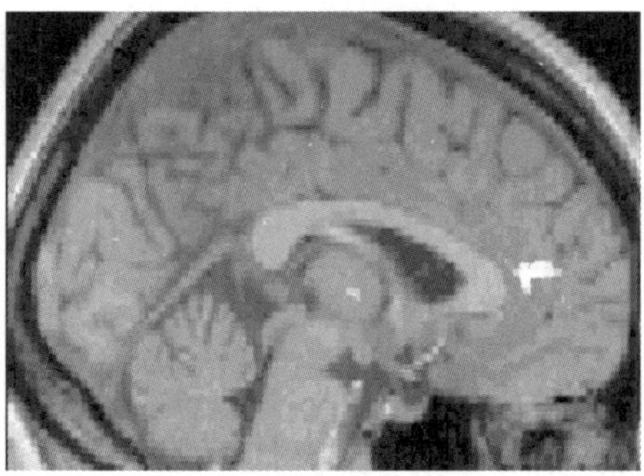

Figure 4: The anterior cingulate cortex was significantly more activated by externally produced tactile stimulation than by self-produced tactile stimulation.

Gabriel 1993) and have shown that rats will self-stimulate this site, suggestin that it is a site of positive reinforcement (Porrino 1993).

While the changes in the anterior cingulate and somatosensory corte might underlie the perception of tactile stimuli, the pattern of brain activity w observed in the cerebellum suggests that this area is the source of the soma tosensory modulation. In somatosensory areas activity was attenuated by al movement: they were equally activated by movement that did and that did no result in tactile stimulation. In contrast, the right anterior cerebellar cortex wa selectively deactivated by self-produced movement which resulted in a tactil stimulus, but not by movement alone, and significantly activated by externall produced tactile stimulation (Figure 5). This pattern suggests that the cerebel lum differentiates between movements depending on their specific sensor consequences. We suggest that the cerebellum is involved in predicting th specific sensory consequences of movements, and in providing the signal tha is used to attenuate the somatosensory response to self-produced tactile stimu lation. The inhibition of somatosensory cortex by self-generated movement could result from the comparison between predicted and actual sensory feed back, which takes place in the cerebellum. When a tactile stimulus is self produced it can be accurately predicted by the cerebellum. In this case ther will be little or no sensory discrepancy between the predicted and actua sensory consequences of a movement, and this accurate prediction provide the signal that is used to cancel the somatosensory response to self-produce tactile stimulation.

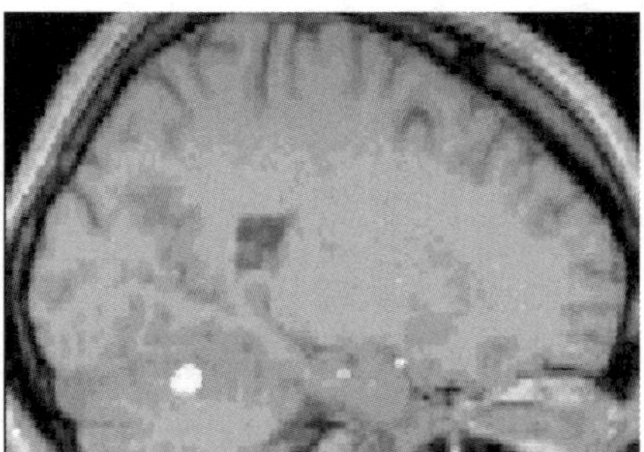

Figure 5: The right anterior cerebellar cortex was significantly more activated by externall produced tactile stimulation than by self-produced tactile stimulation.

2.3. *Perceptual responses to parametric manipulations of the sensory consequences of movement*

We then investigated whether normal subjects' perceptual ratings are affected by perturbing the correspondence between the movement of the left hand and the tactile stimulus on the right hand. In order to investigate this, we introduced parametrically varied degrees of delay between the movement and the tactile stimulation. We predicted that increasing the delay would increase the intensity of the sensation since the stimulus would no longer correspond exactly to the efference copy produced in parallel with the motor command, and therefore could not be accurately predicted.

16 normal subjects were asked to rate the perception of a tactile stimulus on their right palm. By using two robots so that the tactile stimulus could be delivered under remote control by the subject, delays of 0, 100, 200 and 300 ms were introduced between the movement of the left hand and the tactile stimulus on the right palm. The 0 ms condition corresponded to the normal situation in which subjects use their left hand to move a physical rod across the palm of their right palm. Subjects were not informed of the presence of these delays. Subjects reported a progressive increase in the tickly rating as the delay was increased between 0 ms and 200 ms ($P<0.0005$; Figure 6). Under all delays the left hand made the same movement and the right hand experienced

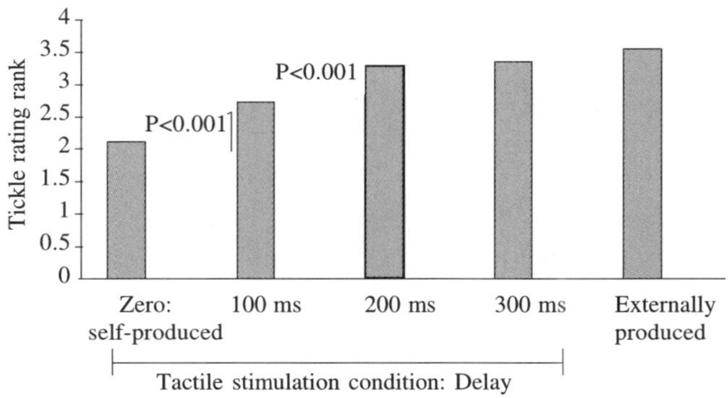

Figure 6: Graph to show that the perception ("tickliness") of a tactile stimulus increase with increasing delay (up to 200 ms) between the movement of the left hand and the tactile stimulus on right hand in normal subjects.

the same stimulus. Only the temporal correspondence between the action of the left hand and the sensory effect on the right hand was altered. These results suggest that the perceptual attenuation of self-produced tactile stimulation is due to a precise attenuation of the sensory feedback, based on specific temporal sensory predictions, rather than a non-specific attenuation of all sensory signals.

We interpreted these results in terms of the sensory prediction errors made by a forward model (Figure 1). Our results demonstrate that the closer the system is to direct contact between the hands the more the sensory re-afference will be attenuated. When there is no delay the model correctly predicts the sensory consequences of the movement, so no sensory discrepancy ensues between the predicted and actual sensory information. In this case the motor command to the left hand can be used to cancel predictively the sensation on the right hand. As the sensory feedback deviates from the prediction of the model (by increasing the delay) the error between predicted and actual sensory feedback increases. This leads to a decrease in the amount of attenuation possible and a relative increase in the intensity of sensation experienced on the right hand. Our results demonstrate that the tickly rating is minimal with zero delay and increases smoothly as the delay increases up to a certain point (200 ms), at which stage the sensation becomes indistinguishable from an externally produced sensation. Interestingly, only two (out of 16) subjects reported being aware of any anomaly of the stimulus in the delay conditions: most subjects were not aware of the delay. Thus, a precise forward model seems to be in operation that is sensitive even to small changes in the correspondence, including those unavailable to conscious awareness.

2.4. *Neural responses to parametric manipulations of the sensory consequences of movement*

We subsequently used $H_2{}^{15}O$ Positron Emission Tomography (PET) to examine brain responses to self-produced tactile stimuli in which the correspondence between movement and its sensory consequences was parametrically varied (Blakemore, S-J et al., 1999b). Six subjects were scanned while self-generating a tactile sensation on the palm of their left hand, by moving a robotic arm with their right hand. Again, delays of 0, 100, 200 and 300 ms were introduced between the movement of the right hand and the tactile stimulus on the left palm. In all conditions the movement made by the subject was the same (the motion of the right hand always determined the tactile sensation on the left palm). Subjects reported a progressive increase in the intense and tickly ratings as the delay was increased from 0 to 300 ms, replicating our previous results (Blakemore et al. 1999a). In addition, in accordance with our predictions, activity in the right cerebellum was positively correlated with delay.

These results support the proposal that the cerebellum is involved in signaling the sensory discrepancy between the predicted and actual sensory consequences of movements. When there is zero delay the model is able to predict correctly the sensory consequences of the movement so no sensory discrepancy ensues between the predicted and actual sensory feedback. In this case cerebellar activity will be low and the motor command sent to the right hand can be used to attenuate predictively the sensation on the left hand. As the sensory feedback deviates from the prediction of the model (by increasing the delay) the sensory discrepancy between the predicted and actual sensory feedback increases, causing an increase in cerebellar activity. This leads to a decrease in the amount of perceptual attenuation possible and a relative increase of the intensity of sensation experienced on the left hand.

3. The perception of self-produced sensory stimuli in patients with auditory hallucinations and passivity

A breakdown in self-monitoring might result in the failure in the modulation of self-produced stimuli that is seen in normal subjects. According to Frith (1992), auditory hallucinations and passivity experiences could be associated with breakdown in self-monitoring, and therefore patients with these symptoms might be abnormally aware of the sensory consequences of their own movements. If this is the case, they would not distinguish between self- and externally produced sensations. We sought to evaluate whether patients with these symptoms differentiate between tactile stimuli that are self- and externally produced (Blakemore, S-J et al. 2000). Age-matched patients with a diagnosis of schizophrenia, depression or manic-depression were divided into two groups according to the presence (n=15) or absence (n=23) of auditory hallucinations and/or passivity experiences according to the P.A.N.N.S. interview (Kay et al. 1987). These patient groups and a group of 15 age-matched normal control subjects were asked to rate a tactile sensation on the palm of their left hand that was produced either by movement of their right hand or by the experimenter. In order to obtain an objective assessment of the ability of subjects to rate a tactile sensation, in a control task subjects were asked to rate the "roughness" of four grades of sandpaper on a scale from 0 to 10. Data from subjects who failed to rate the sandpaper correctly were excluded from the analysis.

The results demonstrated that perceptual ratings are modulated by a causative self-generated actions in patients only in the absence of auditory hallucinations and passivity experiences. Subjects without these symptoms consistently rated a self-produced tactile sensation as being less intense, tickly and pleasant than when the sensation was externally produced. Their ratings were similar to those of normal controls. In contrast patients with these symptoms did not distinguish perceptually between the two types of tactile stimulation. Figure 7 shows the difference between the ratings for self-produced and externally produced tactile stimulation for the three subject groups. These results support the proposal that auditory hallucinations and passivity experiences are associated with a lack of awareness of the predicted limb position based on the forward model. This aspect of the forward model enables the distinction between self- and externally produced sensations, which did not occur in patients with these symptoms. Instead, in patients with these symptoms self-produced tactile stimulation was perceived just as tickly and intense as externally produced tactile stimulation.

Summary

In conclusion, it has been proposed that we are able to recognize the sensory consequences of our own actions using a forward model of the motor system. Our studies demonstrates that self- and externally produced tactile stimuli are perceived differently in normal subjects. This might be due to the differential brain activity associated with the two types of stimuli, self-produced stimuli being gated in the anterior cingulate and somatosensory cortex, a process that might involve the cerebellum. Subsequent experiments, which used a delay between the subject's movement and the resultant tactile stimulation, demonstrated that the perception of a tactile stimulus is proportional to the sensory discrepancy produced by the comparison between the predicted and actual sensory feedback from the movement. We have proposed that as the tactile stimulus diverges temporally from the motor command producing it, its prediction becomes less accurate, so the sensory discrepancy signal between the predicted and actual sensation increases. Finally, preliminary results demonstrated that patients with auditory hallucinations and passivity symptoms showed no perceptual distinction between self- and externally produced sensations. This supports the proposal that these symptoms are associated with an impairment of the forward model.

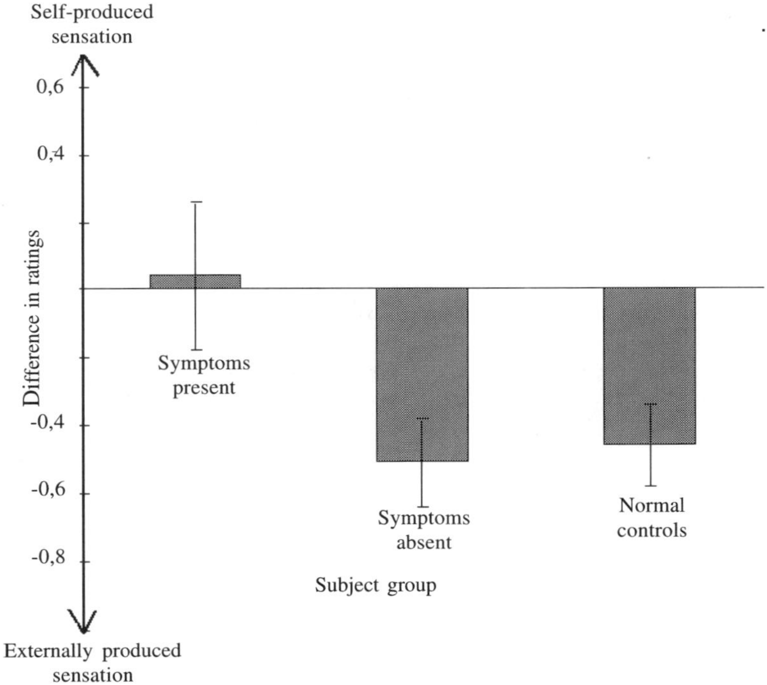

Figure 7: Graph showing mean rating differences between self-produced and externally produced tactile stimulation conditions for the three subject groups: patients with auditory hallucinations and/or passivity experiences, patients without these symptoms, and normal control subjects. There was no significant difference between the perceptual ratings in these two conditions in patients with auditory hallucinations and/or passivity, hence the mean rating difference was close to zero. In contrast, there was a significant difference between the perceptual ratings in the two conditions in patients without with these symptoms and in normal controls: both groups rated self-produced stimulation as less tickly, intense and pleasant than externally produced stimulation.

Acknowledgments

This work was carried out with Chris Frith and Daniel Wolpert. The work was supported by the Wellcome Trust. S-J.B is supported by a Wellcome Trust 4 year PhD Program in Neuroscience at University College London.

References

Andersson, G. & Armstrong, D. M. (1985). Climbing fibre input to b zone Purkinje cells during locomotor perturbation in the cat. *Neurosci. Letts. Supp* 22: S27.

Andersson, G. & Armstrong, D. M. (1987) Complex spikes in Purkinje cells in the lateral vermis of the cat cerebellum during locomotion. *J. Physiol. (Lond.)* 385: 107–134.

Angel, R. W. & Malenka, R. C. (1982). Velocity-dependent suppression of cutaneous sensitivity during movement. *Experimental Neurology* 77: 266–274.

Blakemore, S.-J., Wolpert, D.M. & Frith, C.D. (1998). "Central cancellation of self-produced tickle sensation." *Nature Neuroscience* 1(7): 635–640.

Blakemore, S.-J., Frith, C.D. & Wolpert, D.W. (1999a). Spatiotemporal prediction modulates the perception of self-produced stimuli. *J. Cog. Neurosci* 11(5): 551–559.

Blakemore, S.-J., Frith, C.D. & Wolpert, D.W. (1999b). How do we predict the sensory consequences of our actions? *Society for Neurosciences.*

Blakemore, S.-J., Smith, J., Steel, R., Johnstone, E. & Frith, C.D. (2000). The perception of self-produced sensory stimuli in patients with auditory hallucinations and passivity experiences: Evidence for a breakdown in self-monitoring. In press. *Psychological Medicine.*

Bick, P.A. & Kinsbourne, M. (1987). Auditory hallucinations and subvocal speech in schizophrenic patients. *Am J Psychiatry* 144(2): 222–5.

Claxton, G. (1975). Why can't we tickle ourselves? *Perceptual and Motor Skills* 41: 335-338.

Chapin, J.K. & Woodward, D.J. (1982). Somatic sensory transmission to the cortex during movement: gating of single cell responses to touch. *Exp. Neurol.* 78: 654–669.

Chapman, C. E., Bushnell, M. C., Miron, D., Duncan, G. H. & Lund, J. P. (1987). Sensory perception during movement in man. *Experimental Brain Research* 68: 516–524.

Chapman, C.E. & Ageranioti-Belanger, S.A. (1991). Comparison of the discharge of primary somatosensory cortical (SI) neurones during active and passive tactile discrimination. *Proc. Third IBRO World Congress of Neuroscience*, August 4–9, Montreal Que. 317.

Chapman, C.E. (1994). Active versus passive touch: factors influencing the transmission of somatosensory signals to primary somatosensory cortex. *Can. J. Physiol. Pharmacol* 72: 558–570.

Collins, D.F., Cameron, T., Gillard, D.M. & Prochazka, A. (1998). Muscular sense is attenuated when humans move. *J. Physiol.* 508, 2: 635–643.

Decety, J. (1996). Neural representation for action. *Reviews in the Neurosciences* 7(4): 285–297.

Friston, K.J., Frith, C.D., Liddle, P.F. & Dolan, R.J., Lammertsma, A.A. & Frackowiak, R.S. (1990). The relationship between global and local changes in PET scans. *J. Cereb. Blood Flow Met.* 10: 458–466.

Frith, C.D. & Done, D.J. (1988). Towards a neuropsychology of schizophrenia. *Br J Psychiatry* 153: 437–43.

Frith, C.D. & Done, D.J. (1989). Experiences of alien control in schizophrenia reflect a disorder in the central monitoring of action. *Psychol Med* 19(2): 359–63.

Frith, C.D. (1992). *The Cognitive Neuropsychology of Schizophrenia.* Lawrence Erlbaum Associates, UK.

Frith, C.D., Blakemore, S.-J. & Wolpert, D.M. Abnormalities of the Perception and Control of Action. Invited article, *Proc. Roy. Soc. Lond.* Submitted May 1999.

Gellman, R., Gibson, A.R. & Houk, J.C. (1985) Inferior olivary neurons in the awake cat: detection of contact and passive body displacement. *J. Neurophysiol.* 54(1): 40–60.

Gould (1949). Auditory hallucinations and subvocal speech. *J. Nervous and Mental Disease* 109: 418–427.

Green, P., Preston, M. (1981). Reinforcement of vocal correlates of auditory hallucinations by auditory feedback: a case study. *Br J Psychiatry* 139: 204–8.

von Helmholtz, H. (1867). *Handbuch der Physiologischen Optik* 1st edition. Voss, Hamburg, Germany.

Hoffman, R.E. (1986). Verbal hallucinations and language production processes in schizophrenia. *Behavioral and Brain Sciences.* Vol 9(3): 503–517.

Ito, M. (1970). Neurophysiological aspects of the cerebellar motor control system. *Int. J. Neurol.* 7: 162–176.

Jeannerod, M. (1988). *The Neural and Behaviourial Organisation of Goal-directed Movements.* Oxford: OUP.

Jeannerod, M. (1997). *The Cognitive Neuropsychology of Action.* Cambridge: Blackwell.

Jiang, W., Chapman, C.E. and Lamarre, Y. (1991). Modulation of the cutaneous responsiveness of neurones in the primary somatosensory cortex during conditioned arm movements in the monkey. *Exp. Brain Res.* 84: 342–354.

Kay, S., Fiszbein, A. & Opler, L. (1987) The Positive and Negative Symptom Scale for schizophrenia. *Schiz. Bull.* 13: 261–276.

Malenka, R.C., Angel, R.W., Hampton, B. & Berger, P.A. (1982). Impaired central error-correcting behavior in schizophrenia. *Arch Gen Psychiatry* 39(1):101–7.

Mellor, C.S. (1970). First-rank symptoms of schizophrenia. *Br J Psychiatry* 117: 15–23.

Miall, R.C., Weir, D.J., Wolpert, D.M. & Stein, J.F. (1993). Is the cerebellum a Smith predictor? *J. Motor Behav.* 25: 203–216.

Milne, R. J., Aniss, A. M., Kay, N. E. & Gandevia, S. C. (1988). Reduction in perceived intensity of cutaneous stimuli during movement: a quantitative study. *Experimental Brain Research* 70: 569–576.

Oscarsson, O. (1980). In *The Inferior Olivary Nucleus: Anatomy and Physiology.* (Eds. Courville, J., DeMontigny, C., & Lamarre, Y). New York: Raven Press.

Paulin, M.G. (1989). A Kalman filter theory of the cerebellum. In *Dynamic Interactions in Neural Networks: Models and Data.* Arbib, EMA and Amari, ES. Berlin: Springer-Verlag, 241–259.

Porrino, L.J. (1993). Functional consequences of acute cocaine treatment depend on route of administration. *Psychopharmacol. Berl.* 112(2–3): 343–51.

Simpson, J.L., Wylie, D.R. & De Zeeuw, CI. (1995). On Climbing Fiber Signals And Their Consequence(s) *Behav. Brain Sci.* 19; 3, 384.

Spence, S.A. (1996). Free will in the light of neuropsychiatry. *Philosophy, Psychiatry and Psychology* 3: 75–90.

Sperry, R.W. (1950). Neural basis of spontaneous optokinetic responses produced by visual inversion. *J. Comp. Physiol. Psychol.* 43: 482–289.

Von Holst, E. (1954). Relations Between the Central Nervous System and the Peripheral Organs. *The British Journal of Animal Behaviour* 2: 89–94.

Vogt, B.A., Finch, D.M. & Olson, C.R. (1992). Functional heterogeneity in cingulate cortex: the anterior executive and posterior evaluative regions. *Cereb. Cort.* 2: 435–443

Vogt, B.A., Gabriel, M., eds. *Neurobiology of cingulate cortex and limbic thalamus* (1993). Birkauser: Boston.

Weiskrantz, L., Elliot, J. & Darlington, C. (1971). Preliminary observations of tickling oneself. *Nature* 230: 598–599.

Wolpert, D.M., Ghahramani, Z. & Jordan, M.I. (1995). An internal model for sensorimotor integration. *Science* 269: 1880–1882.

Wolpert, D.M. (1997). Computational approaches to motor control. *Trends in Cognitive Sciences* 1:6; 209–216.

Wolpert, D.M., Miall, R.C. & Kawato, M. (1998). Internal models in the cerebellum. *Trends in Cognitive Sciences* 2(9): 338–347.

Self-Reference and Schizophrenia

A Cognitive Model of Immunity to Error through Misidentification

Shaun Gallagher
Canisius College

n certain symptoms of schizophrenia, such as thought insertion, delusions of ontrol, and auditory hallucinations, various aspects of self-awareness are lisrupted. In this paper I intend to sort out what these different aspects are, and o explore their underlying mechanisms. Specifically, I will begin with a listinction between the sense of ownership and the sense of agency with espect to motor action and cognition. I will also consider whether schizo-hrenic experiences involve the kind of first-person self-reference character-zed by what philosophers call immunity to error through misidentification. In vorking out the underlying dynamics of schizophrenic experience I move etween phenomenological and cognitive levels of analysis. Following a ritical examination of a cognitive model of schizophrenia developed by hristopher Frith (1992), I offer an alternative model inspired by a phenom-nological analysis of time-consciousness, and consistent with empirical stud-es of the temporal experience of schizophrenic patients.

. Ownership, Agency, and the Immunity Principle

n the normal phenomenology of voluntary or willed action, the sense of gency and the sense of ownership coincide and are indistinguishable. The otion of agency, as I will use it in this paper, refers to the initiation or source f the act. It involves a sense of generating or being the willful initiator of an action. When I reach for a cup, I know this to be my action. When I think about the cup, I know this thinking to be my own. This coincidence may be what leads us to think of ownership of action in terms of agency: that the owner of an action is the person who is, in a particular way, causally involved in the production of that action, the one who is the author of the action. In the case of *involuntary* action, however, it is quite possible to distinguish between sense of agency and sense of ownership. I may acknowledge ownership of a movement — for example, I have a sense that I am the one who is moving or is being moved — and I can self-ascribe it as *my* movement, but I may not have a sense of causing or controlling the movement, that is, no sense of agency. The agent of the movement is the person who pushed me from behind, or the physician who is manipulating my arm in a medical examination. In the case of involuntary *cognitive* processes, I may acknowledge that I am the one who is thinking, but claim that the thoughts are not willfully generated by me. For example, certain unbidden thoughts or memories may impinge on my consciousness, even if I do not intend for them to do so, or even if I resist them (see Frankfurt 1976). We are all familiar with melodies that seem to stay in our heads when we would rather think of something else. In such cases, of course, we may not want to say that there is a specific agency at all. It is not that I think someone else is causing my thoughts or my experience. Nonetheless, my claim of ownership (my self-ascription that I am the one who is undergoing such experiences) may be consistent with my lack of a sense of agency.

What remains intact in all of the cases mentioned — voluntary and involuntary — is what Shoemaker (1968) has called *immunity to error through misidentification* relative to the first-person pronoun (for short, the "immunity principle"). The immunity principle is based on what Wittgenstein called the use of the first-person pronoun "*as subject.*" He suggests that if a person says that she has a certain experience, it would be nonsensical to ask "are you sure that it's *you* who are having the experience?" (1958: 67). If you claim to have a toothache, it makes no sense to ask, "Are you sure that it's *you* who have the toothache?" There are grammatical interpretations of this principle, but I think that they fail to capture its full sense. Wittgenstein's characterization points to a more experiential sense of immunity to error through misidentification. His examples are cognitive or experiential ones: "I see so-and-so," "I try to lift my arm," "I have a toothache," and "I think it will rain." It would be nonsensical to ask, "Are you sure that it is *you* who think it will rain?" This is nonsensical, not because it concerns an issue pertaining to grammatical structure, but because it concerns a noetic integrity, the surety of access to one's own experience, or more precisely, to one's own *ipseity*, an access that Shoemaker calls "non-observational."

It is important to keep in mind that for Shoemaker immunity to error through misidentification applies to forms of self-reference in which there is no need for identification, and thus no chance of misidentification. In other words, we are immune to error in this regard, not because we are so proficient, or so infallible at judging who we are, but because this kind of self-awareness doesn't involve a judgment at all. We are not in a position to get it wrong, or to get it right; we are simply, in principle or by default, always correct on this score. According to this view, the immunity principle would seem to apply equally to both the sense of ownership and the sense of agency. My use of the first-person pronoun to signify agency or ownership does not require me to verify that I meet certain criteria in order to judge, on the basis of observation, that I am the one who is acting.

In contrast to uses of the first-person pronoun *as subject*, however, uses of the first-person pronoun *as object* can be open to sensible questions about identification. If, for example, I claim that "I am the most handsome philosopher in the room," one may quite sensibly ask "are you sure that it is *you* who are the most handsome." Such a claim would be based on criteria that observationally (perceptually) I would have to match up with my own appearance. Consider the following example, which more clearly involves misidentification. In response to a statement such as "I have a bump on my forehead," one may sensibly ask, "Are you sure that it's *you* who have a bump on your forehead." For example, in an odd circumstance I may look in a mirror at several people who share my similar features, see that one has a bump on his head, and proclaim "I have a bump on my head," and be quite wrong about it being me.[1]

We can clarify this, and also see that the immunity principle pertains to more than grammatical form, by considering Shoemaker's observation that "whereas the statement 'My arm is moving' is subject to error through misidentification, the statement 'I am waving my arm' is not" (1984: 8). Shoemaker's claim requires some qualification. Whether one or the other statement is or is not immune to error through misidentification depends on the experiential basis for the statement. It is certainly true that if the statement 'My arm is moving' is made solely on the basis of visual perception then there is a possibility of misidentification. By using mirrors or videotape to manipulate visual perception, a deafferented or "proprioblind" subject — for example, one who lacks proprioceptive awareness of his arm — may be easily tricked into thinking that his arm is moving. But that same subject, in such circumstances of deafferentation, could equally be led to say 'I am waving my arm', and be quite wrong about who it is who is waving an arm.[2] In contrast the statement 'My arm is moving', even if meant to express an involuntary movement (i.e., without agency), *is* immune to error through misidentification if the basis for the statement is proprioceptive experience. This is the case even if one is experimentally fooled into thinking that one's arm is moving in a way that it is not (as done, for example, in experiments that use muscle vibration techniques), or even if there is no arm (as in the case of a phantom arm). In such cases I may be wrong about what my arm is doing, or even that it is an arm that is doing it, but I could not be wrong about the fact that it is I who experience it. What the statement 'My arm is moving' means in such cases is 'I feel my arm is moving', and one cannot sensibly ask, 'Are you sure that it is *you* who are feeling your arm moving?'[3]

The application of the immunity principle does not depend on there being intact for action both a sense of ownership and a sense of agency. In the cases of involuntary action, where I lack a sense of agency, there is still a sense of ownership, so I cannot deny that I experience my arm moving, or that it is my tooth that is aching, or that I am the one who is thinking. In such cases the immunity to error through misidentification which is linked to the sense of ownership remains intact. If, on the other side of this distinction, we consider cases in which the sense of agency remains intact, but there is no sense of ownership, it may be tempting to argue that the sense of agency is not as robust as the sense of ownership in regard to the immunity principle, that is, that we can find cases in which the sense of agency is not immune to error. Consider a case of delusion. A delusional subject may report that he is causing other people to act or to think in a certain way: "It is not my action — she is the one acting — but I am causing the action, I am the one willing her to do it." In this case, where there is a sense of agency but not a sense of ownership for action (I do not self-ascribe the action), the immunity principle does not hold for the sense of agency, that is to say, I am not immune from error in such cases — after all, we call this a delusion, and it turns out that it is a delusion that involves misidentification. It would make perfect sense to ask: "Are you sure that it is *you* who are causing that action?" But we need to be careful here. The sense of agency at stake in the delusion example does not involve the subject's own motor action and in that regard is more remote and conceptual than the sense of agency a normal subject might have in reaching to pick up a glass. This example of delusion and, more generally, first-person judgments pertaining to remote agency involve what Wittgenstein calls use of the first-person pronoun *as object*, and no claim is made that the immunity principle holds in such cases. In contrast, where the sense of agency is immediately linked to motor action, or to the subject's own stream of consciousness, and is expressed by the first-person pronoun used *as subject*, the sense of agency remains immune to error through misidentification.[4] Part of what I want to explain in this paper is why this is so. In the remainder of the paper I will understand 'sense of agency' to involve this sort of immediate linkage to action rather than remote agency.

If this is right, it would follow that by asking what mechanisms underlie the senses of ownership or of agency for action we would be asking what mechanisms underlie the immunity principle. To explore this issue, then, we would do well to look at cases in which either of these senses for action is disrupted or missing. It has been suggested that schizophrenic experiences such as thought insertion and auditory hallucination involve a lack of a sense of ownership and/or agency. John Campbell (1999) further suggests that these phenomena represent a failure of the immunity principle.[5] He writes, citing the work of Christopher Frith:

> What is so striking about the phenomenon of thought insertion as described by schizophrenic patients is that it seems to involve an error of identification. … A patient who supposes that someone else has inserted thoughts into his mind is right about which thoughts they are, but wrong about whose thoughts they are. So thought insertion seems to be a counterexample to the thesis that present-tense introspectively based reports of psychological state cannot involve errors of identification. (Campbell 1999: 609–610)

Frith himself puts the point succinctly. He says:

> Thought insertion, in particular, is a phenomenon that is difficult to understand. Patients say that thoughts that are not their own are coming into their head. This experience implies that we have some way of recognising our own thoughts. It is as if each thought has a label on it saying 'mine'. If this labelling process goes wrong, then the thought would be perceived as alien. (Frith 1992: 80)

Campbell goes on to claim that Frith's model of schizophrenia as a disruption of basic self-monitoring processes provides the most parsimonious explanation of how self-ascriptions of thoughts are subject to errors of identification. My intention is to examine these claims. I want to suggest that Frith's mode may not be as parsimonious as Campbell thinks. I also want to clarify the issu concerning whether it is the sense of ownership or the sense of agency, o something more than this, that is disrupted in cases such as thought insertion and whether or not the immunity principle is or is not still intact in such cases If Campbell is right that something like schizophrenic experiences of though insertion violate the immunity principle, then the claim is more serious tha simply finding a counterexample or an exception to the rule. It would involv admitting (in contrast to Shoemaker's characterization) that first-person self awareness *as subject* does involve identification, that schizophrenics get i wrong and that normal subjects get it right. So if the immunity principle i subject to exception in the case of schizophrenia, then the principle itself i threatened.

2. Dynamics of Agency and Ownership in Motor Action

Frith's basic thesis is that the schizophrenic's hallucinatory and delusiona experiences are due to a breakdown of *self-monitoring*. Frith is led to this view from observations of motor behavior in schizophrenia. Let us take that as ou starting point.

It is well known that chronic schizophrenic patients suffer from a variet of movement disorders. They may make peculiar involuntary movements grimaces, with lips and mouth (Frith 1992; Owens et al. 1982; Crow et al 1982). They are unable to maintain synchrony between finger tap and rhyth mic auditory stimuli (Manschreck 1986). They sometimes suffer from povert of action, often manifested in poverty of speech, and this may involve problem with self-generated action (Frith 1992). More relevant to our con cerns, schizophrenic patients make mistakes about the agency of variou bodily movements. The patient suffering from delusions of control may repor that their movements are made or caused by someone or something else. Her is an example cited by Frith: 'The force moved my lips. I began to speak. Th words were made for me.' (Frith 1992: 66). The motor action responsible fo the speech was in fact the patient's own motor action, and the patient acknowl edges that they are his lips that are moved, but he makes an error of identifica tion concerning who produced this motion. Here the sense of agency, rathe ıan the sense of ownership, is disrupted. That is, the patient knows that it is is lips and that he speaks, but his lips were moved and the words were made y someone else. Another example provided by Mellor (1970: 17; cited by pence 1996: 82) makes this clear: 'A 29 year old shorthand typist described er actions as follows: "When I reach my hand for the comb it is my hand and rm which move, and my fingers pick up the pen, but I don't control them."'

How can one explain this disruption in the sense of agency? The classic ıeory in this case involves the notion of a comparator. When a motor ıstruction to move is sent to a set of muscles, a copy of that instruction, the fferent copy, is also sent to a comparator or self-monitoring system. Held 1961) suggested that efferent copy sent to a comparator is stored there, and ıen compared to the reafferent (proprioceptive or visual) information about hat movement was actually made. On this explanation, the sense of agency ould seemingly have to wait for perceptual feedback and would come after ıe fact as verification that it was I who did the moving. This verificationist xplanation is clearly put by Campbell:

> [I]n the cases in which we do have a sense of agency, in which the movement performed is felt to be your own, what grounds that sense of agency is match at the relevant comparator between the efferent copy and the sensory feedback you have about the movement. What explains the feeling that it is you who moved your arm is that at the comparator, an efferent copy was received of the instruction to move your arm which matches the movement you perceive. (1999: 612)

ı the case of the schizophrenic's motor experience, what explains his lack of sense of self-agency, on this model, is the absence of a match between ıovement and efferent copy at the comparator. This *sensory-feedback comarator* account corresponds in part to explanations of motor action and selfwareness in ecological terms. The control of motor action depends in part on roprioceptive and visual feedback, and more generally a perceptually defined cological sense of one's own self-movement (Gibson 1987). If something eems to be going wrong with the action, it is quite possible to correct for it on ıe basis of this concurrent[7] self-awareness, which is implicit in or built into asic perceptual aspects of the short-term body image (O'Shaughnessey 1995; ermúdez 1995). This kind of proprioceptive, ecological sense involves not nly perceptual information and working memory, but also a non-observaonal and pre-reflective differentiation between self and non-self, and a sense f one's own capacities for action (see Gallagher and Meltzoff 1996). For my purposes here, I will treat the sensory-feedback comparator model as more or less equivalent to the *ecological, perceptual-feedback model,* although I think there are important differences between them.[8]

A second component to the control of movement also makes use of the comparator model. In this respect, the comparator is understood to be part of a non-conscious pre-motor system responsible for the control of movement operating *prior to* the actual execution of movement and *prior to* sensory feedback. On this "*forward* model" motor control does not depend on perceptual feedback, although its result is still a conscious sense of agency for action (Jeannerod 1994; Georgieff & Jeannerod 1998). In this case the comparator functions as a central monitor which registers the efferent copy as correctly or incorrectly matching motor intentions and makes automatic corrections to movement prior to any sensory feedback. This *forward comparator model* is quite consistent with an *anticipatory, pre-action model* of motor action. On such accounts, a nonconscious, pre-action process, part of an automatic body schema function, anticipates motor action and provides an online sense of agency complementary to the ecological sense of self built into perception. Marcel (in press) has argued that in one's immediate phenomenology during action, agency is not represented as separate from the action, but is an intrinsic property of action itself, experienced as a perspectival source. Experimental research on normal subjects suggests that an agentive awareness of action is based not so much on actual feedback from movement itself or from peripheral effort associated with such movement, but more on that which precedes action and translates intention into movement — high-level motor instructions, experienced as a sense of agency (Marcel, in press; Fourneret and Jeannerod 1998). In addition, research which correlates initial awareness of action with recordings of the lateralised readiness potential and with transcranial magnetic stimulation of the supplementary motor area, strongly indicates that one's initial awareness of a spontaneous voluntary action is underlain by the anticipatory or pre-movement motor commands relating to relevant effectors (Haggard and Eimer 1999; Haggard and Magno 1999). That is, although the content of experience is a sense of agency for the action, its source is in fact what lies between intention and performance.

Frith (1992) cites evidence that schizophrenics have problems with this forward, body-schematic monitoring of movement, but not with motor control based on perceptual feedback. Normally, subjects required to use a joystick to follow a target on a computer screen may use either visual feedback or the pre ction, more automatic process for correction of movement. In the first case, o correct a mistaken movement one could depend on visual feedback, recog-ize the error, and move to correct it. If visual feedback is unavailable, owever, the normal subject makes a quicker and smoother correction of rrors at the level of the body schema. On the comparator model, such rapid rror corrections presumably depend on the central monitoring of the motor ntention, prior to any perceptual feedback.[9] Experiments show that schizo-hrenic patients have a problem monitoring their own motor intentions at this evel (Malenka et al. 1982). Schizophrenic patients, like normal subjects, orrect their errors when visual feedback is provided, but, unlike normal ubjects, often fail to correct their mistakes when deprived of visual feedback Frith & Done 1988). These findings are consistent with controlled studies hat show abnormal premovement brain potentials in schizophrenia, which ingh and his colleagues associate with elements of a neural network involv-ng supplementary motor, premotor, and prefrontal cortexes (Singh, et al. 992).[10]

Consider how close the schizophrenic's delusional experience of control, n which he feels under the influence of others, is to normal experience of nvoluntary action. In both cases there is a loss of a sense of agency, but not a oss of a sense of ownership, as I've characterized it above. Now the loss of a ense of agency is explained by Frith as a problem with efferent copy in the entral monitor, some sort of dysfunction of the forward, pre-action aspect of he non-conscious body-schema system. This makes good sense with respect o normal involuntary action where a subject does not intend the action; there ould be no pre-action preparation, no efferent copy sent to the comparator. n the case of the schizophrenic' s delusion of control, however, since he is in act the agent, the disruption of the sense of agency is explained by something oing wrong with efferent copy or the comparator. Yet, as we see from the xperimental situation, the schizophrenic does still seem able to correct move-ent errors if perceptual feedback is available. Likewise, in the case of nvoluntary action, the ecological sensory feedback system still seems to do its ob (Gibson 1986). This suggests that the distinction between ecological ontrol (via a perceptual short-term body image or sensory-feedback com-arator) and forward, pre-action control (via body schema mechanisms or orward comparator) corresponds to the distinction between sense of owner-hip and sense of agency, respectively. That is, both in the schizophrenic's elusional experience of control and in the normal experience of involuntary action, the ecological sensory feedback system tells the subject that it is he who is moving or being moved (providing a sense of ownership for the movement), but absent efferent-copy at the comparator, or absent any pre action preparatory processes at the neurological level, the body-schemati system fails to register a sense of agency, a sense that it is the subject himself who is the willful generator of the movement.[11]

3. Dynamics of Agency and Ownership in Cognition

Frith (1992) also applies his model of self-monitoring, which consists of subpersonal cognitive mechanisms ultimately intended to be cashed out in terms of neurophysiology, to thinking. In this context I want to take a closer look at the specifics of his model. As noted, he conceives of the monitoring system in terms of a comparator mechanism, and specifically in terms of its use in an explanation of visuo-motor coordination. The visual system can distinguish between movements on the retina that are due to movements in th world, and movements on the retina that are due to movements of our own body. In the latter case stability of the visual image is achieved by the motor system sending a corollary discharge or efferent copy "to some monitoring system at the same time as a message is sent to the eye muscles" (Frith 1992: 74). The efferent copy alerts the visual system to compensate for self generated or self-initiated movement (Figure 1).

Frith refers to this as a monitoring of *intentions to move* (1992: 74 and 81). To have an intention to move would surely signify something voluntary or as Frith says, "self-initiated" (1992: 43). Frith's analysis focuses precisely on such self-generated or willed action. Our previous considerations of motor action indicate that for the normal subject the sense of ownership of action and the sense of agency coincide in the case of willed action. The schizophrenic however, may experience a loss of a sense of agency when in fact he is th agent, and this can be explained by the forward, body-schematic comparator model that Frith is citing.

Frith finds that this sort of self-monitoring mechanism is traditionall used in explaining motor, perceptual, and linguistic behavior (for example Sperry 1950; Von Holst and Mittelstaedt 1950). Following Feinberg (1978) however, he postulates a similar mechanism for cognition — specifically, for thought and inner speech. He suggests that defects in such mechanisms can

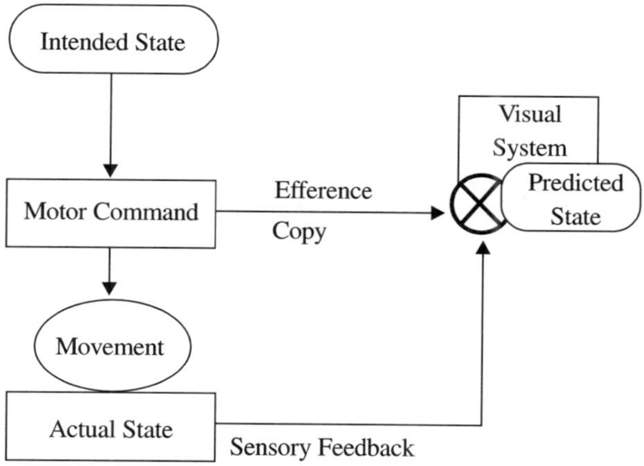

igure 1: Visual-Motor Comparator. Efferent copy enables visual system to predict self-
ovement

xplain hallucination and delusion in the case of schizophrenia. Phenomena ıch as thought insertion, hearing voices, perceiving one's own acts as alien, tc., suggest that something has gone wrong with the central monitoring echanism.

Thought insertion, for example, might be explained in the following way.

> Thinking, like all our actions, is normally accompanied by a sense of effort and deliberate choice as we move from one thought to the next. If we found ourselves thinking without any awareness of the sense of effort that reflects central monitoring, we might well experience these thoughts as alien and, thus, being inserted into our minds. (Frith 1992: 81)

rith's model assumes not only that thinking is a kind of action, but that, as in e case of a motor action, we experience an effortful intention. The intention think, according to Frith, is the element that bestows a sense of "mineness" n the thought, or perhaps more precisely we should say, a sense of agency for e thought. Normally, an efferent copy of the intention to think is sent to the omparator or central monitor, which also registers the occurrence of think-g, and matches up intention and thought (Figure 2). So if the intention (the ferent copy) is somehow blocked from reaching the central monitoring echanism, thought occurs which seems not to be generated by the subject. If e efferent copy is blocked or goes astray, or is not properly generated,

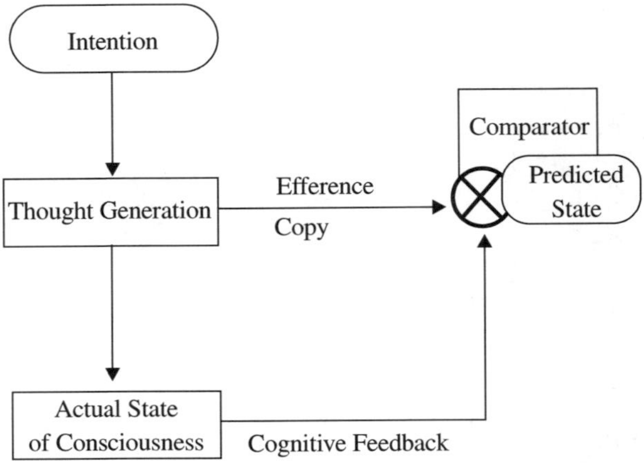

Figure 2: Cognitive Comparator. Match at the comparator identifies thought as one's ow

thinking still occurs, but it is not registered as under my control — it appears t be an alien or inserted thought. There fails to be a match between intention an thinking.

4. Some Phenomenological Problems with Frith's Model

Several aspects of Frith's model are phenomenologically problematic. A fir set of problems pertains to Frith's characterization of the intention to think. I the case of thinking or conscious experience what role does something like a "intention to think" or efferent copy play? It is difficult to conceive of a intention to think prior to thinking itself, unless it is entirely a consciou preparation, as when I might decide to sit down and start thinking about th essay. In that case, however, the intention to think is itself a thinking, and a infinite regress begins to loom — do I require an intention to think in order t intend to think? Frith speaks of a *conscious* feeling of effort or intention t think (or "willed intention"), and equates this with a *conscious* monitoring o efferent copy (1992: 86). Frith's analysis relies, not just on an intention to ac (move or think), but an *awareness* of the intention to act, and he defines th awareness as a case of "metarepresentation." Metarepresentation is "the abil ity to reflect upon how we represent the world and our thoughts," that is, econd-order reflexive consciousness. This is part of what it means to monitor ur actions and, he claims, it is precisely what is missing or disrupted in the chizophrenic's experience. Surely, however, most cases of normal thinking re neither prefaced by conscious intentions to think, nor followed by an ntrospective metarepresentation. Indeed, Louis Sass (1998) suggests that recisely such hyperreflective phenomena are what we find in the case of chizophrenia. In the normal phenomenology, at least in the large majority of ases, there is not first an intention and then a thinking, nor thinking plus a oncurrent but separate awareness of effort or intention to think. Campbell 1999) rightly suggests that, contra to Frith's characterization, the efferent opy (and thus the intention to think) is not itself available to consciousness. Ve should treat efferent copy as a *subpersonal* and non-conscious process which generates an awareness of effort. So as a first attempt to get the henomenology right, let us give this subpersonal mechanism an obscure ame like "thought-generator mechanism" (TGM) and say that as thoughts are enerated (and I suppose this can happen in any number of ways) an efferent opy is normally sent to the central monitor. These are subpersonal processes hat subtend the thinking process (ultimately they are to be cashed out in terms f neuroscience rather than phenomenology).

What Frith calls 'intention to think', then, may be a subpersonal, noncon-cious process. Even if this is the case, like the intention to move, it is not lways the case that my thinking is characterized as something I intend. There re unbidden thoughts that, as Frankfurt puts it, "strike us unexpectedly out of he blue; and thoughts that run willy-nilly through our heads" (1976: 240). I nay just find myself thinking of something. I may just find, without a onscious act of recollection, certain memories coming to the fore, invading or isrupting my thoughts with elements of my past that may or may not be elevant to my present circumstance. Is there any kind of intention to think hen someone suddenly starts shouting instructions at me and causes me to tart thinking? Yet, even in such cases I do not attribute my thoughts to omeone else.[12] This means that the intention to think and its efferent copy are ot doing all the work that Frith would like them to do. The absence of an ntention to think, and hence, the lack of efferent copy generated to represent hat intention at the comparator level do not explain anything more than a elatively normal lack of a sense of agency. It does not explain the attribution f thought to another agency, or why some thought might seem inserted for he schizophrenic. We can also note that in such cases I do not have an intention to think, but I nonetheless retain a sense of ownership, a first-person sense, immune to error through misidentification, which tells me that I am the one who is thinking. So a preliminary or preparatory non-conscious intention to think, if necessary for a sense of agency, seems unnecessary to guarantee immunity to error through misidentification in regard to the sense of ownership — that I am the one who is thinking.

What purpose could *efferent copy* have in the realm of thinking? In the case of visuo-motor control, efferent copy serves a very pragmatic, one would almost say an executive function rather than a verificational one — that is, one system informs another system to make adjustments, with very practical effects — for example, stability of the visual field, postural balance, and so forth. The function of efferent copy is to inform the visual and vestibular systems that the organism, rather than the world, is moving. Even in the case where the motor system is simply updating and correcting itself, the purpose of efferent copy is for motor control. Its purpose is not to verify, simply for the record, that movement is taking place, nor is it *primarily* an information stream that discriminates between intended movement and non-intended movement.[13] Its purpose is rather to instruct the motor or sensory system to make important adjustments. Is there anything like this happening in the thinking process? One can certainly distinguish different cognitive systems — the memory system, the perceptual system, and so on. But we are not talking of efferent copy playing a communicative role among these systems. It does not seem to be a communication between two different systems, unless, of course, one creates an extra system and calls it the comparator or central monitor. On the Feinberg-Frith model, the cognitive system seems to be sending *itself* messages. Thus Campbell (1999: 616) suggests, following Feinberg, that efferent copy has the primary function of keeping thoughts on track, checking "that the thoughts you actually execute form coherent trains of thought." Keeping thoughts coherent and on track, however, could only mean keeping them on a semantic track, that is, on a certain track of meaning, and it would be odd to assign this task to a subpersonal, non-semantic mechanism when, simply put, we seem to be consciously aware of our thoughts and can keep track of them and keep them on track at a conscious level. So the question is whether one really needs a comparator or anything like an observational metarepresentation to verify that I myself am doing the thinking.

Campbell has argued that Frith's model provides the most parsimonious explanation of the sense of agency in thinking. Yet Frith's model would make ıe normal sense of agency for thinking the work of a separate mechanism — comparator. Is this necessary in a system that already involves conscious-ess? The matching process in the comparator supposedly involves a curious ıix of conscious and non-conscious elements. If we follow Campbell rather ıan Frith, the efferent copy is not something we are conscious of, but the ther element of the match — the stream of thought itself — is already a ıatter of consciousness. Supposedly the *outcome* of the match, the sense of gency, must also be conscious in some way — a conscious sense that I am the ne who is thinking. One might suppose, however, that the verifying match in ıe subpersonal comparator would not be conscious, (otherwise there would ave to be a consciousness of something that remains non-conscious — the fferent stream).

Campbell describes the comparator process as involving a form of intro-pection: "it is the match between the thought detected by *introspection*, and ıe content of the efferent copy picked up by the comparator, that is respon-ible for the sense of ownership of the thought."[14] Campbell's use of the term ntrospection' in this context is, I think, relatively innocuous. He is part of a adition that follows Shoemaker's use of the term to mean something like the nmediate reflexive access ("from the inside") which allows us to report our n-going experience, rather than anything like a full-fledged act of reflective ıtrospection.[15] Frith, however, invokes the notion of metarepresentation, as a ıll-fledged act of reflection. But a metarepresentational introspection again ıreatens infinite regress — introspection, in this sense, is itself a thinking rocess and would generate its own efferent copy, to be matched up on top of ıe original match. It seems to me that either the metarepresentation or the omparator's match is redundant. Wouldn't metarepresentational introspec-on be an extra level of consciousness added to the comparator's verification rocess? Not only does this not seem phenomenologically parsimonious, but, s I have already noted, some theorists suggest that precisely this kind of yperreflective introspective concern about verifying that one's own thought indeed one's own is a characteristic of schizophrenia rather than normalcy ee Sass 1998; Zahavi & Parnas 1998).[16]

A second set of problems involves the static nature of Frith's model. That , he takes no account of the temporal flow-structure of thought. To be clear bout this claim, I acknowledge that Frith may very well understand that the ıbpersonal mechanisms involve issues of timing (for example, when does the fferent copy arrive at the comparator relative to the conscious thought; or when precisely does the comparator do its job?),[17] but what he does no account for is the temporal structure of the thinking itself, which would be pa of the input to the central monitor.

It is quite possible to incorporate temporality into the comparator mode and I think to do so would help to address another serious objection that ha been raised against it: If in the case of schizophrenia one of these mechanism goes wrong or is put out of operation, why do not all thoughts seem alien.[18] I either the TGM fails to generate efferent copy or if the central monitor fails t register efferent copy, how do we explain that these mechanisms do seem t work normally sometimes, since not all of the schizophrenic's thoughts ar experienced as inserted thoughts? I'll refer to this as the problem of th occasionality of inserted thoughts. Quite obviously the phenomenology i here going to constrain the cognitive explanation.

5. Two strategies

To address these problems, I want to pursue two strategies. First, I wi propose a solution to the occasionality problem using a less static version c Frith's model, taking into account the temporal structure of the stream c consciousness. Second, because even this enhanced account still fails to me all of the phenomenological constraints, I want to suggest an alternativ model. In either case, however, it will be clear that any explanation whic stays on a strictly subpersonal level, the level of cognitive mechanisms, i inadequate to explain the phenomenology of the schizophrenic.

Following the first strategy, if we conceive of cognition as a Jamesia stream of thought, or as a Husserlian flow of consciousness, then underlyin cognitive mechanisms would have to take into account the temporal flo structure. To take this flow structure into account in Frith's model, we woul have to say that the TGM generates two *streams*–the conscious thinking and th efferent copy — which need to be matched up in the central monitor. Th means, of course, that they need to be in synchrony with each other. If, for som reason, these two streams go out of sync and then back into sync, then *som* thoughts will seem alien (as in the case of thought insertion) and others will no One possible answer to the occasionality problem, then, involves the idea th on occasion the two streams go out of sync and there is a failure to match. On way this might happen is if one of the mechanisms occasionally sputters, and i

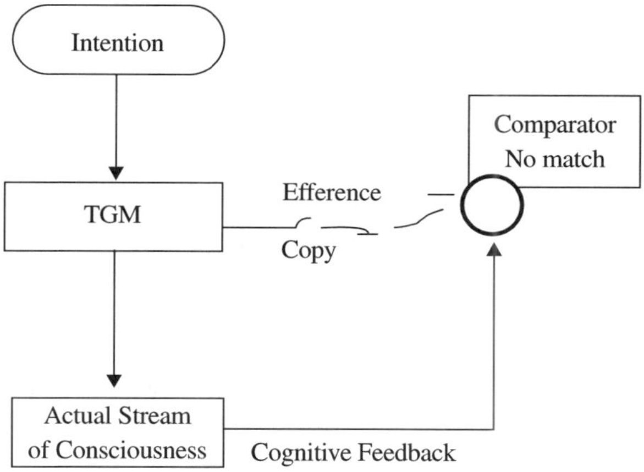

Figure 3: Sputtering Mechanism. No match at the comparator results in the experience of inserted thoughts

the mode of sputtering, either the two streams go out of sync, or the efferent copy is not properly generated, or the central monitor does not properly register it (see Figure 3).[19] Whether the desynchronization is the result of a sputtering mechanism, or not, it is quite possible that one stream simply slows down relative to the other one. There is good evidence that neuronal processes (and information processing) may slow down in circumstances of brain injury and under the influence of alcohol and/or various drugs. Many times these neurophysiological distortions are accompanied by distortions in the experience of time — distortions not unlike those experienced by schizophrenics (see Pöppel 1994; Pöppel et al. 1975). Quite relevant to the phenomenon of auditory hallucination, there is evidence to suggest that auditory centers are susceptible to such slowing, on the order of over three times difference from normal (Pöppel 1994). Slowing of such processes, if, for example, affecting one sense modality more than others, or affecting certain functions of the neuronal underpinnings of cognitive mechanisms, could easily cause a form of "temporal diplopia" (Pöppel 1994: 192) in which efferent copy comes to be out of joint with the conscious stream. This discrepancy might also explain the break down in experienced continuity suffered in some schizophrenics (Pöppel 1994: 199).

Several questions remain: What could cause the subpersonal desynchronization? Why are specific thought contents rather than a large variety of contents always thought inserted? The effects of subpersonal distortions, even if they only occasionally caused the disruption of efferent copy or of the synchrony between the two streams, would have to involve a relatively sophisticated sputtering or neurophysiological slowing in order to account for the actual phenomenology of the schizophrenic. The occasionality problem is actually more complex than our first formulation would indicate. It is not simply that in thought insertion patients occasionally experience thoughts coming into their minds from an outside source, but their experiences are very specific and sometimes associated with specific others. Schizophrenics may experience a certain consistency amid the inconsistency of their inserted thoughts. That is, inserted thoughts often seem to be of a similar mind-set, and seem to have a certain semantic and experiential consistency which cannot be adequately explained by the disruption of subpersonal processes alone. For example, a schizophrenic will report that the thoughts are inserted by a particular person and that they are always about a specified topic or that, in auditory hallucination, the voice always seems to say the same sort of thing. Frith gives the following example: "Thoughts are put into my mind like "Kill God". It's just like my mind working, but it isn't. They come from this chap, Chris. They're his thoughts" (1992: 66). Some patients feel controlled by other people, or even by machines (see, e.g., Bovet & Parnas 1993). Part of the explanation, then, would seem to depend on the intentional content of the thought, and not simply on a subpersonal disruption of efferent copy. Although there is no question of explaining the full and various phenomenologies that one finds in schizophrenic patients, if certain subpersonal mechanisms are predisposed to malfunction in schizophrenic patients, one possible trigger for this malfunction may be intentional content.

Thus, a subpersonal explanation does not entirely resolve the occasionality problem, which may in fact have its proximate cause on the level of semantic intentional content. There are good arguments and good evidence to show that intentional content has an effect on the temporal structure of experience (James 1890; Friedman 1990; Gallagher 1998). Experience speeds up or slows down according to *what* we are experiencing. Consider, for example, the ordinary experience of how time passes when we are with different people. In some cases time passes too quickly, in other cases too slowly. Complicate this picture with emotion and/or the unconscious (whatever you take that to be). If boredom can slow the system down; and enjoyment and interest speed it up, perhaps anxiety or some such emotion can cause a desynchronization between the phenomeno ogical stream and the stream of efferent copy. Although I do not propose to dentify any one aspect of experience as a fundamental cause of schizophrenia, or even as an exclusive cause of a particular symptom, is it not possible that in he presence of certain significant individuals, or in certain kinds of situations, or confronted with certain objects, or on the occasion of certain unbidden houghts, an unruly emotion, for example, anxiety or fear, triggers (unconsciously) a disruption in predisposed cognitive mechanisms that would cause a lesynchronization between thought processes and their efferent copy? This lisruption would be cashed out in terms of embodiment, physiology and ieurophysiology, but would also depend on the intentional content of experince. Just in such cases or similar circumstances, frequently linked to an motional encounter, a schizophrenic subject would then (but not always) xperience thought insertion.

. An Alternative Model

lthough the introduction of temporality and intentional content into Frith's nodel can help to address the occasionality problem, it leaves some of the ther phenomenological problems noted above unresolved. To resolve, or void these problems, I want to propose an alternative to Frith's model. It will elp us to return briefly to the context of motor action. There we distinguished sense of ownership from a sense of agency, and we suggested that this same listinction could be worked out in the context of cognition. In terms of nderlying dynamics, we distinguished two basic models in regard to motor ction.

1. An ecological, perceptual-feedback model that works as a built-in, *concurrent* self-awareness delivering a sense of ownership for action;
2. An *anticipatory* pre-action or forward model that delivers a sense of agency for action which is intrinsic to action.

he two points that I want to emphasize are, first, that both the sense of wnership and the sense of agency for action are normally intrinsic, and often ndistinguishable properties of willed action itself. Second, the built-in sense f agency is based on anticipatory, pre-action specifications (cashed out eurologically in premotor processes). This, as we saw, is consistent with rith's observations that normal subjects, but not certain schizophrenics, can correct movement errors in the absence of visual feedback (1992: 82–83). Something of this sort is also suggested by Georgieff and Jeannerod (1998), in reference to the comparator model of motor action: the efferent copy is said to create an "anticipation for the consequences of the action." The sense of agency, then, is not based on a *post factum* verification or sensory-feedback match (although such factors might enhance it) but on an executive or control function that anticipates action. In this way it is complementary to the ecological non-observational sense of ownership for action, which likewise involves no metarepresentational self-consciousness.

Thought is a different matter, a different kind of action, but it seems that it would be much more parsimonious if one could explain the senses of ownership and agency in this realm as being intrinsic or built into the stream of thought itself rather than introducing a second system involving efferent copy and a comparator or central monitor. As we indicated, efferent copy may indeed play an important practical (executive) role in the case of visuo-motor systems, but it is not clear what role it would play in explaining thought.

In my view, part of the explanation for the senses of ownership and agency for thought, and the loss of the sense of agency in schizophrenic thought insertion can be advanced by employing Edmund Husserl's model of the retentional-protentional structure of time-consciousness. Starting with Husserl's analysis of the temporal structure of consciousness, one can develop a phenomenologically-based cognitive model. In this model, what he calls 'retentions' and 'protentions' may be regarded as subpersonal operations that generate the flow-structure of consciousness. My conscious experience includes a sense of what I have just been thinking (perceiving, remembering, etc.) and a sense that this thinking (perceiving, remembering, etc.) will continue in either a determinate or indeterminate way. This phenomenological temporal sense is based on retentional and protentional dynamics that ultimately need to be cashed out in terms of neurological processes. Although this suggestion goes beyond Husserl's phenomenological analysis, it follows the same logic of time-consciousness that he outlines.

I will explicate in a succinct and relatively rough manner Husserl's phenomenology of time-consciousness. I can do this most expeditiously by referring to a diagram (Figure 4). This diagram and Husserl's theory not only explain how the experience of temporal objects is possible given an *enduring* act of consciousness, they also explain how consciousness unifies *itself* across time.[20] The horizontal line ABCD represents a temporal object such as a

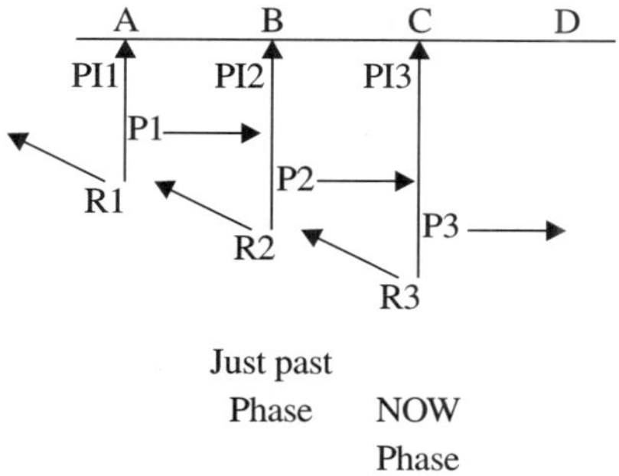

Figure 4: Husserlian Model of Time-Consciousness

melody of several notes. The vertical lines represent abstract momentary phases of an enduring act of consciousness. Each phase is structured by three functions:

- *primal impression* (pi), which allows for the consciousness of an object (a musical note, for example) that is simultaneous with the current phase of consciousness;
- *retention* (r), which retains previous phases of consciousness and their intentional content;
- *protention* (p), which anticipates experience which is just about to happen.

In the now-phase there is a retentioning (r3) of the previous phase of consciousness. Of course the just-past phase includes its own retentioning of the prior phase. This means that there is a retentional continuum — r3(r2[r1]), and so forth — that stretches back over prior experience. The continuity involved in retention has two aspects. The first provides for the intentional unification of consciousness itself since retention is the retention of previous phases of consciousness. Husserl characterizes this as the longitudinal intentionality (*Längsintentionalität*) of retention. But since the prior phases of consciousness contain their respective primal impressions of the previously sounded notes, there is also established a continuity of the experienced object. This is the retentional function which Husserl calls the "transverse intentionality" (*Querintentionalität*) of retention (1991: 85).

The example of speaking or listening to a sentence may help to clarify some things. Consider the beginning of a sentence:

I often think that Julia. …

When in uttering this sentence I reach the word 'Julia' I am no longer saying the previous words, but I still retain a sense of what I have just said. For a sentence to be meaningful, the sense of the earlier words must be kept in mind in some fashion when I am uttering the later words. *Retention,* or what cognitive scientists call working memory, keeps the intentional sense of the words available even after the words are no longer sounded. Built into this retentional function is the sense that *I* am the one who has just said these words. The words do not become part of a free-floating anonymity, they remain part of the sentence that *I* am in the process of uttering. Also, at the moment that I am uttering 'Julia', I have some anticipatory sense of where the sentence is going, or at the very least, that the sentence is heading to some kind of ending. This sense of knowing where the sentence (the thought) is heading, even if not completely definite, seems essential to the experience I have of speaking in a meaningful way. It helps to provide a sense that I am speaking in a sentential fashion, and not speaking a disconnected or meaningless set of phrases.

Protentioning provides consciousness with an intentional direction toward the future. Although Husserl provides an exhaustive explication of retention, he says very little of protention, except that it is like retention in the direction of the future. Husserl does point out that the protentional aspect of consciousness allows for the experience of surprise. If I am listening to a favorite melody, there is some sense of what is to come, a primal expectation of the notes to follow, and the best indication of this is that if someone hits the wrong note, I am surprised or disappointed. If someone fails to complete their sentence, I experience a sense of incompleteness. This kind of perceptual disappointment is based on a lack of fulfillment of that primal expectation which Husserl calls protention. In some sense we might speak here of a failure to match my anticipation with what actually happens. The content of protention is not always completely determinate, however. Indeed, to the extent that the future itself is indeterminate, the content of protention may approach the most general sense of "something (without specification) has to happen next."

Husserl's analysis of protention doesn't go much further. As we saw above, however, in his analysis of retention he suggests that there is a double intentionality — one aspect that is directed at the content of experience and another that is directed at consciousness itself. This double intentionality of retention involves a structure that is similar to a Gibsonian ecological self-awareness. That is, I am not only aware of the melody, I am aware of myself being aware of the melody, so that my perception of the passage of melody is at the same time a non-observational, pre-reflective awareness of my own flowing consciousness — and it is this which delivers a sense that this thinking process is mine[21]–that *I* am the one who is listening to the melody or uttering the sentence. Without meaning to suggest any other kind of symmetry, is there not something like a double intentionality involved in protention as well? That is, isn't my anticipatory sense of the next note of the melody, or of where the sentence is heading, or that I will continue to think, also, implicitly, an anticipatory sense that these will be experiences *for me*, or that *I* will be the one listening, speaking, or thinking. In effect, protention also has what Husserl calls a longitudinal aspect — it involves a projective sense of what *I* am about to do or experience. In fact, regardless of how indeterminate the content of protention may be, the anticipatory sense of self is relatively determinate.

In the normal case the sense of agency with respect to my own thought comes not retrospectively, as if I had to stop to think whether I am really the one who is thinking (this in contrast to Frith's metarepresentation). Rather, it is a sense that is built-into thinking itself. It is part of the very structure of consciousness. The fact that it is not retrospective, or a matter of verification, suggests that it is not initially a matter of the retentional aspect of this structure. Rather, following the clues from our considerations of motor action, I want to suggest that the dynamics of *protention* underlie the sense of agency for thought, or more precisely, that the protentional registration is a necessary but not a sufficient condition for the sense of agency. The function of *retention*, on the other hand, is, in part, to provide a sense of ownership for thought.

Consider, first, that thought may be generated by the subject in a willed and controlled fashion. Problem solving, thinking through a set of instructions, and narrating a story are good examples. I may intend to solve a problem and to do so by following precise steps in a known procedure. I have a sense of where I am going in the procedure, and I push the thinking process along from one step to another in a controlled manner. When I follow a set of instructions, or when I tell a story (perhaps just to myself), I have the same sense that I am promoting my thinking along a path that is, or is becoming, relatively well-defined. In such cases, the protentional aspect of consciousness operates to give me a sense of where the thinking process is going *in its very making*, that is, as it is being generated and developed. It provides a sense that the thinking process is being generated in my own stream of consciousness and, to some degree, under my control.

A second kind of thinking may be more passive. We have referred to unbidden thoughts, memories, fantasies that invade our current stream of consciousness. These are thoughts for which we may have no sense of agency. Still, in such cases, we have a sense that these thoughts are coming from ourselves, rather than from some alien source. Not only do they appear to be part of my stream of consciousness, but, despite the fact that I am not willing them, and may even be resisting them, they still seem to be generated within my own cognitive experience. Protention, in such cases, may be operating perfectly well, providing a sense of where these thoughts are coming from and where they are heading, as they are being passively generated, even within the framework of an unwanted memory or an unwelcome fantasy. Protention may also function to provide a sense of *not knowing* where we are heading, that is providing a sense of uncertainty, or indeterminacy with respect to where such thoughts will lead. For such thoughts, even though I do not intend them, and even though I do not have a sense of where they are heading, I nonetheless have a sense that they are originating and developing within my stream of consciousness. Protention provides some kind of expectancy for them, even if it is completely indeterminate.

What would happen, however, if, in such cases, the protentional function itself failed? In the case of unbidden thoughts, thinking would continue to happen, but there would be neither a sense of agency, nor a sense that these thoughts were being passively generated in my cognitive system, even though they were appearing in my stream of consciousness. I would be unready for such thoughts. They would appear as if from nowhere, and their occurrence would be sudden and unexpected. I would be able to make sense of them only in their retentional train, in retrospect, but not as something self-generated. Protention normally puts me in the forefront of my thoughts and allows me to take up these thoughts as my own product, as they develop.

Consider listening to a sentence uttered by someone else. Normally protention allows me to make sense of the sentence as it is being uttered. I might even be tempted to complete the sentence because I know what the person is going to say. Or, even if I don't know what the person is going to say, I could quickly organize a reasonable end to the sentence — as I often do when someone seems unable to find the right words to finish the thought. But consider a case in which I am caught completely by surprise, as when someone close-by, but out of sight, suddenly yells "Surprise!" In this case, there is no anticipation of the event, even of the most indeterminate kind. The event passes before I realize it is happening. In listening to someone form a sentence, I have a sense of how it is being formed; but in the case of the sudden shout, I catch onto it only in retention. Absent a properly directed protention, the sudden and quickly formed event is *already made* by the time I come to grasp it. Over the course of a second or two, however, an adjustment of attention will bring this event and whatever follows into the proper protentional framework, that is, I will regain a sense of where the voice is coming from and its significance, and my experience is quickly put back on track.

A similar effect may be had, however, if, instead of an external event catching the protentional function off guard, something goes wrong with the protentional mechanism itself. If in the case of an unbidden thought for which I have no sense of agency, something goes wrong with the normal anticipatory sense of what my own thinking will be, the result will be a sense that the thought is not being generated by me.[22] Without protention, thought continues, but it appears already made, not generated in my own stream of consciousness, but appearing suddenly, already formulated as it enters into retention. It is a thought that is neither intended nor anticipated; it will seem to be a thought, but not a thought generated by me. In some way I am not open to it; I am not projected or absorbed into it; it feels alien and less than transparent to me.

Indeed, this may also be the case with intended thoughts for which I would normally have a sense of agency. Without protention, whatever intention I may have, whatever sense I would have of what I will do or think, what I *will* to do or to think, is disrupted. My non-observational, pre-reflective sense of agency, which is tied to control over my own actions, and control over my own thoughts, and which I normally experience within a protentional framework, will be deferred by the lack of protention. That is, I will become aware of my agency only after the fact (as it is captured in retention). In this case, I will experience thoughts that seem to anticipate what I would have thought. Schizophrenic patients sometimes report that some other person seems to know what they are thinking before they actually think it. The thought seems to match up with their own intention, but it still seems to them that they are not the agentive cause of the thought.[23]

Thus, *without protention,* in cases both of thinking that is intended and of thinking that is unintended (unbidden), thoughts will seem to occur within the stream of consciousness that are not experienced *in the making*, but are nonetheless captured by a retentional mechanism that continues to function and to provide a sense of ownership for that stream. I will experience what is actually my own thinking, as a thinking that is not generated by me, as a thinking that is *already made* or pre-formed for me. It is only then that a metarepresentational element might be initiated in the patient, a reflective introspection that is likely to become the hyperreflection characteristic of schizophrenic experience, motivated by something gone wrong with the flow of consciousness. In metarepresentation the patient may start to ascribe the thought to some particular force or individual and report that it is inserted.[24]

A breakdown in the protentional function is consistent with the schizophrenic's experience of time. Minkowski, who describes schizophrenia as involving "acts without concern for tomorrow," "fixed acts," "short-circuit acts," and 'purposeless acts," quotes one of his patients: "There is an absolute fixity around me. I have even less mobility for the future than I have for the present and the past. There is a kind of routine in me which does not allow me to envisage the future. The creative power in me is abolished. I see the future as a repetition of the past" (1933: 277).[25]

Empirical studies show that schizophrenics experience difficulties in indexing events in time, and these difficulties are positively correlated to inner-outer confusions (manifested in symptoms such as auditory hallucinations, feelings of being influenced, delusional perceptions, and so forth), problems that involve distinguishing between self and non-self (Melges 1982; Melges & Freeman 1977). Other studies suggest that future time-perspective is curtailed in schizophrenia (Wallace 1956; Dilling & Rabin 1967). Schizophrenics have difficulty planning and initiating action (Levin 1984) and problems with temporal organization (Klonoff et al. 1970; DePue et al. 1975) and experienced continuity (Pöppel 1994). Bovet and Parnas describe these problems in general terms as an "impairment of self-temporalization" (1993: 584), and they are certainly symptoms we might expect if the protentional mechanism malfunctions. It is suggestive, and perhaps important, that Singh and his colleagues have linked these temporalization problems with the same neurological dysfunctions involved in the schizophrenic's voluntary movement (Singh et al. 1992; also see Graybiel 1997).

What we have outlined in this alternative model is still a subpersonal account, however, and as such it is inadequate to explain the occasionality problem. So one must go on to ask what could cause such a malfunction of protentional mechanisms which in the schizophrenic patient would lead to first-rank symptoms? As I have suggested above, content has an effect on the temporal structure of experience. Emotional content complicates both the phenomenological and neurological pictures. So again, it is quite possible that in schizophrenia, in the presence of certain significant individuals, or in a certain kind of situation, or confronted with a certain object, or in rehearsing certain thoughts, unruly emotions, such as anxiety or fear, trigger a disruption in cognitive mechanisms, specifically a disruption of the protentional dynamic. Just in those cases or similar circumstances a subject would then (but not always) experience thought insertion or similar loss in the sense of agency. It is also possible that this disruption of the protentional function could cause a looping effect that would reinforce the affective trigger. Without protention, for example, it is quite possible that patients would experience the world as being invasive, "on top of them," too close, etc., which are, in fact, anxiety-causing experiences, and experiences reported by schizophrenics.

This analysis links up closely to Francisco Varela's explication of protention in terms of emotional tone. Building on original insights made by Husserl and by Depraz (1994, 1998), Varela (1999a, 1999b) bestows on protention the function of providing a felt tension or readiness for action. This readiness is clearly dependent on current disposition and past experience, which help to define what a subject takes to be emotionally significant. Just such emotional significance may work to upset affective disposition and to leave the subject quite indisposed for whatever is to come. If Varela is right, if the protentional mechanism is essentially linked to affective-tonality, and if affective tonality is, as he suggests, "a major boundary and initial condition for neurodynamics" more generally (1999b: 133),[26] then a disruption of protention is likely to involve widespread cognitive and emotional problems of the sort found in schizophrenia, including incongruity of affect, flat affect (athymia), and "grossly inappropriate affect" (DSM-III-R).[27]

On this account, one does not need to postulate a central monitor — self-monitoring is built into consciousness as the longitudinal aspects of the retentional-protentional structure. In this regard, this explanation requires no mechanisms over and above the mechanisms that account for the temporal structure of consciousness itself. I do not need a separate stream of efferent copy to verify that I am the one who is thinking; the sense of ownership is already included in the original stream of consciousness. The "intention to think" is not something separate from thinking itself; it is included in the very structure of thought. The schizophrenic does not discover alien thoughts by means of a metarepresentational introspection; rather he will have an immediate, non-observational sense that something is wrong, a sense that might in fact motivate metarepresentation as a result.

7. Conclusion

I have argued, against Feinberg, Frith, and Campbell, that with respect to cognition and consciousness the comparator/efferent copy model makes little phenomenological sense and is in some respects redundant or extraneous. I have suggested that the sense of ownership for action (both motor action and cognition) can be distinguished from the sense of agency for action, and that for cognition the sense of agency, although not etiologically explained by protentional mechanisms, depends on the protentional function for its proper registration at the level of consciousness. In contrast, the sense of ownership is closely related to the retentional function.

With respect to the schizophrenic's experience of inserted thoughts, it is necessary to distinguish a sense of ownership from a sense of agency. But this distinction is not itself sufficient to explain thought insertion. Two further steps are required. First, to distinguish inserted thoughts from passively generated, unbidden thoughts, one needs something more than simply a lack of a sense of agency. I've suggested that a failure of the protentional mechanism may account for the fact that the inserted thought seems not to be generated within the subject's own cognitive system. Rather, thanks to retention, it appears "ready made" in the subject's stream of consciousness. Second, the impression that such thoughts are actually generated by someone other than the subject is the result of a delusional, metarepresentational interpretation, motivated by the failure of protention, but explainable only by personal level phenomena.

In conclusion I want to return briefly to the issue of immunity to error through misidentification, which Campbell suggests breaks down in the case of schizophrenic symptoms like inserted thoughts. There is good reason to believe that the immunity principle remains intact even in cases of inserted thoughts. When the schizophrenic reports that certain thoughts are not his thoughts, that someone else is generating these thoughts, he is also indicating that these thoughts are being manifested, not "over there" in someone else's head, but within *his own* stream of consciousness, a stream of consciousness for which he claims ownership. In other words, his complaint with regard to inserted thoughts is not that he is suddenly telepathic, but that someone else has invaded his own mind. The sense of ownership is still intact, despite the feeling that he is no longer the agentive cause of the thoughts.[28] For that reason the schizophrenic should provide a positive answer to what he might rightly regard as a nonsensical question: Are you sure that *you* are the one who is experiencing these thoughts? After all, this is precisely his complaint. *He* is experiencing thoughts that seem to be generated by others. His phenomenology is this: he has a sense of ownership for the stream of consciousness which is impossible to misidentify (and is, in fact, in no need of identification, since it is his own), but into which are inserted thoughts for which he has no sense of agency. His judgment that it is *he* who is being subjected to these thoughts is immune to error through misidentification, even if he is completely wrong about who is causing his thoughts. In the latter case, with respect to agency, he is in a position to make only statements in which he uses the first person pronoun as object — and in such cases the immunity principle is not at stake, and therefore cannot be violated.

Acknowledgments

Research for this paper was supported by a sabbatical leave from Canisius College and by a grant from the National Endowment for the Humanities as a participant at the Summer Institute on Mind, Self, and Psychopathology, directed by Jennifer Whiting and Louis Sass, at Cornell University in 1998. Earlier versions of the paper were presented at the Joint Philosophy and Psychology Project on Consciousness and Self Consciousness, Sponsored by the British Academy, University of Warwick (October 1998) and at the seminar on Exploration de l'expérience et pratique de la description phénoménologique at the University of Paris (April 1999). I thank the following individuals for helpful discussion and comments on earlier versions: Timothy Bayne, José Bermúdez, Sarah Blakemore, Natalie Depraz, Naomi Eilan, Christopher Frith, Christof Hoerl, Teresa McCormack, Josef Parnas, Louis Sass, Galen Strawson, and Francisco Varela.

Notes

1. The example is from Wittgenstein (1958: 67). Galen Strawson (private correspondence) has suggested that all uses of the first-person pronoun are "*as subject*," and that there are no uses that are not immune to error. Even when I mistakenly refer to myself as the person who has a bump on his head, I am still self-referring in the proper way, and indeed, I can only be said to be in error in some respect because I have correctly self-referred. In such cases, it is precisely myself about whom I am wrong. Others have argued that any use of the first-person pronoun *as object* depends on a first-person content that is immune to error through misidentification (see Bermúdez 1998). I do not believe that these alternative ways of viewing the immunity principle substantially affect the arguments found in this paper.

2. In this case the statement "I am waving my arm" is different from Wittgenstein's example, "I try to move my arm," which *is* immune from error through misidentification. Shoemaker distinguishes between absolute immunity and circumstantial immunity, and claims that the statement 'I am waving my arm' is absolutely immune (that is, regardless of circumstances). It is clear from cases of deafferentation, however, that the statement is only circumstantially immune.

3. See Evans (1982) and Cassam (1995) for versions of this argument.

4. This motivates the following question: Does there exist a class of actions that involve an immediate sense of agency that can be expressed in statements which are immune to error through misidentification, but that involve no sense of ownership. I have not been able to think of an appropriate case to fit these requirements. One might think that we could rephrase the delusional case as follows. The delusional subject could state: 'I feel that I am the cause of the action in that other person'. Then one would end up with Wittgenstein's nonsensical question: 'Are you sure that it is *you* who are feeling that way?' But this would still not involve immunity to error through misidentification for the sense of agency. Rather, the subject is actually expressing a sense of *ownership* to which the immunity principle applies. It is a sense of ownership for the feeling (his sense) of remote agency that he experiences (he is self-ascribing the sense of agency) not a sense of ownership for the action. The proper response to the question would be 'Yes it is definitely *my* sense of agency', rather than the response 'Yes I am definitely the cause of the action', i.e., the delusional response to the question 'Are you sure that it is *you* who are causing the action? This raises the possibility, which I shall not explore here, that a sense of agency depends on some form of a sense of ownership for its immunity to error through misidentification.

5. As this paper was being readied for publication, Timothy Bayne called my attention to an essay by Stephens and Graham (1994) in which they discuss schizophrenic thought insertion and make a distinction between sense of agency and sense of subjectivity, where by "sense of subjectivity" they mean what I am calling sense of ownership. Although it is not clear whether what they call the "inseparability thesis" includes the immunity principle, I agree with their conclusion, as far as it goes, that thought insertion involves a failure in the sense of agency rather than a sense of ownership. Campbell does not distinguish between ownership and agency in precisely these terms. He does, however, distinguish two senses of ownership/agency: One tied to self-ascription, and one tied to cause of action. The latter is what I am calling agency; the former, ownership. Campbell

acknowledges that these two senses come apart in schizophrenia. "... we often want to think of the owner of a psychological state as the person who is, in a particular way, causally involved in the production of that state; the person who is, in a sense, the author of the state. This is a separate strand in the notion of ownership of a state to the strand that has to do with the possibility of self-ascription of the state. The two can, on occasion, seem to come apart. This is what happens in the case of the schizophrenic patient who seems to find himself able to self-ascribe a thought of which he is not the author, and who consequently feels that alien thoughts — thoughts which are not his — are being inserted into his mind" (in press).

6. "On reflection, it also seems that this is not just one possible theory; it is the simplest theory which has any prospect of explaining the sense of agency, and we ought to work from it, introducing complications only as necessary" (Campbell 1999: 612).

7. Concurrency here is defined as falling within the same specious present, rather than as absolute simultaneity. The idea is that this sense of agency is built into the action itself, and does not involve a post-factum verification.

8. The differences involve both timing and neurophysiological details. The ecological model implies a self-awareness that is concurrent and "on-line" with the action; the comparator model seemingly introduces an extra and slower verificational mechanism, the comparator. The related neurophysiological issue involves the question of whether the relevant neurological mechanisms are intermodal (with immediate communication between sensory and motor processes) or involve an extra step of translation. My preference is for the ecological model and intermodal neurology. For more on the notion of body schema, and the intermodal relations between sensory and motor systems, see Gallagher & Meltzoff (1995), Gallagher & Cole (1996), and Gallagher et al. (1998).

9. Again I will not try to resolve the question of whether the description in terms of a comparator and efferent copy is the best one in this case. It is also clear that in the absence of vision, proprioception still plays some role in monitoring or correcting movement. But proprioception is precisely an intermodal bridge between sensory and motor systems (see Gallagher & Cole 1996).

10. For more on the involvement of the prefrontal cortex and its complex interrelations with other cortical areas, see Goldman-Rakic & Selemon (1997). For the role of the supplementary motor area in the anticipation and preparation of action, see Passingham (1996) and Tanji & Shima (1994).

11. Marcel points out that often in schizophrenia, as well as in Tourette's Syndrome and Obsessive-Compulsive Disorder, an action is itself experienced as owned, but the source of the action, an intention or command, is dis-owned. Indeed stimulation of the central thalamic nucleus produces hand movements, and although subjects have no idea why they did them, the actions themselves are not dis-owned (Hécaen et al. 1949). Having an intention, or having a sense of agency is not crucial to having a sense of ownership for action (Marcel, in press; Gallagher & Marcel 1999).

12. Of course it is possible to attribute thoughts in my mind to someone else, but in a very ordinary way — for example, in listening closely to a speaker, one might say that the speaker's thoughts are being inserted into one's mind.

13. As we have noted, however, efferent copy is sometimes thought to perform a verificational role (Held 1961; Campbell 1999).

14. Campbell (in press) — emphasis added. He also states: "You have knowledge of the content of the thought only through introspection. The content of the efferent copy is not itself conscious. But it is match at the monitor between the thought of which you have introspective knowledge and the efferent copy that is responsible for the sense of being the agent of that thought. It is a disturbance in that mechanism that is responsible for the schizophrenic finding that he is introspectively aware of a thought without having the sense of being the agent of that thought."

15. See, e.g., Shoemaker 1986. Although Shoemaker begins by discussing Hume's reflective-introspective search for the self he criticizes the perceptual model of introspection as an "inner sense" that would take primary consciousness as an object, or that would involve an identification of self. He is not committed to regarding introspection as a separate act of reflective consciousness. Shoemaker's notion of introspection is clearly stated by Cassam: "introspective awareness, properly so called, is a form of awareness that serves as the basis for making first-person statements in which the first-person pronoun is used as subject. First-person statements in which 'I' is used in this way are those that, in Shoemaker's terminology, are immune to error through misidentification relative to the first-person pronoun" (1995: 315).

16. "What happens here [in the case of the schizophrenic] is that the *ipseity*, the normally tacit or unnoticed 'myness' of the experience, which is a precondition or a medium of any natural, spontaneous and absorbed intentionality, is deranged, and becomes an object of introspective intentionality" (Zahavi & Parnas 1998: 700).

17. Georgieff & Jeannerod (1998), referring to the same kind of comparator model in the context of explaining motor action, describe it in implicitly temporal terms. The efferent copy is said to create an "anticipation for the consequences of the action." Their description raises a number of issues that would need to be explored: Does the efferent copy reach the comparator prior to the registration of the motor action so that there is a real basis for anticipation; or does it reach the comparator simultaneously with the registration of the motor action, so that a simultaneous matching occurs? Spence (1996) raises a slightly different set of issues involving timing.

18. This objection was raised by Louis Sass at the NEH Institute on Mind, Self, and Psychopathology, Cornell University, 1998. One can see this problem in Frith's description of the neurophysiology associated with the positive symptoms of schizophrenia: "Positive symptoms occur because the brain structures responsible for willed actions no longer send corollary discharges to the posterior parts of the brain concerned with perception. This would be caused by disconnections between these brain regions" (1992: 93). One would need to explain why these disconnections are only manifested in some but not all instances.

19. To be more specific, however, if the TGM sputters, then it would seem plausible that both the generated thought and the efferent copy would suffer the effects of the sputtering, and there would still be a synchrony between them. Further, the schizophrenic's phenomenology, if we think of it as being somewhat isomorphic with the mechanism of thought generation, does not seem to indicate anything about the thought that would suggest sputtering. It is not a sputtering thought, but a relatively lucid and intelligible thought that seems inserted. If it is not the TGM that sputters, then either, as Frith suggests, the efferent copy, once generated, fails to reach the comparator (or as I want to suggest, fails to reach it in proper sync), or the comparator sputters. These alternatives would leave the

thought intact, but, lacking a match with efferent copy at the comparator, it would be experienced as inserted.

20. A more detailed account can be found in Husserl (1991). For an extended analysis of Husserl's model and its similarities and differences from James's notion of the specious present, see Gallagher (1998).

21. Gibson himself was inclined to think of his ecological model as applying to thinking as well as to perceptual and motor functions. "Awareness of the persisting and changing environment (perception) is concurrent with the persisting and changing self (proprioception in my extended use of the term). This includes the body and its parts and all its activities from locomotion to thought, without any distinction between the activities called 'mental' and those called 'physical'" (1987: 418).

22. Something along this same line happens when one is falling asleep. Both protentional and retentional mechanisms seem to close down. Consider what happens to comprehension when one is falling asleep while reading. In dreaming too, one does not have a good sense of what will happen next, or a good sense of what has been happening.

23. Spence (1996: 82) cites a case which he interprets in this way. He indicates, however, that this kind of experience resembles something that is more frequently found in autarkic hand syndrome.

24. Spence (1996: 81) suggests that thought insertion involves two elements: First, alienation from one's own thoughts; second, "a delusional elaboration" which seeks to explain the former. The delusional elaboration takes place at the metarepresentational level and follows the initial alienation which has already occurred at the level of pre-reflexive consciousness.

25. This explanation may also account for the perseverative repetitious responses that are often found in schizophrenic patients. A failed protentional mechanism may explain difficulty in generating spontaneous actions, a negative symptom in schizophrenia, as well as difficulties in performing self-directed search (see Frith 1992: 48).

26. On the neurological level, the sort of mechanism that underlies protention is more appropriately thought of in terms of widely distributed and dynamical processes than in terms of localized functions. As a result, the conceptual framework for thinking about the neurological mechanisms responsible for schizophrenia is quite different from the one involving concepts of comparator, central monitor, efferent copy, etc. Even in the realm of motor action, where such localized mechanisms may be involved in generating the sense of agency, since what is at stake is precisely a *sense* of agency, that is, an experience of agency, it is likely, according to the Husserlian model, that the protentional-retentional structure has a role to play in the conscious registration of that sense of agency for movement, or in its failure, for example, in delusions of control.

27. Bovet & Parnas (1993) summarize a number of premorbid characteristics of schizophrenia patients, which include difficulties in interpersonal relations, anxiety, neophobia, and defective emotional rapport.

28. We noted that although Campbell does not make a precise distinction between ownership and agency he does distinguish two senses of ownership: One tied to self-ascription, and one tied to cause of action, and he acknowledges that these two senses come apart in

schizophrenia (in press). Once this distinction is admitted, however, then for the reason outlined here, thought insertion (understood as a problem in regard to the sense o agency) cannot be considered a counterexample to the immunity principle. Stephens an Graham (1994) make the right distinction in this regard, but their analysis of th attribution (to self or to another) of agency for thought (7) suggests that the immunit principle would not apply to the sense of agency even in the normal case. In contrast have maintained (following Wittgenstein and Shoemaker) that expressions that use th first-person pronoun to express the sense of (immediate) agency are immune to erro through misidentification.

References

Bermúdez, J. (1998). *The Paradox of Self-Consciousness*. Cambridge: MIT Press.

Bermúdez, J. (1995). Ecological perception and the notion of a nonconceptual point o view. In J. Bermúdez, A. J. Marcel, & N. Eilan (Eds.), *The body and the self*. Cam bridge: MIT Press, 153–173.

Bovet, P. & J. Parnas (1993). Schizophrenic delusions: A phenomenological approach *Schizophrenia Bulletin* 19: 579–597.

Campbell, J. (1999). Schizophrenia, the space of reasons and thinking as a motor process *The Monist* 82 (4): 609–625.

Campbell, J. (In press). Immunity to error through misidentification and the meaning of referring term. *Philosophical Topics* 26.

Cassam, Q. (1995). Introspection and bodily self-ascription. In J. Bermúdez, A. J. Marcel & N. Eilan (Eds.), *The body and the self*. Cambridge: MIT Press, 311–36.

Crow, T. J., A. J. Cross, E. C. Johnstone, F. Owen, D. G. C. Owens, & J. L. Waddingto (1982). Abnormal involuntary movements in schizophrenia: Are they related to th disease process or its treatment? Are they associated with changes in dopamine recep tors? *Journal of Clinical Psychopharmacology* 2: 336–40.

Depraz, N. (1998). Can I anticipate myself: Self-affection and temporality. In D. Zahav (Ed.), *Self-awareness, temporality, and alterity*. Dordrect: Kluwer, 83–97.

Depraz, N. (1994). Temporalité et affection dan les manuscrits tardifs sur la temporalit (1929–1935) de Husserl. *Alter* 2: 63–86.

DePue, R. A. , M. D. Dubicki, & T. McCarthy (1975). Differential recovery of intellectual associational, and psychophysiological functioning in withdrawal and activ schizophrenics. *Journal of Abnormal Psychology* 84: 325–30.

Dilling, C. & A. Rabin (1967). Temporal experience in depressive states and schizophrenia *Journal of Consulting Psychology* 31: 604–608.

Evans, G. (1982). *The varieties of reference*. Ed. John McDowell. Oxford: Oxford Univer sity Press.

Feinberg, I. (1978). Efference copy and corollary discharge: Implications for thinking an its disorders. *Schizophrenia Bulletin* 4: 636–40.

Fourneret, P. & M. Jeannerod (1998). Limited conscious monitoring of motor performanc in normal subjects. *Neuropsychologia* 36: 1133–40.

Frankfurt, H. (1976). Identification and Externality. In A. O. Rorty (Ed)., *The Identities of Persons*. Berkeley: University of California Press, 239–51.

Friedman, W. (1990). *About time: Inventing the fourth dimension*. Cambridge: MIT Press.

Frith, C. (1992). *The cognitive neuropsychology of schizophrenia*. Hillsdale, NJ: Lawrence Erlbaum Associates.

Frith, C., D., & D. J. Done (1988). Towards a neuropsychology of schizophrenia. *British Journal of Psychiatry* 153: 437-443.

Gallagher, S. (1998). *The inordinance of time*. Evanston: Northwestern University Press.

Gallagher, S., G. Butterworth, A. Lew, & J. Cole (1998). Hand-mouth coordination, congenital absence of limb, and evidence for innate body schemas. *Brain and Cognition* 38: 53–65.

Gallagher, S. & J. Cole (1995). Body schema and body image in a deafferented subject. *Journal of Mind and Behavior* 16: 369–390.

Gallagher, S. & A. J. Marcel (1999). The self in contextualized action. *Journal of Consciousness Studies,* 6, (4), 4–30.

Gallagher, S. & A. Meltzoff (1996). The earliest sense of self and others: Merleau-Ponty and recent developmental studies. *Philosophical Psychology* 9: 213–236.

Georgieff, N. & M. Jeannerod. (1998). Beyond consciousness of external events: A "Who" system for consciousness of action and self-consciousness. *Consciousness and Cognition* 7: 465–77.

Graybiel, A.M. (1997). The basal ganglia and cognitive pattern generators. *Schizophrenia Bulletin* 23: 459–469.

Gibson, J. J. (1987). A note on what exists at the ecological level of reality. In E. Reed and R. Jones (Ed.) *Reasons for realism: Selected essays of James J. Gibson*. Hillsdale, NJ: Erlbaum.

Goldman-Rakic, Patricia S. & Lynn D. Selemon. (1997). Functional and anatomical aspects of prefrontal pathology in schizophrenia. *Schizophrenia Bulletin* 23: 437–458.

Haggard, P. & Eimer, M. (1999). On the relation between brain potentials and the awareness of voluntary movements. *Experimental Brain Research* 126: 128

Haggard, P. & Magno, E. (1999). Localising awareness of action with transcranial magnetic stimulation," *Experimental Brain Research* 127: 102.

Hécaen, H., J. Talairach, M. David, & M. B. Dell (1949). Coagulations limitées du thalamus dans les algies du syndrome thalamique: résultats thérapeutiques et physiologiques. *Revue de Neurologie* 81: 917–31.

Held, R. (1961). Exposure-history as a factor in maintaining stability of perception and coordination. *Journal of Nervous and Mental Diseases* 132: 26–32.

Holst, E. von and H. Mittelstaedt (1950). Das Reafferenzprinzip (Wechselwirkungen zwischen Zentralnervensystem und Peripherie). *Naturwisenschaften* 37: 464–76.

Husserl, E. (1991). *On the phenomenology of the consciousness of internal time (1893–1917)*. Trans. J. Brough. Collected Works IV. Dordrecht: Kluwer Academic.

James, W. (1890). *The principles of psychology*. New York: Dover, 1950.

Jeannerod, M. (1994). The representing brain: Neural correlates of motor intention and imagery. *Behavioral and Brain Sciences* 17: 187–245.

Klonoff, H., C. Fibiger & G. H. Hutton (1970). Neuropsychological pattern in chronic schizophrenia. *Journal of Nervous and Mental Disorder* 150: 291–300.

Levin, S. (1984). Frontal lobe dysfunction in schizophrenia — Eye movement impairments *Journal of Psychiatric Research* 18: 27–55.
Malenka, R. C., R. W. Angel, B. Hampton & P. A. Berger (1982). Impaired central erro correcting behaviour in schizophrenia. *Archives of General Psychiatry* 39: 101–107.
Manschreck, T. C. (1986). Motor abnormalities in schizophrenia. In H. A. Nasrallah and D K. Weinberger (Eds.), *Handbook of schizophrenia, Vol. 1: The neurology of schizophrenia*. Amsterdam: Elsevier, 65–96.
Marcel, A. J. (In press). The sense of agency: Awareness and ownership of actions an intentions. In J. Roessler & Naomi Eilan (Eds.), *Agency and self-awareness*. Oxford Oxford University Press
Melges, F. T. (1982). Time and the inner future: a temporal approach to psychiatri disorders. New York: Wiley
Melges, F. T., & A. M. Freeman (1977). Temporal disorganization and inner-outer confusion in acute mental illness. *American Journal of Psychiatry* 134: 874–877.
Minkowski, E. (1933). *Lived time: Phenomenological and psychopathological studies* Trans. Nancy Metzel. Evanston: Northwestern University Press, 1970.
O'Shaughnessy, B. (1995). Proprioception and the body image. In J. Bermúdez, A. J Marcel, & N. Eilan (Eds.), *The body and the self*. Cambridge: MIT Press, 175–203.
Owens, D. G. C., E, C, Johnstone & C. D. Frith (1982). Spontaneous involuntary disorder of movement. *Archives of General Psychiatry* 39: 452–61.
Passingham, R. E. (1996). Functional specialization of the supplementary motor area i monkeys and humans. In Lüders, H. O. (Ed.), *Advances in Neurology*, vol. 70 (105-116). Philadelphia: Lippincott-Raven.
Pöppel, E. (1994). Temporal mechanisms in perception. *International Review of Neurobiology* 37: 185–202.
Pöppel, E., D. von Cramon, and H. Blackmund (1975). Eccentricity-specific dissociation o visual functions in patients with lesions of the central visual pathways. *Nature (London* 256: 489–90.
Sass, L. (1998). Schizophrenia, self-consciousness and the modern mind. *Journal o Consciousness Studies* 5: 543–65.
Shoemaker, S. (1968). Self-reference and self-awareness. *The Journal of Philosophy*, 6 (19): 555–567.
Shoemaker, S. (1984). *Identity, cause, and mind*. Cambridge: Cambridge University Press
Shoemaker, S. (1986). Introspection and the self. In P. A. French, T. E. Vehling, & H. K Wettstein (Eds.), *Studies in the philosophy of mind*. Minneapolis. Midwest Studies i Philosophy, 10, 101–120.
Singh, J. R., T. Knight, N. Rosenlicht, J. M. Kotun, D. J. Beckley, & D. L. Woods (1992) Abnormal premovement brain potentials in schizophrenia. *Schizophrenia Research* 8 31–41.
Spence, S. (1996). Free will in the light of neuropsychiatry. *Philosophy, Psychiatry, an Psychology* 3: 75–90.
Sperry, R. W. (1950). Neural basis of the spontaneous optokinetic response produced b visual inversion. *Journal of Comparative and Physiological Psychology* 43: 482–89.
Stephens, G. L. & G. Graham (1994). Self-consciousness, mental agency, and the clinica psychopathology of thought insertion. *Philosophy, Psychiatry, and Psychology* 1: 1–12

Tanji, J. & K. Shima (1994). Role for supplementary motor area cells in planning several movements ahead. *Nature* 371: 413–16.

Varela, F. J. (1999a). The specious present: A neurophenomenology of time consciousness. In J. Petitot, F. J. Varela, B. Pachoud, & J.-M. Roy (Eds.), *Naturalizing phenomenology: Issues in contemporary phenomenology and cognitive science*. Stanford: Stanford University Press, 266–312.

Varela, F. J. (1999b). Present-time consciousness. In F. J. Varela and J. Shear (Eds.), *The view from within: First-person approaches to the study of consciousness* (111–140). Exeter: Imprint Academic.

Wallace, M. (1956). Future time perspectives in schizophrenia. *Journal of Abnormal and Social Psychology* 52: 240–45.

Wittgenstein, L. (1958). *The blue and brown books.* Oxford: Basil Blackwell.

Zahavi, D. & J. Parnas (1998). Phenomenal consciousness and self-awareness: A phenomenological critique of representational theory. *Journal of Consciousness Studies* 5: 687–705.

PART IV

Questionable Psychopathology

John Cutting

'he human being is a being that asks questions. That is what Heidegger said in is latter phase (Heidegger 1967). So, what questions does a human being sk? It can ask anything it likes, but there are two questions which are undamental to the rest — Who am I? and What is there? These are the two nost fundamental philosophical questions, but we are here mainly concerned vith the man-in-the-street and his questions. Nevertheless, as we shall see, the ort of answers he gets back in different psychopathological states reveals a lot bout philosophical questions and answers.

What answers does the normal man-in-the-street receive when he asks nese two questions? The answer to our question about the man-in-the-street's uestions is that it depends on who asks them and to whom they are addressed. 'ou might think that it also depends on whom or on what the question refers), but these are the very issues at stake in the initial questions and therefore nese do not concern us yet. But if Heidegger is correct in his formulation, and believe that he is very profound here, then for any questioning to go on there nust be an audience or at least an interlocutor. There is no point in asking a uestion if the questioner knows the answer and there is no point in asking a uestion if there is no possibility of receiving an answer. If the human being is being that asks questions, then the minimal requirements — and these are ecessary preconditions — are that the questioner does not know the answer) some question at some time, is invited or even compelled in some way to sk the question, and expects to receive an answer to at least some of the uestions it poses. In other words, the very fact of asking questions requires nat that part of the questioning being (the human being) which asks questions ; not the same as whatever being or part of a being answers them.

So, where do the answers come from, if not from the questioner? Could ney come from the realm of things? One can certainly address a chair, for example, as to its colour, history, value, etc., and at a pinch one could say that the chair answers questions of this nature. What colour are you? Oh, a reddy brown, not a yellowey-brown, as you thought yesterday. The chair is of course only an ontic being and not an ontological being like a human being. But even if you were to say, almost metaphorically, that it can answer these sort of ontic questions, it cannot answer the sort of questions posed early on. It cannot possibly answer on its own questions about whether it has an ontological status and cannot help in answering questions about the human being's status — ontological or ontic. In fact, the best philosophical formulation of this matter is, in my view, Benjamin's (1979) which is to consider things *mute*. Nor can another non-human animal answer in the way I am exploring, although it can give richer answers than a chair can (by way of sounds and movements) to the sort of ontic questions put to it. So we are left with only two general possibilities for the source of our answers. Either the answer comes from some source outside oneself — God (if you are a theist), a real person, or some real person with whom one has an imaginary connection, or it comes from some aspect of the questioning self, but not that aspect which asks questions. At this point, we are not in a position to give an opinion on the issue because the original question — Who am I? — is seeking this very answer.

We have merely been setting up the preconditions for the two questions. But there are two more matters in this context which need to be tackled before we can start asking our questions with full confidence. One concerns the way in which the question is posed, the other is the invitation or compulsion to ask the question.

The way in which questions are asked is rarely considered in this context. But it is clear that I can ask questions in words or merely look questioningly at some matter. Not all my questions are verbal and therefore not all of any answers I receive are given in language. In fact, it seems quite sensible to me to assume that I can question my environment and receive some sign as an answer without there being any consciousness of the matter, never mind some verbal exchange.

On the issue of invitation, compulsion, or what Heidegger refers to as "calling", this seems to me a quite central problem. "What is called thinking" is one of his later lecture courses, the chief concern of which is what calls thinking. What calls us to think or question something? When one first reads this (or in my case reads it over and over again), it makes no sense. Why should anything call us to think? But the more one thinks about the matter, the nore it seems absolutely correct. If there were not some compulsion or nvitation or call, then why bother to do anything? Something must precede hinking, or, in terms of what concerns us in this lecture, questioning, other-vise it would have no point.

We have dealt with what I regard as some of the chief preconditions for uestioning to occur — that there be a questioner who doesn't know the nswer to the question, and who expects some sort of answer from "some-ody" else, and who has a repertoire of questioning modes, not all of which nvolve language, and, at root, is compelled to question by he knows not what.

After all this preamble, what answer does the normal man-in-the-street et to the simple questions — Who am I? and What is there?

The man-in-the-street and the woman-in-the-street are thing-oriented. he man-in-the-street, at this place and time (late 20th century Europe), is iven the answers — *I am John Smith* and *There are things*. In other places nd at other times, the answer would undoubtedly be different. The man-in-he-jungle might say that he is the spirit of his father. Our common European urnames reflect this — Johnson, O'Leary, MacIntosh. Lord knows what the an-in-the-street thinks emotions are, but, as professional thinkers on these atters cannot tell us either, the man-in-the-street is in good company.

Of course, the professional philosopher is grossly dissatisfied with the an-in-the-street's answers and, in the case of the Who am I? question, starts idening them:

I am a thinking being;
I am an experiencing being;
I am a cognising being, not all of which cognitions I experience;

r in the case of Heidegger:

I am a concerned being.

n the case of the What is there? question, the philosopher's repertoire of nswers is considerable:

I cannot be certain that there are things;
There might be nothing;
There must be something, though not an actual thing;
There's nothing;
No, there's not nothing.

Let us now see how the man-in-the-street asks or answers these question when in a state other than normal, in other words, in a psychopathologica state. I shall consider only the Who am I question and three nosologica entities — depression, mania and schizophrenia. I shall start with depressio because it is, in my view, the most illuminating for our theme.

Over 20 years ago, I conducted a study on schizophrenics' experience c their self. I needed some controls and I chose depressives. What th depressives said about themselves was as follows:

> There was something about me that other people saw but I couldn't figur out what it was that made them that way toward me.
>
> One chap's eyes looked watery as if he were upset about looking at me I'm just linking it now as if there was something about me which couldn't say.
>
> I think I look peculiar because of the way people look at me. I imagine that people thought I was dangerous.
>
> Other people saw a change in me. They said I was snappy. To me, wasn't really snappy.
>
> My missus brought it to my notice. She said I wasn't the same person a the days before.
>
> I keep thinking that people are saying things with hidden meanings or tha people are looking at me to say what a pathetic idiot wasting our time.
>
> I kept thinking people thought I was a gangster.
>
> They were all telling me I was sick.
>
> Recently I've noticed that they notice I've had a stare.

What struck me about these comments was that there was something simila about them, but at the time I could not work out what it was. Moreover, it wa very different from what schizophrenics tended to say — which I will come t later — and it was clearly common. Nine of 20 consecutive depressives sai this sort of thing, whatever it was I have puzzled about it over the intervenin years. What is obvious is that they sensed something different about them selves which they might or might not know what it was, and that the evidenc for this was coming from someone else. The last case is a good example. H idn't primarily notice that he had a stare; he noticed that other people noticed his. It was a puzzle for the depressive, or as I would say now *a question* mposed on him or her about himself or herself coming from outside — *entripetally*, as it were.

These 20 patients were not all psychotic. In conventional psychopathologial terms they had ideas of reference. Subsequently I collected a large sample f consecutive psychotic depressives (with delusions or hallucinations of some ort), 100 in all, and analysed what were in essence *delusions* of self-reference. s you can see in Table 1, 39 had such delusions and I analysed them according o what I thought at the time might be an interesting method. I considered the elusion to be a bipartite Saussurian sign with a signifier and a signified, and ooked at the composition of the sign in the three different psychopathological onditions. Essentially (Table 1) the delusions fell into four categories — either ne signifier was vague or non-existent, or the signified was vague or non-xistent, or both were vague, or both were clear-cut. In depression, the chief ifference from schizophrenics or manics from this point of view was that what *vas* signified was much clearer than the signifier through which it was signified. 'his is clearer in Table 2 where I have compared the three psychopathological onditions according to the presence or absence of a clear-cut signifier or ignified. Depressives overwhelmingly have a signified without much in the vay of a signifier. The question in these psychotic depressives, as opposed to ne non-psychotic, is not that they don't know what the matter with them is, but ather how they know — the source — is vague.

The next issue I want to consider in this sort of way is that of delusions of uilt and unworthiness in depressive psychosis. The general view of these elusions is that the depressive feels so wretched that he deserves to be unished and magnifies some past pecadillo into the reason why he deserves nis. But no one, to my knowledge, with the exception of the British psychiaist, Lewis in 1934, has noted that in many such cases the subject feels ggrieved and resentful of the accusations. As one of his patients said:

> What have I got to blame myself for … There was no truth in it whatsoever. He died a natural death.

ewis comments:

> It is sufficient to point out that scarcely any writers recognize the occurrence of paranoid ideas with resentment or protestations of innocence, as a common feature of depressive states.

Here are some of my sample of 100 psychotic depressives.

> Felt that people didn't want to go to the pub with her — saw it in thei eyes.

> He believed he would go to prison for crimes he had *not* committed.

> He had more money in his pocket than he should have had — might hav stolen it; I'm in a position where I can be blamed for anything!

Moreover, they often express their guilt in the form of a question, or wit considerable doubt:

> Guilty for something *she doesn't know what.*

> Terrified she *might* harm someone.

> Wondered if someone *might* be planning to show him dirty films.

Or their guilt is conditional on some chance event:

> If the next car he sees is red, he is the worst person in the world.

> Feels guilty if someone sits near him.

Again, the whole issue is puzzling, uncertain and chancey, in short questionable.

Table 1: Depressive Psychotics (n = 100)

		S	**M**
No. with delusions of reference	39	*102*	**33**
Clear-cut signified and vague or non-existent signifier, e.g. conscious of an unpleasant attitude by other patients that she had been making up to a doctor.	13	*10*	**1**
Clear-cut signifier and vague or non-existent signified — e.g. peculiar way in which a friend sniffed meant something.	3	*16*	**6**
Clear-cut signifier and clear-cut signified, e.g. handkerchief on a scaffolding was a message telling her to escape.	5	*13*	**6**
Vague signifier and vague signified. E.g. comments on TV referring to her.	18	*63*	**20**

Fourthly, on the depressive's questionable experiences, I want to mention the condition of depersonalisation. This psychopathological term, in my view, has been completely devalued by its use in a number of disparate situations. Its original description by Schilder in 1914 emphasises what, in my view, is more a schizophrenic experience:

> A person afflicted by depersonalisation complains he is no longer the same, no longer himself. Indeed, in clear-cut cases, the patients complain that they no longer have an ego, but are mechanisms, automatons, puppets… All depersonalised patients observe themselves continuously and with great zeal … self-observation is compulsive in these patients.

Mayer-Gross (1935) too stressed the "augmented introspection":

> Sitting by the fire, I suddenly realised: I was me! I suddenly got outside myself and saw myself. I am since then absolutely conscious of being conscious.

But other reports of depersonalisation focus on the questionable nature of the person. Klages (1959), for example:

> Everything seems strange to me now; when I lie in bed I ask myself sometimes, who is it lying in my bed? Is it another person? Sometimes I wonder whether there are three of me — the real me, a self composed of my left side, and a third of my right side.

Fifthly, and finally on the topic of depressive questioning, I want to consider another psychopathological entity almost invariably linked with depression. In the newspapers recently the following headline caught my eye — Who is the real Santa Claus? It was the story of a small-town Scottish solicitor who was well-known to everyone because he always played Santa Claus for the town's children at Christmas. One morning, he told his wife that he was going

Table 2: Analysis of Depressives' Delusions of Reference

	% of 39	*% of S*	**% of M**
Any signifier	20 *	*90*	**97**
Any signified	92 *	*23*	**21**
Signifier without signified	8 *	*77*	**79**
Signified without signifier	80 *	*10*	**3**
Signified with signifier	13	*13*	**18**
Any verbal signifier	3 *	*46*	**82**
Any non-verbal signifier	21	*44*	**15**

N.B. * $P < 0.05$ chi square

to a meeting in Edinburgh and that was the last anyone heard of him for a year until the police were investigating a murder in Cornwall at the other end of the British Isles. They rounded up the usual suspects — casual flower pickers — and the fingerprints of one of them matched those of someone wanted in a small Scottish town for non-payment of a drink-driving offence over a year previously. He was not the murderer but the man, whom locals referred to as a hippie, with dyed red hair, living in a caravan with a girlfriend, was none other than the small-town Scottish solicitor who used to play Santa Claus at Christmas. When the police interviewed those who knew him in Scotland, they discovered that in the year before his disappearance he had become morose, had taken to drinking heavily, that his marriage was failing and that there were irregularities in his business along with the charge of drink-driving, Of course we know the condition as a depressive fugue but what does it tell us about depressive identity. As the newspaper headline put it, Who was the real Santa Claus? Was he a small-town Scottish solicitor with a mid-life crisis who chose to sort himself out in the furthest county away from him that he knew? Or was he really a Cornish hippie living a lie in Scotland? Or was he really Santa Claus all along, tarrying a while here and there on his way to Lapland?

Such is the questionable state of depressive selfdom, which I shall return to later.

Next I want to turn to schizophrenia, which I shall not cover in such detail, but rather contrast it with depression in respect of the questions posed by them or forced on them.

To the simple question which I put to a group of remitted schizophrenics of 20 years ago:

> When you first experienced a change in the way things were — did you feel different in yourself'?

Their answers were very different from those given by depressives. They themselves had personally noticed a definite change in some respect — unlike the depressives who said that they had been made aware of some change through others, by proxy, as it were.

> I felt like a freak.
> I definitely felt more masculine.
> I lost sense of my own self.
> Different personality; split personality.

I experienced homosexuality; I took on the feelings of a woman.
Felt as if part of myself was coming out of me; split in two.
Ninety per cent (90%) man, ten per cent (10%) woman.
Sometimes I think there's two of me.

Setting aside the differences in thematic content, it is the schizophrenic who primarily experiences the change — a change, moreover, which, in most of these examples, is not the sort of change that could be observed anyway. The answers may be extremely questionable to us, but did not appear so to the subject.

Turning to the pattern of their delusion of self-reference, I alluded to the differences between depressives and schizophrenics earlier. Over the years, I collected a series of 250 acute schizophrenics and the general pattern was as in Table 3–there was a definite something in almost all cases (someone sniffing peculiarly, some word said in a certain way) the precise meaning of which for themselves was only identified in under a quarter. The commonest was a signifier without a signified — the converse of the situation in depression — and the signifier was as likely to be a word or number as it was a person or a pictorial thing — unlike depression where it was usually a person or a pictorial thing. Here there were questions, but questions put to the world, almost like a scientist asking why people sniff in such a way, for example, and unlike depressives whose, largely unanswered, questions concern themselves — Why am I like this? Why am I deemed responsible for all the nasty events in the world?

As for the main sorts of morbid selfhood in schizophrenia, I have categorised these elsewhere (Cutting 1997) as either misidentification of self, misclassification of self or misattribution of self, respectively, self as a different identifiable person (e.g. I am my father), self as a different sort of person (e.g. I am a witch, God, animal of some kind) and self with some distinct qualitative

Table 3: Schizophrenics' (n=250) Delusions of Self-Reference (n=102)

	% of 102	*% of D*	**% of M**
Any signifier	90	*20*	**97**
Any signified	23	*92*	**21**
Signifier without signified	77	*8*	**79**
Signified without signifier	10	*80*	**3**
Signified with signifier	13	*13*	**18**
Any verbal signifier	46	*3*	**82**
Any non-verbal signifier	44	*21*	**15**

change (e.g. supernatural powers, exceptional abilities, mission, altered sexual orientation or gender, altered genealogy, altered mental status, altered biography). In all such cases, there is little in the way of questioning, but, as I said at the beginning of this section on schizophrenia, the schizophrenic is being given questionable (only to us normals) answers as to who they are. Together with their unanswered questions put to the world — as in their delusions of reference — their morbid selfhood is a combination of questionable answers and unanswerable questions — compared with, as I see it, the depressive's position in the questions and answers game as unanswered questions.

What of the manic? The manic's delusions of self-reference are shown in Table 4. I did not include manics in my study long ago of subjective experience in psychosis but I did subsequently collect 100 manics, and their pattern of self-referential delusions is very similar to the schizophrenics' except in one respect — the nature of the signifier, which is almost invariably verbal, in which category I placed numbers as well as words. The typical manic delusion of self-reference is a number (e.g. car registration number) or a word (e.g. some advertising slogan on a hoarding) whose meaning for them is a question. Otherwise, their main delusions of selfhood are, as everyone knows, to do with what I called earlier self-misattribution — crediting myself with supernatural powers, exceptional abilities, and altered marital or biographical status. Misclassification of self (e.g. being some high-status person) is also common. In terms of our questions and answers framework, the manic's questions are very limited — to the meaning of words and numbers in their environment — and their overall problem is having too many answers about themselves and the pictorial world to bother about questions. They are, with respect to the depressive's morass of unanswered questions about himself and the schizophrenic's enigma of questionable answers about himself and unanswerable questions about the world, rather in the position of having unquestioned answers about most matters which they feel compelled to follow up.

To return to the philosophical framework with which I started this lecture, what, if anything, has this tour of psychopathology taught us about the fundamental question — Who am I?

There were three main issues which I raised: Who is the questioner? Who does the answering? and Who or what invites, compels or calls us to question in the first place, or, as we saw in the case of manics, check out the answers? A subsidiary issue concerns the mode of the questioning and answering.

Table 4: Manics' (n=100) Delusions of Self-Reference (n=331)

	% of 33	*% of S*	**% of D**
Any signifier	97	*90*	**20**
Any signified	21	*23*	**92**
Signifier without signified	79	*77*	**8**
Signified without signifier	3	*10*	**80**
Signified with signifier	18	*13*	**13**
Any verbal signifier	82	*46*	**3**
Any non-verbal signifier	15	*44*	**21**

We are, of course, reliant on extant philosophical theories to explain all these matters. But in the case of the depressives, there is a quite extraordinary coherence between Heidegger's notion of *Dasein* in *Being and Time* (Heidegger 1927) and the depressive's formulation of who he is. The depressive, as I have presented the matter, is a *being who cares*, reluctantly, in some cases maybe, but nevertheless he is compelled to care, exactly as Heidegger said was true of Dasein. He should have helped the man on the park bench, he is being blamed for giving the striking firemen £5–as two of my patients said. He cares more about the welfare of his fellow humans than any normal person does; that is for sure.

But where does this compulsion come from? It comes, apparently, from the people around him. He is exquisitely sensitive, it seems, to the facial expression of others. Heidegger's "conscience as the call of care" is imposed upon him, as it were, by an exaggerated sense of the plight of others.

What about the answers to his questions? Who is the answerer? In fact, the answers to his questions are pretty paltry. He is forever in a questioning mode — wondering why other people should be the judge of what he is, wondering why he should be so culpable, wondering what his identity really is – and being prepared to swop it when the going gets tough. He is a question looking for an answer. It is, in fact, my view that the answering part of the human self is knocked out in depression. That is their problem. At a philosophical level this is reason; at a neuropsychological level, this is the left hemisphere. There is no one to answer their questions. As Hannah Arendt (1978) said, in *The life of the mind: Thinking:*

> Thinking, existentially speaking, is a solitary but not a lonely business; solitude is that human situation in which I keep myself company. Loneliness comes about when I am alone without being able to split up into the two-in-one, without being able to keep myself company.

As for the mode of questioning, the depressive is thrown back on the non-verba mode. There is no carefully worded proposition, only a look, at the most, to th world, and an answer in the same mode — watery eyes, disdain, etc.

The schizophrenic, more complex than any normal or any other perso afflicted by a psychopathological condition, is a peculiar mix of a questione who cannot evaluate the answers and an answerer who cannot satisfy th questioner. That is why I say that he is an enigma plagued by questionabl answers and unanswerable questions.

What is the schizophrenic's compulsion to pose questions and be trouble by the answers? Here we have to say that he is doubly compelled — once b whatever conditions the questions (as in the case of the depressive) and secondl by whatever conditions the drive to follow up the answers (those put to him b the world).

Where do the answers come from? They come, apparently, from th world, but are, at root, reason's, in his case, anomalous constructions of wha the world is. In other words, they are reason's contribution to thingness, but, i his case, distorted in such a way that they seem to demand attention.
What mode are the questions posed in? They are posed in both nonverbal an verbal mode, hence the answers come back in both modes.

The manic is scarcely interested in questions. It is answers that h receives, answers in the verbal mode, and answers which are all but certain. ' am a thinking being' is the manic's credo, and whatever I think is, and there i no question about that.

References

Arendt, H. (1978). *The life of the mind: thinking*. London: Martin Seckeer & Warburg.

Benjamin, W. (1979). *On language as such and on the language of man. In one-way stree* London: Verso.

Cutting, J. (1997). *Principles of psychopathology*. Oxford: Oxford University Press.

Heidegger, M. (1927/1962). *Being and time,* trans. by J. Macquarrie & E. Robinso Oxford: Blackwell.

Heidegger, M. (1967/1978). *What is metaphysics?* Trans. by D.F. Krell. In D.F. Krell (Ed. *Basic writings. Martin Heidegger*. London: Routledge, Kegan & Paul.

Klages, W. (1959). Depersonalisationserscheinungen bei hirnorganisch Kranken ur Schizophrenen. *Archiv für Psychiatrie und Zeitschrift für die gesamte Neurolog* 199:266–79.

Lewis, A. (1934). Melancholia: a clinical survey of depressive states. *Journal of Mental Science* 80:277–378.

Mayer-Gross, W. (1935). On depersonalisation. *British Journal of Medical Psychology* 15:103–26.

Schilder, P. (1914). *Selbstbewusstsein und Persönlichkeitsbewusstsein.* Berlin: Springer.

Pathological Selves

Michael Alan Schwartz
Case Western Reserve University

Osborne P. Wiggins
University of Louisville

. Self and World

ıt the outset we would like to assert a thesis regarding the self: *The living self ; necessarily related to the world while it at the same time remains separate 'om the world.* This essential feature of selfhood, we shall maintain, can be ɔund at all levels of organic life. At the different levels of organism, however, assumes different forms. We shall sketch some of these differences, but we hall focus on the human self and its differences from other living forms. We ɛcognize the distinctiveness of the human self when compared with other, on-human selves. But we also believe it important to remember that the roots f the human self extend down to the deepest biological levels. Once we ɛcognize what is distinctive of the human self, we shall see how this distinc- veness can assume pathological forms. The *hypernomic,* the *agonomic,* the *yponomic,* and the *idionomic* are the four forms of pathology we shall escribe. Having outlined these four different forms, we shall focus on the *ypernomic* self and characterize it in some detail.

. The Phenomenon of Life

et us begin at the organic level and note some basic constituents of all living eings. The fundamental task of every living organism consists in securing its wn continuing being. Threatened as it always is by the possibility of non-being, death, this possibility will become its actuality if the organism does nc constantly elude this possibility by *doing something*. Because the being of th organism is never insured, that being must be *achieved* and repeatedly *re achieved* through the organism's own *activity*. Non-being threatens the livin being because the organism is a creature of *need:* the organism alway remains *non-self-sufficient*. The living being cannot perpetuate its own contin ued being within itself: in order to continue to exist it must *relate itself to th other, the world*. The organism depends on the world for the resources tha will satisfy its needs. The activity of the organism, then, consists in a interaction with the environment. If this interaction stops, the organism dies Lacking the self-sufficiency that would allow it to continue to exist complet within itself, the organism is a world-dependent being (Jonas).

And yet the organism must also remain *independent* from its environ ment. If the boundaries that separate the life of the organism from the worl should vanish, the organism would die. The living being must then maintai its own *distinct identity* apart from the environment. In order to preserve it own individuality separate from the world, the organism must interact with th world. The self-world relationship is therefore complex: the continued exist ence of self depends on its relationship to the world, and the continue existence of self depends on its separateness from the world (Jonas).

3. World-Relatedness

We may now inquire further into the nature of the world-relatedness of livin beings.

Already at the level of plants, the living being is related to its enviror ment. Through roots, leaves, and its sensitive surfaces the plant registers an interacts with its external surroundings. But because it is primarily throug roots, leaves, and sensitive surfaces that it encounters the environment, th plant's relationship to the world is relatively *immediate:* those parts of th environment which the plant encounters are often contiguous with the sur faces of organism, and those parts of the world that matter to it are greatl limited in quality and quantity (Jonas).

It is different with animal life. The non-human animal encounters th world through perception, emotion, and movement. As a result, far mor aspects of external reality are available to the animal. The animal perceives it rey at a distance and runs across that distance to capture it. Because of erception and motility, then, significant spaces can separate the animal from hose components of the environment that concern it. But those sizable istances must be traversed by perception and movement, or else the animal ails to secure the sustenance necessary for its continued being. Moreover, esire for food must motivate the animal to chase the prey and kill it. Just, ierefore, as perception and movement must span the spatial distance, so esire must bridge the temporal distance that separates the first perceiving of ie prey from the eventual capturing and devouring of it. Desire must endure iroughout and keep the animal going despite the effort and frustration in-olved in the hunt. The animal's relationship to the world is thus a *mediated* elationship: space is mediated by perception and motility, and time is medi-ted by emotion (Jonas).

These forms of world-relatedness of the non-human animal are governed rimarily by the creature's biology. In lower animals the forms of world-elatedness can be conceived as largely mechanistic: thanks, for instance, to a iechanistic reflex, a tick in a tree drops on the human being walking below recisely when the air temperature and the concentration of butyric acid in the erson's evaporating perspiration surpass a threshold level. In more evolved nimals the forms of world-relationship are primarily instinctual, and it is the reature's biology that determines these instinctual forms. Once the instincts merge, they are relatively fixed and inflexible, and whatever learning occurs alls within a narrow range. Consequently each species of animal has its own species-specific environment," i.e., an environment *relative to* that particular pecies and its set of mechanisms and instincts. The animal's "world-relation-iip," then, is in reality *a species-specific environment-relationship.*

In the human animal, however, biology does not achieve this much. uman biology does not fully delineate our forms of world-relatedness. Our iology in fact leaves our forms of world-relationship relatively *open* and *nder-determined.* The indeterminacy of our biological conditioning renders s "instinct-poor." And therefore, the instincts which narrowly define the ivironment-relationships of non-human animals play a smaller role in human xperience and action. As a result, the human being has no species-specific ivironment. Insofar as he is determined by his biological makeup, the human idividual is capable of living in a very wide variety of different environ-ients. This is what is meant by Max Scheler's phrase "world-openness": hile the non-human animal is limited to a relatively narrow environment, the human animal is open to a far broader range of multifarious realities. Throug its biology, therefore, the human being remains unfixed, indeterminate, plastic, and malleable (Portmann, Gehlen).

For this reason, human *culture* must and can come to supplement huma biology. And culture *can* come to supplement biology because our biolog leaves us plastic and malleable enough to be molded into a variety of differer ways of being human. Culture imposes its man-made forms on human existence, and in this way it helps to close the world-openness left by our biolog alone. By internalizing social values and learning social roles, our experienc is molded into more or less definite patterns. Culture determines what biolog left indeterminate (Portmann, Gehlen).

Culture *mediates* our forms of world relatedness primarily by providin us with schemes of interpretation, configurations of meaning, that allow us t make sense of reality and thus carry on our activities in it. Language is, c course, the central system of reference through which the world is given to u But there are other cultural frameworks of meaning that inform and guide us i what would otherwise be an unmanageably complicated reality. In fact one c the main functions of meaning is that of reducing the complexity of th external stimuli to which the human organism is subjected. By reducing th complexity of these stimuli, cultural meanings structure consciousness an behavior (Gehlen).

By mediating the human encounter with the world, cultural meaning als broadens the scope of human life into ever larger spans of space and tim Through meaning human beings can know about past, present, and future a well as near and far. Meaning even extends the reach of humans into imaginary and purely possible realms. And it directs consciousness toward th sacred and transcendent.

Yet culture too still leaves human beings partially "open," under-determined, malleable, and unfixed. In this gap of indeterminacy left by bot biology and culture lives *individual freedom of choice.* After culture an biology have both done their work, the remaining indefiniteness of our form of world-relatedness must be rendered definite by *voluntary decisions.* Bu since the self has already been shaped by its biology and enculturation, it freedom is a "bounded freedom."

. Self-Relatedness

.1. *Helmut Plessner: Eccentric Positionality*

'he self-world relationship may appear at first as inviting schematization in erms of the simple subject → object relationship. And such is probably dequate, at least roughly, when we consider the relationship between the on-human animal and its environment. The non-human animal, governed, as is, largely by its instincts, responds *as a whole* when a specific direction of s behavior is triggered by an item in the environment. Instinctive behavior is ehavior which *unifies* all aspects of the animal's being by focusing them on ie target object. Helmut Plessner has thus called the animal self a *centered* elf.

By way of contrast with this animal centeredness, Plessner has described ie *eccentric position* of the human self. Schematized with reference to the ubject-object relationship mentioned above, the eccentric position of humans 'ould have to be delineated as a subject → subject/object → object relation- hip. In other words, the self as subject is related to itself as object and through iis self-relationship is related to the world.

But let us go back now and describe the eccentric positionality of hu- ians.

The eccentric position means that the person both coincides with his own eing and fails to coincide with his own being. The human self is both entered in its being and not centered in its being: I am both identical with iyself and different from my self. Take my relationship to my own body, of xample. To a certain extent, I *am* my body; I coincide with my body; my ody and I are one. But in other ways my body is something *different from* me: is an *object* or *thing* which *I* use. I use my hands to type on my computer. Vhen I now type, I am unaware of my hands. In this case I *am* my hands; I do ot distinguish between my consciousness which thinks the thoughts and the ands which type these thoughts. My consciousness and hands are one reality; iey perform together as an indivisible unit. But my hands could not always 'pe on a computer. Years ago I had to teach myself, i.e., my hands, how to 'pe. My hands were then objects about which I had to think, and I had to onsciously guide them in each movement. Now that my hands have learned ow to type, I do not think about them and I do not consciously direct them. hey have become so thoroughly unified with my thinking that my thoughts *immediately* appear as words on the computer screen. But, of course, thi *immediate* appearance of the words my mind thinks is *mediated:* it is mediate by my typing hands. Hence Plessner speaks of my relationship to my ow body as one of "mediated immediacy."

Or take the emotions I feel as another example. When I am feeling certai strong emotions, I simply *am* those emotions: my being is enveloped in thos emotions. But I can also decide to "get a hold" on my emotions and chang them. I may tell myself to calm down or to not get so excited. Of course, I ma not succeed entirely when I try to control my emotions. But this partial succes perfectly demonstrates the eccentric position of human beings: my emotion are not identical with me because I can *control* them, but they are to a certai extent identical with me because I cannot completely control them; I ar compelled to simply *be* them.

Now notice that it is precisely through aspects of myself like my typin hands and my self-shaped emotions that I relate myself to the world. M connection with the world is mediated by those aspects of myself that I contrc and use. My world-relatedness is mediated by my self-relatedness.

4.2. *Harry G. Frankfurt: First-Order and Second-Order Desires*

In his much discussed essay, "Freedom of the Will and the Concept of Person," Harry G. Frankfurt attempts to define a characteristic that distir guishes human beings, i.e., persons, from other animals. Frankfort writes tha

> one essential difference between persons and other creatures is to be found in the structure of a person's will. Human beings are not alone in having desires and motives, or in making choices. They share these things with the members of certain other species, some of whom even appear to engage in deliberation and to make decisions based on prior thought. It seems to be peculiarly characteristic of humans, however, that they alone are able to form what I shall call "second-order desires" or "desires of the second order." (1988: 12)

Non-human animals have desires and these desires frequently motivate the to act in particular ways. These are "desires of the first order." The anim desires to eat the prey, for instance. But the animal has no control over thi desire. If the desire is sufficiently powerful, the animal will chase the pre kill, and eat it. Persons, on the other hand, have some *control* over the desires. They may feel a certain desire, and it may even be an especiall powerful desire. But they may dislike having this desire and strive to chang

t. Human beings can thus desire to have certain desires or desire not to have articular desires. Persons are accordingly capable of "desires of the second rder."

Through their capacity to desire their desires, humans can *identify them-elves* with some of their desires and not with others. I may have two onflicting and equally powerful desires, for instance. But I can will that one f these and not the other be *my* desire. I thus *identify myself* with the desire I vill to be mine, and I *withdraw myself* from the desire I will not to be mine 18–19). I may, of course, continue to have this other (undesired) desire, and it nay even be sufficiently powerful to motivate me to act to satisfy it. But even vhen this desire motivates my action, I can still will that it not do so. I can thus eel that I have not remained true to myself, that I have betrayed myself; and I nay feel guilty for this act of self-betrayal. This capacity to identify our own elves with some aspects of our mental lives and not with others will occupy s later.

Frankfurt goes on to argue that it is this human capacity to desire or not esire our desires, i.e., it is the human capacity to have desires of the second rder, that makes possible genuine freedom of the will. Persons, according to rankfurt, are distinctive in having freedom of will. Other animals may be free to act"; i.e., non-human animals may be free to do what they want to do. or example, "an animal may be free to run in whatever direction it wants" 20). But animals do not have freedom of will because they are not able to etermine their wants. Persons have freedom of will if they are able to will vhat they want to will, or humans have free will if they are free to have the vills they want (20).

We need not follow Frankfurt's analysis of free will further here. We only vish to point out that Frankfurt too recognizes the distinctively human capac-y of the self to take a stand toward components of itself. Because the ccentric position entails that I do not coincide with myself, I may not have the esires I desire to have. *My* desires may not be the desires *I* desire; and yet they re still *my* desires. And it is because of this inner distance of myself from nyself which can be bridged by desire and choice that we can call the human vill free or unfree.

There exists a clear connection between the eccentric position of humans nd the fact that they are instinct-poor. Because my instincts are much too veak to structure my experience and behavior, *I* must structure them. *I* must ave control over aspects of myself because otherwise these aspects of myself would lack patterning and directionality. The inner distance opened up by the eccentric position exists because of the need for a conscious and directive agency within the self to organize the life of the self.

5. One Form of World- and Self-Relatedness: Social Roles

Our discussion of the determinants of world- and self-relatedness has thus fa moved on a very general plane. We would like to narrow our scope somewha by focusing on that form of world- and self-relatedness that goes by the name of "social roles."

Biology, culture, and freedom shape persons differently. For example some people enjoy their social roles, and they are able to conform thei behavior to the requirements of these roles easily and comfortably. Such people are able to identify themselves with their roles, at least during the time they are performing them. Other people, however, feel uneasy and awkward while enacting social roles. These people experience considerable "role distance" even when they force themselves to play the role. These alternatives role-identification and role-distance, are the results of biological, cultural, and personal determinants. These determinants shape us differently so that we each have different attitudes toward our social roles.

Notice, however, that we humans, unlike non-human animals, *can* play social roles, and we can play them because of our eccentric positionality When I am enacting a social role, the role is both something I am and something I am not. When I am teaching, I *am* a teacher. And yet I am also *manipulating* my role: I *adjust* it and *modify* it; I *shape* it and *mold* it. I have control over how I play the role, but I do not have complete control becaus the role is also something I *am.*

Roles are, of course, patterns of cultural meaning. As such patterns, role mediate my relationship to other people and to the social world in general. By playing an accepted social role I expect to be understood by other people and to have a recognizable social identity within the world. And I expect othe people to respond to me by performing their reciprocal roles. But roles also mediate my relationship to myself: I understand myself in terms of my role and I control myself in accordance with the requirements of the role. Th social role is a constituent of my personal identity. Through roles, then, mediate my relationship to the cultural world, and through roles cultur mediates my relationship to myself.

6. Dispositional Vectors

As we pointed out above, different people have different relationships to themselves and to the world. I can identify myself with aspects of my being, and I can distance myself from aspects of my being. Likewise, I can identify myself with aspects of the world, and I can distance myself from aspects of the world. To some extent this tendency to identify ourselves or to distance ourselves is biologically determined. But to some extent it is determined by culture and also by personal biography. Through the biological, cultural, and biographical forces that shape us, then, there arise within us tendencies to move in one direction or the other, tendencies to move *toward* identification with social roles and norms, or tendencies to move *away from* identification with social roles and norms. We shall refer to such basic tendencies within the self as "dispositional vectors."

Normal people experience such tendencies within themselves: they are drawn toward identifying themselves with social roles or away from such identification. However, most people, in their daily role-performances, are able to *balance* role-identification with role-distance: they play the roles naturally enough but they do not fully identify their personal being with the roles. Such an equilibrium in the individual's relationship to his social roles manifests an equilibrium in the dispositional vectors we mentioned. Of course, such an equilibrium is rarely constant in human life. The individual vacillates: he is able to identify with his roles sometimes but feels deeply alienated from them at other moments. The vectors, as tendencies in human life, change: they move the person in different directions at different times. But precisely in this change and vacillation is disclosed the unfixed and plastic character of human existence. Indeed it is in the change and vacillation that we must "come to terms" with ourselves and make a decision that selects one alternative from the open range of possibilities confronting us.

Selfhood thus emerges as a broad spectrum of possible ways of being human. This spectrum is broad because our biology leaves us world-open, and our culture as well as our personal history, supplementing biology, shape us in a vast variety of ways. And even after biology, culture, and personal biography have placed each of us in different regions along this wide spectrum of humanity, the indeterminacy that remains must rely on individual free will to decide finally how we shall live.

7. Toward Pathology: Extreme Forms of the Dispositional Vectors

The dispositional vectors within us can assume extreme forms. For example, the tendency to *identify* with social roles and norms may become a tendency to *over-identify* with them. In such a case the person would have no self apart from the social roles she plays and the social norms she obeys. We shall call this extreme form of identification with social roles and norms "hypernomia." By contrast, another person may remain *unable* to identify with social roles and norms. This person may struggle to play social roles or conform to social norms. But ultimately she lacks the capacity to do so and consequently fails. We shall call this extreme form of distance from social roles and norms "agonomia." On the other hand, we can imagine a person who *under-identifies* with social roles and norms. This person may be able to play social roles and conform to social norms. Indeed the person may be able to perform the roles extremely well. But the person may still not identify himself with the social roles he so effectively plays. We label such under-identification with social roles and norms "hyponomia." And finally we can conceive of a person who strongly identifies herself with her own *personal* roles and norms. We shall call such a person "idionomic."

8. Pathological Selves

Having now defined these four different extreme forms that the dispositional vectors can assume, we are prepared to discuss specific kinds of mental illness. We would first like to note, however, that it is the "world-openness" of human beings that makes it possible for those people who behave in ways we call "mentally ill" to survive. Human life can assume many different individual forms and continue to exist in the world because each form inherently retains the indefiniteness and lack of fixity that allow it to adapt to its surroundings. If a "deviant" form of non-human animal appeared in the world, it could probably not survive. Its "deviant instincts" would lead it to behave in ways that, because of their fixed structure, remained too maladaptive. "Deviant" forms of human behavior, however, remain sufficiently open to adjust to a variety of situations.

We shall now draw upon the philosophical anthropology we have sketched above to indicate some central components of four different "mental disorders."

closer to the human center, should be heard. For all of us together constitute a plurality of forms of world- and self-relatedness enabling humans to inhabit this world as well as countless and unfathomable past and present worlds.

Indeed these existential types may and do have crucial and even essential roles to play in human history. The hypernomic type performs an invaluable conservative function in maintaining social standards and in disapproving of deviations from those standards. Deviations from the culture's values are seen by the hypernomic individual as shortcomings and as therefore requiring redress. Hypernomic persons provide strong and selfless support for social norms and institutions. Without them, the inherent flimsiness of cultural standards could easily lead to social breakdown. In times of social breakdown, however, the agonomic type can play a crucial, even a revolutionary historical role. Agonomic human beings may envision innovative value systems. In their alienation from accepted norms, their intense authenticity, their capacity to perceive details that others miss, and their metaphysical preoccupations, they may expound other and newer values. They may see themselves as having the "saving knowledge" which can deliver humankind from its deepening crisis. More than once in human history the agonomic's vision of a "new heaven and earth" has rescued communities from the dead-ends into which their traditional values have led them. Hyponomic individuals, on the other hand, are supremely adaptable to the rapid shifts in values and mores that characterize times of change and crisis. Outstanding performers, they may pick up the values of the moment and express them passionately and perfectly. And with equal gusto they undermine the old as they embrace the new. Finally, idionomic persons may retain for all of us what appears to be no longer of value in the present but which may regain value in the future. With seriousness of purpose, devotion to their tasks, a strong capacity for work, and scrupulous attention to detail, they preserve that which is of value and would otherwise be obliterated.

We certainly recognize that extraordinary suffering is often associated with these types. Nonetheless, if we are right about the important historical functions that are performed by the individuals who embody them, it would be a grave mistake to seek to eliminate from the human gene pool all of the genes which produce such persons. Indeed, if we are right, these genes need to remain in the gene pool in order to continue to give rise to persons of these types. Humanity needs hypernomic individuals to strive forcefully to maintain its existing standards. It also needs agonomic people who may envision radically new ways of life as well as hyponomic individuals who undermine the old and make way for the new and embrace it. In the meantime, idionomic persons preserve that which is of old but unnoticed value: tomorrow such value may once again become essential to us. Without hypernomic people our traditional social structures will lack their main human support and will be threatened with collapse, and without agonomic individuals we will lack the new vistas that we will need when our traditional institutions do inevitably collapse. Hyponomic people can facilitate this collapse while idionomic individuals hold back the tide and preserve that which may prove useful again in the future. The human race needs such extreme qualities: our continued existence may even depend on them.

We would now like to explicate in greater detail one of these types, the melancholic type. We would like to do this in order to clarify the complexity of the world-dependency that one finds in the melancholic personality.

9. The Hypernomia of Typus Melancholicus

The person with melancholia, as we have said, exhibits an excessive dedication (relatedness) to particular social roles and norms. Indeed, there is an *over-identification* with certain social roles and norms. Following Tellenbach and Kraus, we have called this *"hypernomia."* To state our point negatively, we might say that this type of person lacks separation (distance) from certain social ideals. Her striving is thus marked by her *conscientiousness,* by her determination to live up to these social norms. One performs one's duties whether agreeable or disagreeable. The individual with melancholia will not settle for less than complete fulfillment of them. She tends to feel guilty or valueless when she fails to fulfill her duties completely.

In the above descriptions we have employed the phrases *"particular* social norms" and *"certain* social norms." We need to specify what we mean by "particular" and "certain." The social norms to which the person with melancholia ceaselessly strives to conform are *primarily the norms of her childhood.* This is so because one of the main characteristics of this type of personality is its relative *lack of development in time.* Her core self exhibits *very little historical evolution.* This kind of personality is from childhood on *relatively unadaptable* to changing circumstances in the sense of assimilating and adapting to the new values that one encounters as one continues to live. Some components of her personality do change and develop, but the norma-ive roots of childhood remain basically unaltered and powerfully determina-ve. For the far greater part, then, the social values in accordance with which he individual with melancholia lives were values internalized in childhood.

To say that the melancholic personality, at least in its fundamental value-tructure, lacks temporal development is to say that this personality is firmly ooted in the past. For her, the present and future are viewed primarily in terms of the imposition onto them of the ideals of her past. In overly simplified erms, we may say that, for her, the normative past endlessly repeats itself: the uture is merely a projection of the value-ideals of the past. For the future to be ike the past she will have to work hard to realize the ideals; the future will not of its own accord conform to the ideals of the past. *Only firmly committed acts of will can make the future what it ought to be, namely, like the past.* Her *will-ower,* then, is called upon to perform resolutely and even heroically.

Another central characteristic of the person with melancholia is her *ntolerance of ambiguity.* The meanings and values which she bestows on ersons and actions are unambiguous, univocal, and definite. A particular ction, for example, is *either* good *or* bad; it cannot be both good and bad. Colloquial English allows us to say that this person inhabits a "black and white vorld": everything is *either* black *or* white; there are few shades of gray Kraus).

These tendencies to view the future as needing to replicate the past and to view this in an unambiguous, unconditional manner leads to what we would ike to call "the utopian demand of the melancholic type." Nothing less than ull realization of the ideal will do. For this reason the person requires that her nvironment be kept *orderly* and *well structured.* Disorderliness in her envi-onment is deemed a personal failing and hence unacceptable.

There is an obvious gap between the utopian demands of the person with nelancholia and the imperfections of reality. Because of this often wide and ersistent gap, her determination to realize her ideals may require serious acrifices in the present. The present, then, because it necessitates hard work or the sake of the future, may be experienced as a time of considerable lifficulty and striving. But this difficulty and striving are experienced as the rices that *must* be paid to create the utopian future. We may thus describe the hases of her *lived experiences of time* as follows: (1) the *past* was the time of he ideal, (2) the *present,* aimed firmly as it is at the future, requires strenuous ffort that may now produces disappointment, and (3) the *future* will embody he idealized past if one only strives diligently enough.

As we have said, the individual with melancholia finds it difficult to adapt to alterations in her environment. As things around the person change, they will probably become more and more unlike the values that she has internalized in childhood. As they become more unlike the childhood values she still firmly holds, they will be experienced as bad. They cannot be seen as simply "different" because the norms of her childhood furnish the values through which the person unwaveringly perceives the world. There is no other acceptable way to view the world than through these pre-established value-ideals.

Hence the individual with melancholia may find herself in conflict with present-day social norms if these have historically moved away from the earlier ideals of her childhood. Present-day values will be perceived as "degenerate," "loose," or simply "immoral." In a pluralistic society in which many incongruous value-ideals co-exist, she will inevitably find most of these ideals to be "wrong-headed" or "bad." She can then become *highly critical* of the way certain individuals live and of the ways in which certain institutions operate. What is striking here is her *lack of self-doubt or self-criticism* regarding her own ideals. We might expect that living in a pluralistic society would lead a person to take a critical look at his or her own values. Not so for the person with melancholia. In her own mind her ideals carry the status of absoluteness or self-evident truth. To her, her own norms are "obviously" the correct ones and should obtain throughout society.

Self-doubt remains impossible for the individual with melancholia because she identifies her very being with the ideals she strives to realize. Any threat to these norms is consequently a threat to her being. Similarly if she fails to live up to these norms, she has failed completely, she is worthless. For the person with melancholia, her own being is the self who constantly realizes the values she deems absolute, values she believes to be society's "true values," however much society may in fact deviate from them. Consequently, a threat to these values, either through her own failure or the failure of others, is a threat of non-being, a threat of annihilation. She will thus find it necessary to respond to this threat by re-stabilizing the ideals which the failure undermined.

This strict adherence to certain value-ideals does not imply, however, that the individual with melancholia cannot be generous, kind, and forgiving to other people. Even when she observes other people fall noticeably short of her own values, she can be magnanimous and amiable to them. Such magnanimity, generosity, and amicability are after all required by her own ideal conception of herself, and she always strives to live up to her ideal conception of herself.

This hyper-identification of the person with social norms — even if they are solely the social norms of her childhood — evinces her commitment to the social whole. Despite her disapproval of present-day social norms because they contradict the norms of her childhood, she does not withdraw from present-day society. Indeed she repeatedly engages in the social world, striving to realize the ideal. This, of course, requires much hard work for two reasons. (1) The present social world, like every *reality,* falls short of the ideal; and in addition (2) the present social world now holds to its own (changed) norms which *contradict* the "correct" ones.

These difficulties do not deter the person with melancholia, however, in her repeated social engagements: she continues to enter this world and to try. This is another basic constituent of this type of personality: *its attempt to play accepted social roles.* She strives to "fit in" to the given social structure. We might even say that the individual with melancholia needs to "fit in" to some acceptable place within society more than the normal person does. The normal person is more self-sufficient *vis a vis* society. The normal person does not need the ratification of his or her place in society as much as the person with melancholia does. The normal person, while playing social roles, is capable of more role-distance.

The relationship of the individual with melancholia to her social role is, however, equivocal. On the one hand, we can say that she *over-identifies* with her social roles. She will strive to play her roles "to the hilt." She will strive to be the best anyone can be in those roles. And therefore, she may be perceived by others as "extremely capable," "remarkably diligent," or "very successful": she greatly impresses other people because she performs her roles so well. On the other hand, it must be emphasized that this determination to play these roles so well issues from her fundamental ego-defect, her lack of self-sufficiency, her powerful need for the ratification of her being by others. To state our point somewhat paradoxically, the individual's superb role performance does not issue from her personal strength as much as it does from her basic ego-weakness. The superlative quality of her social role performance is a "compensation" for her inability to be a self by herself.

Because the person's determined striving to perform her roles well issues from her ego-weakness, she does not want people to expect too much from her. She fears failure, and consequently she fears the high expectations of others which she may possibly not meet. For this reason there is a tendency to refuse these expectations in advance. She will be demurring and deferring to others. She therefore rarely exhibits pride before others. If she is proud, then others can expect her to be good at what she does. Since she fears such high expectations, she does not publicly appear proud. She will rather appear modest and even self-abnegating.

Because her eagerness to conform to society's requirements arises from an ego-weakness, the role performance of the person with melancholia i "inauthentic": the self playing social roles so well is not her true self. It i rather "an invented self," a self she has created for now in order to have a self she otherwise lacks. But notice that it is a self she has created "for now." I placed in extremely different social circumstances, she could come to perform extremely different roles superbly. This facile ability to "switch" social selve — each of which is very capable and impresses others — arises from the fac that the self of the typus melancholicus lacks fixity; it lacks internal definition

We wish to reiterate however: the person with melancholia suffers deepl from social change. Therefore, she will struggle to avoid change in he environment. When change is forced upon her, she will strive to keep it at minimum. Moreover, even in the midst of change she always remains commit ted to her basic norms. Although her social roles may change in extreme ways they will be fashioned by demands issuing from her own unchanging ideals These ideals remain persistently unadaptable and stable.

Because the individual with melancholia feels a powerful need to create self through role performance, she can appear to be *highly gregarious:* sh seems to like being with others and to enjoy getting along well with them. But for her, this social congeniality requires will and effort: it does not aris naturally and spontaneously from the innermost depths of who she is. At th innermost depths of who she is lies a powerful need to have her being ratified by others, and this need leads to the willed gregariousness through which sh tries to "fit in" well to the given social situation.

We spoke earlier of a distance from present-day social norms on the par of the person with melancholia: because present-day social norms have prob ably changed from the norms of her childhood and because she views the presen through the lens of the norms of her childhood, she will probably feel alienate from present-day social norms. From what we have written just above, howeve we see the powerful need for her to play "to the hilt" social roles with thei *present-day* normative requirements. Now, for her, the one need is as compel ling as the other, i.e., the need to perceive the world from the viewpoint of earlie norms and the need to conform to the requirements of contemporary norms

Because of the ego-blindness of the typus melancholicus, she will probably not become aware of this discrepancy; she may at some level uneasily experience it, but it will probably not come to her attention. The discrepancy is usually glossed over without difficulty.

The normal person can choose between individual *freedom* of behavior and *conformity* to the requirements imposed by social roles. The individual with melancholia does not enjoy the same degree of freedom. She needs to conform to social requirements much more than the normal person does. Because her ego is too weak to be a self without social connections, she can only create a self by playing her roles very well, by conforming to their requirements "to the hilt." Hence the point we made earlier: the person with melancholia lacks role-distance.

Because she brings her self into being by playing a role for others, i.e., because she can be a self only when it is a self-for-others, she cannot feel that the other person values her for simply *being* who she is. She must actually *accomplish* something, *do* something good, in order to obtain the needed ratification of her being by the other. Only her action-for-others manifests her being; her simple being-for-others cannot manifest her being.

This need to *accomplish something* for the other in order to cement the alliance extends even to the intimate sphere of sexuality. The act of love-making cannot be simply an expression of feeling for the other. It must rather be an *active achievement* through which she secures a claim to the other's love (Tellenbach 1961: 82).

Living alone is very difficult for the person with melancholia because she needs strong alliances with other people who *confirm* her activities and the values which guide those activities. Only when such social support is directly furnished by significant others in her immediate environment can she feel that strong connection with the social world that she profoundly needs. And only when she feels firmly connected to society does the individual with melancholia feel that, through her role-participation in it, she is a full self. She then feels that her values and beliefs are not just hers but are rather general values grounded in *a reality transcending her.*

Notice that the person with melancholia seeks solely *confirmation, agreement,* from others. Disagreement, conflict, with others throws into uncertainty both her own being and the truth of those norms she strives to realize. As a result, she detests and strives to avoid *conflict.* She wants to live therefore only with people who *positively value* her and *affirm* her ideals. She cannot long stand to be around people who explicitly question or deny her values. Because of her lack of self-questioning, it is very difficult for her to engage in a detached and impartial debate concerning her ideals. Any debate or argument which touches on her values is one which she *must* win. She consequently tends to avoid such discussions; and, if debates do unavoidably arise, she never doubts that the other person is in the wrong. Indeed, she never doubts that the other person is misguided and she is in the right even when she withdraws rapidly from the debate because she cannot bear conflict.

The person with melancholia, we have said, feels strongly tied to the social world and therefore finds it very difficult to live alone. She therefore needs to live with someone, but not with just anyone. For we have also claimed that she needs other people around her who positively value her and her ideals. At least at the outset of her relationship with a person she will tend to over-idealize him in the light of her own ideals. Because of her intolerance of ambiguity, she will see this person as *only* embodying these ideals; her intolerance of ambiguity will automatically screen out those features of the other which contradict her ideals. For her at the outset, the perceived being of this significant other *is* the reality of her ideals.

We have sought to describe a type of personality whose core characteristic lies in its deep embeddedness in the structures of the social world. The type of person lacks any free play between her own individuality and her social roles. The self-image which this type of person carries does not distinguish between her individual qualities and her social roles: in her self-conception, her true being *is* her social roles. Her very existence as a self therefore depends upon her role-performance.

10. Conclusion: Social Conformity and Individual Autonomy

We have concluded our description of the existential type, *typus melancholicus*. In our description we have sought to understand the peculiar nature of the self-world relationship in the person with melancholia. The deficiencies in this mode of world-relatedness help to illuminate the need for both role-identification and role-distance in normal role performance. Conformity to the norms of society is necessary, but freedom from these norms remains equally necessary. The human self needs to be involved in the social world but at the same time separate from it. The individual with melancholia lacks the role-distance that provides a dimension of autonomy and flexibility in normal life. But it should also be noted that too much distance from society and its requirements is also undesirable. Hence what is best is a healthy equilibrium, an equilibrium that is occasionally difficult to maintain in the daily lives of all of us.

References

Dörr, O. (1992). Herméneutica, Dialéctica y Psiquiatria. *Rev. Chil. Neuro-Psiquiat.* 30: 179–188.

Frankfurt, H. G. (1988). *The Importance of What We Care About.* Cambridge: Cambridge University Press.

Gehlen, A. (1993). *Der Mensch: Seine Natur und seine Stellung in der Welt, Gesamtausgabe, Bd. 3.1 und 3.2.* Frankfurt am Main: Vittorio Klostermann.

Gehlen, A. (1988). *Man: His Nature and Place in the World,* translated by Clare McMillan and Karl Pillemer. New York: Columbia University Press.

Jonas, H. (1966). *The Phenomenon of Life: Toward a Philosophical Biology.* New York: Dell.

Kraus, A. (1977). *Sozialverhalten und Psychose Manisch-Depressiver: Eine existenz- und rollenanalytische Untersuchung.* Stuttgart: Ferdinand Enke.

Plessner, H. (1981). *Die Stufen des Organischen und der Mensch, Gesammelt Schriften IV.* Frankfurt am Main: Suhrkamp.

Plessner, H. (1982). *Ausdruck und menschliche Natur, Gesammelte Schriften VII.* Frankfurt am Main: Suhrkamp.

Plessner, H. (1970). *Laughing and Crying: A Study of the Limits of Human Behavior,* translated by James Spencer Churchill and Marjorie Grene. Evanston: Northwestern University Press.

Portmann, A. (1956). *Biologie und Geist.* Frankfurt am Main: Suhrkamp.

Portmann, A. (1973). *Vom Lebendigen.* Frankfurt am Main: Suhrkamp.

Portmann, A. (1990a). *A Zoologist Looks at Humankind,* translated by Judith Schaffer. New York: Columbia University Press.

Portmann, A. (1990b). *Essays in Philosophical Zoology: The Living Form and the Seeing Eye,* translated by Richard B. Carter. Lewiston, Ny: The Edwin Mellen Press.

Spitzer, M. (1999). *The Mind in the Net.* Boston: MIT Press.

Tellenbach, H. (1961). *Melancholy.* Pittsburgh: Duquesne University Press.

Phenomenology of the social self of *the schizotype and the melancholic type*

Giovanni Stanghellini
Dipartimento di salute mentale, Università degli Studi – Firenze

He who awakens this perilous anarchy is always its first victim
A. Artaud
Héliogabale ou l'anarchiste couronné

1. Introduction: Distinguishing schizotropic from schizotypal vulnerabilities

Clinical psychiatry, like general medicine, has always sought out those elements that foreshadow the onset of a full-blown syndrome. Hypothetically, these elements represent both a syndrome's *primary* phenomena in a pathogenetical sense and its *prodromal* symptoms. The idea of "vulnerability" applies precisely to this pre-clinical condition, preparing the terrain for the development of more characteristic clinical phenomena. Nevertheless, when applied to the realm of major psychoses, and especially to those defined as "schizophrenic", the idea of vulnerability hides an ambiguous and potentially fertile duplicity.

Vulnerability to schizophrenia has been approached from two distinct, though complementary viewpoints, the first stressing attenuated forms of schizophrenic symptoms, the second regarding personality features (Kendler 1985). This twofold assessment of schizophrenic vulnerability coincide more or less with two traditional areas of psychopathological research: the analyses of phenomena occurring in a person's field of experience, and that of his or her value and belief structure. This distinction between modifications of phenomenal consciousness and of the structure of moral conscience is of fundamental importance, and as such has been studied by leading figures in psychopathology (Janzarik 1959; Ey 1963). Psychopathology distinguishes between two psychological domains, on the one hand the field of consciousness, or presence of experience (*champ de la conscience ou l'actualité du vecu*) and, on the other hand the domain of the Self, i.e., the axiological system standing behind a person's worldview. Disordered phenomena occurring in the first domain are abnormal *experiences*, in the second — eccentric *beliefs*. Disorders of the field of consciousness involve acute psychiatric syndromes (such as *bouffées délirantes*), while disorders of the Self entail alienated long-lasting conditions. Thus, in H. Ey's nosology, for instance, full-blown schizophrenias, being pathologies of the Self, are alienated worldviews. The person's pattern of attitudes and convictions positively contributes to the constitution of schizophrenias no less than the passive subjective experience of the decomposition of phenomenal consciousness.

Table 1. The two areas of psychotic vulnerability

Field of consciousness Phenomenal consciousness Experiences	Individual axiological system Moral conscience Beliefs
Schizotropic vulnerability Depersonalization/derealization Passive changes in awareness of the world/self	Schizotypal vulnerability Eccentric philosophy of life Active constitution of one's own worldview

Schizophrenic prodromes can thus be explored and conceptualized either in terms of abnormalities in the field of consciousness, or in terms of eccentricities in mentality or worldview.

Schizotropic vulnerability refers to those disturbances in one's field of subjective experience foreshadowing schizophrenic decomposition. These are disorders of experience falling in the broad category of depersonalization and de-realization phenomena. These feelings of quasi-ineffable strangeness in the perception and conceptualization of one's self, body and world reach a critical threshold at the onset of clinical schizophrenia, but may also occur long before its overt manifestation. Different authors have demonstrated the predictive validity of abnormal experiences and their relevance for the pathogenesis of schizophrenic psychoses (Huber 1983; Klosterkötter 1988; Klosterkötter et al 1997; Chapman 1980), although these phenomena may be observed in persons who never progress into a frank psychosis (Parnas 1994).

Schizophrenic vulnerability, however, cannot be confined to these basic alterations in the field of consciousness; it also involves profound changes in the realm of personal values. This is what we shall call *schizotypal* vulnerability. With the construct of schizotypal vulnerability we view a person's anthropological make-up, his or her existential orientation — in other words, the individual's *attitude* towards ordinary perception and common sense categorization of the world. Schizotypes may hold opinions and convictions that are critical of common sense conventions, and *therefore* attempt to deliberately situate themselves outside of the restraint of shared beliefs and values. This eccentric attitude towards common sense cannot be accounted for as derealization/depersonalization, as these symptoms relate primarily to disturbing changes in the awareness of the world/self that *passively* affect the person.

The eccentric attitude of the schizotype has scarcely been investigated, although this issue seems to be quite relevant for complete comprehension of the schizophrenic's alienation. The schizotype's philosophy of life may contain elements that could foreshadow the onset of a frank schizophrenic syndrome, in its clinical vestiges, and will eventually be its stubborn, perpetual core. Hence, schizotypal vulnerability could be the best vantage point for viewing schizophrenic existence — the *embryo* of a schizophrenic's life project and the ethical and epistemological fingerprint of his/her world.

2. The discontinuity between the schizotype and common sense

In earlier papers (Stanghellini 1997a, 1997b), I have analyzed the conditions of schizophrenic and manic-depressive patients together in terms of an excessive proneness (schizophrenics) or excessive resistance (manic-depressives) to the bracketing of natural evidence of commonsensical everyday experience. Pre-schizophrenic depersonalization/de-realization phenomena (i.e. basic-symptoms, Huber 1983), impairments of intentionality (failure in constituting reality, Mundt 1985) and the experience of the loss of self-evidence (Blankenburg 1971) were interpreted as three different facets (noematic, noetic and eidetic respectively) of an accentuated proneness to lose one's rootedness and at-homeness in one's life-world. This interpretation led us to an anthropological characterization of psychoses as impairments of the dialectical movement between suspending one's natural attitude and conforming to it. Individual and social health is dependent upon a dialectical tension and balance between these tendencies (Minkowski 1927; Blankenburg 1969; Triandis 1995; Stevens and Price 1996). "Normals" seem to spend much of their lives ruling out oddity from their life-world. Schizophrenics, who are hypo-connected to common sense, may be puzzled by ordinary life situations and be unable to act according to what is commonly expected. They seem to lack, ignore, or sometimes refuse, common sense categories to typify their experiences. Vice versa, manic-depressives are hyper-connected to common sense and can hardly act autonomously since they over-identify with it. Here it is assumed that the schizophrenics' hypo-connectedness may also spring out of a *deliberate attitude*–a critical positioning towards common sense. In what follows, the vulnerable condition of the schizotype — together with the analysis of the corresponding and antithetical characteristics of the melancholic type (Tellenbach 1961; Kraus 1977) — will be described along with his or her eccentric attitude towards commonsensical social roles and norms.

Two main objections can be moved to this project. The first objection is an epidemiological one concerning the relationship between schizotypy and schizophrenia on the one hand, and melancholic type and affective psychoses on the other. Schizophrenias and manic-depressive psychoses seem to be final common pathways (i.e., syndromes) arising from a multiplicity of predisposing factors; it is most certainly not true that all full-blown schizophrenics show (or have shown) schizotypal features (at least in the sense of current diagnostic manuals), and that all major depressives (not to speak of manic-depressives) are melancholic types. In the latter case, for instance, it has been established that not more than 50% of major unipolar depressives have melancholic type personality features (Mundt et al. 1997).

The second objection is a psychopathological one. Full-blown schizophrenic and manic-depressive psychoses often seem to have features *opposite* to schizotypy and to melancholic type conditions respectively. For instance while melancholic types, outside of their clinical episodes, would sincerely maintain that they are authentically engaged in helping and protecting their partner, during acute episodes melancholic patients would stigmatize their own behavior as insincere and non-authentic. Melancholic types are overly concerned with their social partners' expectations and convinced that this style of behavior is the only right way to achieve authentic relations with them. Acute melancholic patients, on the contrary, often complain about their own (past and present) incapacity to sincerely "love" their partners and to actually be involved in their lives (Kraus 1994).

These two objections may give rise to a critique: this "model" of psychotic vulnerability — based on self-reports about one's own personal philosophy of life — does not have enough of a clinical grounding (i.e. epidemiologically and psychopathologically). It is simply speculation leading to a quasi-metaphysical conception of psychotic vulnerability. Its value may only lie in the field of anthropology, with no real implications for the assessment of predisposition to and prevention of major psychoses.

I, however, suggest that a positive and non-stigmatizing description such as this could improve our knowledge of the vulnerability to schizophrenic and manic-depressive psychoses, through acknowledgment of the schizotype's and the melancholic type's world-views.

3. Towards a description of the "basic relational deficit" of the schizotype

Do pre-schizophrenics share a common "basic relational deficit" (Maj 1998)? Is it a distinctive feature and a precondition of the schizophrenic syndrome? What are its characteristics? How does it manifest itself? What theory of the mind provides a suitable frame for interpreting it?

It is a matter of debate whether abnormalities in social adjustment and social knowledge in pre-schizophrenic people are simply correlates or consequences of mild psychotic symptoms, or rather, if they are risk factors in a pathogenetical sense. DSM-IV quite vaguely states that schizophrenia "involves" dysfunctions in interpersonal relations (Criterion B). *To involve* means both *to include* as a part of a whole with no pathogenetical implication, and *to imply* or *entail* in a causal sense. In the former sense social dysfunctions are seen as simply co-occurring with other schizophrenic symptoms, such as psychotic ones; in the latter, social dysfunctions are interpreted as consequences of the schizophrenic syndrome, although not as direct results of any other single feature.

Recent longitudinal studies have suggested that the relationship between interpersonal difficulties and schizophrenia is *causal* (Malmberg et al. 1998), since interpersonal difficulties are the only predictors of future psychotic breakdowns. The direction of causality seems to go from interpersonal difficulties — seen as a *primary phenomenon*–to the schizophrenic syndrome as a whole. Accordingly, some authors (Broks 1997; Malmberg et al. 1998) hypothesize that schizophrenia can be construed essentially as a disorder of social cognition — i.e., a disorder of the accurate perception of the dispositions and intentions of other individuals (Brothers 1992).

Besides the issue of the pathogenetical relationship between social dysfunctions and schizophrenic syndrome, two more methodological problems arise. We can call the first one the problem of the *normative concept* of social dysfunction. It concerns the questionable background assumptions that shape the DSM-IV's concept of "social dysfunction". The second relates to one possible solution of the first problem: the paradigm shift from current operationalized criteria of social dysfunction to the phenomenological comprehension of the schizotypal basic relational deficit. We may call this the problem of the *hermeneutic complementarity* between empirical and eidetic approaches.

Problem 1. The current definitions of social functioning seem to be anchored to sociological models in which the normative character of behaviors is emphasized (structural functionalism, see Parsons 1951). According to the normative paradigm the relationship between individual and environment is seen in terms of adjustment of the first to the second, not as an interaction between two entities regarded as mutually influencing one another. In the normative model of social functioning it is assumed that deviant behaviors are manifestations of a pathological state occurring within the individual who is not able to perform social skills and to play social roles. Normative models focus on overt behaviors more than on individual mental states motivating human actions. They assess modes of functioning that are deviant from social norms or expectations and proscribe behaviors that should be avoided. Two criticisms. The first is of an ethical nature: normative models are obviously conservative and proscriptive. They equate deviant behaviors with pathological ones. As a matter of fact these models are also known as *defect* models (see Wine 1980). The second one is an epistemological observation: normative definitions of social dysfunction place emphasis on behaviors and not on subjective experiences, motivations and the individual's value system underlying behaviors, which are the focus of phenomenological research.

Problem 2. In phenomenological literature, concepts like lameness (Kretschmer 1955), eccentricity (*Verstigenheit*), thwartness (*Verschrobenheit*) and mannerism (*Manieriertheit*) (Binswanger 1956) are used to represent the schizotype's oddity and social and interpersonal "deficits" (APA 1994). These are metaphors that eidetically enlighten the schizotype's position in life and attitude towards life. As eidetic categories they are concerned with the phenomenon of schizotypy as a whole. Here we are confronted with a methodological dilemma: Should we fully depend on this pre-conceptual apprehension, or should we attempt to translate this holistic impression into analytical categories suitable for falsification and empirical research?

The approach that I propose here relies on the complementarity between eidetic and empirical research (Blankenburg 1982; Sadler 1992). My goal is to sketch a naturalistic description of the schizotype's attitude — in contrast to that of the melancholic type, which is its mirror image — which involves exactly these specific kinds of abnormalities in social relationships. I propose a phenomenology of the social selves of the schizotype and of the melancholic type. I call this approach *phenomenological* because the patients' first-person accounts of their own attitudes provide the epistemological vantage point. It is a phenomenology of *social* selves because it focuses on the problem of intersubjectivity, that is on the patients' personal attitudes towards societal standards such as social roles and norms.

The question of the schizophrenics' basic relational deficit is faced here as an attitudinal disorder. This view is complementary and not opposed to other kinds of phenomenological analyses focusing on the decomposition of the field of consciousness (e.g., disorders of perception and/or conceptualization of the self/body and external world). That which "awakens this perilous anarchy", in the words of Antonin Artaud, of the schizophrenic world can be seen either in a bottom-up perspective (i.e., abnormal perceptions and the crisis of commonsensical conceptualization of reality affect the personal structure of values and beliefs), or in top-down perspective. In this paper the latter is privileged and the changes in attitude are explored. The concept "attitude" is used here to refer to distinctive features of the individual's value structure which define a specific type of existential orientation. "Values" are conceptualized as principles and standards which substitute instincts in the human species. One's value-structure is the design underlying one's purposes and intents.

4. The attitudes of the melancholic type and of the schizotype

If we view the life-world as a chessboard, whatever the melancholic type's position may be, its range of movement is precisely that of a pawn, limited and predictable. The stubbornness and heaviness of the melancholic type's existential core make him a basically *centric* type: Enmeshed in common sense, hyper-identifying with social norms, intolerant of ambiguity (and, thus, of reality's complexity), hyper-syntonic, with a tendency to be hypo-critical towards the decreed social customs and therefore, in this context, hypo-reflexive. The melancholic type seeks harmony rather than truth in interpersonal relationships, is intent on endorsing the pre-established order and adapting to it rather than challenging it, or even simply imagining a possible alternative. In other words, the melancholic type succumbs to the gravitational pull of the Law, which he equates with Nature. Here the words of Minkowski (1927) are quite appropriate, where he states that the utmost normality is found in syntonia — as well as the utmost pathology in schizoidia.

The schizotype's position is, in contrast, completely outside of the chess-board. It can be seen as reflecting his inclination towards bracketing ready-made social roles and rules. This is all related to the schizotype's tendency to be placed, but also to actively place himself, outside of the boundaries of the social game. The schizotype as an existentially-vulnerable type is quite weakly anchored to common sense, and as a result finds it difficult to adjust to social norms. He is enslaved by individualism to the same degree that the melancholic type is a hostage of a collectivistic attitude. The schizotype may be trapped by the complexity and contradictions of reality, to the point of being displaced, disoriented and even paralyzed by the multiplicity of alternatives. Hyper-reflexive (Sass 1994) to the point of bewilderment by the possibilities that in the end resemble a fun-house mirror game, "he can stand there with a puzzled face and hanging arms, like a note of interrogation" (Kretschmer 1955).

In the schizotype's world-view, the *evanescence* of the foundation of social life (that is, the loss of self-evidence) lives side-by-side with the *refusal* of impersonal and anonymous norms. Thus, it is possible that a schizotype might consider it worth placing himself on the outskirts of social life. In fact, his actual *position* in life may end up coinciding with his *attitude* towards life (for the "position vs. attitude" distinction, see Binswanger 1928) — the disdainful and angry rejection of artificiality in the world, and furious nostalgia for authenticity.

Just as the melancholic type embodies being hostage to *centricity*, the schizotype incarnates propelling himself into extreme *eccentricity*.

5. Centricity and eccentricity in the melancholic type and in the schizotype

I shall sketch out a description of the melancholic type's centric attitude and the schizotype's eccentric attitude, with respect to the issue of their social selves, and two basic categories: attitudes towards (i) social roles and (ii) norms.

5.1. *Attitudes towards social roles*

Social roles can be defined as external representations of identity. Role-identity is the position one assumes in the social game. It is this identification with a social role that allows self-consciousness; one becomes self conscious playing someone else's role (Mead 1938). The establishment of one's Self concept is the positive side of role playing, since putting oneself in someone else's shoes contributes to seeing oneself from another person's perspective, and thus permits the Self-Other distinction. In contrast, its negative side is over-identification with an external representation of identity (which characterizes pre-melancholic personality, Kraus 1977).

Table 2. Attitude towards social roles

Social role = *external representation of identity*
Role-distance = *ability to play a role without completely identifying with it*

Melancholic type	*Schizotype*
Hyper-identification with social roles	Hypo-identification with social roles
Lack of role-distance	Lack of role-playing
Urge for social role	Search for ego-identity
Integration	Isolation
Affiliation/Assimilation	Differentiation
Insider status	Outsider status
Linking orientation	Spacing orientation
Allocentric attitude	Idiocentric attitude

Role-distance is what defends a person from the over-fulfillment of normative role expectations. Role-distance is *not* lack of involvement in one's social role, the "as-if" involvement characterizing sociopaths ("I know the game, and I pretend to play it to my advantage"). It is the ability to play a role without completely identifying with it.

The ability to role-play *plus* role-distance is the precondition for the balance between ego-identity and role-identity, i.e., the dialectical movement between identity and non-identity, which is the prerequisite of mental health and freedom (Blankenburg 1982; Kraus 1982).

On the one hand, the lack of role-distance entails rigid over-identification with social role expectation. This is the condition of the melancholic type who might be thought of as saying "This is the only game I know".

On the other hand, lack of role-playing entails the dissolving of I-World relations, and ultimately of any identification — a condition leading to "a painful cramping of the self into the self" (Kretschmer 1955). "I'd rather not" Melville's *no-man* Bartleby would say, or in Montaigne's words, "Je m'abstiens" (*I abstain*). This is the situation of the schizotype who would say something like, "I know the game, it's merely a simulation, I do not want to play".

As far as their divergent attitudes towards social roles are concerned, the melancholic type's and the schizotype's existential styles can be described with antithetical conceptual pairings. The melancholic type is characterized by the following elements: the urge for a social role, tendency towards integration, affiliation, and attachment, need for assimilation, insider status and linking orientation, collectivistic, mutualistic, and allocentric attitude. For the schizotype, instead, the opposite concepts can be applied: the search for ego-identity, tendency towards isolation, separation, and withdrawal, need for differentiation, outsider status and spacing orientation, individualistic and idiocentric attitude.

5.2. *Attitudes towards social norms*

Social norms can be defined as the connections between situation and action. Empirical studies (Mundt et al. 1994; Mundt et al. 1997) as well as conceptual analyses (Kraus 1987; Stanghellini and Mundt 1997) have demonstrated that the melancholic type has a *hypernomic* and *heteronomic* style of behavior. Hypernomia means exaggerated norm adaptation, and heteronomia exaggerated norm receptiveness (in the sense of passive imprinting). Hypernomic/heteronomic persons are unable to transcend the social norms they once adopted. The melancholic type fails in autonomy in order to keep his hyper-identification with these norms, which mimic verbatim the socially accepted ones. *Orderliness* and *conscientiousness* dominate the social behavior of the melancholic type. Orderliness is the need for a meticulous organization of one's work and environment, as well as the fixation with harmony in interpersonal relationships. Avoiding all disagreement is the dominating thought of the melancholic type. Conscientiousness is the commitment to prevent guilt attribution and guilt feelings.

Table 3. Attitude towards social norms

Social norm = *connection between situation and action*	
Attunement = *capacity to get involved in the other's mental life*	
Melancholic type	*Schizotype*
Hypernomia	Hyponomia
Heteronomia	Resistence to heteronomia
Hyper-attunement	Rejection of hyper-attunement
Heteronomic vulnerability	
Heteronomia is a solution (melancholic type)	Heteronomia is a problem (schizotype)

For the melancholic type, social norms come prior to single social interactions. If you ask melancholic types the reason for their behavior, even if they contribute to forcing themselves into indisputable pathogenic situations (e.g. *includence* and *remanence* melancholies, see Tellenbach 1961), they all answer that even if they are aware that such action will lead them to the edge of a depressive breakdown, nonetheless they *must* do it. But if you inquire into the reasons for this rigid normative behavior, you realize that, for the melancholic type, only at first glance are norms something *out there*, so to speak, something objective and impersonal. The polestar, the center of attraction of the melancholic type's hypernomic/heteronomic actions are not social *norms per se*, but his attunement to the mind of the other. The melancholic type does not simply conform to impersonal social norms, he gets attuned to the expectations of his social partner. The melancholic type's life goes by in an attempt to get attuned to the expectations of others. The melancholic type's hyper-attunement is conceptually distinct from "empathy", since in that case taking of the other's perspective is accompanied by the capacity to distance oneself from the other's perspective, which is lacking here.

If we now recall the previous definition of the concept of "norm" (the connection between situation and action) we see that one acts according to one's perception of a given situation, and that the melancholic type is somehow more embroiled in "a real Bergsonian-type intuitively appreciated world" — as Cutting would say (1997). The melancholic type cannot distance himself from the other's mind, in which social expectations guaranteeing interpersonal harmony are embodied. Melancholic types are hyper-connected to their perception of the mind of their social partner and afflicted by a sort of *hyper-attunement* —, i.e., over-involvement in the other's mental life.

The concept of "melancholic type" is like a mould for the notion of schizotype; the former has a concave shape where the latter is convex. In fact, *hyponomia* is an appropriate concept to define the schizotype's behaviour, in contrast to the melancholic type's heteronomia. As a matter of fact, the schizotype's main concern is *fighting against heteronomia* — and it must be stated clearly that this conflict against exaggerated norm receptiveness is not a synonym of autonomy, i.e., self-governing behavior.

The schizotype's behavior lies between the two extremes of extraordinary emotional resonance and lameness. Schizotypes may say such things similar to the claims of the patient (V.V.) who reported feeling too emotionally involved when she got in touch with other people. She *rejects her tendency to identify* with the point of view of the person she is speaking with, and thus avoids close contacts with other people. Another schizotype (M. Mo.) says that what he *hates most is to be persuaded* by the opinions of others and, therefore, he avoids all discussions. Another tells of how she is *scared to dive into somebody's head*, because she is afraid of getting lost and getting caught in it (M.Ma.).

These sentences express different degrees of *heteronomic vulnerability*, feeling over-involved in the mental lives of others, which melancholic types and schizotypes hold in common. The main difference between the two seems to be that, given the question "How to deal with the Self-Other dilemma?", the melancholic type judges heteronomia to be the *solution*, whereas for the schizotype heteronomia is itself the *problem*. The difference lies in the value systems of the two existential types; for the melancholic type, the urge for interpersonal agreement and fear of isolation are more important than autonomy, while for the schizotype, fear of assimilation and need for differentiation are more important than relatedness.

6. Conclusions: The soteriologic drama of eccentricity

Each historical epoch is confronted with its own *soteriologic drama* — the drama of one's own physical and spiritual salvation. Perhaps in our time this soteriologic drama takes the form of the *drama of eccentricity*, that is, the never-attained goal of coinciding with oneself and with one's own social world. Most of the philosophical anthropologies of the last hundred years emphasize that the phenomenon of eccentricity is indigenous to human existence, and characterize Man as "the still undefined animal" (Nietzsche 1886), or as the being capable of taking a position with respect to himself and making something of himself (Gehlen 1944). Man as an eccentric being "is never entirely what he 'is'" (Plessner 1970).

This condition of eccentricity is at the same time the root of freedom and of psychoses. Eccentricity is the root of the possibility to bracket conventional social roles and norms, thus establishing autonomously one's own Self without losing the historical connectedness with the social world. Yet it is also the root of either being displaced into absolute eccentricity, or of being inexorably enmeshed in commonsensical roles and rules.

Thus, the soteriologic drama of eccentricity is the drama that unfolds when the constitution of personal identity is caught in the cross-fire of collectivistic and individualistic values. In the context of this drama, the dialectical movement between these two polarities is the prerequisite of mental health and freedom. But when this dialectical movement is impaired, existence may become restricted to only one polarity: hyper-identification with external representations of identity (role-identity) and heteronomia, on one end; rejection of social roles and attunement, on the other. The melancholic type's heteronomia can be contrasted to the schizotype's *antagonomia* (opposition to norms, see also Wiggins and Schwartz in this volume). These polar characteristics of the melancholic type and the schizotype, however, should by no means be understood as attitudes towards social ceremonies. Here the problem does not only concern mere compliance to or rejection of objective, taken-for-granted and commonsensical norms of behavior, but also the attitude towards one's attunement to the mind, in short the expectations, of one's social partner.

As I have argued in this paper, the melancholic type's vulnerability fundamentally consists in his or her own hyper-compliance to his attunement to the other's expectations, whereas the schizotype rejects his or her own hyper-attunement. Psychotic vulnerability is the polarization into one of these two opposite tendencies.

Perhaps it is not due to chance that Psychiatry at the end of this Millennium represents Madness — in its nosological forms: manic-depressive and schizophrenic psychoses — as the crystallization of either a lack or an excess of eccentricity.

Bibliography

APA (1994). *Diagnostic and Statistical Manual of Mental Disorders — Fourth Edition.* Washington DC: APA.

Binswanger, L. (1928). Lebensfunktion und innere Lebensgeschichte. *Monatschrift für Psychiatrie und Neurologie* 63: 57–79.

Binswanger, L. (1956). *Drei Formen missglückten Daseins*, Tübingen: Niemeyer.

Blankenburg, W. (1969). Ansätze zu einer Psychopathologie des "common sense". *Confinia psychiatrica* 12: 144–163.

Blankenburg, W. (1971). *Der Verlust der natürlichen Selbstvertständlichkeit. Eine Beitrag zur Psychopathologie Symptomarmer Schizophrenien.* Stuttgart: Enke.

Blankenburg, W. (1980). Phenomenology and Psychopathology. *Journal of Phenomenological Psychology,* 1, 50–78.

Blankenburg, W. (1982). A dialectical conception of anthropological proportions. In A.J.J. De Koning, & F.A. Jenner (Eds.), *Phenomenology and Psychiatry*. London: Academic Press.

Broks, P. (1997). Brain, self, and others: the neuropsychology of social cognition. In: G. Claridge (Ed.) *Schizotypy. Implication for Illness and Health.* Oxford: Oxford University Press.

Brothers, L.A. (1992). Perception of social acts in primates cognition and neurobiology. *Seminars in Neurosciences* 4: 409–414.

Chapman, L.J., & Chapman, J.P. (1980). Scales for rating psychotic and psychotic-like experiences as continua. *Schizophrenia Bulletin* 6: 477–489.

Cutting, J. (1997). *Principles of Psychopathology. Two Worlds — Two Minds — Two Hemispheres*. Oxford: Oxford University Press.

Ey, H. (1968). *La conscience*. Paris: Desclée de Brouwer.

Gehlen, A. (1944): *Der Mensch. Seine Natur und Seine Stellung in der Welt.* Wiesbaden : Athenaion.

Huber, G. (1983). Das Konzept substratnaher Basissymptome und seine Bedeutung für Theorie und Therapie schizophrener Erkrankungen. *Nervenarzt* 54: 23–32.

Janzarik, W. (1959). *Dynamische Grundkonstellationen in endogenen Psychosen*. Berlin: Springer.

Kendler, K.S. (1985). Diagnostic approaches to schizotypal personality disorder: A historical perspective. *Schizophrenia Bulletin* 11: 538–553.

Klosterkötter, J. (1988). *Basissymptome und Endphänomene der Schizophrenie.* Berlin-Heidelberg-New York: Springer.

Kraus, A. (1977). *Sozialverhalten und Psychose Manisch-Depressiver.* Stuttgart: Enke.

Kraus, A. (1982). Identity and psychosis of the manic-depressive. In A.J.J. De Koning, & F.A. Jenner (Eds.): *Phenomenology and Psychiatry.* London: Academic Press.

Kraus, A. (1987). Dynamique de role des maniaque-dépressifs. *Psychologie Médicale* 19: 401–405.

Kraus, A. (1994). Le motif du mensonge et la dépersonnalisation dans la mélancolie. *L'Evolution psychiatrique* 19: 401–405.

Kretschmer, E. (1955). *Körperbau und Charakter.* Berlin-Göttingen-Heidelberg: Springer.

Malmberg, A., Lewis, G., David, A., & Allebeck, P. (1998). Premorbid adjustment and personality in people with schizophrenia. *British Journal of Psychiatry* 172: 308–313.

Mead, G.H. (1934). *Mind, Self, and Society.* Chicago: University of Chicago Press (13th ed. 1965).

Minkowski, E. (1927). *La schizophrénie. Psychopathologie des schizoides et des schizophrènes.* Paris: Payot.

Mundt, Ch. (1985). *Das Apathiesyndrom der Schizophrenen. Eine psychopathologische und computertomographische Untersuchung.* Berlin-Heidelberg-New York: Springer.

Mundt, Ch., Backenstrass, M., Kronmueller, K.-T., Fiedler, P., Kraus, A., & Stanghellini, G. (1997). Personality and endogenous/major depression. An empirical approach to Typus melancholicus. 2. Validation of Typus melancholicus Core-properties by Personality Inventory Scales. *Psychopathology* 30: 130–139.

Nietzsche, F. (1886) *Jenseits von Gut und Böse. Vorspiel einer Philosophie der Zukunft.* Italian translation Milano: Adelphi 1972.

Parnas, J. (1994). Basic disorder concept from the viewpoint of family studies in schizophrenia. In G. Gross (Ed.), *Perspektiven psychiatrischer Forschung und Praxis.* Stuttgart: Schattauer.

Parsons, T. (1951). *The social system.* New York: Glencoe.

Plessner, H. (1970). *Philosophische Anthropologie.* Frankfurt a.M.: Fischer.

Sadler, J. (1992): Eidetic and Empirical Research: A Hermeneutic Complementarity. In M. Spitzer, F.A. Uehlein, M.A. Schwartz, Ch. Mundt (Eds.), *Phenomenology, Language & Schizophrenia.* New York: Springer.

Sass, L.A. (1994). *The Paradoxes of Delusions. Wittgenstein, Schreber and the Schizophrenic Mind.* Ithaca and London: Cornell University Press.

Stanghellini, G. (1997a). For an anthropology of vulnerability. *Psychopathology* 30: 1–11.

Stanghellini, G. (1997b). *Antropologia della vulnerabilità.* Milano: Feltrinelli.

Stanghellini, G., & Mundt, Ch. (1997). Personality and endogenous/major depression. An empirical approach to Typus melancholicus. 1 Theoretical issues. *Psychopathology* 30: 119–129.

Stevens, A., & Price, J. (1996). *Evolutionary Psychiatry. A New Beginning.* London-New York: Routdledge.

Tellenbach, H. (1961). *Melancholie. Problemgeschichte, Endogenität, Typologie, Pathogenese, Klinik* (3rd ed. 1983). Berlin: Springer.

Triandis, H.C. (1995). *Individualism and Collectivism*, Boulder-San Francisco-Oxford: Westview.

Ühlein, F.A. (1992). Eidos and Eidetic Varation in Husserl's Phenomenology. In M. Spitzer, F.A. Ühlein, M.A. Schwartz, Ch. Mundt (Eds), *Phenomenology, Language & Schizophrenia*. New York: Springer.

Wine, J.D. (1980): From defect to competence models. In J.D. Wine, & M.D. Smye (Eds.), *Social competence*. New York London: Guildford.

Index

In the series ADVANCES IN CONSCIOUSNESS RESEARCH (AiCR) the following titles have been published thus far or are scheduled for publication:

1. GLOBUS, Gordon G.: *The Postmodern Brain.* 1995.
2. ELLIS, Ralph D.: *Questioning Consciousness. The interplay of imagery, cognition, and emotion in the human brain.* 1995.
3. JIBU, Mari and Kunio YASUE: *Quantum Brain Dynamics and Consciousness. An introduction.* 1995.
4. HARDCASTLE, Valerie Gray: *Locating Consciousness.* 1995.
5. STUBENBERG, Leopold: *Consciousness and Qualia.* 1998.
6. GENNARO, Rocco J.: *Consciousness and Self-Consciousness. A defense of the higher-order thought theory of consciousness.* 1996.
7. MAC CORMAC, Earl and Maxim I. STAMENOV (eds): *Fractals of Brain, Fractals of Mind. In search of a symmetry bond.* 1996.
8. GROSSENBACHER, Peter G. (ed.): *Finding Consciousness in the Brain. A neuro-cognitive approach.* n.y.p.
9. Ó NUALLÁIN, Seán, Paul MC KEVITT and Eoghan MAC AOGÁIN (eds): *Two Sciences of Mind. Readings in cognitive science and consciousness.* 1997.
10. NEWTON, Natika: *Foundations of Understanding.* 1996.
11. PYLKKÖ, Pauli: *The Aconceptual Mind. Heideggerian themes in holistic naturalism.* 1998.
12. STAMENOV, Maxim I. (ed.): *Language Structure, Discourse and the Access to Consciousness.* 1997.
13. VELMANS, Max (ed.): *Investigating Phenomenal Consciousness. Methodologies and Maps.* n.y.p.
14. SHEETS-JOHNSTONE, Maxine: *The Primacy of Movement.* 1999.
15. CHALLIS, Bradford H. and Boris M. VELICHKOVSKY (eds.): *Stratification in Cognition and Consciousness.* 1999.
16. ELLIS, Ralph D. and Natika NEWTON (eds.): *The Caldron of Consciousness. Motivation, affect and self-organization - An anthology.* n.y.p.
17. HUTTO, Daniel D.: *The Presence of Mind.* 1999.
18. PALMER, Gary B. and Debra J. OCCHI (eds.): *Languages of Sentiment. Cultural constructions of emotional substrates.* 1999.
19. DAUTENHAHN, Kerstin (ed.): *Human Cognition and Social Agent Technology.* 2000.
20. KUNZENDORF, Robert G. and Benjamin WALLACE (eds.): *Individual Differences in Conscious Experience.* 2000.
21. HUTTO, Daniel D.: *Beyond Physicalism.* 2000.
22. ROSSETTI, Yves and Antti REVONSUO (eds.): *Beyond Dissociation. Interaction between dissociated implicit and explicit processing.* n.y.p.
23. ZAHAVI, Dan (ed.): *Exploring the Self. Philosophical and psychopathological perspectives on self-experience.* 2000.
24. ROVEE-COLLIER, Carolyn, Harlene HAYNE and Michael COLOMBO: *The Development of Implicit and Explicit Memory.* n.y.p.
25. BACHMANN, Talis: *Microgenetic Approach to the Conscious Mind.* n.y.p.
26. Ó NUALLÁIN, Seán (ed.): *Spatial Cognition. Selected papers from Mind III, Annual Conference of the Cognitive Science Society of Ireland, 1998.* n.y.p.

27. McMILLAN, John and Grant R. GILLETT: *Consciousness and Intentionality.* n.y.p.
28. ZACHAR, Peter: *Psychological Concepts and Biological Psychiatry. A philosophical analysis.* n.y.p.
29. VAN LOOCKE, Philip (ed.): *The Physical Nature of Consciousness.* n.y.p.